INTERNATIONAL HANDBOOK OF EDUCATIONAL LEADERSHIP
AND ADMINISTRATION

Kluwer International Handbooks of Education

VOLUME 1

International Handbook of Educational Leadership and Administration

Part 2

Edited by

Kenneth Leithwood
Ontario Institute for Studies in Education, Canada

Judith Chapman
University of Western Australia

David Corson
Ontario Institute for Studies in Education, Canada

Philip Hallinger
Vanderbilt University, U.S.A.

Ann Hart
University of Utah, U.S.A.

KLUWER ACADEMIC PUBLISHERS
DORDRECHT / BOSTON / LONDON

A C.I.P. Catalogue record for this book is available from the Library of Congress

ISBN 0-7923-3530-9

Published by Kluwer Academic Publishers,
P.O. Box 17, 3300 AA Dordrecht, The Netherlands.

Kluwer Academic Publishers incorporates
the publishing programmes of
D. Reidel, Martinus Nijhoff, Dr W. Junk and MTP Press.

Sold and distributed in the U.S.A. and Canada
by Kluwer Academic Publishers,
101 Philip Drive, Norwell, MA 02061, U.S.A.

In all other countries, sold and distributed
by Kluwer Academic Publishers Group,
P.O. Box 322, 3300 AH Dordrecht, The Netherlands.

Printed on acid-free paper

Printed in the Netherlands

Table of Contents

SECTION 3: COGNITIVE PERSPECTIVES ON
EDUCATIONAL LEADERSHIP AND ADMINISTRATION
(KEN LEITHWOOD - SECTION EDITOR)

SECTION 4: CONCEPTIONS OF LEADERSHIP AND ADMINISTRATIVE PRACTICE (PHILIP HALLINGER - SECTION EDITOR)

Section 4

Conceptions of Leadership and Administrative Practice

Philip Hallinger – Section Editor

Chapter 19: Building Innovative Capacity and Leadership

RUDOLF VAN DEN BERG AND PETER SLEEGERS

Catholic University of Nijmegen, The Netherlands

In Western Europe, educational innovations can be characterized as increasingly large scale. Nevertheless, in every innovation one always confronts the question of the appropriate strategy for introducing the innovation. With regard to large-scale innovations, it is also important to search for supplemental support strategies.

Within this perspective, it is also important to consider the shift in Western Europe from a traditional to a transformational policy of innovation. It is exactly such conditions of uncertainty and continual change that call upon the innovative capacities of schools, and this demand has consequences for the form of leadership required by schools. In particular, it is becoming increasingly necessary for schools to call upon their own strategic policies and capacities.

These issues will be considered in the following discussion. First, the demand for new educational designs and concepts will be considered. Second, the generally large-scale nature of the educational innovations undertaken in Western Europe will be described. Third, the limitations inherent in a large-scale approach to innovation will be discussed; the concomitant significance of strategic re-orientation will then be sketched. Fourth, the most important results of three research studies will be described. The results of these studies show transformational leadership to be of particular importance for innovation along with more attention to the concerns of those involved in implementation.

THE DESIRABILITY OF EDUCATIONAL REVIEW IN LARGE-SCALE FRAMEWORKS

Various studies, workshops, and publications concerned with the quality of education have all called for major reviews of educational functioning (Rolff, 1993; Sleegers & Wesselingh, 1993). Our society and educational systems are undergoing major changes as a result of –

K. Leithwood et al. (eds.), International Handbook of Educational Leadership and Administration, 653-699.
© 1996 Kluwer Academic Publishers. Printed in the Netherlands.

among other things – new information technologies, demographic shifts, and the changing position of educators in our society. Educational experts have pointed to a number of cultural shifts including an increasing degree of individualization, changing and/or decaying morals, changing relations between parents and children, changing patterns of socialization, changing patterns of youth interaction, increased emancipation, and growing cultural transfer in a variety of forms. In order to respond to these changes adequately, one must develop a tremendous innovative capacity.

Policy institutes tend to talk about an educational crisis and, indeed, one of the major sources of tension in schools is the current clash between pedagogical aims and efficient policy measures. Should the school opt for a mission or a market? Or can these different options perhaps be combined? The needs of society and those involved in the educational system can no longer be met in the old familiar manner; educational innovation is needed. It is time to consider a new and more contemporary educational design.

The following social changes will most certainly confront education on its way to the year 2000: increased economic growth, increased internationalization, continued technological advancement, further emancipation for women, and increased cultural pluralism. The demand for a new and contemporary educational design, moreover, is not exclusively European. School leaders and educational experts all feel that there is a clear need for fundamental educational reform, and this need is fuelled by the many complaints about the quality of education (Elmore, 1988; Timar, 1989). In particular, the possibilities for professional growth need to be expanded. This may involve a fundamental change in the content of the educational curriculum, the greater delegation of authority and decision making, and the development of educational accountability at the level of the school.

The search for new educational designs should also be stimulated by the visible shift from a traditional policy of innovation to a transformational policy of innovation. A transformational policy gives people the room to experience and realize a change (van den Berg, 1992). Various schools and networks of schools have also indicated a need for a transformational approach and *the fundamental change in education represented by a transformational approach* (Mesenburg, 1991; Hallinger, 1992). The notion of transformation has received increasing interest in educational circles because of what Fullan calls an ultimately fruitless uphill battle. The solution is not to keep trying to climb the same old hill of getting more innovations or reforms into the educational system.

We need a different formulation to get at the heart of the problem, a different hill, so to speak. We need, in short, a new mind-set about educational change' (Fullan, 1993, p. 3).

Transformation can be described as a process in which the individual capacities and responsibilities of people to change the context in which they live and work are intensely appealed to and enhanced, as well (i.e., the expertise and energies of different individuals are utilized) (van den Berg, 1992). It is thus assumed that the individual can influence events significantly. The most important starting points for transformation appear to be space to experience and realize the change, a desire for growth, and the capacity to mobilize energy. In much of the literature within this framework, this notion is referred to as *entrepreneurship* (van den Berg, 1992). If one wants to be an entrepreneur, then the richness and dynamics of the daily reality should be kept in mind rather than the planning, standardization, and control of activities. The facilitation of creativity and problem-solving abilities should predominate. The concept of *entrepreneurship* clearly reflects the disillusionment that has grown over the years with the classic methods of innovation (Sundbo, 1992).

In the framework of traditional policies of innovation, schools often appear to function simply as the enacting organization. They enact that which has been externally specified. In the framework of a transformational policy of innovation, schools are considered learning organizations (Mintzberg, 1987; 1989; Senge, 1993). Schools are considered centers of change, and both professional and personal growth should be possible for teachers as well as school leaders. Government initiatives can then be viewed as opportunities for development rather than as threats to a school's own goals. The central concepts in this shift from a constructivist to a transformational policy are *restructuring* and *empowerment*, which are assumed to foster the growth of self-esteem, autonomy, and action. In the USA, school leaders and teachers feel that there is a growing need for the increased autonomy of schools (Chubb & Moe, 1987; Timar & Kirp, 1989). In The Netherlands, deregulation and delegation have also played a major role in current discussions of education. Deregulation means a decrease in the degree of central regulation, and an important consequence of this is that schools will have a greater amount of autonomy and a greater say in policy formation. Delegation involves the transfer of authority, responsibility, and tasks from a higher 'level' (for example, the Department of Education and Science) to a lower 'level' (for example, the local School Board).

The increased autonomy of schools means that schools will – more than ever – have develop their own policies and take on more of the characteristics of a strategic organization. There are also increasing efforts to provide a more bottom-up or school-focused approach to innovation. Improvements are more likely to take root and grow if they are established in the schools themselves. Development occurs best when teachers recognize the need for change and are willing to undertake the work needed to achieve this change. And a great deal of school-focused support is needed for such innovation to succeed.

At the same time, the governments of many countries continue to play a central role in the development of the frameworks for innovation. As a result of this centralized approach, large-scale change continues to be a characteristic of the educational process in a variety of Western European countries (Louis & Loucks – Horsley, 1989). However, the paradox represented by continued centralization and the drive for decentralization creates a high level of insecurity and tension (Caldwell, 1993, p.158).

The large-scale nature of the educational innovation process in Western Europe is a typical product of constructive government policy and has produced a series of national projects (van den Berg & Vandenberghe, 1986). Within these projects, special attention is paid to – among other things – alternative educational structures, major curriculum changes, the changing roles of teachers, the integration of multiple innovations, and radical changes in class practices (Goldwasser, 1992; Murphy & Hallinger, 1993; Sashkin & Egermeier, 1992). The large-scale nature of the innovation projects directed by the government, however, has left the schools to develop their own specific innovation activities. In The Netherlands, innovations are characterized by a unique (and complex) combination of centralized administration/ organization and decentralized educational content. Through the active participation of thousands of elementary schools and hundreds of cooperating agencies, the innovations take on a large-scale character.

According to Beare and Boyd (1993), large-scale innovations represent a special type of reform. They are typically justified on the grounds that they will influence the educational curriculum, encourage the adoption of alternative programs, and improve educational results. They do not stem from the teachers or educational advisors, however. The source of such large-scale reforms is external policy with the goal of adequate management of the schools within a national framework.'[The reforms] appear to have been imposed from outside, at least initially. Furthermore, the current efforts seem to aim primarily at the control and governance of both schools and school systems' (Beare & Boyd, 1993, p.2).

In not only the innovation operations in The Netherlands but also the large-scale innovation projects in other Western European countries, the innovations are system-wide attempts at change. Their justification and influence is often wider than the particular educational system itself. In Great Britain, for example, attention is paid to a national curriculum and program of evaluation for both the elementary – and secondary – school systems. A comparable centralized approach to educational innovation can also be found in the Scandinavian countries.

LARGE-SCALE INNOVATIONS FROM THE POINT OF VIEW OF IMPLEMENTATION

The Larger Point of View

As a consequence of a centralized approach to large-scale educational reform, those in the field of education are confronted by a number of descriptions and plans for the realization of this reform. The options considered by the government in the creation of this policy cannot normally be traced by outsiders. In The Netherlands, Belgium, and the United Kingdom, for example, there are innovation committees and advisory committees responsible for important preparatory work with regard to policy but the manner in which these committees reach their decisions is not apparent to the outside world.

Long-range policies are usually outlined with the manner of implementation indicated in general terms. Such official descriptions usually emanate from the Ministries of Education. In most cases, however, there are no indications or suggestions for how to achieve the objectives. That is, those concerned with the creation of policy and enactment of legislation *seldom look down the track to the stage of implementation.* The central government appears to assign the task of implementation to others. Others must see to the translation of the general starting-points for implementation at the level of school and classroom practice, which may create a wide gap between the intentions of the policy designers and the perceptions of the implementers.

A large-scale reform may also be a bundle of innovations. The Renewed Secondary School in Belgium, for example, asks the school and teachers to group students in a manner that deviates – sometimes drastically – from the present graded system (the problem of intra-class differentiation). At the same time, the teachers are asked to implement a new kind of evaluation (the so-called formative evaluation). New manuals are put into use; the teachers are expected to cooperate more than before; the school and teachers are confronted by a new system of external support; and new relations with other schools are also imposed. An important characteristic of such large-scale projects is, thus, their *multidimensionality*. A number of important objectives must be accomplished *simultaneously* and *coherently*.

The proposed innovations may also be so pervasive at times that Gene Hall (1992) speaks of *hyperinnovations*. Such innovations are extremely complex (often accompanied by numerous slogans and little extra money) with, as a result, little influence on the teacher in the average school with 35 or more students in a class (Hall, 1992, p.889). In his opinion, popular slogans must be translated into concrete changes. If this does not occur, then the broad support for the proposed reforms will not be found. Each innovation often points to a significant array of objectives. The expectation is that these objectives will not only be adopted at the same time but also applied in an integrated manner, which is extremely difficult if not impossible. It is also hard to avoid the impression that the authorities are simply not aware of these limitations, moreover.

Taking into account this multidimensionality, it is not surprising that the participants in educational reform may emphasize different aspects of large-scale projects. The external facilitators of change may stress different goals than the principals, and teachers may be most interested in innovations related to actual class practice. As already mentioned, this can produce a relatively wide gap between the plans outlined by the policy makers and the decisions made by the school. In other words, the proposed projects are filtered, various choices are made, and different aspects are stressed at each school to produce different realizations of the same policy, which the authorities do not sufficiently recognize.

In investigations of the implementation of large-scale projects, it is expected that the schools and teachers will not provide a single, clear answer. The schools will probably assign different priorities to the proposed innovations. Also, the same innovation – such as continuous diagnosis or remedial teaching – may be included at the level of the classroom but nevertheless occur in very different configurations depending on the classroom. In our opinion, greater attention should be paid to the influence of initial decisions on later implementation, the potential diversity of the reactions to proposed policy, and the variability in the practical realization of large-scale innovation.

The multiplicity of the objectives contained in large-scale projects along with the local realities of the school districts, the personal experiences of the teachers, and the opinions of the school leaders raise many questions about the way in which implementation should be conceptualized. We underline the importance of local circumstances, the innovative history of the school, the form of leadership, and the influence of certain teachers or groups of teachers in the realization of large-scale projects (Fisher & Schratz, 1990). Implementation is evolution. A large-scale project represents an interesting starting point but should be considered as the launching pad for the deployment of a school's innovative capacities. Large-scale innovations should be aimed at making small-scale innovations possible.

The Individual Point of View

In large-scale projects, different people are involved at different levels (national, regional, local) and each individual has a more or less specific task. It is therefore important to pay attention to the way in which these people personally define the requirements of the project and the consequences of participation in the innovation. What are the reactions, experiences, and opinions of those involved in the realization of such projects? In our opinion, more researchers and educational facilitators should attempt to document the *different* reactions and interpretations of those involved in such large-scale projects and thereby illustrate the dynamic aspects of such innovation rather than the static or supposedly 'correct' interpretation of such innovation.

Multidimensionality characterizes the reactions of the school leader or the individual teacher as much as the project itself. The implementation of large-scale innovations is a very complex process. Teachers often experience the implementation of such large-scale innovations as an ongoing negotiation process. These negotiations and discussions with regard to a number of new tasks sometimes produce clear answers and sometimes do not. This leaves the teachers to make a number of implementation decisions on their own. In other words, the teachers may have to translate the general aims of a large-scale project into specific innovation activities.

The personal definition of the goals of a large-scale innovation project may be coloured by the individual's positive or negative experiences with earlier innovations, ideas about the objectives and functions of a particular instructional method, and the organizational context in which one is working. The different participants in an innovation – the teachers, school leaders, and so on – can be conceived as different cultures or subcultures. An innovation may be developed by a group of policy makers with a particular set of norms and values. As the policy is disseminated to the teachers, it enters a new culture with significantly different norms and values. The policy will therefore be interpreted differently when applied in this new culture. As a consequence, attention must be paid to the significance of the different aspects of innovation for the individuals and groups involved in such a project. An analogous line of thought is proposed by Fullan and Stiegelbauer in *The New Meaning of Educational Change* (1991). In different places, these authors elaborate on the most important thesis of their book – namely, the transformation of subjective realities as the essence of change.

As should be clear by now, the implementation of a (complex) educational innovation requires the attachment of some personal significance to the new situation. As already mentioned, however, large-scale projects can give rise to a number of conflicting interests particularly when viewed from the perspective of implementation. For the individual and as outlined in Figure 1, these conflicts may actually constitute a dilemma (van den Berg & Vandenberghe, 1986, p.45)

Examination of Figure 1 shows the following dilemmas to be associated with the implementation of large-scale innovation projects. a) As opposed to the relatively simple implementation of an innovation in one's own school, large-scale innovation projects entail a greater degree of complexity. This complexity not only concerns the organization of the project but also the content of the project. b) Instead of adapted facilitation for each school, more or less general strategies are used for large-scale innovations. c) Contrary to viewing innovation in terms of desirable evolution, which means adjustment to the needs of the people at each site, large-scale projects tend to impose standardized cooperative links and ignore the individual difference between teachers and schools. d) While the agents of change are very much aware of the fact that innovation is a process, it is often very difficult – if not impossible – to fit large-scale projects into such a perspective. The support of large-scale projects tends to be based on actions that cannot possibly be tuned to an implementation perspective.

Implementation Dilemmas

Implementation perspective	Large-scale perspective
(a) a concrete design of the innovation in one's own school must be developed, which details both content and process	(a) large-scale innovation projects are very complex in nature; as a result it is not clear what priorities (objectives) should be set
(b) an adjusted facilitation plan for each school should include diagnosis of teachers' concerns and skills as well as norms, structures, and procedures that can constitute the basis for decisions with regard to the interventions	(b) large-scale innovations dictate action according to more or less general strategies; feelings of discontent can grow as a result and lead to a diminished commitment by individual schools
(c) desirable evolution should be emphasized; this enhances the realization of the innovation adapted to the teacher and to the school, who control its design themselves in their schools	(c) large-scale innovations should foster cooperation and the development of materials; it therefore results in little consideration of the individual teachers and schools
(d) process facilitation occurs on the influencing factors and it lasts for several years	(d) change facilitators do not have an adequate basis to plan strategies, procedures, and instruments or the time for implementation

Figure 1: Some dilemmas associated with the implementation of large-scale change

Van den Berg and Vandenberghe (1986) have suggested that the most important goal of large-scale change should be to optimize the conditions for small-scale change. In other words, large-scale changes should place schools in a position to work on the concrete and tangible implementation of educational reforms. The latter is nevertheless difficult to realize, and many of those involved in educational practice argue that large-scale reform simply provides them with too few opportunities for real and substantive innovation.

The Behaviour of Individuals as the Target of Policy

On the basis of experience and research in Western Europe, we know that the agents of change in large-scale projects are confronted by a number of specific problems that are clearly profiled in the *Concerns-Based Adoption Model* (Hall & Hord, 1987; van den Berg, 1993). Despite the increasing complexity of large-scale projects, the *concerns* of the individual schools and teachers still appear to be of paramount importance. The question is whether or not a system of support can be developed for each individual school. This brings us to the heart of the implementation-perspective. 'In response to the demand, our minds explore ways, means, potential barriers, possible actions, risks, and rewards in relation to the demand. All in all, the mental activity of questioning, analysing, considering alternative actions and reactions, and anticipating consequences is *concern*. An aroused state of personal feelings and thoughts about a demand as it is perceived is *concern*' (Hall, George, & Rutherford, 1977, p.5).

The concept of *concern* refers to the personal experiences of teachers when involved in important projects. The composite representation of the feelings, preoccupations, thoughts, and considerations related to a particular issue or task is called a *concern*. If one wants a person to change, his or her abilities, needs, and concerns should first be considered. One should then act in such a way as to satisfy those needs.

In 1981, the *Concerns-Based Adoption Model (CBAM)* was applied in The Netherlands and Dutch-speaking Belgium (i.e., Flanders) by van den Berg and Vandenberghe. The *CBAM* was designed for the diagnosis of the needs of those teachers and school leaders involved in the implementation of innovation, and the instruments associated with the model have been used in several American states (Hall & Hord, 1987), parts of Australia, and a number of Western European countries (Harrison, 1991; Hopkins, 1990; Janssens, 1987). In the Dutch-Belgian situation, the set of instruments developed in the USA was not just translated but also reassessed and to an important extent adapted, revised, and supplemented. Given the socio-cultural differences between the countries, simple translation would not have been valid. In The Netherlands, significant attention was also paid to the validity of the 'developmental' theory behind the instruments.

At the end of the eighties, re-examination of the performance of educational organizations was increasingly considered to be of importance. New organizational concepts and management philosophies had developed, and schools were now perceived as learning organizations rather than just the implementers of – for example – government policy. Within this framework, attention needed to be paid to the development of school policy that appeals to the responsibilities and creativities of the individuals involved in the implementation of innovations. One way of giving shape to this approach was offered by the *CBAM*. The *CBAM* can be used to assist schools in more competently dealing with the many changes confronting them. The model also offers an interesting framework for the study of changing organizations.

The instruments associated with the *CBAM* are:
- the Stages of Concern questionnaire;
- the Levels of Use interview (including interview schedule, interview questions, scoring method, model interviews, and coding exercises);
- a procedure for describing the configurations of innovations; and
- a procedure to help the facilitator of change adapt the interventions to the particular situation.

The first two instruments will be briefly described in the following as these were used in our examination of the innovative capacity of a number of schools.

Stages of concern

The *Stages of Concern questionnaire* is structured around three areas of concern: self (concerns about personal ability), task (concerns about the performance of the task) and other (concerns about cooperation among colleagues). In the area of *self-concern*, for example, the teachers often wonder what the innovation actually means for themselves. Recurring considerations are:
- Can I manage this?
- Am I functioning well enough?
- I have just reorganized things. Do I have to change again?
- How much more does it demand of me and will I benefit in the end?

The *task-concern* is related to the possible impact of the innovation on one's task. The most pervasive questions and problems in this area are:
- Is that being newly introduced also efficient?
- Is the invested time proportionate to the required results?
- Are the means for the realization of the innovation lacking?
- Is the innovation proceeding too rapidly?

The final area of concern usually pertains to the functioning of others – that is, *other-concern*. These others can be parents, colleagues, the head school leader, or the governing body of the school. At the same time, there is also often concern for the pupils involved in the innovation. The primary concern, however, usually is about the cooperation between colleagues. Problems arising in this area can be:

- Is it always the same group of people who participate in an innovation?
- Is it difficult to exchange ideas with regard to an innovation?
- What more can be asked of the teachers as far as teamwork is concerned?
- Are observations or alternative interpretations unappreciated by colleagues?

In sum, the areas of concern refer to the attitudes, problems and the experiences of the teachers and schools involved in an innovation. As this brief overview has hopefully illustrated, these attitudes can be either positive or negative, but anyone confronted with an innovation will have concerns.

In the meantime, a new version of the questionnaire has been constructed. About 1,400 people from The Netherlands and Belgium have been involved in this. A scale meeting the methodological requirements of the Rasch-Model (van den Berg, 1993) has been developed, and the name of this scale is *Intensity of Concern*. The scale is presented in the form of a thermometer and runs from -3 to +3. A three-year longitudinal study was then undertaken to examine the extent to which the scale actually indicates the stages of concern. Using this scale, research into high and low innovation schools could also be undertaken (see section 4).

Levels of use

The *Levels of Use interview* makes it possible to analyse the way in which teachers actually apply an innovation and give shape to it. The following levels of use can be distinguished:

Level 0   : non-use
Level I   : orientation
Level II   : preparation

These levels concern the early stages of innovation. The people involved are still orienting themselves towards the innovation.

Level III   : mechanical
Level IVa : routine

The main occupation at these levels is with the conduct of the task and the way in which it should be carried out.

Level IVb : refinement
Level V   : integration

When these levels are reached, there is a clear orientation towards the other people involved in a particular innovation (colleagues, pupils, parents).

Level VI   : refocusing

With the help of the interview, it is possible to make the levels of use for an innovation visible (using diagrams) and observe any differences in the manner in which an innovation is used among the teachers. This has been done with several improvement projects.

The Stages of Concern questionnaire and Levels of Use interview provide two key ways of describing and better understanding the behaviour of individual school leaders or teachers involved in change. Many innovation projects have been analysed using the *CBAM*-instruments. For example, three years after the initiation of the large-scale innovation projects in the Netherlands, 40% of the schools were still found to be at the stage of self concern. This is a plausible explanation for why many large-scale innovation projects fail to produce the results intended by the policy.

Another way of thinking and doing is needed, one that takes the motivations and concerns of the individual regarding capacity to make a unique contribution to the organization. We are increasingly faced with the task of making schools organizationally more competent. In order to realize these goals, schools must become places in which the various people involved in an innovation are motivated to work on it. In many cases, this will call for reconsideration of the roles and positions of the personnel within a school. In this context, we believe that the *CBAM* offers a number of useful assumptions and instruments.

In the near future, organizational self-government and self-control will become increasingly important. We have linked this development to the concept of transformational policy. Transformation refers to a fundamental change in the culture of an organization during periods of uncertainty. Via transformation one tries to find the solution for external challenges and uncertainties (Leithwood & Jantzi, 1990). The responsibility of the individual should then be seen as a guiding principle, and the behaviour of the individuals within an organization should be considered an important target of policy development.

Schools can be given enough policy space to undertake the numerous small steps that produce incremental transformation. It will be necessary for those involved in the innovation, however, to regularly reflect on their individual professional functioning and the functioning of the school as a whole. The diagnosis of the needs of the individuals and schools involved in a particular innovation will become an important part of such policy development, and the *CBAM* can provide the necessary tools.

TWO PERSPECTIVES ON SCHOOLS AND LARGE-SCALE INNOVATIONS:
THE RESULTS OF SOME DUTCH RESEARCH

The restructuring debate, now in full voice in most developed countries, is also taking place in the Netherlands where the reformist (New Right) government has pursued a policy of decentralization in education since the mid-eighties. This policy takes the form of an increased market orientation and the introduction of a new system of lump-sum financing. The policy of decentralization has also presupposed increased autonomy for schools. That is, schools should have greater opportunities to develop and carry out their own policy.

As in other countries in Western Europe, however, this shift towards the decentralization of education also has been accompanied by an increased tendency towards centralization. The interest of the Dutch government in maintaining control over the schools has been manifested, for example, in the implementation of a national curriculum (*basisvorming*) for secondary education. The tension created by the tendencies towards decentralization and centralization occurring at the same time is not just a Dutch dilemma. Hargreaves and Reynolds (1989), for example, have observed that *'we are entering a period of reduced state support for education overall, together with increasing state control over what remains (...)' (p.2).*

These policy developments clearly call upon those characteristics that pertain to the capacities of a school as an organization. Of major importance, then, is that schools be able to give form to their strategic capabilities (van den Berg, 1992; Sleegers, 1991). Besides giving the innovations imposed by the government a greater chance of succeeding, schools can also more easily implement the innovations which they consider important for local reasons. An important question in this light is whether or not schools are actually in a position to handle such changes. In order to answer this question in the Netherlands context, three studies have been undertaken. The first study concerned the capacity of secondary schools to develop policy. The second and third studies concerned the innovative capacities of both primary and secondary schools. These studies reflect two quite different perspectives on change: a 'managed change' or structural-functionalist perspective, and a perspective that is much more subjective and sensitive to the individual.

A Study of Schools and Policy Making: A Structural-Functionalist Perspective

Despite strong interest in the allocation of greater autonomy to schools, there is very little research into the ability of schools to utilize this autonomy. In the Dutch literature, for example, it is frequently assumed that the policy-making capacity of the school will determine its exploitation of these new opportunities (Marx, 1987). Marx argues that the attitude of schools towards such autonomy (i.e., the space available for policy-making) largely depends on the capacity of the school to actually make policy. Marx assumes that schools with relatively little policy-making capacity will make less use of available opportunities than schools with relatively greater policy-making capacity. Schools must have sufficient policy-making capacity for decentralization to succeed, and recent Dutch research has examined the relation between the policy-making capacity of schools and the extent to which these schools make use of such opportunities for policy-making (Sleegers, 1991).

The policy-making capacity of schools

The policy-making capacity of schools can be defined as the extent to which the schools are capable of independently performing their policy-making tasks. This policy-making capacity demands a certain level of development of the organizational structure of schools. By the 'organizational structure of schools,' we mean – among other things – the specification and distribution of the tasks involved in policy making. The organizational structure of schools clearly can influence the effectiveness of their policy making, and the organizational structure of schools can thus be regarded as an important indicator of their policy-making capacity (Marx, 1988).

Marx distinguishes three sets of variables that influence a school's policy-making capacity. The *first* set is concerned with mechanisms of coordination:

–   Size of the school.
–   The nature of student guidance.
–   The structure of student guidance.

The *second* set of variables influencing the extent to which schools are equipped for policy-making include:

–   School management support. School management should not only support policy-making activities but also steer these processes.
–   Management skill. School management should be sufficiently skilled with respect to organization, social leadership and the generation of a strategic viewpoint.
–   Structure for consultation. This should be formalized with more rather than fewer teachers involved in such consultation.
–   Coordination tasks. Such tasks should be distributed widely among the teachers.

A *third* set of variables concerns the authority relations within the school:

–   Teacher autonomy. The teaching staff must not function too autonomously.

The scope of policy-making of schools

The scope of policy making can be defined as the total number of opportunities that schools have to create or carry out their own policy. These opportunities are limited in The Netherlands by the laws and rules that pertain to the constitutional responsibility of the Dutch government for the quality of education in the country.

It is frequently assumed that Dutch schools do not make full use of the opportunities available to them for policy making. A possible explanation for this situation might be the schools' perception of the scope of policy-making. If schools judge the scope of policy-making to be quite small, then they will see very few opportunities for the making of policy (Sleegers and van Rooyen, 1989). Complete exploitation of the range of opportunities for policy making clearly depends on a desire to be actively involved in development of policy.

Thus, the use of policy-making opportunities (space) was indicated in this study the perceived space available for policy-making, and the actual development of policies (i.e. the actual policy-making of schools).

Research questions and design

The central questions in this study were as follows:
- Is it possible to distinguish between schools on the basis of their policy-making capacity?
- And does use of the opportunities for policy-making differ for schools with different policy-making capacities?

In order to address these issues, questionnaires were developed for school leaders and middle managers (i.e., teachers with supervisory and coordination tasks). The questionnaires addressed the following issues: student guidance and counselling, school organization, and the of policy-making space. The school was the unit of analysis.

Of the 196 schools initially approached, 26 agreed to participate in the study, (a response rate of 13.3%). As a result of insufficient response to the questionnaires within three schools, only 23 schools were included in the final analysis. In the selection of the schools for the analyses, the following two criteria were used: at least four people had to have responded within each school, and both school leaders and middle managers within each school had to have completed the questionnaire. Given the particularly low response rate in this study, however, its external validity can be questioned and the results should therefore be interpreted with caution.

Results

This section describes the main results of the survey. For a full account of the research we refer to Sleegers, Bergen & Giesbers (1994).

On the basis of a hierarchical cluster analysis (procedure CLUS-
TER; method WARD from SPSSX), three clusters of schools could be
distinguished, based on their policy-making capacity.

Cluster 1 can be typified as having a *hierarchically-oriented* policy-
making capacity. This cluster contains schools where management
dominates the policy-making process.

Cluster 3 can be typified as having a *collegial-oriented* policy-making capacity. This cluster contains schools where teachers dominate the
policy-making process.

Cluster 2 can be typified as having a *reduced collegial-oriented* policy-making capacity. This cluster contains schools in between the clusters of schools mentioned above. It should be noted that the schools in
Cluster 2 were more similar to the schools in Cluster 3 than the schools
in Cluster 1.

The relation between policy-making capacity of schools and the
scope of policy making (second research question) was examined in a
one-way analysis. Result of these analyses show the Cluster 3 schools
to be most active in the development of instructional and administrative policies. These schools differed significantly from schools with a
hierarchically-oriented approach to policy-making (Cluster 1 schools):
these schools were the least active with regard to the development of
instructional and administrative policies. Finally, Cluster 2 schools
were found to judge the opportunities (space) available for policy making to be great but were not most active in the development of instructional and administrative policies. This result was contrary to the
researchers' expectation that greater use of the opportunities for policy
making would be made when schools perceived the scope of policy
making to be extensive. It can be concluded that schools not only differ
in their policy-making capacity but also in their utilization of the
opportunities for policy making (i.e., the available space for policy-
making).

**From Policy-Making Capacity to Innovative Capacity: Implications for
Leadership**

The policy-making capacity of schools appears to be related primarily
to those organizational characteristics that are of particular importance
for the independent development of policy by schools. A major underlying assumption, then, is that schools operate rationally and are goal-
directed organizations (see Giesbers & Sleegers, 1994). The develop-

ment of policy, then, can be construed as a systematic and methodic method for leading a school. In an extension of this, the policy-making capacity of a school concerns the capacity of the school to develop explicit policy and the capacity of the school to steer the implementation of the policy that has been formulated (Marx, 1987, 1988). In other words, coordination and steering constitute central aspects of a school's policy-making capacity.

The perspective on the role of the principal is essentially managerial in nature. The need for the leader to maintain at least an oversight role, which involves initiating the development of explicit policy, an active monitoring of the implementation of the policy, the creation of a formalized structure for consultation and communication, and the generation of a strategic view is emphasized. The development and implementation of policy is centrally coordinated within the school. Although active engagement of teachers in the policy-making process (participatory decision-making) is advocated, decision making at the school level is reserved to the principal. The centrality attributed to the principal's role expresses a view of the principal as the manager of others in the school.

According to Marx (1988), schools with a greater policy-making capacity will also make greater use of the space available to them for policy making. Research by Sleegers (1991) (see also Sleegers et al., 1994) has refined this claim by showing that the use of the policy space in schools is more likely to be determined by the type of policy-making capacity than by the degree of policy-making capacity. Schools with a collegial-oriented policy-making capacity make greater use of their policy-making space than schools with a hierarchically-oriented policy-making capacity. This suggests that the schools, at least in The Netherlands, will be better equipped to take advantage of increasing autonomy as they become more collegial. The central assumption behind this line of reasoning is that the possibilities for schools to adequately deal with large-scale changes such as increased school autonomy will be promoted by the capacity of the schools to develop and implement their own policy. Viewed in this manner, issues of educational development and innovation can be reduced to questions of policy-making structure.

This analysis of the policy-making capacity of schools and the role of the principal gives rise to a vision of educational development and innovation that, according to Louis (1994), falls 'into a paradigm that might be best called managed change' (p.4). This structural-functionalist perspective which views managed change as an effective strategy for educational improvement has been largely undermined by research into large-scale change processes in schools (Louis, Lagerweij & Voogt, 1994). Research has shown, for instance, change processes to be unpredictable, evolutionary, and difficult to manage as a result (Louis & Miles, 1990; Louis & Smith, 1991, 1992; Rosenblum, Louis & Rosmiller, 1994).

In the change process, the effective principal's role is described as a facilitator, freeing the staff and the school to reach its own potential. In restructured schools, effective leaders focus on helping staff to confront, make sense of, and interpret the problems facing the school so that teachers and administrators can work with each other to reach goals that are never well-defined (Louis, 1994).

School restructuring calls for a greater emphasis on collective problem solving, teacher empowerment, experimentation and teacher reflection. This implies a different role for the principal which calls more attention to the enhancement of the individual and collective problem-solving capacities of all members of the school community; a role often referred to as transformational leadership. The perspective on the role of the principal is essentially leadership, not managerial, in nature.

In addition to the preceding considerations with respect to the capacity of schools for innovation, it was recognized that the policy-making capacities of schools are too infrequently analysed from the perspective of the involvement and contribution of the individual people involved in the organization. As the research reviewed in section 3 has shown, the involvement of the individual teacher is of great importance for the effective completion of an innovation trajectory by a school and success of the more general innovation program. In other words, a more personal perspective should be adopted in the study of change processes in schools.

It was these insights that in fact prompted us to ask if the concept of policy-making capacity was appropriate for our study of weather or not schools are in a position to handle the large scale educational changes confronting them.

The preceding considerations with regard to the policy-making capacity of schools led us to speak of the *innovative capacity of schools*. In the following sections, this concept will be considered in greater detail. The results of two studies of the innovative capacity of schools will also be presented, and two central aspects of the innovative capacity of schools will be considered in particular: the functioning of the school as a learning organization and the role of the transformational school leader.

The Innovative Capacity of Secondary Schools: An Individual Perspective

A first qualitative study. In light of the large-scale innovations taking place in The Netherlands and the rest of Western Europe, it is useful to consider the potential and possibilities of schools for the actual realization of these innovations and the large-scale innovations in particular. Of particular concern are: just how large the innovative capacity of the schools may be, what educational possibilities are available to them, and the role that good leadership plays in such innovation (van den Berg & Sleegers, 1995).

The *innovative capacity of schools* is defined as the competence of schools to implement innovations initiated by either the government or the school itself and the competence to bring both types of innovation into relation with each other when necessary. A review of the literature on the functioning of innovative organizations shows the following components to be of particular importance and thus of significance to a school that wants to make optimal use of its innovative capacities:
- the context of the school;
- collaboration among the teachers;
- transformational school leadership; and
- the functioning of the school as a learning organization.

The context of the school

On the one hand, school context refers to those features of the external environment of the school relating to markets, the political climate, and economic circumstances (Mintzberg, 1991). On the other hand, a number of internal features are also of significance and thus part of the context of the school. The school is currently confronting a strongly changing environment that compels innovation. The school is also confronting legislation and government policy that provide a greater degree of freedom, and the school leadership is concerned with teachers who are already used to a great degree of autonomy (which either may or may not be stimulated by internal regulations).

Within the classroom, teachers are free to work as they choose. Nevertheless, it is important for schools to attune policy and daily practice to each other (Kievit & Vandenberghe, 1993), and it should be noted that complex, large-scale innovations are simply no good without central regulation (Rolff, 1993, Sleegers & Wesselingh, 1993). When a school wants or needs to expand its innovative capacity, it will have to stimulate teachers to contribute within the existing contextual framework.

Collaboration among the teachers

A well-functioning team of teachers is the basis for a good school. Stimulating school leadership is naturally a prerequisite for a good teacher team (Fullan, 1992), but the team determines the functioning of the organization and its innovative capacity. It is important that the team not functions as a group of individual teachers. 'Advanced innovation requires that experts from different disciplines be combined into flexibly functioning ad hoc project groups' (Mintzberg, 1991, p. 205). Teachers must collaborate intensively on the content of their subject matter but also across subject matters. One may think in terms of thematic or project teaching, which clearly requires collaboration. Any hesitation to attend each other's lessons or ask each other for advice is minimized.

In the area of school organization, teachers also should collaborate with each other and work together with the school leaders. Within such a framework, attention should be devoted to the collective responsibility of the school team without losing sight of the individual's freedom and creativity. As will be seen below, this form of collaboration is of central importance for 'the school as a learning organization.'

Transformational school leadership

In a study of the factors that foster a collaborative culture, à Campo (1993) found a relation between the strategies that the school leadership employed in the determination of policy and the existence of a collaborative culture. One of the forms of leadership found to accompany the development of a high innovative capacity in particular is referred to as *transformational leadership* (Conger & Kanungo, 1994; Leithwood, 1992; 1994; Lovell, Lynch & Hart, 1994; Sergiovanni, 1990, 1992). Transformational school leaders see themselves 'as responsible more for redefining educational goals than for implementing existing programs' (Mitchell & Tucker, 1992, p. 34).

In the Centre for Leadership Development in Toronto (Canada), Leithwood and others have conducted a great deal of research into the position, characteristics, and effects of transformational leadership. This form of leadership has been related by Leithwood to the great changes facing education. Leithwood, Tomlinson and Genge (1995), reviewed six qualitative and 15 quantitative studies of transformational school leadership. This led to the identification of 12 dimensions of such leadership. On the basis of research with 74 secondary-education teachers (Leithwood, 1995), this number was reduced to the following four dimensions:

- the *identification of goals* including the development of a school-wide *vision*, the inspirational dissemination of this vision (charisma) and the establishment of high expectations with regard to the functioning of teachers and students;
- the *involvement of people* including the guidance and stimulation of individuals;
- the development of *structures bottom-up*; and
- the development of a *culture of collaboration*.

Leithwood concludes on the basis of his research, that transformational school leaders pursue three fundamental goals: first, the stimulation and development of a collaborative climate within the school; second, contribution to the continuous professional development of the teachers; and, third, expansion of the problem-solving capacity of the school. Transformational school leadership clearly occurs within the framework of maximizing the potential of those involved in a particular organization.

Fullan (1992) sees the creation of a collaborative culture as the most important task of the transformational leader. The transformational school leader must stimulate a collaborative culture by establishing the prerequisites necessary for such collaboration and stimulating the teachers to continue developing, collaborating, and striving to realize the school's mission and target goals.

Sagor (1992) also has reported on the results of research into schools where there is evidence of transformational leadership. No matter how different the schools and school leaderships were, a high level of teacher involvement was found even in tasks other than teaching in every case. Participation in joint projects, delegation of responsibility by the school leaders and appreciation of the contribution of every individual were found to significantly increase the degree of involvement. 'Yet, in each case these principals provide teachers with the meaningful personal support that creates a willingness to go above and beyond the call of duty' (Sagor, 1992, p. 18).

Confirmation of the foregoing insights can be found in research by Hopkins (1994). This research, performed by a team from Cambridge University, showed the need to conceptualize leadership in a manner other than the traditional manner. Leadership is seen by these authors as a source for teachers to optimally develop themselves on the basis of their own, individual expertise. In this connection, one speaks of 'working with' rather than 'working on.' Working with teachers thus means:

- seeing that the teachers continue to look ahead: letting them see what works; negative experiences should not, however, be disregarded;
- emphasizing what they already have mastered and are capable of doing: paying attention to that manner of working that has been experienced as positive in the past;
- encouraging teachers to work in partnerships where relative differences nevertheless are recognized and honoured; and
- using reinforcement in whatever form.

These characteristics are considered crucial by the research team from Cambridge. The opinions and work of the teachers are thus confirmed and reinforced in a positive manner. The researchers refer to this process as *empowerment* and see this as the basis for the developing of the school as a learning organization. Transforming teacher perspectives is seen as the essential principle of school improvement. In sum, research has shown transformational leadership to exert a positive influence on the course of school-improvement processes.

The functioning of the school as a learning organization

For the optimal development of the innovative capacity of a school, it is important that the school conducts its own policy and thus takes on the character of a *strategic organization*. Such organizations are directed at the possibility of continually generating new knowledge, expertise, and skills in order to play off of the changing circumstances around them (Senge, 1993). The notion of a strategic organization is closely related to a notion that is currently of great interest, namely the *learning organization* (van den Berg, 1992).

A *learning organization* is an organization that consciously executes policy intended to expand its learning capacity at all levels and on a continuous basis in order to optimize its effectiveness. In much of the literature on innovative organizations (Mintzberg, 1991; Sundbo, 1992, and others), an *organic* structure is identified as the best for survival in a complex and dynamic environment. It seems reasonable then, that schools should also develop in this way. Within a strategic or learning organization, one can speak of such an organic structure. This structure identifies itself in the first place with the use of strategy formation for policy determination and in the second place with coordination based on attuning the various sections of the school to each other. These two aspects will be further specified below.

Every organization needs strategies for determining its policies. The manner in which these strategies are developed can differ. One possibility for policy determination is *strategic planning*, where management establishes plans for the long term. A danger of such tight planning and fixed long-term policy is organizational rigidity. Another possibility for the determination of policy is *strategy formation*. In this case, policy determination has an incremental character starting at the base. Strategies are not determined in a single place (the top) nor are they consciously formulated. Rather, strategies are *formed* in an implicit manner during the activities that occur in the organization (Mintzberg, 1991). Teachers play a crucial role in *strategy formation*. They can indicate what is happening in a school and what is needed, which we call the *personal perspective* (van den Berg, 1993). From a personal perspective, policy is developed on the basis of the problems, initiatives, and needs of the teaching staff and school leaders. With and through the contribution of teachers, strategies can be formulated for realization of the school's mission. School leaders play an important role in the development of this collective perspective.

Different authors also plea for incremental policy development (van den Berg, 1992, Louis, Lagerweij & Voogt, 1994). One should be occupied with the solution of the problems that present themselves based on the existing situation and what is attainable in the short term. A number of alternatives must be considered when the goals are not always explicit (van den Berg, Hameyer, & Stokking, 1988). An innovative process is extremely difficult to control because innovation implies detaching oneself from established patterns (Mintzberg, 1991). Innovation also implies disturbance of the equilibrium, which brings

678

uncertainty and inconsistencies along with it. Innovations cannot, therefore, develop under rigid planning circumstances. They require a different climate. One should not attempt to avoid or eliminate the chaos that occurs. One should, however, try to control chaos. Under such circumstances, one cannot fall back on the forms of standardization applicable in a more stable environment (van den Berg, 1992).

One way of coordinating the activities in a learning organization is to appoint contact individuals or key persons to attune the various activities within the organization to each other. Not only formal school leaders but also teachers should help appoint these people (Mintzberg, 1991), who are then responsible for coordination of the different project teams and the maintenance of various contacts. These people are constantly in touch with what is happening in the organization and can therefore function as an excellent intermediary between the various parties involved. In such a way, the different activities can be well-tuned to each other. This has proved to be of importance for the development of policy in schools (Sleegers et al, 1994).

Just how the components of the innovative capacity described above relate to each other is schematically represented in Figure 2.

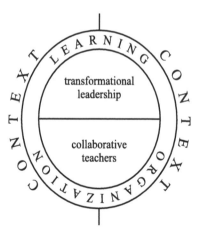

Figure 2: Conceptual model of the innovative capacity of schools

The relation between the four components of an innovative capacity can be sketched as follows. The context forces schools to follow a different-less dependent-(local) school policy. An important element in this policy is knowing how to give form to internal and external innovations. In order to do this, two conditions are of particular importance:

a specific form of leadership and a collaborative culture. The presence of these two components can lead to a learning organization. The school leader should also foster strategy formation and mutual harmony, which are two critical aspects of a learning organization.

Research questions and research design

In order to empirically describe the concept of innovative capacity, a preliminary study of the innovative capacity of secondary schools was undertaken (N teachers = 46). The following research question was formulated as the basis for this research: *To what extent do schools with a high innovative capacity differ from schools with a low innovative capacity?*

A group of secondary schools with a high innovative capacity and a group of secondary schools with a low innovative capacity were identified. For the selection of the schools with a *high* innovative capacity, two criteria were formulated:
  - the school began early with the preparation of the core curriculum, and
  - the school has a tradition of quickly and frequently implementing innovations.

The selection criteria for schools assumed to have a *low* innovative capacity stand in direct contrast to the preceding:
  - these schools started on the preparation of a core curriculum at a late stage, and
  - these schools generally demonstrated strong resistance to the implementation of innovations.

Interview questions were grouped under a number of topics and served as a guide for the interview. For each of the four components in the model, a number of questions were formulated. The implementation of a core curriculum as the basis for innovation was taken as the starting point in posing the questions.

All of the interviews were audio recorded. The interview took approximately one study period. For a more detailed description of the research design and methods of data collection, the reader is referred to van den Berg and Sleegers (1995).

Results

In this section, the most important results of the foregoing study will be considered. Of particular interest will be the results with regard to two of the central components of an innovative school capacity: transformational leadership and the school as a learning organization. For a description of the other results, the reader is referred to van den Berg and Sleegers (1995).

The results with regard to transformational leadership are presented in Table 1. The absolute number of statements related to a variety of key words is presented in the data matrices. In Table 1, those key words with a relatively large difference in the number of statements produced by the high and low innovation schools are presented. (These differences were evaluated by a number of independent judges.) For each of the key words, two columns are indicated. The left column represents the total number of statements for the group of teachers from the high innovation schools. The right column indicates the total number of statements for the group of teachers from the low innovation schools.

School leaders in schools with a high innovative capacity attempted to create and realize a target idea (realization of a target idea). In schools with a low innovative capacity, this proved to be much less the case (no shared educational vision). School leaders in schools with a high innovative capacity also appeared to create a supportive atmosphere among the members of the teaching team (team building). The contact between the school leaders and the teachers was also judged to be satisfactory in the high innovation group; the barrier to contact was low (low supportive school leaders). The barrier to approaching the school leaders was higher in the low innovation group (supportive school leaders). In addition, initiatives in schools with a high innovative capacity were stimulated by the school leaders (stimulated); this was less so in schools with a low innovative capacity (not stimulated).

In schools with a high innovative capacity, the school leaders considered it important to maintain or improve the existing culture. School leaders also paid a lot of attention to the well-being of the teachers (personnel care). In the high innovation group, final strategic decisions predominantly were made in the staff meeting (decision making on the basis of staff meeting).

Key word	Total number of statements for high innovation group	Total number of statements for low innovation group
Task construction		
Realization of a target idea	53	18
No common /educational vision	5	20
Team building	33	2
Contact		
Supportive school leadership	11	5
Low supportive school leadership	7	11
Initiatives		
Stimulated	34	8
Not stimulated	3	14
Personnel policy		
Cultural Maintenance	7	0
Personnel care	12	3
Decision making		
On the basis of staff meetings	14	4

Table 1: Overview of key words relevant to transformational leadership for each group of secondary schools

Results with regard to the school as a learning organization are presented in Table 2. More tasks and authority were delegated to the teachers in the schools with a high innovative capacity (sufficient delegation) than in the schools with a low innovative capacity. The teachers also were found to directly influence policy in schools with a high innovative capacity. In addition, the conduct of policy was found to be the most flexible under these circumstances (flexibility in the implementation of policy), and the conduct of policy was found to occur incrementally from the bottom up (bottom-up influence) under such circumstances. Committees responsible for particular activities (functioning of committees) and middle management were found to occupy key positions (middle management as key figure) in the schools with a high innovative capacity. Together, these authorities saw to the coordination of the different activities. Finally, the teachers in the high innovation group were found to have the need to continually develop themselves, (need for in service training) and the school leadership had clearly outlined a policy for this purpose (policy for in service training).

A striking result is that the teacher was found to influence policy by being a member of a committee or the middle management in both groups of schools. The development of middle management is being observed more and more in secondary education and appears to be prompted by the changing tasks of the school leadership. Such a structure clearly allows the functions being created to be finely differentiated and the coordination of the various activities within the school to occur in a less top-down manner than before. It is also important, however, that the tasks and responsibilities of the middle management be clearly specified.

The Innovative Capacity of Primary Schools: A Second Qualitative Study

Results of the first investigation into the innovative capacity of secondary schools were used to create an initial model of the innovative capacity of schools (see Figure 2). In a second study, the innovative capacity of primary schools in The Netherlands was examined. Central to this research was the innovative program *Together Again to School* (*Weer Samen Naar School*), a large-scale school-innovation project in (van den Berg and Vandenberghe, 1984). It is intended to jointly realize a number of goals at both the school and classroom levels of organization. The major goals of the program are: to reduce the number of students receiving referral for special education; to set up a system of integrated student care; to increase the diagnostic and remedial capacities of teachers; and to develop more strategic school policy.

Key words	Total for high innovation group	Total for low innovation group
Strategy		
Sufficient delegation	15	6
Bottom-up influence	28	4
Flexibility in the implementation of policy	15	1
Coordination		
Functioning of committees	13	5
Middle management as key figure	18	9
Learning		
Need for in service training	21	6
Policy for in service training	18	5

Table 2: Overview of key words relevant to the school as a learning organization for each group of secondary schools

The purpose of this second study was to validate the model developed in the initial study and to go one step further by examining the possible relation between the innovative capacity of schools and the intensity of their concerns with regard to the innovation. As mentioned above, examination of the concerns of individual teachers is an important step in understanding the process of educational change and innovation.

The following research questions were formulated for this second study.

1 What concrete differences can be observed between high – and low – innovation primary schools for each component of innovative capacity?

2 Is there a relation between the innovative capacity of a primary school and the concerns of the school leaders and teachers within the school?

In the preliminary study of secondary schools, a group of high-innovation schools was found to clearly differ from a group of low-innovation schools with respect to the components of their innovative capacity. In the present study, we wanted to examine these differences in greater detail. In particular, it was expected that high-innovation schools would differ from the low-innovation schools in terms of their concerns.

Method

A number of *high-innovation* and *low-innovation* schools were once again sought. The 64 teachers, internal advisors and directors who agreed to participate in this study were interviewed twice and administered a questionnaire. The actual innovative capacity of the school was examined with an adapted form of the interview used in the first preliminary study. Questions in this interview pertained to the four components of the model of innovative capacity (see Figure 2). All of the interviews were tape recorded and then transcribed by a third person.

The prevalence of a concerns-based approach within the school was examined in a second interview and a questionnaire. The interview was the *Levels of Use of an Innovation* (van den Berg & Vandenberghe, 1981) and the Rasch – questionnaire was the *Intensity of Concern* (see section 3.3.; van den Berg, 1993). On the basis of the interview, the particular phase of an innovation's implementation can be determined. Rasch – scores from the questionnaire describe the degree of concern for the innovation. For a more elaborate description of the research design, the reader is referred to van den Berg, Sleegers and Geijsel (in preparation).

As mentioned above, the content of the innovation program was *Together Again to School* (*Weer Samen Naar School*)

Results

The key words identified with respect to the innovative capacity of schools in the previous study (about 70) also constituted the basis for the analyses of the interviews in the present study (van den Berg et al., in preparation). In keeping with the discussion of the results of the previous study, the most important results with regard to transformational leadership and the school as a learning organization are reported.

Key words	Total for high innovation group	Total for low innovation group
Vision	38	17
No vision	1	43
Charisma	22	0
No charisma	0	38
Innovation	62	7
Traditional teaching	0	26
Sufficient individual feedback	27	5
Insufficient individual feedback	4	12
Adequate delegation	48	5
Inadequate delegation	12	38
Joint goals	41	2
Collaborative culture	41	2
Joint responsibility	7	2
No joint responsibility	0	47

Table 3: Overview of key words televant to transformational leadership for each group of primary schools

The results for the categories pertaining to the presence or absence of a transformational leadership are summarized in Table 3. The school leaders in the high-innovation schools can be characterized by their vision of education and the school. Leaders in these schools have a certain charisma that can inspire others, but they can also take firm position of their own when necessary. The school leader is continually working on the realization of his or her vision, consciously initiating innovations in the school, and using his or her powers of persuasion to motivate the team. At the same time, the leader shows respect for the ideas of others and understanding for their personal needs and feelings.

Such leaders also are in a position to delegate responsibilities, without neglecting them, because a great deal of attention is paid to the creation of a joint plan of responsibility. In such a way, collaboration becomes self-evident and can be further stimulated. The joint responsibility of the team for both students and their parents is also appealed to.

Examination of the low-innovation schools reveals a very different image of the school leader. Many of the respondents in these schools were of the opinion that their school leader had no educational vision. Questions with regard to this issue were largely answered with 'no idea' or 'I don't understand the question.' The school leader is much less of an initiator than in the high-innovation schools; he or she does not motivate or inspire the team. The teachers indicated a desire for more energy from their school leader, which would include pushing for the conclusion to a lengthy discussion (but not at the cost of the plans of the teachers). The school leader in the low-innovation school was often more conservative than the school leader in a high-innovation school. School leaders in low-innovation schools also appeared to consciously slow down certain innovations at times. Personal needs and desires of teachers were rarely considered. The delegation of responsibility was either neglected or viewed as a means of leaving the work to someone else. These school leaders make little attempt to create a shared plan of responsibility for innovation and change. Also there was far less that was jointly-shared in the low-innovation schools when compared to the high-innovation schools.

One of the low-innovation schools provided an exception to this image. A year prior to the initiation of this study, a new school leader was appointed to the school. Among other things, improvement of collaboration within the school was identified as a major goal and an exception to the low-innovation group was thus created.

Data pertaining to the schools as a learning organization are summarized in Table 4. Initiatives from the teaching team are stimulated more in the high-innovation schools than in the low-innovation schools. One can also speak of greater strategy formation in the high-innovation schools than in the low-innovation schools. The task descriptions from the internal advisor, for example, are clearer in the high-innovation schools than in the low-innovation schools. There is a clear difference between the groups with regard to the availability of information. The libraries in the high-innovation schools are much better equipped than the libraries in the low-innovation schools, and people clearly know about the materials available in the high-innovation schools. The comments from the respondents in the high-innovation schools indicate a clear educational policy while in the low-innovation group relatively less attention is paid to the sorts of courses, for example, that may be of importance to the future of the school. Much less of a need for in service training was also observed in the low-innovation schools when compared to the high-innovation schools. Keeping on top of new developments is apparently less important in the low-innovation schools than in the high-innovation schools.

Key words	Total for high innovation group	Total for low innovation group
Influence stimulated	70	14
Influence not stimulated	6	38
Clear task description	19	12
Unclear task description	5	14
Sufficient availability of information	32	7
Insufficient availability of information	9	36
Educational policy	20	2
No educational policy	3	12
Large need for in service training	31	7
Minimal need for in service training	14	43
Decisions in team meeting	57	12
Little say in decisions	2	24
Little agreement on decisions	0	21
Middle management	33	7
Need for personal growth	32	14

Table 4: Overview of key words relevant to the school as a learning organization for each group of primary schools

Differences between the two groups can also be observed with regard to decision-making. In the high-innovation group, this occurs in the team meeting and consensus is attempted particularly when it comes to policy decisions. In the low-innovation group, decisions are also made in a team setting but the voicing of one's opinion is much less encouraged than in the high-innovation group. One can also speak of a middle-management framework within the high-innovation schools; the internal advisor appears to have a clearly established position within these schools. Finally, the comments with regard to the need for personal growth suggest that the respondents in the high-innovation schools strive to develop on all fronts and continue to critically examine themselves.

In sum: The differences between the two groups with regard to the functioning of the school as a learning organization predominantly concern the influence of the team members, the availability of information, educational policy, and the manner in which important decisions are made.

Intensity of concern and levels of use

On the basis of the *Concerns-Based Adoption Model (CBAM)*, the intensity of the concern and level of use for an innovation was expected to be higher for the respondents in the high-innovation schools than for the respondents in the low-innovation schools. The interview *Levels of Use of an Innovation* and the questionnaire *Intensity of Concern* were used to examine the relation between the innovative capacity of a school and the degree of involvement in the program *Together Again to School*. In the present discussion, we will limit ourselves to the most relevant results. For a more extended description of the results, the reader is referred to Geijsel (1994).

As described in section 3, the *CBAM* distinguishes eight different levels of use for an innovation, which can then be measured by the interview *Levels of Use of an Innovation*. The results of this interview are presented in Table 5 and show a significant relation to exist between the innovative capacity of a school and the level of use for the innovation program *Together Again to School*. When compared to the low-innovation schools, the high-innovation schools appear to be more concerned with how the innovation program can best be implemented. The respondents in the high-innovation group also appear to be more aware of what the program can mean for students and colleagues; the respondents in the low-innovation schools continue to be in the preparatory phase and preoccupied with the initial phase of implementation in particular.

Levels of use (N = 64)		High Innovation group		Low Innovation group	
0/I/II	Orienting use	1	(2%)	11	(58%)
III	Mechanical use	10	(22%)	5	(26%)
IVa	Routine use	14	(31%)	3	(16%)
IVb/V	Integrated use	20	(45%)	0	(0%)

Chi-square = 36.03, df = 3. p = 0.00

Table 5: Distribution of the different levels of use for each group of primary schools

The results for the questionnaire *Intensity of Concern* are summarized for the two groups of schools in Table 6. The purpose of this questionnaire was to determine the intensity of the concern with the innovation among those involved in the provision of educational services. This concern can run from a relatively passive knowledge of the innovation, which reflects marginal involvement, to inclusion of the innovation in the daily teaching routine, which clearly reflects active involvement (van den Berg, 1993). The maximum values for the scale used to measure the intensity of the concern were -3 and +3. The higher the score on the scale, the greater the intensity of the concern with the innovation. A t-test revealed the difference between the two groups to be significant with the high-innovation schools demonstrating a greater degree of concern with the program of innovation *Together Again to School* than the low-innovation schools.

CONCLUSION

Reflecting upon the results of the preceding studies of the innovative capacity of schools, the following conclusions can be drawn.

Innovative capacity	Average	Standard deviation	N
High innovation group	- 0.65	1.54	45
Low innovation group	- 1.65	1.49	19

$t = 2.43$, df. $= 35$, $p = 0.02$

Table 6: Average scores for the questionnaire 'Intensity of Concern' for each group of primary schools

Transformational Leadership

Large differences were found between the leaders of high-innovation and low-innovation schools. These differences were also found to correspond to the major dimensions of transformational leadership (Leithwood, 1994). The following four features appeared to be of particular importance.

Mission

When asked about the vision of the school leader, the respondents in the low-innovation schools frequently did not answer or mentioned a general educational goal such as 'the provision of a good education.' In contrast, everyone appears to be completely full of the leader's vision in the high-innovation schools. The teachers also appear to stand behind this vision; they can clearly describe the task of the school and specify the foundations of the vision. In other words, the vision of the leader has become a school mission. The following statements from two different teachers about the same school leader are illustrative.

> With regard to educational vision, our school leader is very child-oriented. The profile of this school was already very child-oriented for the outside but the organization was not structured in such a manner. The school leader has organized things here without losing sight of the principles that we stand behind. That is not always easy. I think he is a steering force.

He is also really busy with the reality, with the developments as they now are within the educational system. There is absolutely no dozing off...things are tackled here...and I think that is really good.

His vision is crystal clear: The child is most important to him...and it is most important to us all. Since he has been at our school, he has been able to bring this more into the foreground. It was always clear, but his strength is that everything now turns around this.

Joint goals

A transformational school leader is responsible for the acceptance of the goals that the school has set for itself. The transformational leader can convince the team of the importance of the goals and inspire them to pursue the goals.

Charisma

Inspiration is largely related to the charisma of the school leader. The transformational leader radiates dedication, which motivates people and was clearly evident in the comments of the respondents from the high-innovation schools.

Individual support

Understanding and respect for personal feelings is a very important characteristic of the transformational leader. Without this capacity, it is impossible to convince teachers about anything.

The School as a Learning Organization

High – and low – innovation schools not only differ with regard to the presence or absence of transformational leaders; they also differ with regard to functioning as a learning organizations. The following two features appeared to be of particular importance.

Need for personal growth

In high-innovation schools, the teachers appear to have a need for personal growth and continued schooling. The opportunity to meet these needs is presented by making information available to the teachers and considering which form of schooling may be of importance to the school.

Strategy formation

The contribution of teachers to policy – and decision – making is clearly stimulated in the high-innovation schools. One of the characteristics of strategy formation is the use of middle management, which helps make everyone's task clear. Strategy formation is further enabled by designating the team meeting as the most important decision-making body and stimulating people to think along with others. Everyone is notified of ongoing matters and therefore sufficiently informed.

Innovative Capacity, Intensity of Concern, and Levels of Use

In the six high-innovation primary schools studied here, the educators clearly demonstrated a more concerns-based approach than the educators in the low-innovation primary schools. Both the *level of use* for the *Together Again to School* program and the *intensity of concern* for the program appeared to be greater in the high-innovation schools than in the low-innovation schools. This confirms the assumption that innovative capacity and degree of concern may be related. The results of the interviews nevertheless suggested that this relation should be further worked out in future research.

IMPLICATIONS

The Need for Transformational Leadership in Large-Scale Innovations

In order to expand the innovative capacity of schools, it is important to train school leaders on aspects of transformational leadership. School leaders must develop in such a manner that they can disseminate a mission, do this in interaction with those involved in the school, and provide the necessary support for individual teachers. In such a way, leadership can be developed that contributes to a greater innovative capacity for the school.

In the context of complex large-scale innovations, one can often see the need for very specific leadership to help the innovations succeed. In particular, large-scale changes may be defined as transitions that significantly disrupt people's expectations (Salisbury & Conner, 1994). Changes that only marginally disrupt people's expectations are relatively easy to implement. Major disruptions of expectations, however, can result in significant self concern: disorientation, confusion, fear, anxiety, and loss of one's emotional equilibrium.

For minor or small-scale changes, traditional leadership appears to be sufficient. For major or large-scale changes, however, the accepted forms of leadership do not appear to be adequate. More specifically: The existing pattern of expectations among the teachers is disrupted to such an extent that transformational leadership appears to be more adequate under such circumstances.

The Importance of Analysing Concern by Transformational Leaders

The disruption of the existing pattern of expectations is related to what we call *concern*. This is a natural reaction in situations where teachers are expected to tackle new problems, use new materials, and apply new forms of teaching. The perception of the nature of an innovation by the actors is a strong determinant of the chances of innovative success. Not only the objective characteristics of the innovation but also the manner in which significance is attached to the innovation by those involved in it are determinants of the innovative capacity of a school. We therefore plead for the adoption of the so-called *personal perspective* in innovations. Using this perspective, the personal concerns with a particular innovation can then be undertaken with the aid of the instruments described in section 3.3 above.

By clearly taking the concerns of those involved in an innovation into consideration, the possibilities for the performance of what they see as their task are appealed to. Anything that can possibly optimize this task – whether internal or external – should be taken as a pretext for the provision of support. It is then important that insight into the exact nature of the individual's personal perspective be acquired in order to provide *concern-based support*. Support means connecting with – and not imposing or dictating – and thus constitutes one of the most important tasks of a transformational leadership.

Incremental Policy Development and Leadership

In the framework of the innovative capacity, schools must be able to operationalize their goals, collect the relevant information, analyse this information in light of their goals, make decisions about the interventions based on the original goals, etc. All of these activities must be conducted in the framework of complex, often large-scale, innovations. Numerous goals must be simultaneously realized within a short time span, and numerous organizations and people are also involved on a variety of levels.

In many of the discussions of educational innovation to date, the emphasis has been on the large-scale aspect of the innovation and the *surrounding optimism* that is expected to come with such innovation. The large-scale emphasis can be found in the national plans to drastically reform the educational system. By *surrounding optimism*, we mean the expectation that (large-scale) improvements in the school and its environment will produce – more or less on their own – the desired effects.

We have questioned the effectiveness of large-scale plans and projects. The number of proponents of a small-scale approach is growing, and the quality of the teacher is being given greater importance within such an approach. This also makes finely-tuned, long-term guidance by school leaders a clear prerequisite for successful innovation. This does not mean that large-scale policy should not be conducted. Rather, national policy should serve to establish the positive prerequisites for the conduct of small-scale, school-related projects.

From such a perspective, it is important to take the changes that are occurring within the individual school into consideration. The notion of the school as a learning organization then becomes relevant, and one can speak of *incremental policy development* from the base. This holds for the innovative capacity of the school as well as for the building of this capacity by the school leader. An innovative capacity is best built systematically, layer-by-layer. We see increasing the innovative capacity of a school as an evolutionary process. It is wise to develop the innovative capacity of a school step-by-step from the inside out. Schools must spell out their own trajectory for development; stepwise development must be made possible within a reasonable span of time; and transformational leadership will be indispensable in this process.

The Need for a Transformational Innovation Policy and Leadership

In Western Europe, the current situation in education inadvertently calls to mind the picture of 'Prisoners in a Prison Yard' (Van den Berg 1992, p. 440). As the executors of government policy in the framework of large scale innovations, school leaders are becoming unsure of themselves. In many situations, school leaders and teachers rarely seem to look toward the future. In combination with diminishing resources, this attitude can cause them to revert to primal survival strategies (high self-concerns). This description is characteristic of educators in the United States as well (Hall, 1992).

Everywhere, school leaders and teachers have high self concerns and task concerns. They are unable to accomplish all that is being asked of them and are feeling increasingly paralyses by the never ending demands for the addition of new large scale innovations. Findings of research in Western Europe indicate that it is extremely difficult to initiate and execute those innovations. To prevent the 'prisoners in the prison yard' syndrome we need transformational leaders with a sense of having much control over their own profession, vision and direction, and a high sense of efficacy for what they personally can do. This is important to address the situation in ways that they believe would result in improved innovative capacity.

A transformational innovation policy is characterized by capacities of school leaders, where vision building, creativity, involvement of people (personal perspective) and individual feedback are key. No two schools are exactly alike. It is necessary for local schools to be empowered by school leaders to create educational inviting settings. One of the primary reasons for the 'prisoner in the prison yard' syndrome is the failure of the policy-making perspective (structural-functionalist perspective) to trust and have confidence in school leaders and teachers to bring about needed improvements. A system of support must be developed in order for teachers and school leaders to be empowered to innovate school in more transformational ways.

REFERENCES

Acampo, C. (1993). Collaborative school cultures: how principals make a difference. *School Organisation, 13*(2), 119 – 127.

Beare, H., & Boyd W.L. (Eds.) (1993). *Restructuring schools. An international perspective on the movement to transform the control and performance of schools.* London: The Falmer press.

Berg, R. van den (1992). Transformational Education Policy. Schools as strategic organizations. *Knowledge: Creation Diffusion, Utilization, 13*, (4), 440 – 459.

Berg, R. van den (1993). The Concerns – Based Adoption Model in the Netherlands, Flanders and the United Kingdom: State of the art and perspective. *Studies in Educational Evaluation, 19*, 51 – 63.

Berg, R. van den, Hameyer, U. & Stokking, K. (1988). *Dissemination reconsidered: the demands of implementation.* ISIP. Leuven: Acco (Belgium).

Berg, R. van den, & Sleegers, P. (1995). The innovative capacity of schools in secondary education. *International Journal of Qualitative Studies in Education, (in press).*

Berg, R. van den, Sleegers, P., & Geysel, F. (1995). *The innovative capacity of schools in primary education. A second qualitative study* (in preparation).

Berg, R. van den, & Vandenberghe, R. (1981). *Onderwijs – innovatie in verschuivend perspectief* (Educational innovation in a changing perspective). Tilburg, The Netherlands: Zwijsen.

Berg, R. van den, & Vandenberghe, R. (1986). *Strategies for large – scale change in education: Dilemmas and solutions.* Leuven: Acco (Belgium).

Caldwell, B.J. (1993). Paradox and uncertainty in the governance of education. In H. Beare & W.L. Boyd (Eds.), *Restructuring schools*, (pp. 158 – 173). London: The Falmer Press.

Conger, J.A., & Kanungo, R.N. (1994). Charismatic leadership in organizations: perceived behavioural attributes and their measurement. *Journal of Organizational Behaviour, 15*, 439 – 452.

Chubb, J., & T. Moe (1987). No school is an island: Politics, markets and education. In W. Boyd & C. Kerchner (Eds.), *The politics of excellence and choice in education. 1987 yearbook of the politics of education association.* London: Falmer.

Elmore, R.F. (1988). *Early experiences in restructuring schools: voices from the field.* Washington D.C.: Center for Policy Research (CPRE).

Fisher, W.A., & Schratz, M. (1990) Transformational Leadership; Impulse fur eine neue Führungs – philosophie in pädagogischen Leistungsfunktionen. *School Management, 21* (4), 34 – 41.

Fullan, M.G. (1992). Visions that blind. *Educational Leadership, 49* (5), 19 – 20.

Fullan, M.G. (1993). *Change forces. Probing the depths of educational reform.* London: Falmer Press.

Fullan, M.G., & Stiegelbauer, S. (1991). *The new meaning of educational change.* New York: Teachers College Press.

Geijsel, F. (1994). *Het innovatief vermogen van scholen in het basisonderwijs.* (The innovative capacity of primary schools). Nijmegen: University, Department of Educational Sciences.

Giesbers, J.H.G.I., & Sleegers, P. (1994). The Marx – models as conceptual models in school effectiveness research. *School organisation, 14* (1), 91 – 102.

Goldwasser, M.L. (1992). *School restructuring and the gap between policy and practice*. Paper presented at the annual meeting of the American Educational Research Association: San Francisco.

Hall, G. (1992). The local educational change process and policy implementation. *Journal of research in science teaching, 29,* (8), 877 – 904.

Hall, G.E., & George, A.A. & Rutherford, W.L.(1977). *Measuring stages of concerns about the innovation: a manual for use of the SoC questionnaire*. Austin, Texas: The University of Texas, Research and Development Center for Teacher Education.

Hall, G.E., & Hord, S.M. (1987). *Change in schools facilitating the process*. Albany, New York: State University of New York Press.

Hallinger, Ph (1992). The evolving role of American principals: From managerial to instructional to transformational leaders. *Journal of Educational Administration, 30,* nr. 3, 35 – 48.

Hargreaves, A., & D. Reynolds (1989). *Educational Policies: Controversies and Critiques*. Lewes. Falmer Press.

Harrison, I. (1991). *Facilitating the development of teacher assessment: using the CBAM – model*. Paper presented at the international conference on educational change, in the Netherlands, at Noordwijkerhout.

Hopkins, D. (1990). Integrating staff development and school improvement: a study of teacher personality and school climate. In: B. Joyce (Ed.), *Changing school culture through staff development*. 1990 Yearbook of the Association for Supervision and Curriculum Development. Alexandria, Virginia: ASCD.

Hopkins, R. (1994). *'Like life itself': Narrative and the revitalization of educational practice*. Paper presented at the annual meeting of the American Educational Research Association, New Orleans.

Janssens, S. (1987). A description of concerns of beginning teachers: the results of a qualitative study with some methodological considerations. In: R. Vandenberghe & G.E. Hall (Eds), *Research on international change facilitation in schools* (pp. 49 – 70). Leuven, Belgium: Acco.

Kievit, F.K., & Vandenberghe, R. (1993). *School culture, school improvement, and teacher development*. Leiden University: DSWO Press, The Netherlands.

Krogt, F. van der (1983) *Probleemoplossing en Beleidsvorming in Scholen*. (Problem solving and policy making in schools.) Leiden: Rijksuniversiteit (The Netherlands).

Leithwood, K.A. (1992). The move towards transformational leadership. *Educational Leadership, 49* (5), 8 – 12.

Leithwood, K.A. (1994). Leadership for school restructuring. *Educational Administration Quarterly, 30* (4), 498 – 518.

Leithwood, K.A. (1995). Leadership for school restructuring. *Educational Administration Quarterly* (in press).

Leithwood, K., & Jantzi, D. (1990). *Transformational leadership: How principals can help reform school*. Paper presented at the Annual Meeting of the Canadian Association for Curriculum Studies. Toronto: The Ontario Institute for Studies in Education.

Leithwood, K.A., Tomlinson, D., & Genge, M. (1995). Transformational school leadership. In K. Leithwood (Ed.), *International Handbook of Educational Leadership and Administration*. Boston: Kluwer Press (in press).

Louis, K.S. (1994). Beyond 'managed change': rethinking how schools improve. *School Effectiveness and School Improvement, 5* (1), 2 – 24.

698

Louis, K.S., Lagerweij, N., & Voogt, J.C. (1994). School Improvement. In: *International Educational Encyclopedia* (pp. 5241 – 5247). London: Pergamon.

Louis, K.S., & S. Loucks – Horsley (Eds.) (1989). *Supporting school improvement: a comparative perspective.* Leuven: Acco (Belgium).

Louis, K.S., & Miles, M. (1990). *Improving the urban high school: What works and why.* New York: Teachers College Press.

Louis, K.S., & Smith, B. (1991). Restructuring, teacher engagement and school culture: Perspectives on school reform and the improvement of teacher's work. *School effectiveness and School Improvement, 2,* 34 – 52.

Louis, K.S., & Smith, B. (1992). Renewing teacher's professional status and engagement: Breaking the iron law of social class. In: I. Newmann (Ed.) *Student Engagement and achievement in American high schools.* New York: Teachers College Press.

Lovell, K.C., Newbrough Lynch, S., & Hart, T. (1994). *Value – added leadership: the experiences of two professional development school principals.* Paper presented at the annual meeting of the American Educational Research Association, New Orleans.

Marx, E.C.H. (1987) Vermogen van scholen tot het voeren van bestuurlijk beleid. In: L. Genemans (Ed.) *Autonomie van scholen en deregulering. (Autonomy of schools and deregulation).* Nijmegen: ITS. (The Netherlands).

Marx, E.C.H. (1988) De uitkomsten van de OTO – gevalstudies, organisatiekundig bezien, (The results of the OTO – casestudies, from the point of organizational view). *Meso, 38,* 20 – 32.

Mesenburg, J. (1991). *Transforming education: The Minnisota plan.* Paper presented at the American Educational Research Association: Chicago.

Mintzberg, H. (1987). Crafting Strategy. *Harvard Business Review, 65,* 66 – 75.

Mintzberg, H. (1989). *Mintzberg on Management: inside our strange world of organizations.* New York: The Free Press.

Mintzberg, H. (1991). *Mintzberg over management.* (Mintzberg on management). Amsterdam: Uitgeverij Veen.

Mitchell, D.E., & Tucker, S. (1992). Leadership as a way of thinking. *Educational Leadership, 49* (5), 30 – 35.

Murphy, J., & Ph. Hallinger (1993). *Restructuring schooling: learning from ongoing efforts.* Newbury Park (CA): Corwin Press.

Pelkmans, A.H.W., & Vrieze, G. (1987). *Meer over co* (More on coordination and management) Nijmegen: ITS. (The Netherlands).

Rolff, H.G. (1993). *Wandel durch Selbstorganisation. Theoretische Grundlagen und praktische Hinweise für eine bessere Schule.* Weinheim/München: Juventa Verlag.

Rosenblum, S., & Louis, K.S., & Rossmiller, R. (1994). School leadership and teacher/ quality of work life. In: J. Murphy and K.S. Louis (Eds.). *Reshaping the principalship: lessons from restructuring schools.* Newbury Park: Corwin Press.

Sagor, R.D. (1992). Three principals who make a difference. *Educational Leadership, 49* (5), 13 – 18.

Salisbury, D.F., & Conner, D.R. (1994). How to succeed as a manager of an educational change project. *Educational Technology, 34* (6), 12 – 19.

Sashkin, M., & J. Egermeier (1992). *School changed models and processes: a review of research and practice.* Paper presented at the annual meeting of the American Educational Research Association: San Francisco.

Senge, P.M. (1993). *The fifth discipline: the art and practice of the learning organisation.* New York: Doubleday, Currency.

Sergiovanni, T.J. (1990). *Value – added leadership: how to get extraordinary performance in schools.* San Diego: Harcourt Brace Jovanovich.

Sergiovanni, T.J. (1992). *Moral leadership. Getting to the heart of school improvement.* San Francisco: Jossey – Bass Publishers.

Sleegers, P.J.C. (1991). *School en beleidsvoering.* (School and policy making). Nijmegen: Universiteit. (The Netherlands).

Sleegers, P., Bergen, Th., & Giesbers, J. (1994). The policy – making capacity of schools: results of a Dutch study. *Educational Management & Administration. 22* (3), 147 – 160.

Sleegers, P., & Rooyen, A. van (1989). Autonomievergroting en het benutten van de beleidsruimte door scholen. (Autonomy and the use of the space available for policy – making of schools). *Pedagogisch Tijdschrift, 14,* 327 – 336.

Sleegers, P., & Wesselingh (1993). Decentralisation in Education: a Dutch Study. *International Studies in Sociology of Education, 3* (1), 49 – 67.

Sundbo, J. (1992). The tied entrepreneur: On the theory and practice of institutionalization of creativity and innovation in service firms. *Creativity and Innovation Management, 1* (3), 109 – 120.

Timar, T.B. (1989). The politics of school restructuring. *Phi Delta, Kappan,* 71, 265 – 275.

Timar, T.B., & D.L. Kirp (1989). Education reform in the 1980's: Lessons from the States. *Phi Delta Kappan,* 71, 504 – 511.

Chapter 20: Leadership for Change

MICHAEL FULLAN

University of Toronto

> Wanted: A miracle worker who can do more with less, pacify
> rival groups, endure chronic second-guessing, tolerate low
> levels of support, process large volumes of paper and work
> double shifts (75 nights a year out). He or she will have carte
> blanche to innovate, but cannot spend much money, replace
> any personnel, or upset any constituency. (R. Evans, Educa-
> tion Week, April 12, 1995)

We have come a long way since the days of valuing leaders who 'run a
tight ship'. We have gone through the phases of the principal 'as
administrator' and the principal 'as instructional leader' to a broader
and more fundamental notion of principal as change agent. In this
chapter I take a critical approach to understanding the nature of the
evolving role of school leadership, why it has changed, and what we
need to know and to be able to do to make the leadership role more
doable. While the focus is on 'school' leadership (principal and teacher
leadership), much of the analysis applies to 'system' leadership involving superintendents and other central office staff.

The premise of the chapter is that we are obtaining a general appreciation of the new work of leaders, but that two problems remain: (1)
the noise function in which misleading conceptions of leadership persist, and (2) to the extent that new conceptions are on the right track,
they remain at a general level of understanding with little practical
meaning about how to carry out the role at the operational level.

The chapter is organized in the following sections. First, the new
context is analysed to identify key underlying reasons why and how the
role of school leadership has changed. Second, I discuss the broad conceptions of leadership with a view to sorting out less productive from
more productive lines of thinking. The intent is to capture how 'leadership for change' might be conceptualized. Although this is still at a
general level, the mindset of effective leadership is clearly articulated.
Third, (and this is the essence of the chapter) I present a number of
'middle level' examples of how key problems of change would be specifically handled. This section on how 'leadership for change in action'

K. Leithwood et al. (eds.), International Handbook of Educational Leadership and Administration, 701-722.
© *1996 Kluwer Academic Publishers, Printed in the Netherlands.*

focuses on what leaders would actually do in real situations of complex change. This, I believe is missing from much of the literature and is obviously crucial for informing both understanding and action.

I will not address here the broad issues of the age of paradox and chaos in postmodern society (although these issues do get introduced in the following two sections). Rather, we are interested in the more specific manifestations of these trends as they directly change the very context within which leadership must work. Eight trends in particular affect school leadership directly (see Fullan and Hargreaves, 1996; Hargreaves and Fullan, 1996).

First, there is a world-wide trend toward *self-managing* schools. This has meant a sea-change in the role of the school leader transforming responsibility towards whole school development, school development planning and the like. Developing collaborative work cultures with a focus on teaching and learning for all students has become a major mandate for school principals. The term self-managing, however, is misleading because the other trends, paradoxically mean that with greater autonomy comes greater permeability of boundaries and more visible accountability and involvement with other constituencies.

Second, part and parcel of the new devolution of authority – from Chicago to New Zealand and points in between – is new forms of *school-community governance*. Most directly this takes the form of legislated 'local school councils' with new responsibilities and powers. The formal governance component as we shall see later, is only the most obvious structural aspect of a much more comprehensive realignment of parental/community-school relationships. In effect, school boundaries are becoming more transparent, and the work of the school not only much more visible but ultimately more intertwined with the family and the community (Epstein, 1995). School leadership, in turn, is radically affected. We are no longer talking about attempting to have cordial relationships with parents but rather developing more comprehensive learning systems in new public arenas, requiring new conceptions and skills that school leaders have hitherto never experienced.

Third, there is a trend to *reduce dependence on outside bureaucracy and regulation*. Because of the ambivalence of the state to 'let go', this trend is difficult to interpret. It is the case, driven partly by the need to reduce expenditures and partly by the new conceptions described here, that there is a widespread reduction in the number of bureaucrats at both the regional and state levels. In these jurisdictions that have district school boards, it is not at all clear that this level of bureaucracy will survive as some of the powers devolve to local school councils while other powers are usurped upward to the state.

Fourth, while middle level bureaucracies are becoming simplified or eliminated, *the state is taking on new centralist roles*. Depending on the degree of centralizing tendencies this takes the form of developing state-wide curriculum frameworks, standards of practice, and accountability of performance and outcomes. School leaders, of course, must constantly negotiate this simultaneous centralization-decentralization terrain.

Fifth, there is more talk and action about *reinventing teacher professionalism* with increased standards of practice that in effect widen and deepen the role of the teacher, transcending the classroom door to new forms of collaboration and partnership within and outside the school. This reduction in the isolation of teachers is accompanied by new opportunities and expectations for teacher leadership. School leadership, then, becomes more complex. Every teacher is expected to exercise such leadership, and particular new teacher leadership roles become established. The principal finds himself or herself participating in the change of the teaching profession itself where the role of the traditional school leader is disappearing.

Sixth, massive expansion of *information technology* brings with it greater global access to ideas and people, and untold opportunities and headaches about how to manage the information explosion in relation to its positive potential and harmful downside.

Seventh, a focus on the *new learning outcomes* continues apace, defined less in terms of traditional content and more in terms of teaching for understanding and performance in a changing world. School leaders become embroiled in debates that are no less fundamental than revisiting the question of the purpose of schools in a social and work world very different from the past.

Eighth, *multi-racial, gender and sexual politics* bring new styles of leadership and more visibility to issues of equity. The socio-political complexity of the role of the school leader comes with the new territory.

In short, to begin to understand 'leadership for change', one must first understand basic changes in the social context.

BROAD CONCEPTIONS OF LEADERSHIP

I wish the reader for the time being to accept the following premise: neither the passive facilitator leader who tries to be responsive to others, or the forceful charismatic leader is effective under the contextual conditions just outlined. The former leader fails to stand for anything, and the latter dominates the agenda.

Since vision-driven leadership tends to be a major component of leadership theory over the last decade, it is necessary to clarify the limitations of this view. Beckhard and Pritchard (1992) provide a succinct version of this conception. There are four key aspects, they say: creating and setting the vision; communicating the vision; building commitment to the vision; and alignment to the vision (p. 25). Similarly, Bennis and Nanus (1985) advocate four leadership strategies: I Attention through Vision; II Meaning through Communications; III Trust through Positioning; IV The Deployment of Self through Positive Self-Regard.

Senge (1990) I believe provides the definitive critique of the above image of leader as saviour:

> Our traditional views of leaders – as special people who set the direction, make key decisions, and energize the troops – are deeply rooted in an individualistic and nonsystemic world view. Especially in the West, leaders are *heroes* – great men (and occasionally women) who 'rise to the fore' in times of crises. Our prevailing leadership myths are still captured by the captain of the cavalry leading the charge to rescue the settlers from the attacking Indians. So long as such myths prevail, they reinforce a focus on short-term events and charismatic heroes rather than on systemic forces and collective learning. At its heart, the traditional view of leadership is based on assumptions of people's powerlessness, their lack of personal vision and inability to master the forces of change, deficits which can be remedied only by a few great leaders. (p. 340)

Yet, we know that strong leadership is required to manage the barrage of problems and potential opportunities to make major reforms. In the remainder of this section I will develop a more balanced view of strong leadership which leads to the following two conclusions: (1) the conception of the leader of the future is becoming more articulated *at the broad level* (2) and a corollary, it is very difficult to obtain from this literature what leaders would do at the operational level if they attempted to follow this conception in their own work.

A good place to start is Champy's (1995) recent excellent book on 'reengineering management'. He claims, I think correctly, that there are four broad issues for managers of the future:

- *Issues of purpose.* Insistently, persistently, relentlessly, the new manager must ask, 'What for?' What is it that we're in business for? What is the process for? This Product? This task? This team? This job? What are we doing here, anyway
- *Issues of culture.* If successful reengineering requires a change in a company's whole culture, as seems to be the case in many instances, how is it to be accomplished by the same management that did so well in the old culture? If it is true (and it is) that reengineering is unlikely to succeed where the corporate atmosphere is charged with fear (and its twin, mistrust), how do we generate another, better environment – one, say, of willingness and mutual confidence.
- *Issues of process and performance.* How do we get the kind of processes we want? How do get the performances we need from our people? How do we set the norms and standard, or measure results – for worker performance, management performance, and the performance of the whole enterprise? Reengineering usually demands radical objectives, leadership, and political skills to realize. But how do we know whether we have the stuff? What does it take to be a good manager today?
- *Issues of people.* Who do we want to work with? How can we find them from both inside and outside the company? How do we get them to want to work with us? How do we know whether they're the kind of people we want? (p. 7)

Champy advocates that we should 'lead experimentally', and that 'linear thinking, general strategy thinking, familiar thinking, conventional thinking, produce only comforting illusions, bland rigidities, complacent passivity, all the slow working recipes for disaster' (pp 32-33). What follows in Champy's book are many illustrations, ideas and insights (and we shall draw upon some of them later), but at the end of the book, one would be hard pressed to answer the question: 'what do I do now, where do I start?'

Senge (1990) also put us on the right track in his description of the new work of the leader: as designer, as steward, as teacher. As designers:

> The leaders who fare best are those who continually see themselves as designers not crusaders. Many of the best intentioned efforts to foster new learning disciplines founder because those leading the charge forget the first rule of learning: people learn what they need to learn, not what someone else thinks they need to learn.
>
> In essence, the *leader's task is designing the learning processes* whereby people throughout the organization can deal productively with the critical issues they face, and develop their mastery in the learning disciplines. this is new work for most experiences managers, may of whom rose to the top because of their decision-making and problem-solving skills, not their skills in mentoring, coaching, and helping others learn. (p. 345, italics in original)

As stewards, leaders continually seek and oversee the broader purpose and direction of the organization:

> In a learning organization, leaders may start by pursuing their own vision, but as they learn to listen carefully to others visions they begin to see that their own personal vision is part of something larger. This does not diminish any leader's sense of responsibility for the vision – if anything it deepens it. (p. 352)

Leader as teacher is not about teaching other people one's own vision:

> Leaders in learning organization have the ability to conceptualize their strategic insights so that they become public knowledge, open to challenge and further improvement... [Leader as teacher] is about fostering learning for everyone. such leaders help people throughout the organization develop systemic understandings. Accepting this responsibility is the antidote to one of the most common downfalls of otherwise gifted learners – losing their commitment to the truth. (p. 356)

As we move directly to the role of the principal we see similar conceptions of the leadership role. Deal and Peterson (1994) argue that principals must possess both technical and symbolic traits (logic and artistry):

> Technical problems require the analytical, rational problem-solving capabilities of a well-organized manager. Symbolic dilemmas require the sensitive, expressive touch of an artistic and passionate leader. (p. 113)

Eight technical roles are identified: planner, resource allocator, coordinator, supervisor, disseminator, jurist, gatekeeper, analyst; as well as eight symbolic roles: historian, anthropological detective, visionary, symbol, potter, poet, actor, leader.

Goldring and Rallis (1993) recommend that principals must in combination be:
- The Facilitator: Enabling Internal Leadership
- The Balancer: Communicating Within the System Hierarchy
- The Flag Bearer and Bridger: Managing the Environment
- The Inquirer: Assessing Effectiveness and Developing School-Based Accountability

Similarly, Patterson (1993) states five values needed for leadership in tomorrow's school as compared to the present:

Value 1: Openness to Participation

Today's Value:	Our organization values employees listening to the organization's leaders and doing what the leaders tell them to do.
Tomorrow's Value	Our organization values employees actively participating in any discussion or decision affecting them. (p. 5)

Value 2: Openness to Diversity

Today's Value:	Our organization values employees falling in line with the overall organizational direction.

| Tomorrow's Value | Our organization values diversity in perspectives leading to a deeper understanding of organizational reality and an enriched knowledge base for decision making. (p. 7) |

Value 3: Openness to Conflict

| Today's Value: | Our organization values employees communicating a climate of group harmony and happiness. |
| Tomorrow's Value | Our organization values employees resolving conflict in a healthy way that leads to stronger solutions for complex issues. (p. 8) |

Value 4: Openness to Reflection

| Today's Value: | Our organization values employees conveying a climate of decisiveness. Firm decisions are made and implemented without looking back. |
| Tomorrow's Value | Our organization values employees reflecting on their own and others' thinking in order to achieve better organizational decisions. (p. 10) |

Value 5: Openness to Mistakes

| Today's Value: | Our organization values employees concentrating on making no mistakes and working as efficiently as possible |
| Tomorrow's Value | Our organization values employees acknowledging mistakes and learning from them. (p 12) |

Patterson concludes with the now familiar refrain of the need to 'lead within paradox' (p. 80).

Finally, in my own *Change Forces* eight lessons are identified derived from the conclusion that change processes these days are inevitably non-linear and chaotic, and that effective leaders are those who are able to foster and/or capitalize on periodic patterns that occur over time. The eight lessons themselves are laced with dilemmas that require leaders to work with opposing tendencies by bringing them into dynamic tension:

Lesson One:	You Can't Mandate What Matters (The more complex the change the less you can force it)
Lesson Two:	Change is a Journey not a Blueprint (Change is non-linear, loaded with uncertainty and excitement and sometimes perverse)
Lesson Three:	Problems are Our Friends (Problems are inevitable and you can't learn without them)
Lesson Four:	Vision and Strategic Planning Come Later (Premature visions and planning blind)
Lesson Five:	Individualism and Collectivism Must Have Equal Power (There are no one-sided solutions to isolation and groupthink)
Lesson Six:	Neither Centralization Nor Decentralization Works (Both top-down and bottom-up strategies are necessary)
Lesson Seven:	Connection with the Wider Environment is Critical for Success (The best organizations learn externally as well as internally)
Lesson Eight:	Every Person is a Change Agent (Change is too important to leave to the experts, personal mind set and mastery is the ultimate protection) (Fullan, 1993: 21-22)

As inspiring as this literature on the new role of leaders is, and as many specific descriptions of leaders that the same literature contains, I maintain that, at the end of the day, it is very difficult for even the committed reader to know what to do. For the latter we need a more middle-level theory of leadership that not only beckons, but also provides insightful examples of how leaders would manage typical paradoxical situations that they increasingly face. In fact, in the absence of more grounded analysis, the literature is misleading at worse and unhelpful at best. In reviewing over 200 studies of the role of the principal as change agent, Christensen (1994) found the literature dominated by prescriptions and sometimes descriptions with a very weak research and analytical base. As we shall see in the next section, in her own carefully documented study of the role of the principal, Christensen's findings provided insights that go beyond and in some cases contradict the characterization of leadership for change found in the literature.

LEADERSHIP FOR CHANGE IN ACTION

Leadership for change requires an internalized mindset that is constantly refined through thinking, and action, thinking, action, etc. This cumulative learning produces an orientation and ability to exercise greater executive control over the forces of change, and a capacity to generate the most effective actions and reactions in accomplishing change. The result is both more specific and to a certain extent different than what the general literature would have us believe about the role of the principal.

Mintzberg (1994) in his definitive critique of strategic planning says 'companies plan when they *have* intended strategies, not in order to get them' (p. 111, his italics). In a related interview he offers this wise advice:

> Never adopt a technique by its usual name. If you want to do reengineering, or whatever, call it something different so that you have to think it through for yourself and work it out on your own terms. If you just adopt it and implement it, it is bound to fail. (1995: 27)

Put differently, there are no shortcuts. Leaders for change must immerse themselves in real situations of reform and begin to craft their own theories of change constantly testing them against new situations and against grounded accounts of others' experiences. In this section, I will illustrate what this new mindset for change looks like in action by taking four typical dilemmas faced by principals:

1. The case of Advocacy and Resistance with respect to given innovations or reforms
2. The case of Whole School Reform
3. The case of School Councils
4. The case of contending with State Policy

Advocacy and Resistance

Leaders are urged to foster experimentation, but what if staff appears uninterested in trying new things? Principals are expected to promote some of the latest innovations but what if staff are not committed to doing so? If we look deeply enough the new conceptions of leadership gives guidance about how to handle these kinds of situations. Gitlin and Margonis (1995) state it this way:

> We believe teachers' initial expressions of cynicism about reform should not automatically be viewed as obstructionist acts to overcome. Instead, time should be spent looking carefully at those resistant acts to see if they might embody a form of good sense – potential insights into the root causes of why the more things change the more they stay the same. (pp 386-387)

Their case study of site-based reform shows how a well intentioned administrator went about promoting the innovation, working with career ladder teachers, attempting to overcome resistance on the part of teachers. On the surface the principal did most things that the literature on transformational leadership would endorse. For Gitlin and Margonis there was a failure to get at two root causes: new authority relations where teachers would indeed have more power; and need for examining the structures and availability of time to manage the new demands.

Let's build the case, however, in a more simple manner. Assume that you are a principal who is strongly committed to the increased use of technology. You are sincerely convinced that it is in the best interest of students to become technologically proficient. To keep the example uncomplicated we must leave aside a number of contextual questions we would have to have answered. We can contrast then, the old and the new way of approaching the situation. By the old I mean the superficial reading of the literature. By the new I mean a deeper understanding of leadership for change.

Your old way of thinking would be like the following: I am sure that technology is one of the keys to the future for my students; parents support it; I know that some teachers favour it, but others are going to be Luddites; How can I get some teacher leaders to support it? What kind of external resources and expertise can I generate to provide support and pressure to move forward? Maybe I can secure a few transfers and new appointments. My whole approach is advocacy and co-optation into an agenda that I am sure is right.

With the new mindset, I am equally convinced that technology is critical, but I approach it differently. Cutting the story short, let's say that I am having a staff session in which I am about to show a video segment that portrays a highly successful technology-based school in action. Instead of showing it to make my case, I present it differently. I randomly ask one half of the staff to view the video with a 'positive lens' noting what might be in it for us; I ask the other half of the staff to view it 'negatively or critically' by identifying what might be problematic or potentially negative for us. If I am sincere, I have legitimized dissent. I have made it easy for staff to speak up about concerns (which would come out later anyway in more subtle and/or inaccessible ways). I listen carefully, suspending my own advocacy, because I know that some fundamental problems will be identified and that people's fears, real or imagined, will need to be examined carefully. This information may lead me to go back to the drawing board or to work with staff on some precondition s that would have to be addressed; or to proceed into action on a 'start small, think big' basis, or to abandon high-profile technology in favour of a different approach.

There is no right answer in this case, but consider the underlying theory. This is what is meant in the new literature by 'disagreement is not bad'.

> A culture that squashes disagreement is a culture doomed to stagnate, because change always begins with disagreement. Besides disagreement can never be squashed entirely. It gets repressed, to emerge later as a pervasive sense of injustice, followed by apathy, resentment, and even sabotage. (Champy, 1995: 82)

The new leader then does not assume that it should go her or his way, values diversity and early disagreement as fundamental to breakthroughs, listens (really listens) to pick up cues and new ways of thinking. Once this becomes internalized it generates myriads of more productive actions and reactions to situations of change. Without this internalization and more sophisticated understanding it is easy to get mislead by the literature.

The Case of Whole School Reform

Christensen (1994) conducted a thorough review of the literature on the role of the principal before launching her own investigation into the role of the principal in transforming an 'Accelerated School' (Levin, 1995). As noted earlier, she analysed over 200 studies. She portrayed the difference in the literature between the role of the principal in the traditional school vs the restructured school. Our interest here is how the conception in the restructured school stacks up against Christensen's findings in her own study – findings carefully documented through the analysis of over 1000 'critical incidents' of behaviour, cross-validated in open-ended questions she asked in the five accelerated schools she studied.

The top behaviours cited in the literature were different in priority compared to those found by Christensen. The literature places 'communicates goals', 'shares decision-making', 'creates/articulates school vision' and 'supports staff' (the one overlap) at the top of the list. Christensen found that 'fostering the process', 'supporting staff', 'promoting learning' and 'promoting parent involvement' were the major behaviour categories with 'promote the vision of the school' as an important, but more distant priority (it ranked 10th in frequency out of 13 categories) (Christensen, 1994:113).

We must be careful not to misinterpret these findings. They do not say, for example that creating a vision is unimportant. But they do put it in perspective, showing that it is subordinate in some ways to a more sophisticated process. Second, although we do not have the specifics here, it is crucial that leaders understand the discrete behaviours that made up the categories. For example, 'use the governance process correctly' was one of 18 subcategories of 'fostering the process' and itself had a dozen types of critical incidents of behaviour such as:
- don't make administrative mandates that affect the whole school without going through the process
- make sure decisions are not made in a hurry
- don't take over meetings; be a co-participant
- get input from all stakeholders
- encourage consensus rather than voting. (ibid., p.120)

Similarly in interviews, the top 'things a principal must do to be a good accelerated school principal' according to principals and teachers were:
- be willing to let go of control
- be supportive of staff
- be present
- stand up to the district
- be a real expert on the accelerated school process
- be positive
- believe every child is a success
- be open-minded; listen to everybody's opinions
- be sensitive to staff morale. (ibid., p. 132)

It is obviously not helpful to try and memorize the list of behaviours, but a pattern is emerging. Effective principals extend as well as express what they value. They nurture a subtle process of enabling teachers to work together to generate solutions. It is easy for principals with good ideas to let themselves get seduced into 'taking over'. Prestine's (1994) study of a 'Coalition of Essential Schools' reform that got bogged down, but eventually regrouped illustrates this problem clearly.

When progress was faltering, the principal became more and more concerned:

> Taking charge of the meetings, the principal assigned a series of discrete tasks, built around authentic assessment ideas, to be completed by faculty groups. In essence, nothing happened. As the principal noted, 'I gave an assignment. I can't believe I tried this. No one read the book. No one understood what I was talking about. It was like I was talking Swahili. The whole thing sort of fell flat. (Prestine, 1994: 134)

Reflecting on this the principal observed:

> I allowed the faculty to push responsibility for their learning onto me. Even worse, I went out and provided the venue in which it would happen. I did something I swore I would never do – take responsibility for a school's behaviour, for the learning of individual teachers. I took direct managerial responsibilities. Worse yet, the model I set up was exactly the kind of instruction I had never done as a teacher – that is, I give you an assignment and you do exactly as I told you to do. It was

terrible as I came to understand what I had been doing. (ibid., p. 135)

As one of the teacher co-ordinators observed:

> We suddenly realized what was wrong. We realized that we did not have ownership anymore... He [the principal] seemed to know everything there was to know about it, so it necessary to push it onto him. Once we did that, it was doomed to failure. (ibid., p. 135)

The point here is not that these mistakes can be eliminated. Rather the message is that you need enough of a working theory of leadership for change combined with mechanisms for personal and collective reflection, so that you inevitably self-correct, thereby deepening the internalization of theory and your capacity to act effectively the next time, and the time after that, and so on.

These developments are part and parcel of a more fundamental change in the culture of schools and in the evolution of the teaching profession itself, which go beyond the terms of reference of this chapter. Schools are not now learning organizations and for them to become so they must engage in a radical process of 'restructuring, retiming and reculturing the school' (Fullan, 1995). The end result of this process is not yet known but the implications for the role of leadership are compatible with the formulations in this chapter. Leaders in learning organizations for example know that *both* individualism and collaboration must co-exist. They know that isolation is bad, but that collaboration has downsides too – not the least of which are balkanization and groupthink (Fullan, 1993). They know that differences, diversity and conflict not only are inevitable, but that they often contain the seeds of breakthroughs. Homogenous cultures are more peaceful, but are also more stagnant than heterogeneous cultures.

In short, the socio-cultural context for teachers' own learning and ownership for reform will change (Gallimore, Goldenberg and Saunders, 1995). The changes in school culture are part of a more fundamental change in the nature of the teaching profession itself. The role of the teacher has widened and deepened over the past decade. Teachers are expected to be 'moral change agents', making a difference in the lives of students while becoming experts in managing change. How far this change will go is as yet undetermined, but there is no doubt that radical changes in the teaching profession and perforce in the principalship are in store (Fullan and Hargreaves, 1996; Hargreaves and Fullan, 1996).

Whole school reform, in other words, changes the culture of the school and the nature of the teaching profession. Principals are front and centre in this transition which goes far beyond conceptions of principals as leaders of site-based management.

School Councils

The establishment of School Councils with parent and community participation in advisory or decision making roles is an international phenomenon of major proportions. What is the principal as change agent to make of these developments? The old way of responding would be to treat it as a necessary evil – something to be tolerated, blunted – or to go about dutifully trying to make the Council work. Both of these responses are narrow and limiting as a broader conception and considerable evidence reveals.

The principal steeped in leadership for change would have a different approach. First, he or she would recognize the emergence of School Councils as part of a systemic shift in the relationship between the communities and schools that is both inevitable and that contains the seeds of a necessary realignment with the family and other social agencies. Put another way, the principal would not take School Councils literally, but would see them as the tip of a more complex and powerful iceberg. Systemic thinking says that boundaries need to be more permeable and operate in interaction and with mutual influence. An abstract way of putting it to be sure, but specifically meaningful in rethinking the relative roles of the family/community and the school.

Second, and to be much more specific, research and best practice are abundantly clear: Nothing motivates a child more than when learning is valued by schools and families/community working in partnership. Furthermore, you can do something to improve this relationship through deliberate action. For the same reason that site-based management (involving teachers) bears no relationship to changes in the culture and learning of the whole school, the presence of School Councils per se does not affect student learning. The establishment of a Council involving a handful of parents (not to mention matters of representation and skill) could not possibly improve the learning for the hundreds of students in the school (see Wylie's (1995) assessment of the New Zealand experience). What does make a difference is the multiple forms of particular involvement deliberately fostered, developed and supported. Summarizing over a decade of research and development of best practice, Esptein (1995) makes the case unequivocally. At least six types of involvement working in concert are needed to make a difference, namely, programs that promote greater:

1. Parenting Skills (improving home environments)
2. Communication (two-way school-to-home)
3. Volunteering or Parent Aides (recruit and organize parent help)
4. Learning at Home (specific home tutoring assistance)
5. Decision-making (involve parents and develop parent leaders)
6. Coordinating with Community Agencies (identify and interpret community services)

Note that involvement in decision-making is only one of six forms (and a skilled form at that). Moreover, these forms of involvement do not happen by accident or even by invitation. They happen by explicit strategic intervention. In other words, both parents and educators need staff development in their new roles and new role relationships in order to become effective. This incidentally is one of the main reasons why programs like James Comer's School Development Program are successful, that is, they succeed in large part because they have a *parent development* component (Comer, 1992; see also the principal's parent involvement role in 'Accelerated Schools,' Christensen, 1994).

Third, in thinking and working through these developments, the principal's theory of change becomes much more powerful. It becomes clearer what Sarason (1995) and Ontario's Royal Commission on Learning (1994), meant when they said that school councils or parent involvement is not an end in itself. Shifts in power are involved, but it is not power in and of itself that counts, but what the new power arrangement can actually do:

> To seek power is to raise and begin to answer the question: to seek power to change *what*? Changing the forces of power in no way guarantees that anything else will change... To seek power without asking the 'what' question is not only to beg the question but to avoid it and, therefore to collude in cosmetic changes. (Sarason, 1995:53, his emphasis)

Both Sarason and Dolan (1994) make it clear that parents are a crucial and largely untapped resources. While there are destructive and hopeless parents, on the whole, parents have (or can be helped to have) assets and expertise that are essential to the partnership. Parents have knowledge of their child that is not available to anyone else, they have a vested interest in their child's success, they have the expertise of the customer who is paying for and experiencing a service, they have valuable knowledge and skills by virtue of their 'special interests, hobbies, vocation, and community' role (see Sarason, 1995: ch. 4; Dolan, 1994: ch. 14).

Dolan draws this powerful conclusion:

> To educate children without a deep partnership of teacher parent is hopeless, and going in we have conditioned everyone to minimal interaction, indifference, maybe even suspicion. This is the Steady State in most of the country. And, it has to change. (p. 159)

Fourth (and once again we see the operational principles of leadership for change in action), ideas about diversity and conflict become a natural part of the creation of something new:

> In a school, where mistrust between the community and the administration is the major issue, you might begin to deal with it by making sure that parents were present at every major event, every meeting, every challenge. *Within the discomfort of that presence*, the learning and the healing could begin. (Dolan, 1994: 60, my emphasis)

Similarly, without knowledge for change, School Councils can easily become diversions where energy is diverted to compliance and power struggles not to capacity building. A School Council, as surprising as this may seem:

> ... is *not* primarily a decision making mechanism. This is not principalship by committee. A Site Council that focuses only on decision-making tends to make the intervention solely a power issue. It often exhausts itself on petty issues and control struggles and never gets to the main business which is *driving* the change. (Dolan, 1994: 131, his emphases)

Rather, the role of the Council is to help mobilize the forces and resources for change by developing the skills of parents, teachers, students and principals as leaders in 'group problem-solving,' 'dealing with conflict,' and 'making content expertise accessible' (ibid. p. 134). This brings new, more complex meaning to the role of the principal in the middle.

State Policy

Two related problems plague educational reform at the system level: overload and fragmentation. In a certain objective sense this is inevitable because post modern societies are non-linear, chaotic, dynamically complex (Fullan, 1993). Under these circumstance leadership for change is essentially a 'coherence-making' proposition. Leithwood and his colleagues' case study of local implementation of state policy in British Columbia is instructive (Leithwood, 1995; Leithwood, Jantzi and Steinbach, 1995). They found that school leadership made the single largest contribution to school restructuring through supporting and helping develop teachers' commitments, capacities and opportunities to engage in reform – findings which are compatible with our discussion above about whole school development.

Viewed in the context of state policy, Leithwood et al.'s additional findings are noteworthy. While school people experienced state policy as lacking coherence, consistency and sustained commitment (an endemic feature of chaotic systems), some schools were able to overcome these limitations. Schools 'with a coherent sense of direction essentially were able to make sense of even relatively large numbers of disparate initiatives undertaken within the school' (Leithwood et al., 1995: 34). In other words, schools with leadership that served to increase the capacity of teachers to engage in individual and collective learning were less troubled by lack of clarity on central policies and made more progress in implementing them.

This represents another example of principals operating effectively in ambiguous, complex environments by getting their own community in order and by being less dependent on the vagaries of system policies. Such principals and their staff become 'critical consumers' of central policies. They see the occasion of state initiatives as representing legitimate if not well worked out concerns. They are willing to stop, think and examine the issues contained in new state policies, and to 'exploit' the potential resources that might be obtained.

I shall use a simple example from our files on 'Vignettes of successful change' from the Ontario Teachers' Federation (1992) project 'Creating a Culture of Change.' In this case, a principal, faced with a newly issued curriculum policy from that state was troubled by the prospect of carrying forward the policy to his staff. He, probably correctly, predicted that the staff would see it as yet another misguided imposition. Instead of introducing the policy, the principal, working with a facilitator, conducted a professional development session designed to identify which curriculum changes the teachers' themselves would like to see in the school. The principal and teachers then connected some of the identified themes with state policies, and began to work upwards in relation to the policies.

This is an oversimplified example because there are a great many additional contextual factors that one would have to take into account. But the example clearly illustrates that educational change is neither top-down nor bottom-up. The role of leaders is to work with teachers and the local community to navigate the complex two-way relationship between the school and the state. These ideas are contained in the literature but it is only when you begin to marshal particular examples and learn from them that you can begin to build a meaningful approach to leadership for change.

CONCLUSION

I have made the case that the literature on school leadership is misleading in some respects, and unhelpful in others. This is largely because many of the new theories of change purportedly formulated to address complex systems requiring leaders to 'manage paradox,' fail to provide particular examples and insights, which in turn can be linked to powerful concepts. Although much more work remains to be done to develop a meaningful action-based theory of leadership, we were able to obtain from the empirical literature a number of problem-based examples which contribute to as well as are informed by the emerging theory. They place the principal (at least in this transition period working toward a learning organization) in the role of what Dolan (1994: 94) calls a 'deep coordinator' working in fundamentally interdependent ways within the school and community, and externally with the wider system.

The role of the school principal has become significantly more complex. Principals are experiencing greater stress and greater mental and physical health problems (Wylie, 1995). In the same way that some people handle stress better than others, principals who develop leadership for change capacities learn to control more of their own and their community's destiny in more healthy and productive ways.

Most of the literature and examples in this chapter were from North American sources, and this is a limitation. The issues, however, are consistent at least across most developed countries. Nor did I address gender differences, which by and large tend to confirm that the directions of new leadership are more congruent with women's socialization and leadership style (see Rothschild, 1990), although the main message is that all leaders need to develop the capacities that we have been discussing.

Differences across cultures is a different story still. There are bound to be major differences in the role of 'school leadership for change' across Eastern and Western, and Northern and Southern cultures, but there is almost a complete absence of specific insights and examples at the level of analysis presented in this chapter – a gap that requires urgent attention in the literature.

Leadership for change in education is a field that has generated enormous interest over the years. It is a tribute to the complexities and dilemmas inherent in this topic to realize that much of the message remains elusive. By working in a self reflective way on real paradoxes of change we can build a more insightful set of theories and develop a richer array of skills and effective practices. There will be no shortage of opportunities to do so.

REFERENCES

Beckhard, R. & Pritchard, W. (1992). *Changing the essence.* San Francisco, CA: Jossey-Bass.
Bennis, W. & Nanus, B. (1985). *Leaders.* New York, NY: Harper & Row.
Champy, J. (1995). *Reengineering management.* New York, NY: Harper Collins
Christensen, G. (1994). *The role of the Principal in transforming accelerated schools.* Unpublished doctoral dissertation, Stanford University.
Deal, T. & Peterson, K. (1992) *The leadership paradox.* San Francisco, CA: Jossey-Bass.
Dolan, P. (1994). *Restructuring our schools.* Kansas City, MO: Systems & Organizations.
Epstein, J. (1995). School/family/community partnerships, *Phi Delta Kappan,* Vol.76, pp 701-712.
Fullan, M. (1993). *Change forces.* London, U.K: Falmer Press.
Fullan, M. (1995). Schools as learning organizations: Distant dreams. In M. Seltzer (Ed.), *Theory into practice.* Columbus, OH: Ohio State University.

Fullan, M. & Hargreaves, A. (1996). *What's worth fighting for in your school?* 2nd edition. New York, NY: Teachers' College Press; Toronto, ON: Ontario Public School Teachers' Federation.

Gallimore, R., Goldenberg, C. & Saunders, W. (1995). The sociocultural context of teacher development. In M. McLaughlin (ed.), *Research reports of the National Centre for the Study of Cultural Diversity and Second Language Learning.* Palo Alto, Stanford University.

Gitlin, A. & Margonis, F. (1995). The political aspect of reform: Teacher resistance as good sense. *American Journal of Education,* Vol. 103, pp 377-405

Goldring, E. & Rallis, S. (1993). *Principals of dynamic schools.* Newbury Park, CA: Corwin Press.

Hallinger, P. (1995). Culture and leadership: Developing an international perspective on educational administration. *UCEA Review,* Vol. 36, pp 1, 4, 5, 10-12.

Hargreaves, A. & Fullan, M. (1996). *What's worth fighting for out there.* New York, NY: Teachers' College Press; Toronto, ON: Ontario Public School Teachers' Federation.

Leithwood, K. (1995). *School restructuring in British Columbia: Summarizing the results of a four-year study.* Paper presented at the American Educational Research Association Annual Meeting, San Francisco, CA.

Leithwood, K. Jantzi, D. & Steinbeck, R. (1995). *An organizational learning perspective on school responses to central policy initiatives.* Paper presented at the American Educational Research Association Annual Meeting, San Francisco, CA.

Mintzberg, H. (1994). *The rise and fall of strategic planning.* New York, NY: Free Press.

Mintzberg, H. (1995). *Strategically speaking.* Acumen.

Ontario Teachers' Federation (1992). *Creating a culture for change.* Toronto, ON: Ontario Teachers' Federation.

Ontario Royal Commission on Learning, *Love of learning,* Vol. I - V. Toronto, ON: Queen's Printer.

Paterson, J. (1993). *Leadership for tomorrow's schools.* Alexandria, VA: Association for Supervision & Curriculum Development.

Prestine, N. (1994). *Ninety degrees from everywhere: New understandings of the principal's role in a restructuring essential school.*

Rothschild, J. (1990). *Feminist values and the democratic management of work organizations.* Paper presented at the 12th World Congress of Sociology, Madrid.

Sarason, S. (1995). *Parent involvement and the political principal.* San Francisco, CA: Jossey-Bass.

Senge, P. (1990). *The fifth discipline.* New York, NY: Doubleday.

Wylie, C. (1995). *School-site management: Some lessons from New Zealand.* Paper presented at the American Educational Research Association Annual Meeting, San Francisco, CA.

Chapter 21: The Principal's Role in School Effectiveness: An Assessment of Methodological Progress, 1980-1995

PHILIP HALLINGER AND RONALD H. HECK

Vanderbilt University, Chiang Mai University; and University of Hawaii, Manoa

There is relatively little disagreement in either lay or professional circles concerning the belief that principals play a critical role in the lives of teachers, students and schools. This belief has led to considerable research into the nature of principals' work, attitudes, values, thought processes, and behaviour (Leithwood, Begley & Cousins, 1990, 1992). When consulting the empirical literature, however, both the nature and degree of principal impact continue to be subject to debate (e.g., Pitner, 1988; Rowan, Dwyer & Bossert, 1982; van de Grift, 1990).

Over the past 15 years several substantive reviews of this research literature have been conducted with the aim of consolidating our understanding of the principal's role in schooling (e.g., Boyan, 1988; Bossert, Dwyer, Rowan, & Lee, 1982; Bridges, 1982; Leithwood & Montgomery, 1982; Leithwood et al., 1990; Murphy, 1988; Murphy, Hallinger & Mitman, 1983; Pitner, 1988). These reviews consistently paint a picture whose broad strokes seem quite clear from afar, but which becomes much fuzzier when viewed up close. While most of these scholars agree on the importance of the principal's leadership, we still lack many details concerning how principals respond to their schools' environmental contexts as they seek to shape organizational processes and student outcomes. Reviewers have concluded that the tradition of research on the impact of principals has not generally done justice to the complexity of the topic in terms of either theoretical or methodological sophistication (Bossert et al., 1982; Bridges, 1982; Murphy, 1988; Rowan, et al., 1982).

For example, following a review that focused focusing primarily on methodological features of research of educational administrators, Bridges (1982) asserted:

> Research on school administrators for the period 1967-1980 reminds one of the dictum: 'The more things change, the more they remain the same'.... Although researchers apparently

K. Leithwood et al. (eds.), International Handbook of Educational Leadership and Administration, 723-**783**.
© 1996 Kluwer Academic Publishers, Printed in the Netherlands.

show a greater interest in outcomes than was the case in the earlier period, they continue their excessive reliance on survey designs, questionnaires of dubious reliability and validity, and relatively simplistic types of statistical analysis. Moreover these researchers persist in treating research problems in an ad hoc rather than a programmatic fashion.... Despite the rather loose definition of theory that was used in classifying the sample of research..., most of it proved to be atheoretical. Likewise the research seemed to have little or no practical utility. (pp. 24-25)

While it was not the specific focus of his review, Bridges (1982) further noted that research on administrator impact was both consistent with the above characterization and plagued by additional problems as well.

The lack of integration of theory with procedures of scientific inquiry in studying the consequences of school administration is especially disheartening. We must have confidence that researchers have accurately described and explained the phenomenon under consideration if this research is to be useful in informing policy efforts to improve schooling. Methodology concerns the process by which we construct knowledge. As such analyses of methodology must address how data are collected, analysed, and interpreted, as well as the theoretical and technical justification for these procedures (Everhart, 1988; Kaplan, 1964). Therefore, we must attend to the underlying assumptions of any scientific approach, as well as to its strengths and weaknesses (see Everhart (1988) for a thorough discussion of the relationship between methodology, method, and techniques of scientific inquiry in educational administration).

Over the past 15 years researchers in educational administration have increased their attention to the study of the principal's leadership role and its impact on a variety of school processes and outcomes. This was stimulated in part by parallel research into processes of school improvement and effectiveness. These efforts have been coupled with analytical innovations such as structural equation modelling. In combination, they have yielded a new generation of research on principal effectiveness.

Findings from this research that have found their way into scholarly and professional publications tend to give the impression that principals make a difference in student learning (e.g., Andrews & Soder, 1987; Bamberg & Andrews, 1990; Cheng, 1994; Eberts & Stone, 1988;

Heck et al., 1990). In our view, however, the interpretation of substantive findings from a body of literature must be considered in light of conceptual and methodological underpinnings. Both are crucial to determining the extent to which findings from research can be accepted as valid.

This chapter reviews research that explores the relationship between the leadership of the school principal and school outcomes concerned with student learning. The period of review extends from 1980 up to 1995. Our lens focuses more on the interplay between methodological and conceptual features of this body of research than upon the substance of the actual findings. Our aim is assess the contribution to knowledge made by these studies by understanding more clearly both the theoretical frameworks and processes of scientific inquiry used to generate the results. The purpose of the chapter, therefore, is threefold:

1) to analyse the theoretical frameworks that have been employed by researchers in the most recent generation of research on the principal's role in school effectiveness;

2) to examine the methodological features of this literature;

3) to propose a theoretical framework and appropriate methodological approaches that might guide future investigations of principal impact.

We begin by discussing the perspective for this review and issues that concern policymakers and researchers with respect to the impact of administrative leadership in schools. We briefly examine how this emerging concern was addressed by researchers during the 1980's and the resulting influence on our thinking about this review. Next, we consider conceptual and methodological issues as they emerged in our analysis of the studies. This analysis rests on the assumption that the way the research problem is conceptualized and the means of studying it both lead to what is observed and how those observations are interpreted. The chapter concludes with an attempt to frame an agenda for research on the principal's role in school effectiveness for the next generation of studies.

THE PERSPECTIVE AND SELECTION OF STUDIES FOR THIS REVIEW

Any attempt to integrate a body of research into a coherent framework that summarizes both conceptual and methodological issues must begin with an acknowledgement of its limitations. First, the field's conceptualization of organizational processes, including the school leadership construct, is constantly evolving (Glasman & Heck, 1992; Hallinger,1992, Leithwood & Hallinger, 1993; Leithwood et al., 1992). Hence, we assert that there is no universal paradigm or theory for examining organizational behaviour that is valid in all contexts. This point is especially salient for the current review since we include studies conducted internationally.

Second, proposed theories often become problematic when they seek to model the actual detail and richness of life in organizations (Bossert et al., 1982; Hallinger & Murphy, 1986b). The complexity of extra- and intra-organizational processes represents a challenge for researchers who seek to study causal relationships (Boyan, 1988; Marcoulides & Heck, 1993; Pitner, 1988). Social scientists who seek to develop valid theoretical models and apply appropriate analytic techniques to assess how those models work in the empirical world confront a formidable set of tasks.

We began this review with the assumption that the number of studies to be included would not be so large as to require a sampling strategy (Bridges, 1982). At the same time, we sought to conduct a highly inclusive review. We first searched the ERIC (Resources in Education) and Current Journals in Education (CJIE) databases and used the resulting sources as well as our personal knowledge of published and presented research to identify additional studies.

Three criteria guided our selection of studies for review. First, we were interested in studies that had been designed explicitly to examine the school principal's beliefs and leadership behaviour. The research must have clearly conceptualized and measured principal leadership as one of the independent variables. While our assumption was that most studies would use some measure of instructionally-oriented leadership, we observed that the definition of principal leadership has changed considerably over the decade and half of our review.

Second, the studies also had to include an explicit measure of school performance as a dependent variable. Most often performance was measured in terms of student achievement data, but occasionally other definitions such as effectiveness were also used. It was our desire, though not a necessary condition for inclusion, to also identify studies that examined the principal's impact on teacher and school level variables as mediating factors. The dual focus reflects the priority that we assign to student outcomes as the goal for school improvement, since we assume that an understanding of principal impact on student outcomes must also account for the operation of classroom and school-level variables. Notably, however, we did not include studies that examined principal impact on intervening variables if they did not also incorporate a measure of school outcomes. This criterion shifted the focus of the review towards quantitative studies of impact, as opposed to studies about the nature of the principal's work.

Third, given both the focus of the Handbook and the growing interest in international perspectives on school improvement, we made an extra effort to seek out studies that examined the impact of principals conducted in a variety of countries. We were reasonably successful in attaining this goal. Although we do not undertake comparative analysis in this chapter, we have included studies conducted in a diverse set of cultural contexts including the United States, Canada, Singapore, England, Netherlands, Marshall Islands, Israel, and Hong Kong. Eleven of the studies reviewed were conducted outside of the United States.

Consequently, the review includes published journal articles, dissertation studies, and papers presented at peer-reviewed conferences. We are reasonably confident that the chapter has captured most empirical studies of principal impact on school effectiveness disseminated internationally between 1980 and 1995. We owe particular debts to the earlier efforts of Bossert and colleagues (1982), Boyan (1988), Leithwood and colleagues (1990), and Pitner (1988) for laying the groundwork for this review.

THE PRINCIPAL'S ROLE IN SCHOOL EFFECTIVENESS: METHODOLOGICAL AND CONCEPTUAL ISSUES

Using these criteria, we identified 40 studies that explored the relationship between principal leadership and school outcomes or effectiveness conducted during this time period. Twenty-two of the studies were published in blind-refereed journals. Eleven were presented as papers at peer reviewed conferences (primarily the annual meeting of the AERA). Five were doctoral dissertations. One was a book chapter and one was a synthesis of several studies conducted by the author. Of the studies identified, we were unable to obtain two papers presented at professional meetings (Edington & Benedetto, 1984; Teddlie, Falkowski, Stringfield, Desselle, & Garvue, 1983).

With this overview in mind, we assess the conceptual and methodological trends that emerged from these 40 studies as a group. We content analysed the studies using a classification scheme suggested by Pitner (1988) (described in further detail later in the chapter). Working independently, we classified each study as one of six model types (see Figure 1). After comparing our completed schemes, we resolved the few discrepancies and triangulated our results with previous reviews (e.g., Bridges, 1982; Pitner,1988).

In this section of the chapter we discuss the major conceptual and methodological features of these studies. First, we briefly overview the philosophical and methodological perspectives of these studies. Then we look more specifically at the range of theoretical models that have been proposed for the study of the principal's role in school effectiveness and the corresponding operationalization of the variables proposed in the theoretical models. Next, we look more closely at a variety of design issues: the nature of the samples chosen, units of analysis, data collection methods, the analytical techniques employed to test the various models. Finally, we address the construct validity of the leadership models presented and generalizability of the knowledge generated from this set of studies.

Frame of Reference

In 1982 Bridges concluded that the frame of reference for studies in educational administration tended to be neither theoretical nor practical in nature. He found meager evidence of any systematic attack on problems of practice. Similarly, there appeared to be little accumulation of knowledge aimed at building theory. This was a bleak conclusion indeed for a field of professional practice.

This next generation of research is but subset of the literature reviewed by Bridges. Yet, it suggests considerable improvement. Perhaps because of the present studies' common lineage from the effective schools literature (Hallinger & Heck, in press), they delineate similar themes concerning the principal's role in promoting school improvement. Early studies of effective schools (e.g., Brookover et al., 1978; Edmonds, 1979) tended to view organizations primarily from a technical/rational perspective (Bolman & Deal, 1992; Ogawa, 1992). Scholars implied that changes could be made in schools by implementing effective schools correlates such as high expectations and strong school leadership. Prolonged positive effects of such change interventions, however, have been difficult to find or to generalize across educational settings. Nonetheless, the studies target an important area of research in educational administration in a positive fashion.

As Everhart (1988) argues, however, research approaches (e.g., purposes, questions, methods) must be seen within the historical and social context in which they are formulated; the answers created are equally contextualized. Thus, it is important to note that as a group the studies included in this review are decidedly functionalist and positivistic in their philosophical tradition. This undoubtedly resulted in part from our very framing of the question that underlies the review – how do principals make a difference in the learning of students?

What we observe in organizations is socially constructed and often reinforces, or at least reflects, dominant social and political ideologies (e.g., Anderson, 1990; Benham & Heck, 1994). While it is true that scholars have paid greater attention to alternative philosophical frameworks over the past decade (e.g., critical theorist, feminist, Marxist, phenomenological, post-modernist perspectives), relatively little of this discourse seems to have worked its way into empirical research on administrative effectiveness [see *Educational Administration Quarterly*, *27*(3) for a discussion of several different frameworks for research]. The lack of diverse philosophical and methodological views manifested in these studies is notable. The implications of the rather limited philosophical perspective and methodological approach taken within 'effective schools' studies, including those reviewed here are, therefore, considerable.

The examination of methodology itself forces one to admit that any particular approach is unlikely to yield universal understanding (Eisner, 1993; Everhart, 1988). From a methodological perspective, we chose to frame our review in terms of administrator effects on school effectiveness (as opposed to, for example, descriptions of principal work). Consequently, our selection criteria weighed heavily towards identifying finding quantitative studies. In contrast, a different approach to conceptualizing effectiveness might have pointed us towards naturalistic inquiry (e.g., fieldwork, ethnography) which tends to be constructivist, holistic, and process oriented (Everhart, 1988). In our view, quantitative methods are essential for the first part of this research program – assessing the extent to which administrative effects seem to be present. The use of qualitative approaches, however, is also essential if we are to understand the more complex processes that underlie this set of observed interactions (Dwyer et al.,1983).

Research Design

Almost all of the studies identified in our search used some form of cross-sectional, correlational design, often employing surveys or interviews as methods of gathering information. Studies of this type have been labelled under the broad design type of 'non-experimental' research (Pedhazur & Schmelkin, 1991). In this research approach, the independent variables are not manipulated as they are in experimental or quasi-experimental designs. Also, as in quasi-experimental designs the subjects are not assigned to groups through randomization. None of the studies in this review were classified as experimental or quasi-experimental in design.

Some may view this as problematic. Experimental and quasi-experimental designs employ stronger procedures for controlling extraneous variables that can confound measurement of the effects of the independent variable. Thus, such designs are often better suited to determinations of causation.

At the same time, the usefulness and feasibility of conducting experiments in the social sciences, often under relatively isolated conditions, has been debated with no clear conclusion (Pedhauzer & Schmelkin, 1991). Experimental research comes with its own set of problems and design limitations, particularly when applied to relatively large sample of schools. Thus, as we shall elaborate throughout this chapter, the over-riding issue is not design type per se, but the extent to which the chosen research design is guided by a strong theoretical model and the data are analysed using appropriate methods.

As has been discussed elsewhere, the use of non-experimental designs to study causal relationships is a dauntingly complex task (Pedhazur & Schmelkin, 1991; Pitner, 1988). A point of departure in understanding distinctions among the three broad classes of designs is the role of theory to help specify the models for testing. In experimental and quasi-experimental designs causal inferences are made from the independent variables to the dependent variables. In contrast, in non-experimental designs causal inferences are generally made in the opposite direction (Pedhazur & Schmelkin, 1991). In non-experimental research attempts are made to account for a dependent variable by 'uncovering' relevant independent variables. Appropriate model specification readily becomes a problem because one must recognize the need to include all relevant independent variables to specify the model properly.

Thus, the major threat to validity in non-experimental research stems from uncontrolled confounding variables. Major approaches to control include subject selection, statistical adjustments (Pedhazur & Schmelkin, 1991), and replication of results through varying conditions (Heck & Marcoulides, 1992). These are critical points to keep in mind when assessing the contribution to knowledge made by this set of studies.

We suggest two further points to consider in judging the contribution of the studies in this review. First, as implied above, in non-experimental research the complexity of relationships explicated in the tested model play an important role in interpreting the results. Empirical research grounded in overly simplistic conceptualizations of leadership effects is unlikely to yield results that are useful, practically or theoretically.

Second, the appropriateness of analytical techniques used by the researcher affect the strength of the conclusions that can be drawn about the effects of the principal's role. Certainly more rigorous analyses may lead to uncovering relationships in the data that are not revealed in more simplistic analyses. At the same time, however, they are also more likely to lead to fewer findings of substance than have often been 'claimed' in studies that employ more simplistic analytical methods (Pedhazur & Schmelkin, 1991).

Classification of Administrator Effects

While granting that there exists a rather narrow philosophical perspective undergirding studies of school and administrator effects, there is still considerable variation in the conceptual modelling of leadership effects. Because the group of studies is essentially confined to one philosophical stance, we found it convenient to apply Pitner's (1988) framework of administrator effects in classifying the studies. In an earlier analytical review, Pitner (1988) sought to conceptualize the possible theoretical approaches that could be used in studying administrator impact through non-experimental research designs. She identified five theoretical approaches to portraying administrator effects: direct-effects, moderated-effects, antecedent-effects, mediated-effects, and reciprocal-effects models (pp. 105-108). These models offer one means of viewing both the impact of the school context on administrative behaviour and the influence of administrative behaviour on the

732

school organization and its outcomes. Our adaptation of Pitner's classification system of administrative effects is depicted in Figure 1.

A *direct-effects model* of administrator effects (Model A, Figure 1) proposes that the principal's leadership actually exerts an influence on

Model A: Direct-effects Model without or with Antecedent Effects (A-1)

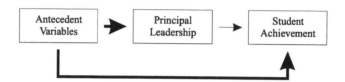

Model B: Moderated-effects Model

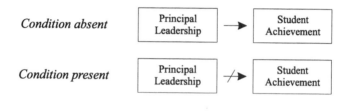

Model C: Reciprocal-effects Model

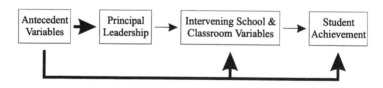

Model D: Reciprocal-effects Model

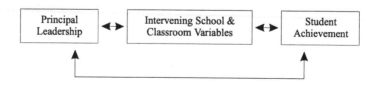

Note: a thick line indicates an antecedent effect.
Adapted from Pitner, 1988, pp. 105-108

students apart from other variables within the school (e.g., teacher behaviour, curricular organization, school culture). The researcher using this model does not normally seek to account or control for the effects of these in-school mediating variables. The researcher may or may not control for the impact of external variables.[1]

In the past, studies employing a direct-effects model were, therefore, typically bivariate in nature (e.g., O'Day, 1983; Ruczieska, 1988; van de Grift, 1987, 1989[2], 1990; see Table 1). More recently, however, sophisticated analytic techniques such as structural equation modelling have also been employed to assess the relationship between leadership and school outcomes (e.g., Hallinger et al., 1990; Heck et al., 1990; van de Grift, 1990; Weil, Marshalek, Mitman, Murphy, Hallinger, & Pruyn, 1984). Two direct-effects studies (i.e., Ramey, 1982; van de Grift, 1990) used structural equation modelling.

While direct-effects studies are quite common in the literature, they have been criticized for making untenable assumptions about the nature of leadership in organizations (Murphy, 1988; Rowan et al., 1982). Moreover, in such studies the process by which administrators achieve an impact is hidden by a 'black box.' Consequently, these studies reveal little that advances our theoretical or practical under-standing of the critical school processes through which the principal achieves an impact on school effectiveness (Leithwood et al., 1990; Leitner, 1994).

Another conceptual framework for examining administrator effects is represented by the *moderated-effects* model (Model B, Figure 1). Here it is proposed that some condition in the school or the environ-ment operates as a third variable *moderating* the relationship between leadership and school outcomes through its presence or absence. One begins by noting a relationship (e.g., a correlation) between the admin-istrator and outcome of interest. A third, usually dichotomous, variable is then added to the model and its effects on the original relationship assessed. Typically, researchers using a moderated-effects model would hypothesize that the administrator effect occurs under one set of conditions but not under another, less favourable condition (Pitner, 1988).

This approach was not widely used by researchers in this set of stud-ies. We would, however, note that several studies in our review did identify third variables that appeared to act as moderating forces on the relationship between principal leadership and school outcomes. The most frequently studied was community socioeconomic factors (e.g., high or low school socioeconomic status). This environmental variable was found to specify the type of leadership principals exercise in an effort to improve school outcomes (i.e., Andrews & Soder, 1987; Hallinger & Murphy, 1986; Rowan & Denk, 1984). This result has implications for the moderated-effects approach, but was derived from studies using the antecedent-effects model.

A third perspective for viewing administrator effects identified by Pitner (1988) is the *antecedent-effects* model. Conceptually this model is more complex than the previous conceptualization. Unlike the moderated-effects model where the administrator is considered as an independent variable, in antecedent-effects research 'the administrator variable stands as both a dependent and an independent variable' (Pitner, 1988, p. 106). As a dependent variable, administrative behaviour is subject to the influence of other variables within the school and its environment. As an independent variable, the administrator is an agent who acts to influence the actions of teachers, the nature of the school organization and the learning of pupils (Bridges, 1970, 1977; Hallinger & Murphy, 1986a; Leithwood et al., 1990; Rowan et al., 1982).

When actually categorizing studies by model type, we found the distinction between moderated effects and antecedent effects often difficult to ascertain. In practice the distinction depends on several factors. These include the specific theoretical model proposed before the data are analysed (sometimes not specified by researchers), the level at which the relevant variables are measured (i.e., often continuous for antecedent-effects and categorical for moderated-effects models), the techniques used to analyse moderated (i.e., correlations, t-tests and analysis of variance) and antecedent (i.e., structural equation modelling or regression with interaction terms) effects, and the findings as interpreted in the published study. Thus, both conceptual and empirical issues influence the choice of model.

As indicated, the two conceptual models imply different approaches to data analysis. For example, the researcher who conceives of socioeconomic status as exerting a *moderating* effect might build data tables to portray and compare the relationship between leadership and outcomes in light of the moderating variable. The first table would analyse the relationship between leadership and outcomes in schools with high socioeconomic status. The other would show the relationship between leadership and outcomes in schools with low socioeconomic status (e.g., Andrews & Soder, 1987; Andrews, Soder & Jacoby, 1986; Hallinger & Murphy, 1986b). The researcher then looks at both tables to determine how the moderating variable affects the original relationship. Although this approach to analysing moderating effects most clearly demonstrates the concept, it should be noted that other analytical approaches can be used as well (Rowan & Denk, 1984).

If we conceive of the antecedent variable(s) (e.g., socioeconomic status) as exerting both a direct effect on school outcomes as well as an indirect effect through intervening variables (e.g., on classroom composition, teacher behaviour, school leadership), an antecedent-effects model may be preferable. This approach is considerably more flexible in that it allows the researchers to included multiple antecedents in the model and to analyse the whole constellation of relationships simultaneously rather than separately.

In fact, only a few analytical techniques are able to measure the indirect effects implied in antecedent-effect models. As we shall elaborate later in the chapter, path analysis and structural equation modelling are the preferred methods for this type of model. There are, selected instances where such relationships can be implied using interaction terms associated with analytical techniques such as analysis of variance or covariance and regression analysis.

An important conceptual point to keep in mind in differentiating these two models is the relative importance attached to the third (moderating or antecedent) variable. In moderated-effects studies this variable remains of secondary concern to leadership. In antecedent-effects studies this external variable is conceived to play a key role in understanding the system of relationships among the variables.

An example serves to illustrate this distinction. Andrews and Soder (1987) tested the direct effects of leadership on school outcomes. They concluded that a significant relationship existed between principal leadership and student outcomes across all schools in their sample for reading and math improvement. Then they introduced school socioeconomic status, conducting separate analyses for high and low SES schools. All significant relationships between leadership and math and reading outcomes disappeared for high SES schools, but some remained for low SES schools. The same general pattern also held when the sample was dichotomized by predominant ethnicity. They were unable to consider the possible interactions between ethnicity and SES, or between these variables and leadership, in their analysis, however, because of the small sample size.

In this study, therefore, the more complete conclusion is that socioeconomic status and ethnicity *moderate* the effects of leadership on school outcomes. Within this model, the direct and indirect effects of environmental conditions could not be optimally tested on both leadership and outcomes simultaneously (as implied in an antecedent-effect model). Therefore, linkages between the antecedent contextual variables and leadership and their resultant combined impacts on school outcomes are hinted at but left unclear. The study illustrates the distinction between the models and the limitations of the moderated-effects approach.

A *mediated-effects* model (Model C, Figure 1) assumes that some or all of the impact attained by administrators on desired school outcomes occurs through manipulation of, or interaction with features of the school organization (e.g., Biester et al., 1984; Crawford, Kimball, & Watson & 1985; Eberts & Stone, 1988; Jackson, 1982; Silins, 1994; see Table 1). This is consistent with Bridges' (1977) contention that managers achieve their results through other people. Mediated-effects studies, therefore, are more useful for theory building than direct-effects studies. They are also of potentially greater value for revealing avenues by which administrators achieve practical results.

A fifth approach Pitner proposed is the *reciprocal-effects* model. Scholars have noted that it is not necessarily the case that the effects of administrative move in only one direction. It is possible, even likely, that the relationship between the administrator and features of the school are interactive. Administrators may cause changes which then cause reciprocal effects in the originating variable (i.e., leadership). Alternatively, it could be hypothesized that the administrator adjusts his or her leadership behaviour to processes and characteristics of the school (e.g., current and changing states of student outcomes).

Where doubts about the direction of causality are expressed, cross-sectional data are unable to resolve the ambiguity inherent in correlations and other measures of association (Davies, 1994). As Davies (1994) argues, "the duration in current state" data often collected in cross-sectional studies are not sufficient to overcome this type of problem. Moreover, with cross-sectional data, one cannot characterize the inertial properties of the assumed reciprocal relationship. A more complete representation, therefore, would require the assumption that the reciprocal effects will only become apparent over time. Thus, in order to specify such models properly, longitudinal data are preferred.

Notably, only two studies tested for reciprocal effects and these are actually more properly conceived of as C_1 studies (Hallinger et al., 1990; Heck et al., 1990). Yet, the approach holds much promise for future investigations that seek to employ dynamic models of principal effects.

We contend that a comprehensive framework for viewing the principal's role in school effectiveness must locate principal leadership within both organizational and environmental contexts. To adapt this view to the framework proposed by Pitner, the effects of the principal on the organization can be modelled by combining antecedent variables with either direct or mediated-effects models (see Figure 1 and Table 1). When antecedent variables are incorporated into the direct-effects model, we will refer to this new model as Model A_1 (e.g., Blank, 1987; Dilworth, 1987; Krug, 1986; see Table 1). When antecedent variables are included in a mediated-effects model, we will term this combination as Model C_1 (e.g., Goldring & Pasternak, 1994; Hallinger et al., 1990; Heck et al., 1990, 1993, Leithwood et al., 1993; Leitner, 1994; Scott & Teddlie, 1987; Weil et al., 1984; see Table 1).

To illustrate two contrasting conceptualizations within this analytic scheme, some studies in the review simply seek to establish whether certain relationships exist between the principal's leadership and other dependent variables including, but not limited to school achievement. The purpose of these studies is often to address a question of practical interest. Thus, the researcher might ask, how do principals in high- or low-achieving schools differ in terms of their attitudes, beliefs, or behaviour? Most of these studies are not primarily concerned with theory in the sense of contributing to our understanding of larger theoretical issues. These studies tend to cluster into what we will later describe as direct-effects studies (see Models A and A_1 in Figure 1).

In contrast, quite a few researchers were explicit in their attempt to link their empirical analysis to theoretical issues involving principal role and the relationship of leadership to the organization and its environment (e.g., Goldring & Pasternak, 1994; Heck et al., 1990; Jones, 1987; Leithwood et al., 1993; Leitner, 1994; Ogawa & Hart, 1985; Silins, 1994). Such studies developed and tested more complete theoretical models. Occasionally, they also tested competing theoretical models about the effects of leadership (e.g., Cheng, 1994; Silins, 1994) and gave greater attention to the replication of findings across a variety of contextual conditions. In general, these studies also tended to employ more sophisticated designs and analytical techniques by which to test their data against the proposed theoretical relationships.

By our measure, approximately one-half of the studies could be classified as being driven by broad theoretical and methodological issues. These studies were disproportionately represented under Model C_1, C, and A_1. In these reports, the researchers addressed issues that went well beyond the common empirical concern about the principal's impact that draws these investigations to our attention. This represents significant improvement over the picture depicted by Bridges in 1982, who termed research in the field as intellectual random events.

Table 1 presents our full classification of the studies included in our review. As summarized in the table, the studies reviewed most frequently incorporated features of the antecedent-effects, direct-effects, and mediated-effects models. Less frequent were studies that used the moderated- or reciprocal-effects models in studying the relationship between principal leadership and school effectiveness (see Hallinger & Heck, in press for a more complete discussion of the conceptual models in use). It may be further noted that there is a general trend over time (i.e., from 1980 to 1995) in terms of the complexity of the model tested. Research tends to be moving from more simple, direct-effects models to more comprehensive models (e.g., mediated effects with antecedents).

Conceptualizing and Operationalizing Variables

Within any of the previously outlined theoretical models, researchers still have numerous choices as to the selection and operationalization of variables for studying the role of the principal in school effectiveness. Foremost, perhaps, for this review is the theoretical orientation and steps taken to model and measure the principal's leadership role. As suggested by our previous discussion, differences in how the theoretical models are conceptualized and variables operationalized have important implications for the ways in which the models are tested. This in turn has an impact on the types of conclusions that we can draw about the nature of principal leadership and its effects. Here we will briefly examine the predominant conceptualizations of variables included in the studies. Consistent with our notion of comprehensive models, we will briefly examine principal leadership, antecedent/context variables, mediating variables, and school outcomes.

Principal leadership

The conceptualization of principal leadership has evolved considerably over the past 25 years (Duke, this volume; Glasman & Heck, 1992; Hallinger, 1992; Leithwood et al., 1992). Predominant notions of the principal's role have evolved from manager, to street-level bureaucrat, to change agent, to instructional manager, to instructional leader, to

| | | | Analytic Technique | | | | | | |
Study Author	Sample Size/Type	Dependent Variable	Desc.	Corrle'n	T-test Chi Squ.	Anova Manova	Regression	Structural/Path Modelling	Outcome Effects
Model A: Direct Effects									
Broughton, 1991*	70 tch/20 es	1					x		none
Cantu, 1994	96 tchrs, 6es	2				x			none
Glasman, 1981	29 studies	1			x				none
Glasman, 1983	210 pr & tch	2	x						yes
Glasman, 1984	302 pr	2	x						none
Glasman, 1992	35 pr	2	x						yes
Glasman/F, 1992	20 pr	2	x						yes
Hunter, 1994*	52 ms; 331 tch, 52 pr	2			x				mixed
O'Day, 1983*	140 tch/19 es	1		x	x	x			none
Ruczieska, 1988*	155 tch/11 es, ms	2		x	x				mixed

Table 1: Characteristics of Principal Effects Studies

Study Author	Sample Size/Type	Dependent Variable	Analytic Technique						Outcome Effects
			Desc.	Corrle'n	T-test Chi Squ.	Anova Manova	Regression	Structural/Path Modelling	
van de Grift, 1989	182 es pr	1		x					mixed
van de Grift, 1987	139 pr	1		x					none
van de Grift, 1990*	104 es	1						x	none
Model A-1: Direct-effects with antecedent effects									
Blank, 1987	32 hs	1, 5				x			mixed
Brewer, 1993	2070 hs st	1					x		yes
Dilworth, 1987	77tch	1					x		none
Krug, 1986	193 tch/11 es	2		x					mixed
Ramey, 1982	193 tch/19 es	1						x	none
Cheng, 1991	64 hs	4				x			yes
Cheng, 1994	190 es	1, 3		x	x				mixed
Model B: Moderated-effects									
Andrews, 1987	33 es	1			x				yes
Hallinger, 1986	10 es	2	x						N.A.

Table 1 (contd.): Characteristics of Principal Effects Studies

Study Author	Sample Size/Type	Dependent Variable	Analytic Technique						Outcome Effects
			Desc.	Corrle'n	T-test Chi Squ.	Anova Manova	Regression	Structural/Path Modelling	
Rowan, 1984	142 es	1					x		mixed
Model C: Mediated-effects									
Jackson, 1982*	8 es	2	x				x		yes
Biester, 1984	8 es	2	x						mixed
Crawford, 1985*	94 es, ms, hs	1						x	mixed
Eberts, 1988*	300 pr	1					x		yes
Silins, 1994*	265 pr	3						x	yes
Model C-1: Mediated-effects with antecedent effects									
Bamberg, 1990	61 es	1				x			yes
Goldring, 1994	34 es	1					x		yes
Hallinger, 1990	87 es	2						x	yes
Heck, 1990	200 tchrs/30 el, hs	2						x	yes
Heck, 1991	71 tch/4 es, hs	2					x		yes

Table 1 (contd.): Characteristics of Principal Effects Studies

Study Author	Sample Size/Type	Dependent Variable	Analytic Technique						Outcome Effects
			Desc.	Corrle'n	T-test Chi Squ.	Anova Manova	Regression	Structural/Path Modelling	
Heck, 1993	138 tch/26 hs	2					x		yes
Heck/Hallinger**	70 tch/20 es	1						x	yes
Heck/Hallinger***	104 es	1						x	yes
Jones, 1987	27 hs	1		x			x		none
Leithwood, 1993	770 tch/272 sch	3		x			x		yes
Leithwood, 1994	varied	3						x	yes
Ogawa, 1985	275 es, hs	1				x			yes
Scott, 1987	250 tch/76 es	1						x	none
Weil, 1984	20 es	1, 2, 6				x		x	mixed

Table 1 (contd.): Characteristics of Principal Effects Studies

Study Author	Sample Size/Type	Dependent Variable	Analytic Technique						
			Desc.	Corrle'n	T-test Chi Squ.	Anova Manova	Regression	Structural/Path Modelling	Outcome Effects
Model D: Reciprocal-effects									
Hallinger, 1990	87 es	2						x	N.A.
Heck, 1990	200 tchrs/30 el, hs	2						x	N.A.

* Antecedent variable(s) were limited to controlling for effects on achievement
** Reanalysis of Broughton & Riley, 1991
*** Reanalysis of van de Grift, 1990

Key for Dependent Variables:
1 = student achievement
2 = school effectiveness
3 = teacher perceptions of school effectiveness
4 = organizational effectiveness
5 = attendance
6 = student self-concept

Table 1 (contd.): Characteristics of Principal Effects Studies

transformational leader. Even within the past decade, we have observed a discernable shift in emphasis in the conceptualization of the principal's role. Thus, we have begun to see less emphasis given to the instructional leadership role and more to various models construed as more consistent with school restructuring such as transformational leadership (Hallinger, 1992; Leithwood & Jantzi, 1993).

As Glasman and Heck (1992) argue, the changing role conceptualizations may result from increasing external demands and reflect the reform of an educational system that is moving from a closed to a more open system of governance. This has implications for management, with a decreased emphasis on centralized, directive management and an increased emphasis on participatory leadership and decentralized decision making. This evolving view of leadership continues to reflect a recognition of the importance of the principal as a leader, but with different expectations of both stylistic and substantive nature.

The evolving conceptualization of the principal's role is captured in the chronological progression of the studies. Studies from the early to late 1980's were dominated by an instructional leadership conceptualization drawn from the effective schools literature (e.g., Andrews & Soder, 1987; Biester et al., 1984; Hallinger & Murphy, 1986; Jackson, 1982; Jones, 1987; Krug, 1984; O'Day, 1983; Scott & Teddlie, 1987). This was not unexpected given the policy context of the past decade or so. Though defined in a variety of ways, 30 of the 40 studies conceptualized the principal's role in school effectiveness in terms of instructional leadership.

When an instructional leadership construct was employed, researchers most frequently drew on comprehensive conceptualizations of the principal's role based on the theoretical models of Bossert and his colleagues [(1982) e.g., Hallinger et al., 1990; Heck et al., 1990; Heck, 1993], Hallinger and Murphy [(1985; Weil et al., 1984) e.g., Andrews & Soder, 1987; Andrews, Soder & Jacoby, 1986; Dilworth, 1987; Jones, 1987; Krug, 1986; Leitner, 1994; O'Day, 1983; Ruczieska, 1988], or the Connecticut State Education Department (Sirois, & Villanova, 1982; Villanova, Gauthier, Proctor, & Shoemaker, 1981). Others also focused on instructional leadership, but were less comprehensive in their approach to conceptualizing instructional leadership. For example, Biester and his colleagues (1984) focused on the effects of 'achievement-directed leadership.' Braughton and Riley (1991) investigated principals' knowledge and involvement in the reading process with school outcomes in reading. In two studies, Glasman (1983, 1984) explored how principals use achievement data to stimulate teachers towards instructional improvement. Both Bamburg and Andrews (1990) and Goldring and Pasternak (1994) employed instructional leadership conceptualizations that relied heavily on the principals' use of goals as an agent for achieving an impact on the school.

The conceptualizations embedded in more recent studies tend to take a less confined approach to the role. Three studies examined transformational and transactional leadership constructs (Leithwood et al., 1993; Leithwood, 1994; Silins, 1994). One used Bolman and Deal's (1992) four frames of organization as the basis for their study of principal leadership (Cheng, 1994). The remaining studies were either not explicit in their conception of principal leadership (e.g., Glasman & Binianimov,1981; Ramey et al., 1982) or relied solely on the principal's role as a proxy for determination of leadership effects (e.g.,Ogawa & Hart, 1985; Rowan & Denk, 1984).

Personal antecedents and school context

Our analysis suggests that the complexity of the relationship between principal leadership and student outcomes overmatched the conceptual and methodological tools being used by researchers. Beyond the simple question of whether principals make a difference, researchers have since sought to further understand how the context in which the principal works influence the expectations and requirements for leadership and the subsequent responses of principals. Our analysis indicates that some progress has been made in increasing our understanding of how contextual factors influence school leadership. Notably, this has been achieved primarily through studies using Model B and C_1 theoretical frameworks.

That said, the surface has only been scratched. There has been a fairly wide range of variation in the operationalization of environmental variables. A few (e.g.,socioeconomic status and school level) have received considerably more attention than others (e.g., district structures, community political conditions, rural/urban, cultural distinctions). Similarly, past personal demographics, (e.g.,experience, education) personal variables have not received much, if any, consideration in the past group of studies (e.g., gender differences, professional and organizational socialization). From our perspective, there is certainly room for future research that incorporates various socialization processes and gender-related research (and alternative theoretical perspectives) into the impact of principals upon school processes and outcomes.

Mediating variables

As a group, the studies offer several hints at promising mediating variables between principal actions and school effectiveness. A multi-level perspective on schools suggests that principals work primarily with teachers across classrooms and teachers with students within classrooms. This makes untangling principal effects relatively complex.

Because organizations are themselves socially constructed, defining potential in-school processes that are affected by leadership depends heavily on the perceptions of those in the organization who contribute to the creation of an organizational reality. The processes we refer to as intervening variables (e.g., student opportunity to learn) are therefore often more perceived than real. Thus, we can only observe these processes indirectly.

Recent methodological innovations such as structural equation modelling provide an important means for investigating the school processes that comprise important mediating variables in our conceptual models. The system of structural relations explicated in a model, (and tested empirically) serves as an intermediary between visible manifestations of the process and the abstract theories or models through which we interpret and understand these processes. The types of in-school processes that these researchers have studied can be referred to in structural equation modelling as latent (or unobserved) variables. These are defined by any number of observed manifestations of the process. Together the observed manifestations serve as a proxy for the hypothesized dimension (e.g., see Hallinger et al., 1990; Heck, 1993; Heck et al., 1990; Leithwood et al., 1993).

Leithwood (1994), for example, focused on psychological dispositions of teachers with respect to leadership actions of the principals. He studied teacher perceptions about school culture, decision-making processes, programs and instruction, school goals, resources, commitment and attitudes toward change, and organizational development. Other studies operationalized aspects of the Bossert et al. (1982) framework. These examined facets of school climate, or culture, and instructional organization.

Weil et al. (1984) concluded that principals in outstanding elementary schools had a strong effect on teachers' perceptions of the learning environment. They explored the effects of high expectations and success with students, student motivation, alignment of curriculum relative to principals in average-achieving schools. The researchers noted differences between effective and average schools in terms of the social environment (sense of community, student involvement, orderly environment) and leadership. Many of these perceptions were triangulated with data from teachers, students, and parents.

Several studies found positive relationships between principals' supervision of instructional processes and outcomes (e.g., Brewer, 1993; Hallinger et al., 1990; Heck et al., 1990; Heck et al., 1991). Our own reanalysis of the Braughton and Riley (1991) study demonstrates that principals' active involvement in supervising the work of teachers has a substantial positive indirect effect on students' reading outcomes. A number of studies also produced consistent findings in terms of the principal's role in setting and communicating school goals (e.g., Brewer, 1993; Heck et al., 1990).

Interestingly, when the studies that report positive findings are reviewed, only one mediating variable shows up with consistency as a significant factor interacting with principal leadership: school goals (e.g., Bamberg & Andrews, 1990; Brewer, 1993; Goldring & Pasternak, 1994; Hallinger et al., in press; Hallinger & Murphy, 1986; Heck et al., 1990; Leithwood, 1994; Silins, 1994). This variable was measured differently in various studies. In some studies the goal variable was measured in terms of goal consensus; in others it was operationalized in terms of the simple presence of school goals, the degree of academic focus, principal vision or focus, or the principal's role in communicating a mission. For the purposes of this chapter, we cannot do more than note that this function of the principal – establishing and sustaining a school-wide purpose – does receive empirical support. Clearly this will represent an area for further investigation within mediated-effects models.

School outcomes or effectiveness

The question that often guides discussions of principal impact - 'Do principals make a difference?' – is subject to widely varying interpretations. While research that examines impact on school outcomes is highly attractive from a policy perspective, it has been fraught with conceptual and methodological problems that are not easily untangled. One of the most salient strengths of this research – its reliance on standardized test scores as the outcome measure – has also come to be viewed as one of its greatest limitations.

During the 1980's many policymakers, preoccupied with quantitative measures of educational productivity, cast the question of principal impact in terms of its effects on a single variable – student achievement. Research adopting this perspective first began to appear in 1984 (e.g., Biester et al., 1984; Glasman, 1984; O'Day, 1984; Rowan & Denk,1984). These early studies of principal impact on student learning foreshadowed the increasing interest among researchers that would emerge over the next decade.

In the mid-1990's it is increasingly accepted internationally that effective education is represented by a wider range of cognitive and affective variables than are measured by the common standardized achievement tests (Leithwood et al., 1990). We believe that the continued reliance on narrow standardized measures for assessing administrative impact distorts the meaning of the question, 'Do principals make a difference? Perhaps more importantly, because of the research shortcomings mentioned previously, the empirical findings that accumulated have often been viewed as ambiguous. At times, they are even contradictory. This may be at least in part a function of how school outcomes have been conceived.

When we inquire into the impact of principal leadership, a wide range of dependent variables is available for study. The dependent variables may be broadly grouped into at least three categories of impact: school and environmental effects (e.g., parent satisfaction, community participation, perceptions of school functioning), intra-organizational processes (e.g., staff morale, curricular organization, instructional effectiveness), and student effects (e.g., student achievement, attitudes, retention). The priority assigned to these variables varies widely, both within and across countries, and is implicitly value-laden.

As restructuring has become a more popular policy solution during the 1990's, we note a corresponding shift in thinking toward a broader view of potential principal impact. The later studies explore the relationship between principal leadership and a wider range of intervening classroom and school level variables in the belief that the impact of principal leadership is likely to be indirect in nature (e.g., Goldring & Pasternak, 1994; Hallinger et al., 1990), or look more specifically at leadership aimed at 'second order,' or restructuring, changes (e.g., Leithwood et al., 1993; Leithwood, 1994; Silins, 1994). These studies tend to group into the second category of concern – intra-organizational processes. As evidenced in Table 1, however, little attention has been directed toward environmental outcomes such as parent satisfaction or community participation.

While the assessment of higher-order cognitive outcomes is not in evidence in these studies, the researchers have sought to move away, to some degree, from exclusive reliance on standardized tests to assess student performance. As shown in Table 1, there is some variation in the ways in which school outcomes have been conceptualized and measured (e.g., test scores, school effectiveness, improving or declining schools, teacher-perceived program, school, and student outcomes).

Most often the dependent variable has tended to be student scores on standardized tests or an overall school effectiveness variable. These measures may or may not include controls for contextual differences in schools [see Hallinger & Murphy, (1986) or Heck et al., (1990) for examples]. The validity and reliability of this range of dependent variables is an important issue in interpreting the findings from these studies. One must consider the extent to which a standardized test score or any number of definitions of effectiveness represent a valid school 'outcomes.'

We believe continued effort must be directed toward broadening the school outcome construct and in considering the findings of individual studies in light of the particular dependent constructs investigated. For example, the psychometric properties of any number of dependent constructs can be reported, but this issue was seldom addressed in this set of studies. While standardized tests, for example, are typically highly reliable, their validity has been open to increasing debate.

Sampling

There are several important issues in sampling. For the purposes of our review we will concern ourselves with the representativeness of samples (i.e., the extent to which the sample represents the populations from which they are chosen) and the precision of estimates based on sample size (Pedhuzer & Schmelkin, 1991).

Nature of the samples

These reports reveal a wide range in the nature of the samples studied. They indicate a distinct preference among researchers for studying elementary school principals. Of these 40 reports, over two-thirds either studied elementary schools exclusively or in combination with schools at other levels. Nine studies included principals at the high school level along with elementary schools, and three additional studies explored leadership solely at the high school level.

The predilection for studying the impact of elementary school principal's leadership is not surprising. Researchers often base their preference for studying the impact of the principal at the elementary level because of the greater likelihood of detecting effects in the smaller, less organizationally complex, venue of elementary schools. Aside from this factor, exploring the relationship between principal leadership and school effectiveness at the high school level also poses greater conceptual and methodological challenges (Firestone & Herriott, 1982; Hallinger & Murphy, 1986a).

Given the non-experimental nature of this research, the sampling design of the studies becomes an important issue when we seek to detect the effects of principal leadership quantitatively (Bridges, 1982; Eberts & Stone, 1988; van de Grift, 1990). How the sample is obtained is central to the validity of results. Samples are broadly of two types: non probability samples, which are based on convenience or accessibility; and probability samples, where assumptions are made about the criteria and procedures for obtaining the sample. Often, however, the use of intact schools, 'statistical tails' consisting of the best and worst schools in a population, or various added criteria regarding the stability of staff and principal precluded the use of true random samples in this body of research.

While several studies employed elements of randomization (e.g., selecting teachers at random within a nonprobability sample of schools), few studies employed truly randomly selected samples. Notable exceptions are Goldring and Pasternak (1994) and van de Grift (1990). Others addressed the sampling issue by attempting to be exhaustive in focusing on a single school system or complex of schools and including every school (or a sample of schools) and their personnel within the unit (e.g., Heck et al., 1991; Leitner, 1994). This approach approximates cluster sampling (Pedhazur & Schmelkin, 1991). There is considerable flexibility in how the samples were selected.

Size of samples

Decisions about sample size are relatively complex and subject to many concerns. These can include sampling strategy, economic, and practical considerations. Of considerable importance in interpreting the findings of any study is the concept of effect size; that is, the degree to which the phenomenon is present in the population (Cohen, 1988). For observing the principal's impact on school processes or outcomes, we must assume that the effect size is relatively small. To detect small effects, therefore, implies the need for larger samples. Otherwise, one may fail to reject the null hypothesis because the research was not designed with sufficient ability to detect the effect due to the small sample size. Power analysis concerns the ability of the statistical analysis conducted to detect the presence of an effect, should one exist, given various effect sizes, levels of significance, and sample size (Cohen, 1988). Other things being equal, small samples, therefore, are only capable of detecting relatively large effects in the population.

The size of the principal or school samples studied ranged widely from a low of 75 teachers and principals in a complex of four schools (Heck et al., 1991) to a high of about 300 principals (Eberts & Stone, 1988; Glasman, 1984). The median sample size was 34 schools or principals studied. Much of the discussion of sample size also depends upon the purposes of the research, the unit of analysis, and analytical techniques used to investigate the data. Our judgment is that many of the studies reviewed had samples that were not selected through optimal sampling methods and were too small to detect leadership effects if they were present. Thus, caution must be employed in evaluating the findings of individual studies in light of the sampling methods used.

In the absence of preferred methods of sampling, however, replication across educational settings and with various instruments becomes an important means of increasing confidence in findings. From this standpoint, while the majority of studies reviewed have sampling problems to some extent when viewed in isolation, the convergence of findings from Model C studies that principals do affect school outcomes at least indirectly is encouraging. This is especially true since they were conducted in a variety of educational settings, with varied samples, using different instruments to operationalize leadership constructs, and a variety of techniques used to analyse the data. Thus, despite the sampling problems of individual studies, as a group these problems become less severe.

Unit of Analysis

Researchers have recently given increased attention to the measurement of variables across levels of organizations. In education, these distinctions are readily apparent, but have been difficult to investigate empirically. Students bring individual abilities to their classrooms. Teachers shape the children's classroom environment. Principals monitor teachers within their schools. Superintendents develop improvement plans for their districts. Theoretically, this has been referred to as a 'nested structure' and represents one example of a hierarchical data structure (Bossert et al., 1982).

When studying the interrelationships among principal, teacher, and student-level variables, this structural feature of educational organizations takes on particular importance. This is the case because principals are likely to influence the school level of the organization more directly than the classroom (e.g., how teachers organize instruction) or student levels (the motivation of particular students). We immediately run into problems in attempting to decide where the appropriate unit of analysis is when looking at data intended for school-level analyses.

One illustration of this concerns whether constructs such as school climate or principal leadership are basic properties of the organization or merely perceptions of the individuals. If we accept the former conceptualization, perceptions should be measured at the school level. in the latter case, they would more appropriately be measured at the individual teacher or student level.

Earlier studies of schools as organizations seldom addressed the problem of variables that are impacted by multiple levels of the organization (e.g., student achievement). In this group of studies, for example, the unit of analysis tended to be either the individual level (e.g., teachers and principal as individuals without regard to their school setting) or the school level. In the latter case, teacher responses were summed to create school means. The researchers would then compare *schools* within the sample.

Neither solution is completely satisfactory. A limitation of a school-level analysis is that every individual in the school is assumed to hold the same perception about the principal. Individual level analyses do not allow us to assess accurately the effects of different levels of the organization on the relevant outcome of interest. For example, if quality of teaching is hypothesized to affect student learning, then we know that some students in our sample of individuals have the same teacher and, further, differ in the quality of teaching that they receive.

To ignore this by disaggregating the data, therefore, we violate the assumption of independence of observations that is basic for classical statistical techniques. That is, systematic groups of students in our sample would have the same value on all variables at the classroom level (Bryk & Raudenbush, 1992).

Several promising analytic techniques have been developed over the past few years (e.g., structural equation modelling, hierarchical linear modelling) that allow the investigation of these effects across organizational levels. One such study (Rowan, Raudenbush, & Kang, 1991) serves as a good example of how this approach can yield useful information about administrative effects. This study was not included in our review because it did not use school achievement as a dependent variable.

Rowan et al. (1991) looked at differences in principal leadership and other organizational processes using a multilevel analysis. Hierarchical linear modelling (Bryk & Raudenbush, 1992) was first employed to separate the variance accounted for in principal leadership practices into within-school and between-school components. From this analysis, they determined that most of the variance in teacher perceptions about principal leadership (roughly 75 percent) was actually the result of within-school variation in how teachers view the principal's actions. Of course, this variation would be lost if measurements were simply aggregated to school level means, and those school-level means used in a between-school analysis. Therefore, studies that do not account for within-school variation can run the risk of over-emphasizing differences in leadership between schools.

Now that the analytic technique is available, one alternative solution proposed through hierarchical linear modelling is to develop a within-school model to determine the relative effects of various factors (e.g., gender, backgrounds of teachers) on teachers' perceptions about the principal's leadership. In this manner, we can also determine whether leadership has been measured with sufficient reliability and validity within each school to permit a school-level analysis of differences in principal leadership. If there is, the adjusted leadership mean for each school can then used as the dependent variable in a between-school comparison.

The smaller proportion of variance in principal leadership due to differences between schools (in Rowan et al.'s 1991 study this was about 25 percent), for example, might be additionally affected by the level of the school, whether it was public or private, and the socioeconomic status of the community. Thus, the estimated effects of independent variables at the individual level of the school can be adjusted simultaneously for effects that may be present at other levels of analysis (Rowan et al., 1991). The approach is illuminating for many research situations in that it allows the variability in important dependent variables (e.g., outcomes, leadership) to be decomposed across different levels of the organization. Although not without its own limitations as an analytical technique (e.g., assessing indirect effects), this application should prove to be useful in instances where researchers are attempting to answer questions about the principal's impact across various layers of the school.

Data Collection Methods

As noted a dozen years ago, surveys continue to be the data collection strategy of choice among researchers who examine the impact of school administrators (Bridges, 1982). Of the 40 studies analysed here, all but four relied on a survey for all or part of the data collected in connection with the school-level variables (i.e., leadership, in-school processes). Six studies incorporated interviews as all or part of their data collection schemes (Biester et al., 1984; Blank, 1987; Jackson, 1982; Glasman, 1992; Glasman & Fuller, 1992; Hallinger & Murphy, 1986).

While most of the studies drew on demographic data to supplement interviews and/or surveys, two investigations appeared to rely solely upon demographic data for their analysis (Ogawa & Hart, 1985; Rowan & Denk, 1984). Although it was hardly a shock to find surveys comprising the predominant mode of data collection, we were surprised by the relative dearth of mixed method studies. Only six of the studies could truly be classified as mixed qualitative and quantitative studies. As we suggested previously, however, our own bias in identifying studies for the review was weighted towards quantitative studies because of our interest in determining the trend of effects uncovered by those who have investigated the impact of the principal's leadership on student achievement.

Given the fact that the majority of studies of principal impact are quantitative and used data collected with surveys, issues of instrument reliability and validity take on great importance. In his review, Bridges (1982) was highly critical of the state-of-the-art when it came to the care with which researchers in educational administrator developed, used, and tested their instrumentation. Issues of instrument reliability are highly germane in the field of principal effects research. Research instruments with low (or undocumented) reliability will have difficulty accurately detecting differences among subjects without samples larger than those that typify most of the research in this field.

Judging from our reading of these studies, some progress has been made in developing reliable instrumentation for measuring principal leadership. Instrumentation for measuring the instructional leadership construct developed by Villanova and his colleagues in Connecticut (1982) was used with documented reliability (e.g., Hallinger et al. 1990; Scott & Teddlie, 1987). Likewise, the reliability of the *Principal Instructional Management Rating Scale* (Hallinger, 1983) was documented in several investigations (Hallinger, Taraseina, & Miller, 1994; Jones, 1987; Leitner, 1994; O'Day, 1983).

The analytic approach taken by Rowan et al. (1991), for example, can also be used to determine how reliably leadership can be measured both within and between schools. Marcoulides and Heck (1992) also presented a procedure for establishing the reliability and validity of observations on the principal. They analysed the variance components (i.e., leadership behaviour, teachers as raters, occasions of measurement) of teachers' perceptions of principal leadership within schools and found that teachers as raters were a substantial source of error variation (in this case representing about 20 percent), but that occasions of measurement were a small source of error (only about 1 percent). The finding indicates increasing the number of teachers sampled within each school reduces the source of error observed, but that measurements about principal leadership can be reliably gathered from each school on one occasion.

Still of concern in this domain is the less frequent documentation of the validity of instrumentation. Very few of the studies that we reviewed gave explicit attention to issues of instrument validity. It should also be noted, however, that while these instruments achieved consistently high levels of reliability, most of the studies were conducted at the elementary level.

To illustrate the importance of this issue, we need only examine one study that did systematically examine the validity of instrumentation as a step in its data analysis. Jones (1987) used the PIMRS (Hallinger, 1983) to collect data on principal instructional leadership in a sample of Canadian high schools. While the instrument possesses documented validity at the elementary school level, Jones' (1987) findings cast doubt on whether the same level of validity is may be expected at the high school level. Given differences in the principal's role at the secondary level, as well as in other community and cultural settings, researchers must continue to be vigilant in testing their instruments across a variety of conditions (Firestone & Herriott, 1982).

Data Analysis

Beyond issues of sampling, unit of analysis, and data collection, we can examine the extent to which the analyses conducted are appropriate for the expressed purpose of the research and the particular theoretical model being investigated (Tatsuoka & Silver, 1988). A wide variety of qualitative and quantitative analytical techniques are currently available for research in educational administration. Some excellent reviews of the application of those techniques have already been provided elsewhere (e.g., Everhart, 1988; Tatsuoka & Silver, 1988). Because of the exclusive use of non-experimental designs in work that is being done in this sub-field of educational administration, we will confine our comments about analytical techniques to those commonly used with this type of research (see Pedhauzer & Schmelkin (1991) for a more complete discussion of appropriate techniques for use with non-experimental research).

Tatsuoka and Silver (1988) categorized available methods of data analysis into four broad categories – descriptive (e.g., means, percentages, cross tabulations), analysis of variance (i.e., ANOVA, MANOVA, analysis of covariance), correlational (e.g., correlation, regression), and causal inference methods (e.g., path analysis, structural equation modelling). Pitner (1988) argued that of these categories of techniques, only causal inference methods are an appropriate means of testing the types of models proposed in Figure 1. She made this claim because these methods are able to provide estimates of both the direct and indirect effects implied in the models. After analysing the studies in this review, however, we have come to believe that the issue is more complicated than a simple right-approach, wrong-approach.

For the most part, the techniques used in analysing the impact of principals over the past 15 years demonstrate greater variation and considerable improvement over those reported by Bridges in 1982. The studies analysed here used techniques in all four broad categories outlined by Tatsuoka and Silver (1988). We do, however, note differences in the extent to which the analytic techniques employed were able to provide a complete test of the models implied in the studies.

Analytical techniques used to test direct-effects models

Any analytic technique must provide an adequate test of the theoretical model implied in the study. Bridges (1982) reported that earlier research on school administrators was inclined to use single factor, correlational analytic techniques for examining relationships between principal leadership and organizational outcomes (see Model A studies, Figure 1). Often such tests were conducted without including relevant control variables. Moreover, Bridges noted that it was often the case that the theoretical models being studied were not fully explicated. These represent severe constraints on the construction of knowledge. Without controlling for relevant variables or explicating the theoretical relationships among variables, analytic techniques offer little hope of shedding light on causal relationships.

As Table 1 indicates, researchers investigating Model A frameworks (direct-effects models) tended to use descriptive statistics, bivariate correlational analysis, and tests of significance between groups of principals. A common approach has been to use common t-tests for two groups or analysis of variance (ANOVA) when there are more than two categories. While several studies isolated some positive (or mixed) differences in principals' actions, these techniques were not fully capable of testing for the direct effects of principal leadership on school outcomes. In some cases, it should be noted, this was not the researcher's primary intent (e.g., Glasman, 1983, 1992).

The frequent use of t-tests, ANOVA and correlational methods in direct-effects research (A and A_1) represents a continuing drag on the accumulation of knowledge in our field. Unfortunately, these are often the only kinds of analytic approaches to which many researchers are exposed (Pedhauzer & Schmelkin, 1991), including those in educational administration (Bridges, 1982; Pitner, 1988). The explanation for this is partially historical. ANOVA and related techniques have been strongly associated with experimental research in psychology. Regression analysis is commonly used for research in natural settings as in sociology and economics (Amick & Walberg, 1978). These disciplines represent the most common methodological bases for studies in educational administration over the past several decades.

The historical context of usage has implications for the appropriateness in which the analyses are carried out in non-experimental research. A bit more discussion of the application of available analytic techniques may be useful here. In terms of non-experimental research, techniques such as correlation and t-tests are not 'causal' in the term's limited sense of referring to an integrated system of relationships. For example, with respect to correlation, any two variables may be correlated but still not exist in a theoretical system of relations. Similarly, because the results of a t-test indicate that two groups of principals are not the 'same' (i.e., they differ 'significantly') in terms of their perceived leadership, it does indicate what might account for this observed difference. The conceptual leaps that often follow from such findings of differences among groups are often made on very shaky analytical (and theoretical) grounds.

Similar arguments can be made about other tests of group differences (e.g., ANOVA, MANOVA) when they are not used in an experimental setting. In experimental research, relevant variables are controlled and the independent variable is actually manipulated as a means of testing for its effects on a dependent variable. Such is not the case in non-experimental studies. Depending upon the interpretation made by the researcher, this can represent a misuse of techniques for analysis of data in non-experimental studies.

The misuse of these analytical techniques is related to the assumptions they make concerning the process of data analysis. In non-experimental designs we work backward from the dependent variable to relevant predictor variables hoping to explain possible outcome variation. These techniques often give the unfortunate impression of having conducting an 'experiment' when in fact one has not done so. This can lead to incorrect conclusions being drawn from the results.

ANOVA-type designs (including analysis of covariance) also make assumptions that the independent variables are truly 'independent' of each other. In fact, in studies of principal and school effects, the variables investigated are quite highly correlated. Thus, the use of such analytical methods in non-experimental research can lead to serious errors and misspecifications when seeking to understand causal relationships [see Pedhauzer & Schmelkin (1991) for a full discussion of this problem].

Moreover, while continuous independent variables (e.g., SES) are common in this field, researchers often 'carve' up such variables into categories and employ an ANOVA design. This represents another misuse of a design that better suited analyzing the effects of varying levels of a treatment administered than arbitrary categories of SES (e.g., high and low). Moreover, within the A_1 model, analysis of variance cannot analyse both the direct effects of antecedents on leadership and their corresponding indirect effects on outcomes (i.e., through leadership). This is a case where the statistical tests were simply inadequate to the demands of the theoretical model and the research design. Approaches based on analysis of variance are, therefore, severely limited. This conclusion extends even to their ability to shed light on the theoretically simple relationships proposed in Model A and A_1 studies.

Model A_1 studies show somewhat more variation in terms of analytic techniques. Recall that the theoretical model implied in these studies includes antecedent variables, leadership, and outcomes (see Figure 1). In addition to correlational analyses and those emphasizing differences between groups of principals, some of these direct-effects studies used regression analysis. The goal of research in regression studies – to explain variation in the dependent variable – is generally more consistent with the logic of non-experimental research designs than is analysis of variance (i.e., that groups are not the same). In multiple regression analysis the relationship among independent and dependent variables must be fixed in advance. Here the categorical independent variables (e.g., strong, average, weak leadership) are treated as a set of coded vectors, and the dependent variable (e.g., outcomes) is continuous.

The multiple regression approach can accommodate categorical, continuous, and combinations of two types of independent variables in the same analysis. Moreover, several independent variables can be considered more efficiently within the same analysis. The lesser risk, therefore, in Model A and A_1 studies, where some type of theoretical framework is at least inferred, is to use regression analysis.

As can be seen in Table 1, regression was used frequently in Model A_1 (antecedent/direct-effects) studies. Where dependent variables (e.g., school effectiveness) were categorical, discriminant analysis was also used occasionally (e.g., Goldring & Pasternak, 1994; Heck, 1993). We classified these two studies as regression studies because their intent was to investigate several sets of variables related to the school outcome variables (i.e., effective and ineffective schools). We make note of this because discriminant analysis is conceptually closer to multivariate analysis of variance than to regression in that its main purpose is the description of group differences.

In terms of its use in the explanation of categorical outcomes, discriminant analysis is now being replaced by newer and more flexible regression programs designed for categorical data (e.g., logistic regression, hierarchical log-linear models). The analysis of categorical dependent variables requires these newer techniques because the observations are generally not from populations that meet the assumption of being normally distributed.

Exploring principal effects through regression analysis

Pitner (1988) argued that causal inference techniques are the most appropriate to use with all of the models in Figure 1. While we do not disagree with this view, we believe the regression model is flexible enough to encourage its use in many, though not all circumstances. This judgment includes those procedures used for categorical dependent variables and nonlinear relationships.

The ultimate value of any regression approach is, of course, dependent on the substantive model it is meant to represent. While in regression analysis it is not necessary to make assumptions about the causal structure linking predictor variables, interpreting the results of these analyses does require some assumptions about the underlying causal relationships (Mueller, Schuessler, & Costner, 1977). Conclusions about the relative importance of predictors must therefore take into consideration both their direct and indirect effects (i.e., effects mediated by other variables). This is true whether or not the full range of effects is actually investigated. Again, this points to the importance of model specification through a proposed theory of the phenomenon under investigation *before* actual testing with data. Analysis should then focus on the extent to which the results are consistent and logical given the model.

Regression-type analyses are, however, not without problems. One of the most serious problems is model misspecification. A common habit among researchers using multiple regression analysis is to fish for explanations. This is especially dangerous in non-experimental research, in which prior theoretical explication of the model is critical to overcoming inherent limitations of the research design. Regression models are also limited in that they are not fully suited to test for indirect effects. At best, such effects can sometimes be implied through the cautious use of varying the entry of variables into the model (or sometimes by specifying interaction terms). An example will serve to illustrate.

In a direct-effects model (Model A), leadership variables are hypothesized to affect school outcomes. When an antecedent variable is added (as in Model A_1), the two independent variables (antecedent and leadership) can be treated in two ways. First, as a single-stage model, the antecedents and leadership can be treated as correlated independent variables, where the correlation is treated as given but not explained. This, for example, is how the van de Grift (1990) study treated the relationship between leadership and SES.

In contrast, in a two-stage model, the antecedent (e.g., SES) can be hypothesized to affect leadership. Now the two independent variables are no longer merely correlated. Order of entry into the equation makes a difference (i.e., earlier entry generally accounts for more variance in the dependent variable). In explanatory research, the decision must be made on the basis of one's underlying theory. One can make a valid case for entering SES first, as it is now hypothesized to affect both leadership and outcomes. Leadership would be entered second and it would be expected that SES would account for the most variance in outcomes (because of its combined direct and indirect effects) and leadership a smaller, incremental amount. It would not make sense to enter leadership first because it would not be hypothesized to affect SES.

As our discussion of research in this chapter has attempted to illustrate, specifying the appropriate theoretical model in advance (as opposed to upon examination of the results) is of utmost importance to determining and interpreting what is found, no matter which analytical technique is used. Regression, and other path-analytic approaches, are therefore most effectively used when guided by strong theory. This discourages the use of procedures such as stepwise entry of independent variables, because such techniques emphasize statistical significance as opposed to an a prior set of defined theoretical relationships.

Interestingly, the same problem arose in the limited instances where structural equation modelling was used in direct-effects studies (e.g., van de Grift, 1990). Here the method was adequate to the test, but the theoretical model was not sufficiently developed. The result in this instance was the inverse: the statistical test was underused. That is, it was not used to reveal the full set of relationships, though it might have (see below). This again highlights the importance of starting with a well explicated theoretical model before choosing and applying the statistical test.

Analytical techniques used to test mediated-effects models

More complex theoretical models require the use of what Tatsuoka and Silver (1988) termed causal inference techniques. These include path-analytic methods, which are increasingly being used to replace multiple regression analysis in Model C and C_1 studies. There are a wide variety of terms used to describe these types of analytic techniques.

Path analysis has been used to refer to models where single (observed) indicators are used to represent the variables in the theoretical model. Covariance structure models, latent variable models, structural equation models (SEM) are all terms that refer to models that have observed and underlying (latent) variables. They are erroneously referred to by the computer programs used to analyse the data (e.g., LISREL, EQS). The growing popularity of these techniques is due to their flexibility in handling a wide variety of theoretical models. These include direct, indirect, and total effects, as well as reciprocal (nonrecursive) and hierarchical relationships.

At the time of Pitner's (1988) review, she could find no study that employed causal inference techniques. From this standpoint, the studies in our review are much improved over those in Pitner's (1988) analysis. The majority of model C studies use some type of causal inference technique. This bodes well with respect to the technical requirements needed to understand how administrative leadership influences organizational processes and performance.

As our discussion of the conceptual and methodological progress in this sub-field of educational administration shows, the formulation of a theoretical model is a long process entailing a great deal of creativity, critical thinking, insight, and empirical validation. While we caution against their indiscriminate use, we also believe that these techniques have the potential to open up exciting new possibilities for research. In order to demonstrate how theoretical and methodological advances combine to create a convergence of findings we will provide two examples from the set of studies.

Two new analyses

To test the potential of path modelling, we decided to reconceptualize and reanalyze two Model A studies (Braughton & Riley, 1991; van de Grift, 1990). Both studies concluded that there was no positive relationship between principal leadership and school outcomes. However, the studies gave little attention to possible antecedent variables and mediating school processes.

Braughton and Riley (1991) used an appropriate technique (i.e., regression analysis) to investigate the effects of a variety of leadership and teacher variables on reading scores. Previous reading scores was included as a control, but not considered in terms of direct or indirect effects. All 14 variables were considered as observed and entered into the regression equation. Within their regression model only direct effects were considered. No relationships were considered between principals and teachers, nor between previous reading grade and principal or teacher behaviour. As we suggested, in a regression analysis (that is not conceived of as a path analysis), such effects might be partially considered through interaction effects or variable entry (e.g., enter principal set, then teacher set).

We recast the study as Model C_1 to consider possible antecedent variables (i.e., previous reading outcomes) on teachers and principals, and the effects of principal leadership mediated by teachers' classroom practices on school reading outcomes. Thus, our redesigned conceptual model considered several paths of theoretical interest that were not investigated in the previous study. Principal leadership, as defined by principal knowledge, attitudes, and supervisory behaviour, consisted of eight observed indicators that formed the latent construct. Teacher classroom practices were also conceived of as a latent variable consisting of four observed indicators of teacher classroom reading practices. We then tested the new proposed theoretical model using structural equation modelling (LISREL 8) and Braughton and Riley's correlation matrix of observed variables as input.

The resulting findings indicated no direct effects of principal leadership (with a standardized path coefficient of .04) on outcomes. Teacher practices were significantly (although negatively) related to outcomes. Our interpretation of this finding is that where student reading scores were lower, teachers were more actively involved in developing students' skills. This is essentially where the previous analysis stopped.

Drawing upon the additional capabilities of structural modelling, we found further that principal actions were significantly (and negatively) related to certain intervening variables: teacher knowledge and practices. The finding indicates that where teachers were less knowledgeable and competent about reading practices, principals were more involved in supervision and direct intervention. Moreover, the total effects of leadership on student outcomes, which considers *both the direct and indirect effects* (i.e.,through teacher practices) were significant and positive (.38).

Thus, almost all of the effects of principal leadership on school outcomes were indirect (.34). The effects resulted from the principals' knowledge and skills in monitoring and supervising teachers, as well as improving the reading curriculum. It was also noted that previous reading scores (an antecedent variable) was found to affect subsequent teacher classroom behaviour significantly, but not to affect principal behaviour significantly. Our results, therefore, supported the theoretical model (Model C, Figure 1) in which principals' actions have an indirect impact on school outcomes through teachers as a mediating factor. The particular antecedent used in the study, however, did not influence leadership practices. The finding demonstrates both the importance of theory in guiding development of empirical model and why it is critical to select the correct statistical method for analysis of the data.

Our reanalysis of one of van de Grift's (1990) studies was similarly illuminating. This was especially true in that this study has often been pointed to as evidence that leadership does not affect school outcomes, at least in The Netherlands (with a reported standardized path coefficient of .002). Van de Grift had previously investigated the direct effects of socioeconomic status and leadership on school outcomes using structural equation modelling (Model A). Therefore, in this instance, we needed only to set up a competing theoretical model and reanalyze his data.

We believe that there is ample evidence to suggest that SES affects leadership practices (e.g.,Andrews & Soder, 1987; Hallinger & Murphy, 1986a, Rowan & Denk, 1984). The van de Grift study did not, however, hypothesize any effect between the antecedent variable (SES) and leadership. SES was used simply as a control variable in relation to student achievement. In our reanalysis, we hypothesized that the antecedent variable, socioeconomic status, should affect leadership directly and outcomes both directly and indirectly (i.e., through leadership). Consequently we set up a C_1 model portraying antecedent- and mediated-effects.

In addition, van de Grift considered leadership as one variable comprised of four observed subscales (initiating innovations, stimulating teachers, supervising teachers, fostering climate). We chose to create two leadership constructs (instructional organization and school climate), following the Bossert et al. (1982) model of mediated effects. The measurement model in our reanalysis, which estimates relationships between the observed variables and latent constructs, was virtually identical to the various parameters reported previously.

The new structural relationships tested, however, indicated that socioeconomic status affected instructional organization leadership significantly (but weakly), but not leadership involving school climate. Socioeconomic status also affected outcomes significantly, as was found previously. Leadership in monitoring the instructional organization of the school was found to affect leadership in developing school climate significantly, but not the other way around [similar to Heck et al.'s (1990) finding]. Principal leadership aimed at developing school climate was positively related to school outcomes, but not significantly. Moreover, instructional organization leadership was found to be significantly (but weakly) negatively related to outcomes. Thus, the substantive conclusions that can be drawn from the data are more extensive and complex than the conclusion of 'no effects' reached in the original study.

The negative coefficient observed between principal leadership aimed at school improvement and teacher supervision (i.e., instructional organization) was somewhat puzzling. One interpretation of the negative coefficient in this study [and the Braughton & Riley (1991) study we reanalyzed] is that where school achievement has been consistently low, teachers perceive that principals are actually working harder to create innovation, stimulate teachers to improve teaching, and supervise school's teaching and learning processes. Interestingly, this path is also similar to Heck's (1993) study in Singapore, where a negative coefficient was also observed between instructional monitoring and outcomes.

It is our belief that this consistency in finding across several studies relates back to how researchers define the dependent variable in their studies. For example, Heck et al.'s (1990) study investigated school effectiveness longitudinally (i.e., over several years) and in relative terms (i.e., relative school outcomes controlled for socioeconomic status and language background), suggesting that 'effective' urban schools might produce lower actual outcomes than effective suburban schools because of student composition factors. The studies in our reanalysis [and the Heck (1993) Singapore study] investigated actual outcomes in terms of the school outcome means unadjusted for composition differences.

In both examples we chose to reanalyze, therefore, we found that our proposed structural models fit the data quite well. As is the case with structural models, a model that is not rejected (i.e., that fits the data reasonably well) is only one of many possible models that might fit the data. This emphasizes the importance that theory plays in developing a model (or set of competing models) to be tested (see also Hallinger, Bickman, & Davis in press; Silins, 1994).

Van de Grift's (1990) and Braughton and Riley's (1991) determination that leadership does not affect school outcomes are correct with respect to the direct-effects models that were tested. Our models, conceived to be relatively consistent with the Bossert et al. (1982) model (i.e., antecedent and mediated effects), also fit the data presented in each study, yet they reveal more about the interrelationships between the theoretical constructs comprising each model. They also yield quite different conclusions concerning the nature of principal impact on school achievement. We believe that these reanalyzes demonstrate the greater potential that emerges when more comprehensive theory is combined with sufficiently powerful methods of research.

Construct Validity and Generalizability

Overall, the most important aspect of any of the studies conducted is the interpretation of results (Tatsuoka & Silver, 1988) in light of the theoretical grounding of the model tested and method employed to test the model. There is a close interplay between substantive theory and statistical method in yielding explanations of results (Tatsuoka & Silver, 1988). This is especially true in the social sciences, where one must often rely on quasi-experimental or non-experimental designs. It is not necessarily the sophistication of the analytic method that primarily determines whether, and to what extent, a study verifies a particular set of theoretical relations. It is rather the manner in which the study is designed and conducted that matters the most (Tatsuoka & Silver, 1988). Ultimately, this process relates to the confidence and validity we can place in the observed outcomes of the investigation.

Of the many approaches to validity that have been discussed in the literature, construct validity is the most general and can be considered to include all others (Cronbach, 1971). Construct validity occurs when the researcher evaluates a set of operations in light of a specified construct (National Council on Measurement in Education, 1984) or set of theoretical relations. The proposed interpretation generates specific testable hypotheses, which are a means of confirming or disconfirming the claim (Cronbach & Meehl (1955). Construct validity is in fact an ongoing process (Heck & Marcoulides, 1992). A variety of statistical procedures have been developed to address this issue [see Pedhazur & Schmelkin (1991) for a complete discussion].

As a group, the studies provide support for the construct validity of the antecedent with mediating-effects model and, more specifically, the mediating-effects model. First, several studies used confirmatory factor analysis, one established means of investigating construct validity (Heck & Marcoulides, 1992) to validate their specific models. This process assesses the extent to which observed variables in a model are related to the theoretical constructs they are hypothesized to measure. The procedure itself forces researchers to define proposed theoretical relationships prior to testing models with data.

Another approach used to establish construct validity is to conduct tests of model invariance across different groups. When group differences are being considered, an assumption is made that the construct(s) being investigated are similar for all groups being examined. If the constructs measured are not similar, this failure to may be due to a lack of construct validity or an indication that the groups are different (Heck & Marcoulides, 1992). The value of a proposed model of leadership is greatly enhanced if the same model can be replicated in subsamples from different populations (Cattell, 1962). This in fact was observed in several studies that reached similar conclusions in different settings and with different subgroups of the population tested.

Finally, there is evidence that researchers are beginning to test competing theoretical model, which is seen as another means of studying construct validity. Given the empirical evidence of effects from the antecedent with mediated-effects model, as well as our further reanalyses, it would appear that this model represents a promising conceptualization. Our brief discussion suggests that researchers should pay greater attention to issues of validity as well as reliability in their investigations of principal leadership constructs. This is reflected in retrospective reviews of the prior work of researchers that focus on examining the construct validity of particular leadership models (e.g., Heck & Marcoulides, 1992; Leithwood, 1994).

CONCLUSION

We began this review of the literature on principal effects with uncertainty as to whether the results would warrant the effort. Several respected reviews had already been conducted of this research literature over the past 15 years (Bossert et al., 1982; Bridges, 1982; Leithwood & Montgomery, 1982; Leithwood et al., 1990; Murphy, Hallinger, & Mitman, 1983; Murphy, 1988). Although the rationale for reviewing the empirical literature once again seemed sound, we were unsure what new information of value it would yield to researchers in this domain.

In our judgment, the results have more than warranted the effort. The review reveals what we would characterize as a 'leap forward' in the quality of empirical research being conducted in this sub-field of educational administration since 1980. In this most recent generation of principal effects research we found substantial progress on both conceptual and methodological dimensions (see also Hallinger & Heck, in press). The evidence of progress is especially notable in that this particular domain presents formidable challenges to the researcher. In our opinion, the methodological issues are as complex as those posed in any other topical area within educational administration. While we cannot generalize the gains found here to the field at-large, our results certainly suggest marked improvement in the research being conducted by scholars who have been working on this particular set of issues.

In contrast to Bridges' in 1982, we found a clear accumulation of knowledge in both methodological and conceptual domains. The recommendations of earlier reviewers of this literature (e.g., Bossert, Boyan, Bridges, Cuban, Glasman, Hallinger, Leithwood, Murphy, Pitner, Rowan, van de Grift) as well as the incremental suggestions advanced by who have conducted programmatic empirical research (e.g., Andrews, Cheng, Glasman, Goldring, Hallinger, Heck, Leithwood, Marcoulides, Miskel, Ogawa, Rowan, van de Grift) are interwoven throughout the studies we reviewed. Not surprisingly, this accumulation of knowledge in the processes of research is also, to a degree, reflected in an increasing consistency of findings that emerge from the studies. As noted in our discussion of construct validity, this type of programmatic effort is necessary to developing the foundations on which knowledge is built.

Drawing upon prior research reviews, we focused our lens upon this one subset of the educational administration literature: empirical studies of administrator effects on student learning. The chapter had three primary aims:

1) to analyse the theoretical frameworks that have been employed by researchers in the most recent generation of research on the principal's role in school effectiveness;
2) to examine the methodological features of this literature;
3) to propose a theoretical framework and appropriate methodological approaches that might guide future investigations of principal impact.

In this last section of the chapter we will summarize the major findings of the review with respect to the first two goals. In doing so, we will use the findings from Bridges' (1982) review as a benchmark both for identifying the progress that has been made to date and key targets for future improvement. Woven throughout the discussion are the implications of our assessment for future investigations in this domain of educational administration.

Theoretical Frameworks for Conceptualizing Principal Impact

This chapter has reviewed research on the principal's role in school effectiveness conducted between 1980 and 1995. Although the studies vary in their conceptualizations of principal impact, all of them included measures of school outcomes, most frequently student achievement. We analysed 40 studies identified by our search on both conceptual and methodological dimensions.

We drew upon a framework proposed by Pitner (1988) for categorizing non-experimental studies of principal impact as a conceptual framework for the review. The framework includes five distinct models plus two variations for viewing principal impact: direct-effects, moderated-effects, antecedent-effects, mediated-effects, reciprocal-effects models. Each suggests a different theoretical perspective for viewing the principal's leadership role in school effectiveness. In addition, the models require different types of analytic techniques for empirical investigation.

When applied to the studies, we found that the most frequently represented models were the mediated-effects, direct-effects, and combined antecedent-effects models. A few studies could be viewed as falling within the moderated-effects category, but this distinction was not always clear. Despite the intuitive logic in support of the reciprocal-effects model, no studies had been explicitly designed to test for these potentially important effects.

One reason for the paucity of reciprocal-effects studies seemed to be the absence of longitudinal data. Such data enhance our ability to validly test reciprocal-effects models. For example, principal leadership can be hypothesized both to depend on features of the school's culture (e.g., teacher resistance to change) and also to shape it (e.g., by promoting collaboration). While reciprocal relationships can be implied at one point in time (i.e., in cross-sectional data), these dynamic relationships are best observed over time. Common approaches to this problem are to pool cross-sectional data or to use time series (panel) data. Unfortunately, longitudinal data on principal impact appears to be in short supply. Given the theoretical importance of the issues that flow from viewing principal leadership effects as reciprocal rather than uni-directional, we see this as a prime target for future study (also see Bridges, 1982; Rowan et al., 1982).

A second pattern illuminated by the classification scheme was the clear trend over time away from simple direct-effects models and towards the use of more complex, comprehensive conceptualizations of the principal's leadership role. In the past half-dozen years, the most popular approach used to study principal impact has been the antecedent/mediated-effects model. As noted above, this model requires researchers to be more explicit and comprehensive in their conceptualization of leadership effects. It also requires more sophisticated analytical methods. This trend suggests definitive progress in the field. This is a very different story than was found in the prior generation of research as reported by Bridges in 1982.

The framework for classification also yielded a striking and rather unexpected result concerning the role of the school principal in school effectiveness. When the studies were grouped in terms of these theoretical models, a clear trend emerged in the direction of their substantive results. The studies that utilized more sophisticated theoretical models yielded more consistently positive findings concerning the positive impact of the principal on school outcomes than did the less sophisticated studies (see Table 1). The studies reporting evidence of principal effects tended to fall into the antecedent/mediated-effects category.

This model hypothesizes that principal leadership is simultaneously a dependent and independent variable. The principal's leadership is exercised in response to features of the school organization and its environment and is aimed towards influencing internal school processes that are more directly linked to student learning. These internal processes range from school policies and norms to the practices of teachers.

Studies based on this model frequently uncovered positive *indirect* effects of principal leadership on student achievement. The finding of positive indirect effects was particularly significant because that such studies put the leadership construct to a more rigorous test than is posed by direct-effects studies. While the findings across studies were neither uniform in direction nor overly powerful in effects, the trend was clear.

Moreover, the studies that reported positive indirect effects of principal leadership on student achievement consistently found those effects acting on the school organization through its goals. Principal leadership that was geared towards the development and sustenance of a school-wide purpose or focus seemed to make a difference for student learning. That said, additional investigation is needed that explores this interaction in more detail.

This substantive finding reinforces our view of simultaneous progress on the dual fronts of theory and methodology. The finding that principal effects, when they occur, are indirect in nature is, in fact, conceptually consistent with accepted notions of how leadership is actually exercised in educational organizations (Cuban, 1988). However, in the absence of theoretical models that force empirical tests to include mediating variables, we are left with the conceptually weak and empirically ambiguous findings that necessarily result from studies that employ a direct-effects model.

Thus, our first task in this review was a fruitful one. The framework used to guide our analysis of the studies (Pitner, 1988) illuminated important theoretical and methodological dimensions of the research in this domain. Moreover, it highlighted the critical interplay between theory, method and results so important in the conduct of valid research. In the next section, we summarize the main findings with respect to the specific methodological issues that emerged from the review.

Conceptual Progress

As a group, the studies demonstrate several conceptual advances over the prior generation of principal impact studies. First, whereas Bridges (1982) noted an absence of theoretically-oriented research, we found a distinctly different trend among these studies. From our reading, almost all of the studies could be counted as theoretically informed. The authors were uniformly explicit about the particular lineage in which their studies were located. They also tended to be quite careful in defining their constructs, particularly the leadership variable.

A more strict definition of theoretical orientation would require the studies to link their empirical efforts to larger conceptual frameworks and issues. It would also require the authors to use theory to guide both selection of variables and placement within hypothesized models. By this standard, well over half of the studies reviewed in this data-set were quite sophisticated in terms of their theoretical orientation. Particularly within the C and C_1 groups, authors took pains to discuss, in advance, how the leadership construct was theoretically linked to the intervening variables and student outcomes (e.g., Goldring & Pasternak, 1994; Hallinger et al., 1990, in press; Heck et al., 1990; Jones,

1987; Leitner, 1994; Leithwood et al., 1994; Silins, 1994; Weil et al., 1984). This theoretical groundwork proved critical in light of the non-experimental research designs that predominate in studying the principal's role in school effectiveness.

The review further demonstrates the importance of beginning with a theoretically informed model of leadership and how it influences school outcomes. If the impact of principal leadership is achieved through indirect means – for example through the school's culture – we need to advance our understanding of how such linkages and norms are shaped by the principal. The studies offer some limited guidance as to the types of intervening variables that may potentially yield fruit. Yet, more work remains to be done in uncovering the nature of this particular path.

We would like to step back and make several recommendations concerning the conceptualization of the principal's role in school effectiveness. First, we strongly recommend that researchers continue using *comprehensive* models of leadership in studies of principal effects. The abbreviated direct-effects model represented in Models A and A_1 simply cannot be defended in light of current theory. Given the availability of appropriate analytical techniques such as structural equation modelling, researchers would be better served by building upon the model C_1 studies conducted to date.

Second, we would argue for researchers to incorporate more comprehensive notions of administrator outcomes into their conceptual models in future studies in this domain. Our own review would appear to 'buy into' the notion that student achievement is the most desirable measure of principal effectiveness. In fact, while we remain committed to understanding how principals influence student learning, achievement tests only represent one proxy for this outcome.

Thus, we would call for more diverse conceptualizations of the goals of administrative behaviour. The current group of studies begins to suggest other outcomes of principal leadership that may be worthwhile exploring. For example, studies conducted by Leithwood and colleagues (1993) and by Silins (1994) analysed effects on a wide range of school improvement variables that should be of interest to scholars of administrator effectiveness. These included program implementation, teacher professional development, and school improvement indices. Where possible, we would suggest that these types of measures be used to supplement direct measures of student learning.

Although it was not a focus for the review, we would be remiss in not returning to an important and related issue that has lurked in the shadows of this chapter. Earlier we noted that this set of studies reflects an exclusively functionalist and instrumental view of the principal's leadership role. This is linked to the criteria we used in defining the purpose of the review: to examine research on the impact of principals on student achievement and school effectiveness. This approach to studying administrator effectiveness reflects a dominant perspective in our educational culture as well as in the field of leadership research (Anderson, 1990; Blase, Dedrick, & Strathe,1986).

This conceptual lens for viewing principal impact narrowed the issue, thereby allowing us to conduct a technically sound literature review. At the same time, it also clouds potentially important discourse about the normative purposes of administrative behaviour. We have seen within this body of literature how conceptual progress can 'work its way into' empirical investigation over a period of time. Thus, we would explicitly urge researchers to undertake studies that are conceived from alternative philosophical frameworks that are gaining currency in this era (e.g., critical and feminist theory, postmodernism, chaos and complexity theory).

Finally, although the studies included in this review were conducted in a variety of countries and cultures, the conceptualizations of leadership were all based on Western notions of how leadership is exercised in organizations. This covers up an assumption that characterizes empirical research as well as theory in educational administration. There has been surprisingly little research that is either cross-cultural in nature or that employs indigenous conceptions of leadership in non-Western cultures (Hallinger, 1995).

This is a glaring shortcoming that needs to be addressed. Such research will need to take into account not only potentially different conceptualizations of leadership, but also different views on the desired outcomes of leadership in other cultures. The serious consideration of non-Western conceptions of leadership and effectiveness have the potential to open our eyes to very different theoretical treatments of this domain. We believe that this will be an increasingly important area of inquiry in future years.

Methodological Progress

Methodological progress reflects a similarly positive trend over time, though some important and quite fundamental issues remain to be addressed. Foremost among our concerns is the continued over-reliance on a single type of research design: non-experimental research designs (primarily cross-sectional survey research). Cross-sectional designs – even ones of high quality – limit our ability to understand the causal relationships involved in studying the impact of school administrators. Interpretation of data from studies of principal impact continues to be further hindered by the absence of longitudinal, experimental, quasi-experimental and qualitative research. We encourage future studies employing greater diversity in research design.

In particular, this should include both quasi-experimental designs and qualitative approaches. We found none of the former in our search of the literature. With respect to qualitative studies, several were uncovered in our initial search, though fewer than we might have expected. We would also argue for more mixed method and two-stage studies. In the latter approach, the researcher engages the basic question of administrator effects issues at a broad level of study through quantitative analysis and then focuses on specific issues through more flexible qualitative methods (e.g., Hallinger & Murphy, 1986b; Jackson, 1982; Leitner, 1994). we see this as a potentially fruitful means of uncovering the more subtle processes that underlie expertise in leadership behaviour (e.g., Dwyer et al., 1983; Leithwood et al., 1992).

We would also note that most of the studies included in this data-set tended to focus on the impact of elementary school principals. This was not a function of predetermined choice on our part; rather, it resulted from the relative paucity of studies of principal impact being conducted at the secondary level. This is an issue of both theoretical and practical importance since secondary schools differ from elementary schools on important contextual dimensions such as size and complexity. Theory, as well as preliminary research in high schools, suggest that these contextual variables influence both how principals exercise leadership and the results of their leadership (e.g., Firestone & Herriott, 1982; Hallinger & Murphy, 1986a; Heck, 1993; Jones, 1987; Saavedra, 1987). While findings from elementary level studies provide clues as to the direction researchers may take at the secondary level, additional theoretical and empirical work is needed to describe and account for the impact of these contextual differences.

Another issue concerns how studies are conducted and analysed. With respect to quantitative studies, sampling remains a problematic area. Probability sampling and adequate sample size were highlighted as key sampling issues of concern. Obtaining an adequate sample size is necessary if we hope to detect effects in this domain where we expect measurable impact to be relatively weak. As we noted, probability sampling is central to non-experimental research. Most of the studies we reviewed fell far short of ideal sampling conditions both on sample size and the nature of the sampling procedures. Improvement is needed in this area.

In the realm of instrumentation, we found clear progress on two fronts. First, researchers showed increased concern and care in assessing and describing the characteristics of their measurement instruments. Many of the studies that we reviewed included some discussion of instrument reliability, at least reporting alpha coefficients or other relevant statistics if not the details of obtaining them. Second, it appears that several instruments have emerged over the past decade with a reasonable track record for use in studies of school administrators. These cover several constructs including instructional leadership, transformational leadership, as well as several perspectives on leadership derived from the work of Bolman and Deal (1992) and Sergiovanni (see Cheng, 1994).

At the same time, while the reliability of measurement scales seems to be less of an issue today than a dozen years ago, researchers must attend with greater care to assessing the validity of their measurement instruments. We illustrated the basis for this concern in pointing out how an instrument that demonstrated high degrees of validity at the elementary failed to replicate similar validation at the secondary level (Jones, 1987). More complicated sets of issues arise in attempting to conduct studies of principal leadership in diverse cultural settings. This instance serves as a cautionary note for researchers to exercise greater attention to validity as well as reliability in the development and use of their research instruments.

To extend the process of validation further, we noted that although these studies were conducted in a variety of countries, the philosophical perspectives and methodological approaches undergirding them has not really opened the field up to solid comparative research. The bulk of the studies were conducted in contexts where Western forms and systems of education predominate. Moreover, even when research has been conducted outside of Western contexts, Western conceptions of leadership and schooling have, in most cases been overlaid onto the other culture.

We would emphasize here that a more culturally diverse orientation to the study of leadership and its effects also has quite specific methodological implications. First it suggests the need to begin with a culturally appropriate definition of leadership. This may be gained most effectively through the use of qualitative methods that stress the inductive generation of culturally grounded theory. The actual investigation of leadership effects from a cross cultural perspective raises a number of interesting methodological issues including obtaining samples across diverse settings, validation of instrumentation, and using analytical techniques that are appropriate for multi-group samples (e.g., structural equation modelling).

The range of analytical techniques for addressing complex research questions and theoretical models has expanded greatly over the past 25 years. At the same time, however, researchers in the field of educational administration have not always taken full advantage of the techniques available (Bridges, 1982; Tatsuoka & Silver, 1988; Willower, 1987). When new analytical techniques have been utilized, researchers have not always fully understood the implications of those approaches for the pursuit of knowledge. As our review bears out, sometimes researchers have applied the wrong analytical techniques to the right theoretical models; at other times they have applied the right techniques to the wrong models.

We believe that researchers of administrative activity will also profit greatly from adopting a multi-level perspective towards schools as organizations (Bossert et al., 1982; Rowan et al., 1991). Treating data within its hierarchical structure may assist in building theory about the nature of administrator impact across levels of the organization. It will also facilitate more refined investigations into a wider variety of theoretical perspectives on how impact is obtained in different types of organizational structure (e.g., restructured schools).

That said, we can also conclude that substantial progress is evident on the analytical front. Even among the less sophisticated Model A and A_1 studies, we found an increased use of control variables, whose relative scarcity was bemoaned in Bridges' (1982) review. Moreover, we also observed a distinct trend towards the use of increasing levels of sophistication in the data analysis techniques in more recent years.

Comprehensive modelling of principal effects requires more powerful analytical tools than have been applied in the past. Several new approaches (e.g., structural equation modelling, hierarchical linear modelling) show particular promise in terms of their appropriateness for addressing key conceptual issues in this domain of research. The frequency of use of these approaches has increased dramatically since 1990 and bodes well for future research in this area.

As our reanalyses of others' data demonstrated, however, the use of these tools is double-edged. It is important to keep in mind that strong theoretical explication must be used to guide the specification of models when applying these techniques or it becomes very easy to fall into the trap of drawing incorrect or over-stated interpretation of the findings. When using these tests, the failure to reject one model is not an indication that there are no other models that could fit the data equally well or better. Thus, it is wise to consider competing structural models in light of theoretical propositions and previous empirical work (see Leithwood et al., 1993; Silins, 1994).

This highlights a major theme that emerged from the review. It returns us to the notion that theory and method play a mutually reinforcing role in the creation of new knowledge. This review suggests that although much work remains in filling out our understanding of the principal's role in school effectiveness, as a field we are making progress in the application of theory and methods of research in attacking this potentially important problem of practice.

Thus, in conclusion, the review supports *both* the potency of Bridges' (1982) highly critical review of methodology in educational administration and the conceptual promise hinted at by other reviewers of this literature (Bossert et al., 1982; Leithwood & Montgomery, 1982; Murphy, Hallinger, & Mitman, 1983). While readers may find the substantive conclusion of the review of interest, we believe that this finding is actually of only secondary importance. For the purposes of researchers, the most salient result is the demonstration of how substantive progress in a field can be achieved when headway occurs simultaneously on methodological and conceptual fronts. If in fifteen years, methodological and conceptual advancements of a similar magnitude can be claimed, we are confident that the field will have made much more significant headway in addressing important substantive problems of interest to practitioners, policymakers and researchers.

ACKNOWLEDGEMENT

The authors would like to acknowledge useful comments made on earlier drafts of this manuscript by Edwin Bridges, Larry Cuban and Ken Leithwood.

FOOTNOTES

1. Two issues arise here. The first involves control of the dependent variable. Some studies include control variables designed to

account for other influences on students achievement such as student SES or students' prior achievement. In other cases, the control variables may also be manipulated as a means of studying the influence of context on the principal's leadership. For our purposes, inclusion of control variables that are used exclusively in connection with the dependent outcome measure is indicated in Table 1 with an asterisk. When the control variable is also used to inform our understanding of antecedent – effects on leadership, this is classified in either Model A1 or C1 in Table 1 and Figure 1.

2. Van de Grift's 1987 and 1989 studies were analysed based upon information provided in van de Grift, 1990, not from the reports of the original studies.

REFERENCES

Amick, D. & Walberg, H. (1975). *Introductory multivariate analysis.* Berkeley, CA: McCutchan Publishing.

Anderson, G. 1990. Toward a critical constructivist approach to school administration: Invisibility, legitimation, and the study of non-events. *Educational Administration Quarterly, 26*(1) 38-59.

Andrews, R. & Soder, R. (1987). Principal instructional leadership and school achievement. *Educational Leadership, 44*, pp. 9-11.

Andrews, R., Soder, R., & Jacoby, D. (1986, April). *Principal roles, other in-school variables, and academic achievement by ethnicity and SES.* Paper presented at the Annual Meeting of the American Educational Research Association, San Francisco.

Bamburg, J. & Andrews, R. (1990). School goals, principals and achievement. *School Effectiveness and School Improvement, 2* (3), pp. 175-191.

Benham, M. & Heck, R. (1994). Political culture and policy in a state-controlled educational system: The case of educational politics in Hawaii. *Educational Administration Quarterly, 30* (4), 419-450.

Biester, T., Kruse, J., Beyer, F., & Heller, B. (1984, April). *Effects of administrative leadership on student achievement.* Paper presented at the annual meeting of the American Educational Research Association, New Orleans.

Blank, R. (1987). The role of the principal as leader: Analysis of variation in leadership in urban high schools. *Journal of Educational Research, 82* (2), pp. 69-80.

Blase, J., Dedrick, C., & Strathe, M. (1986). Leadership behaviour of principals in relation to teacher stress, satisfaction, and performance. *Journal of Humanistic Education and Development, 24* (4), 159-171.

Bolman, L. & Deal, T. (1992). *Reframing organizations.* San Francisco, CA: Jossey-Bass.

Bossert, S., Dwyer, D., Rowan, B., & Lee, G. (1982). The instructional management role of the principal. *Educational Administration Quarterly, 18* (3), pp. 34-64.

Boyan, N. (1988). Describing and explaining administrative behaviour. In N. Boyan (Ed.), *Handbook of research in educational administration.* New York: Longman.

Braughton, R. & Riley, J. (1991). *The relationship between principals' knowledge of reading processes and elementary school reading achievement.* ERIC: ED341952.

Brewer, D. (1993). Principals and student outcomes: Evidence from U.S. high schools. *Economics of Education Review, 12* (4), pp. 281-292.

Bridges, E. (1970). Administrative man: Origin or pawn in decision-making? *Educational Administration Quarterly, 6* (1), 7-25.

Bridges, E. (1982). Research on the school administrator: The state-of-the-art, 1967-1980. *Educational Administration Quarterly, 18* (3), pp. 12-33.

Bridges, E. (1977). The nature of leadership. In L. Cunningham, W. Hack, & R. Nystrand (Eds.), *Educational administration: The developing decades.* Berkeley: McCutchan.

Brookover, W. & Lezotte, L. (1977). *Changes in school characteristics coincident with changes in student achievement.* East Lansing: Michigan State University Press.

Brookover, W., Schweitzer, J., Schneider, J., Beady, C. Flood, J., & Wisenbacker, J. (1978). Elementary school climate and school achievement. *American Educational Research Journal, 15*, pp. 1-18.

Bryk, A. & Raudenbusch, S. (1992). *Hierarchical linear models: Applications and data analysis methods.* Newbury Park, CA: Sage.

Burns, J. M. (1978). *Leadership.* NY: Harper & Row.

Cantu, M. (1994). *A study of principal instructional leadership behaviours manifested in successful and nonsuccessful urban elementary schools.* Unpublished doctoral dissertation, University of Texas, Austin.

Cattell, R. (1962). The basis of recognition and interpretation of factors. *Educational and Psychological Measurement, 22*, 667-669.

Cheng, Y. C. (1991). Leadership style of principals and organizational process in secondary schools. *Journal of Educational Administration, 29* (2), pp. 25-37.

Cheng, Y.C. (1994). Principal's leadership as a critical factor for school performance: Evidence from multi-levels of primary schools. *School Effectiveness and School Improvement, 5* (3), pp. 299-317.

Cohen. M.R. (1988). Statistical power for the behavioural sciences (2nd edition). Hillsdale, NJ: Lawrence Erlbaum.

Crawford, J., Kimball, G., & Watson, P. (1985). *Causal modelling of school effects on achievement.* Paper presented at the annual meeting of the American Educational Research Association, Chicago, March.

Cronbach, L. (1971). Test validation. In R. Thorndike (Ed.) *Educational measurement* (2nd edition). Washington, DC: American Council on Education. (166-195).

Cronbach, L. & Meehl, P. (1955). Construct validity in psychological tests. *Psychological Bulletin, 52*, 281-302.

Cuban, L. (1988). *The managerial imperative and the practice of leadership in schools.* Albany: Suny Press.

Davies, R. (1994). From cross-sectional to longitudinal analysis. In A. Dale & R. Davies (Eds.), *Analyzing social and political change: A casebook of methods.* Albany: SUNY Press.

Dilworth, R. (1987). *A study of the relationship between student achievement and the variables of teacher-perceived instructional leadership behaviours of principals and teacher attendance.* Unpublished doctoral dissertation, University of Southern Mississippi.

Duke, D. (this volume). Perception, prescription and the future of school leadership. In K. Leithwood (Ed.). *The international handbook of research in educational leadership and administration.* Kluwer Press.

Dwyer, D. (1986). Understanding the principal's contribution to instruction. *Peabody Journal of Education, 63* (1), pp. 3-18.

Dwyer, D., Lee, G., Rowan, B., & Bossert, S. (1983). *Five principals in action: Perspectives on instructional management.* San Francisco: Far West Laboratory for Educational Research and Development.

Eberts, R. & Stone, J. (1988). Student achievement in public schools: Do principals make a difference? *Economics of Education Review, 7* (3), pp. 291-299.

Edington, E. & Dibenedetto, R. (1988). *Principal leadership styles and student achievement in small and rural schools of New Mexico.* Paper presented at the annual meeting of the American Educational Research Association, New Orleans, April.

Edmonds, R. (1979). Effective schools for the urban poor. *Educational Leadership, 37,* pp. 15-24.

Eisner, E. (1993). Forms of understanding and the future of educational research. *Educational Researcher, 22* (7), 5-11.

Everhart, R. (1988). Fieldwork methodology in educational administration. In N. Boyan (Ed.) *The handbook of research on educational administration.* NY: Longman, pg 703-727.

Glasman, N. (1983). Increased centrality of evaluation and the school principal. *Administrator's Notebook, 30* (1), pp. 1-4.

Glasman, N. (1984). Student achievement and the school principal. *Educational Evaluation and Policy Analysis, 6* (3), pp. 283-296.

Glasman, N. & Binianimov, I. (1981). Input-output analyses of schools. *Review of Educational Research, 51* (4), pp. 509-539.

Glasman, N. & Fuller, J. (1992). Assessing the decision-making patterns of school principals. *The International Journal of Educational Management, 6* (3), pp. 22-30.

Glasman, N. & Heck, R. (1992). The changing leadership role of the principal: Implications for principal assessment. *Peabody Journal of Education, 68* (1), pp. 5-24.

Glasman, N. & Heck, R. (this volume). Role-based evaluation of principals: Developing an appraisal system. In K. Leithwood (Ed.) *The international handbook of research in educational leadership and administration.* New York: Kluwer.

Goldring E. & Pasternak, R. (1994). Principals' coordinating strategies and school effectiveness. *School Effectiveness and School Improvement, 5* (3), pp. 239-253.

Hallinger, P. (Spring, 1995). Culture and leadership: Developing an international perspective in educational administration. *UCEA Review.*

Hallinger, P. (1992). Changing norms of principal leadership in the United States. *Journal of Educational Administration, 30* (3), pp. 35-48.

Hallinger, P. (1983). *Principal instructional management rating scale.* Palo Alto: Stanford University.

Hallinger, P., Bickman, L., & Davis, K. (1990). *What makes a difference? School context, principal leadership and student achievement.* Occasional paper #3. The National Center for Educational Leadership, Cambridge, MA: Harvard University.

Hallinger, P., Bickman, L., & Davis, K. (in press). School context, principal leadership and student achievement. *Elementary School Journal.*

Hallinger, P. & Heck, R. (in press). Reassessing the Principal's Role in School Effectiveness: A Review of Empirical Research, 1980 -1995. *Educational Administration Quarterly.*

Hallinger, P. & Murphy, J. (1985). Assessing the instructional management behaviour of principals. *Elementary School Journal, 86* (2), pp. 217-247.

Hallinger, P. & Murphy, J. (1986a). Instructional leadership in school contexts. In W. Greenfield (Ed.), *Instructional leadership: Concepts, issues and controversies.* Lexington, MA: Allyn & Bacon.

Hallinger, P. & Murphy, J. (1986b). The social context of effective schools. *American Journal of Education, 94* (3), pp. 328-355.

Heck, R. (1993). School context, principal leadership, and achievement: The case of secondary schools in Singapore. *The Urban Review. 25* (2), pp. 151-166.

Heck, R. (1992). Principal instructional leadership and the identification of high- and low- achieving schools: The application of discriminant techniques. *Administrator's Notebook, 34* (7), pp. 1-4.

Heck, R. & Marcoulides, G. (1992). Principal assessment: Conceptual problem, methodological problem, or both? *Peabody Journal of Education, 68* (1), pp. 124-144.

Heck, R. & Marcoulides, G. (1989). Examining the generalizability of administrative allocation decisions. *The Urban Review, 22* (4), pp. 247-265.

Heck, R., Larson, T., & Marcoulides, G. (1990). Principal instructional leadership and school achievement: Validation of a causal model. *Educational Administration Quarterly, 26*, pp. 94-125.

Heck, R., Marcoulides, G., & Lang, P. (1991). Principal instructional leadership and school achievement: The application of discriminant techniques. *School Effectiveness and School Improvement, 2* (2), pp. 115 -135.

Hunter, C. (1994). *Los Angeles Unified School District Middle School principals' instructional leadership behaviours and academic achievement.* Unpublished doctoral dissertation, Peppardine University, Los Angeles.

Jackson, S. (1982, April). *Instructional leadership behaviours that differentiate effective and ineffective low income urban schools.* Paper presented at the convention of the International Reading Association, Chicago, IL.

Jones, P. (1987). *The relationship between principal behaviour and student achievement in Canadian secondary schools.* Unpublished doctoral dissertation, Stanford University, Palo Alto, CA.

Kaplan, A. (1964). *The conduct of inquiry: Methodology for behavioural science.* San Francisco: Chandler.

Krug, F. (1986). *The relationship between the instructional management behaviour of elementary school principals and student achievement.* Unpublished doctoral dissertation, U. of San Francisco, San Francisco, CA.

Leitner, D. (1994). Do principals affect student outcomes? An organizational perspective. *School Effectiveness and School Improvement, 5* (3), pp. 219-239.

Leithwood, K. (1994). Leadership for school restructuring. *Educational Administration Quarterly, 30* (4), pp. 498-518.

Leithwood, K., Begley, P., & Cousins, B. (1992). *Developing expert leaders for future schools.* Bristol, PA: Falmer Press.

Leithwood, K., Begley, P. & Cousins, B. (1990). The nature, causes and consequences of principals' practices: A agenda for future research. *Journal of Educational Administration, 28* (4), pp. 5-31.

Leithwood, K. & Hallinger, P. (1993, Fall). Cognitive perspectives on educational administration: An introduction. *Educational Administration Quarterly, 24* (3), pp. 296-301.

Leithwood, K. & Jantzi, D. (1990). Transformational leadership: How principals can help reform school cultures. *School Effectiveness and School Improvement, 1*, (1), pp. 249-280.

Leithwood, K., Jantzi, D., Silins, H., & Dart, B., (1993). Using the appraisal of school leaders as an instrument for school restructuring. *Peabody Journal of Education, 68* (1), pp. 85-109.

Leithwood, K. & Montgomery, D. (1982). The role of the elementary principal in program improvement. *Review of Educational Research, 52* (3), pp. 309-339.

Marcoulides, G. & Heck, R. (1992). Assessing instructional leadership effectiveness with 'g' theory. *International Journal of Educational Management, 6* (3), pp. 4-13.

Marcoulides, G. & Heck, R. (1993). Organizational culture and performance: Proposing and testing a model. *Organization Science, 4* (2), pp. 209-225.

Mueller, J., Schuessler, K. & Costner, H. (1977). *Statistical reasoning in sociology* (3rd edition). Boston: Houghton Mifflin Company.

Murphy, J. (1988). Methodological, measurement and conceptual problems in the study of instructional leadership. *Educational Evaluation and Policy Analysis, 10* (2), pp. 117-139.

Murphy, J., Hallinger, P., & Mitman, A. (1983). Research on educational leadership: Issues to be addressed. *Educational Evaluation and Policy Analysis, 5* (3), pp. 297-305.

National Council on Measurement in Education. (1984). *Standards for educational and psychological testing.* Washington, DC: American Psychological Association.

O'Day, K. (1983). *The relationship between principal and teacher perceptions of principal instructional management behaviour and student achievement.* Unpublished doctoral dissertation, Northern Illinois University, Normal, Illinois.

Ogawa, R. (1992). Institutional theory and examining leadership in schools. *International Journal of Educational Management, 6* (3), 14-21.

Ogawa, R. & Hart, A. (1985). The effect of principals on the instructional performance of schools. *Journal of Educational Administration, 22* (1), pp. 59-72.

Pedhazur, E. & Schmelkin, L. (1991). *Measurement, design, and analysis: An integrated approach.* Hillsdale: NJ: Lawrence Erlbaum Associates.

Pitner, N. (1988). The study of administrator effects and effectiveness. In N. Boyan (Ed.), *Handbook of research in educational administration.* New York: Longman.

Ramey, M., Hillman, L., & Matthews, T. (1982, March). *School characteristics associated with instructional effectiveness.* Paper presented at the annual meeting of the American Educational Research Association, New York.

Rowan, B. & Denk, C. (1984). Management succession, school socioeconomic context and basic skills achievement. *American Educational Research Journal, 21* (3), pp. 17-537.

Rowan, B., Dwyer, D., & Bossert, S. (1982). *Methodological considerations in the study of effective principals.* Paper presented at the annual meeting of the American Educational Research Association, New York.

Rowan, B. Raudenbush, S. & Kang, S. (1991). Organizational design in high schools: A multilevel analysis. *American Journal of Education, 99* (2), pp. 238-266.

Rucziska, J.K. (1988). *The relationships among principals' sense of efficacy, instructional leadership and student achievement.* Unpublished doctoral dissertation. San Francisco: University of San Francisco.

Saavedra, A. (1987). *Instructional management behaviours of secondary school administrators.* Unpublished masters dissertation, Bukidnon State College, Malaybalay, Bukidnon, Malaysia.

Scott, C. & Teddlie, C. (1987, April). *Student, teacher, and principal academic expectations and attributed responsibility as predictors of student achievement: A causal modelling approach.* Paper presented at the annual meeting of the American Educational Research Association, Washington D.C.

Silins, H. (1994). The relationship between transformational and transactional leadership and school improvement outcomes. *School Effectiveness and School Improvement, 5* (3) pp. 272-298.

Sirois, H. & Villanova, R. (1982). *Theory into practice: A theoretical and research base for the characteristics of effective schools.* Paper presented at the annual meeting of the American Educational Research Association, New York.

Tatsuoka, M. & Silver, P. (1988). Quantitative research methods in educational administration. In N. Boyan (Ed.) *The handbook of research on educational administration.* NY: Longman, 677-701.

Teddlie, C., Falkowski, C., Stringfield, S., Desselle, S., & Garvue, R. (1983, April). *The study of principal and teacher inputs to student achievement.* Paper presented at the annual meeting of the American Educational Research Association, Montreal.

van de Grift, W. (1990). Educational leadership and academic achievement in elementary education. *School Effectiveness and School Improvement, 1* (3), pp. 26-40.

van de Grift, W. (1989). Self perceptions of educational leadership and mean pupil achievements. In D. Reynolds, B.P.M. Creemers, & T. Peters (Eds.). *School effectiveness and improvement.* Cardiff/Groningen: School of Education/RION, pp. 227-242.

van de Grift, W. (1987). Zelfpercepties van onderwijskundig leiderschap. In F.J. Van der Krogt (Ed.). *Schoolleiding en management.* Lisse: Swets & Zeitlinger, pp. 33-42.

Villanova, R., Gauthier, W., Proctor, P., & Shoemaker, J. (1981). *The Connecticut school effectiveness questionnaire.* Hartford, CT: Bureau of School Improvement, Connecticut State Department of Education.

Weil, M., Marshalek, B. Mitman, A., Murphy, J., Hallinger, P., & Pruyn, J. (1984, April). *Effective and typical schools: How different are they?* Paper presented at the annual meeting of the American Educational Research Association, Chicago.

Willower, D. (1987). Inquiry into educational administration: The last twenty-five years and the next. *Journal of Educational Administration, 25* (1), pp. 12-27.

Chapter 22: Transformational School Leadership

KENNETH LEITHWOOD, DIANA TOMLINSON AND MAXINE
GENGE
Ontario Institute for Studies in Education

> Out of the varying motives of persons, out of the combat and
> competition between groups and between persons, out of the
> making of countless choices and the sharpening and steeling
> of purpose, arise the elevating forces of leadership and the
> achievement of intended change (Burns, 1978, p. 432).

Transformational leadership is a term which has appeared with increasing frequency in writings about education since the late 1980's. Sometimes it has been used to signify an appropriate type of leadership for schools taking up the challenges of restructuring now well underway in most developed countries throughout the world (Leithwood, 1992). In this context, a common-sense, non-technical meaning of the term is often assumed. For example, the dictionary definition of transform is 'to change completely or essentially in composition or structure' (Webster, 1971). So any leadership with this effect may be labelled transformational, no matter the specific practices it entails or even whether the changes wrought are desirable.

This chapter is not concerned with transformational leadership defined in this loose, common-sense fashion. It is concerned, rather, with a form of leadership by the same name that has been the subject of formal definition and systematic inquiry in non-school organizations for at least several decades. The small but rapidly growing body of evidence, which has emerged quite recently, inquiring about such leadership in elementary and secondary school settings is reviewed in this chapter. Much of this research takes the non-school literature on transformational leadership as a point of departure, both conceptually and methodologically. So it is important, at the outset, to appreciate the general nature of that literature.

Downton's (1973) study of rebel leadership is often cited as the beginning of systematic inquiry about transformational leadership in non-school organizations. However, charisma, often considered an integral part of transformational leadership, has substantially more dis-

K. Leithwood et al. (eds.), International Handbook of Educational Leadership and Administration, 785-840.

tant origins - typically attributed to Max Weber's (e.g., 1947) efforts almost five decades ago.

James McGregor Burns's (1978) prize-winning book first drew widespread attention to ideas explicitly associated with transformational leadership. Based on a sweeping historical analysis, Burns argued that most understandings of leadership not only overemphasized the role of power but held a faulty view of power, as well. There were, he claimed, two essential aspects of power - motives or purposes and resources - each possessed not only by those exercising leadership but also by those experiencing it. The essence of leadership is to be found in the relationships: between motives, resources, leaders, and followers: '... the most powerful influences consist of deeply human relationships in which two or more persons *engage* with one another' (p. 11). Burns's distinction between transactional and transformational types of leadership hinges on this appreciation of power-as-relationships.

In contrast to transformational leadership, transactional leadership occurs when one person takes initiative in making contact with others for the purpose of exchanging valued things (economic, political, or psychological 'things', for example). Each person in the exchange understands that she or he brings related motives to the bargaining process and that these motives can be advanced by maintaining that process. But because of the nature of the motives at issue, those involved are not bound together in any continuing, mutual pursuit of higher purposes. With this form of leadership, motives or purposes may well be met using the existing resources of those involved in the exchange. Neither purposes nor resources are changed, however.

Transformational leadership entails not only a change in the purposes and resources of those involved in the leader-follow relationship, but an elevation of both - a change 'for the better'. With respect to motives or purposes: 'transforming leadership ultimately becomes *moral* in that it raises the level of human conduct and ethical aspiration of both leader and led, and thus has a transforming effect on both' (Burns, 1978, p. 20). This form of leadership, according to Burns's view, also aims to enhance the resources of both leader and led by raising their levels of commitment to mutual purposes and by further developing their capacities for achieving those purposes.

Burns's seminal work provided a solid conceptional footing on which to build the distinction between transactional and transformational types of leadership[1]: it also illustrated the meaning of these forms of leadership in many different contexts. Not to be found in this work, however, was a testable model of leadership practices or any empirical evidence of their effects. The prodigious efforts of Bass and his associates have been largely in response to these limitations. Bass's (1985) book *Leadership and Performance Beyond Expectations* provided an impressive compendium of survey research evidence about the effects of one model of transformational leadership. Among the most important features of this model are the dimensions of leadership practice it includes and the proposed relationships among these dimensions.

Referred to in more recent publications as the four i's (e.g., Bass and Avolio, 1993, 1994) Bass and his colleagues define transformational leadership as including: charisma or idealized influence, inspirational motivation, intellectual stimulation, and individualized consideration. In addition to these dimensions of transformational leadership, three dimensions define the meaning of transactional leadership: contingent reward, management-by-exception, and a laissez-faire or 'hands off' form of leadership.

Whereas Burns considered transformational and transactional practices as opposite ends of the leadership continuum (essentially more and less effective forms of leadership), Bass offers a quite different conception, a 'two-factor theory' of leadership: transactional and transformational forms of leadership, in his view, build on one another (e.g., Avolio & Bass, 1988; Waldman, Bass & Yammarino, 1990; Bass & Avolio, 1993; Howell & Avolio, 1991). Transactional practices foster ongoing work by attending to the basic needs of organizational members. Such practices do little to bring about changes in the organization, however. For this to occur, members must experience transformational practices, in addition. Enhanced commitment and the extra effort usually required for change, it is claimed, are consequences of this experience.

Transactional practices were the traditional focus of attention for leadership theorists until the early 1980's. Disillusionment with the outcomes of that focus, however, gave rise to a number of alternative approaches, among them transformational leadership. These approaches have been referred to collectively by Bryman (1992), Sims and Lorenzi (1992), and others as the 'new leadership paradigm'. Empirical studies of transformational leadership, reflecting this pessimism with transactional practices, often give them minimum attention. This is the case with Podsakoff, MacKenzie, Moorman, and Fetter (1990) for example. While Podsakoff and his associates adopted a quite limited conception of transactional leadership for their research, they offered arguably the most comprehensive set of transformational leadership dimensions available to that point, dimensions based on a synthesis of seven prior perspectives on transformational leadership. These dimensions, which helped organize parts of the subsequent review, include: identifying and articulating a vision; fostering the acceptance of group goals; providing an appropriate model; high performance expectations; providing individual support; providing intellectual stimulation; contingent reward; and management-by-exception.

This brief and selective introduction to the formal study of transformational leadership in non-school organizations is intended to assist readers in better appreciating the initial perspectives adopted by many of those whose research in elementary and secondary school settings is reviewed. Subsequent sections of this chapter describe: the framework and methods used for this review; the nature of transformational leadership as it is experienced in schools; what is known about the effects of such leadership; and the antecedents of (or influences giving rise to) transformational school leadership.

FRAMEWORK AND METHODS FOR THE REVIEW

Framework

Figure 1 is a comprehensive framework for understanding leadership and an indication of the particular focus for this review. Relationships among the constructs in the framework are conceptualized as forming a causal chain with *Leadership Practices* in the centre of the chain. These practices are the more or less overt behaviours engaged in by leaders and, moving backwards in the chain, are a direct product of leaders' *Internal Processes*: the personality traits, demographic characteristics, and capacities, skills and thought processes which figure into leaders' choices of overt behaviour. While internal processes are, in part, autonomous (a product of innate traits as well as personal experiences), they are shaped also by many kinds of *External Influences*, the far left construct in Figure 1. Formal training, informal socialization experiences, district policies, staff preferences, the weather, community opinion and a host of other factors have the potential for such influence. Neither set of antecedents to leadership are considered in this review. *Leadership Practices*, according to Figure 1, potentially contribute to both organizational outcomes and outcomes which schools aspire to for students (the far right construct). There is nothing

Figure 1:
A Framework for Guiding The Review of Research
on Transformational School leadership

especially unique about this framework. Variants on it have been proposed, for example, by Bossert et al. (1982) and Yukl (1989).

Methods

Our intention was to conduct an exhaustive review of both published
and unpublished research on transformational leadership in elementary
and secondary school organizations up to approximately August 1993.
In the early stages of the search, we also located about two dozen
empirical studies carried out in non-school settings which were read as
background to this review. Electronic searches were made of ERIC, a
comparable Ontario data base called ELOISE, Sociological Abstracts,
Psychological Abstracts, and Dissertation Abstracts. The reference
lists of all studies located through these sources were read and manual
searches conducted for all promising study titles. Dissertation
Abstracts yielded by far the largest proportion of studies finally
selected for the review, an indication of the recency of attention
devoted to inquiry about transformational leadership in schools.

To the studies identified in this way, we added a half dozen studies
reported by others after the completion of the searches carried out, by
this time a year earlier. A comparable number of studies completed by
the first author and his colleagues were also available by this point.

This three-staged search resulted in a final set of 34 empirical and
formal case studies (see Table 1) conducted in elementary and secondary school organizations. Of these 34 studies, 12 were conducted using
qualitative methods, 17 relied on quantitative methods alone, and 5
studies employed some mixture of qualitative and quantitative techniques. Information in the 34 studies were derived from a single source

(e.g., a sample of teachers) in 17 of the studies; sample sizes ranged from 1 (single case studies) to 770. Surveys, interviews, document analyses and observations were among the instruments or procedures used for collecting information. Sixteen studies relied on survey instruments alone, 6 on interviews alone, and 11 studies employed multiple data collection procedures. In one study (Kirby, King and Paradise, 1992) data were collected through a content analysis of the narrative writings of those who were able to identify exceptional leaders with whom they had worked.

Finally, the 34 studies of transformational leadership were largely concerned with the leadership of school principals (22 studies), but described transformational leadership offered by those in a number of other educational leadership roles, as well. These other roles included superintendents and other central office staff (5), some combination of school and district roles (4), and multiple roles across schools and districts (2). One study examined multiple roles, not only in schools but in other organizations, as well.

Taken as a whole, the methodological features of these studies avoid some of the most critical threats to the confidence an aggregated body of evidence permits. The studies are not distributed across so many roles as to provide little evidence about any single role: there is clearly much evidence about principals, in particular. Nor are the methods used exclusively of one type; a surprising number of studies used qualitative or mixed designs. And while many studies use only survey instruments, a reasonable variety of data collection procedures were used in the remainder. These qualities of the aggregate body of research reviewed in this chapter provide initial optimism about the robustness of conclusions that might be drawn.

THE NATURE OF TRANSFORMATIONAL SCHOOL LEADERSHIP

This section identifies specific dimensions of transformational leadership found to be relevant in school contexts and describes the specific school leadership practices or behaviours associated with each dimension.

Authors	Design	Sample	Instruments/Data Collection Methods	Organizational Role
Bass (1985)	Qualitative	23 central administrators	– survey (MLQ)	central office
Brown (1994)	Qualitative	– 7 principals – 18 VP's – 21 dept. heads	– interviews	– principal – vice principal – dept. head – teacher
Bright (1987)	Quantitative	– 78 board members – 187 principals – 30 superintendents	– surveys – MLQ – other	– superintendent
Buck (1989)	Qualitative	– 51 superintendents	– interview	– superintendents
Darling (1990)	Qualitative	– 174 teachers – 53 principals – 10 principals	– Survey (School Work Culture Profile) – Survey (The Leadership Report) – Survey (The Principal Report) – interview	– principals

Table 1: Methodological Features of Studies of Transformational School Leadership

Authors	Design	Sample	Instruments/Data Collection Methods	Organizational Role
Genge (1993)	Qualitative	10 secondary principals	– interviews	– principal
Helm (1989)	Mixed	– staff in 29 schools – 4 schools – unspecified # – teachers – parents – others – 4 elementary principals	– Survey (MLQ) – observation – interviews – school artifacts – documents	– principal
Hoover (1987)	Quantitative	– 45 schools – 151 staff and faculty members	– Survey (MLQ)	– principals
Kendrick (1988)	Qualitative	– 155 superintendents – 670 'followers'	– Surveys	– superintendent
King (1989)	Quantitative	– 208 (variety of roles)	– Survey (MLQ) – Survey (Organizational Climate Index)	– principals – superintendents – central office administrators – university administrators

Table 1 (contd.): Methodological Features of Studies of Transformational School Leadership

Authors	Design	Sample	Instruments/Data Collection Methods	Organizational Role
Kirby, King & Paradise (1992) *Study A*	Quantitative	– 103 educators (teachers, VP's, principals)	– Survey (MLQ)	– principals – superintendents – other central office roles
Study B	Qualitative	– 58 educators (teachers, administration)	– Narrative writing	– multiple K-12 roles
Koh (1990)	Quantitative	– 814 teachers – 846 teachers – 89 principals	– Survey (MLQ) – Survey (Organizational Citizenship Behaviour) – Survey (Organizational Commitment) – Survey (Index of Organizational Reactions) – Survey (Index of Perceived Org. Effect)	– principals
Kushner (1982)	Quantitative	– 61 elementary principals – 656 elementary teachers	– Survey (Leadership Posture Questionnaire)	– principal

Table 1 (contd.): Methodological Features of Studies of Transformational School Leadership

Authors	Design	Sample	Instruments/Data Collection Methods	Organizational Role
Lehr (1987)	Qualitative	– 31 persons, multiple roles in and outside education	– interviews	– leaders of schools and other types of organizations
Leithwood, Cousins & Gérin-Lajoie (1993)	Quantitative	– 350 secondary teachers – 3557 secondary schools	– survey – survey	– principal
Leithwood, Dart, Jantzi & Steinbach (1993a)	Mixed	– 509 intermediate teachers (168 schools) – 48 intermediate teachers – 5 principals (5 schools)	– surveys – interviews	– principal
Leithwood, Dart, Jantzi & Steinbach (1993b)	Mixed	– 74 secondary teachers (6 schools) – 534 secondary teachers (77 schools) – 2045 secondary students	– interviews – survey – survey	– principal
Leithwood & Jantzi (1990)	Qualitative	– 133 teachers (12 schools)	– interviews	– principal

Table 1 (contd.): Methodological Features of Studies of Transformational School Leadership

Authors	Design	Sample	Instruments/Data Collection Methods	Organizational Role
Leithwood, Dart, Jantzi & Steinbach (1991)	Mixed	– 44 teachers (12 elementary schools) – 247 teachers (35 elementary schools) – 31 principals	– interviews – survey – survey	– principal
Leithwood, Jantzi & Fernandez (1994)	Quantitative	– 168 secondary teachers (9 schools)	– survey	– principal
Leithwood, Jantzi, Silins & Dart (1993)	Quantitative	– 770 elementary teachers (272 schools)	– survey	– principal
Leithwood & Steinbach (1991)	Qualitative (expert vs. typical)	– 9 elementary principals	– stimulated recall	– principal
Leithwood & Steinbach (1993)	Mixed	– 9 secondary principals	– stimulated recall	– principal
Orr (1990)	Quantitative	– 155 supts. – 670 'followers'	– surveys	– superintendent

Table 1 (contd.): Methodological Features of Studies of Transformational School Leadership

Authors	Design	Sample	Instruments/Data Collection Methods	Organizational Role
Roberts (1985)	Qualitative, longitudinal	– 1 superintendent – 45 staff (multiple roles)	– archival searches – participant observation – interviews	– superintendent
Sashkin & Sashkin (1990)	Mixed	– 12 principals – ? VP's – ? lead teachers and others – 16 central office – 12 schools	– Survey (Leadership Behaviour Questionnaire) – Survey (School Culture Assessment Questionnaire)	– school and district leadership roles
Silins (1992)	Quantitative	– 678 elementary teachers (256 schools)	– survey	– principal
Silins (1994a)	Quantitative	– 679 elementary teachers	– survey	– principal
Silins (1994b)	Quantitative	– 458 primary teachers (23 schools)	– survey	– principal
Silins & Leithwood (1994)	Quantitative	– 350 secondary teachers	– survey	– principal

Table 1 (contd.): Methodological Features of Studies of Transformational School Leadership

7

Authors	Design	Sample	Instruments/Data Collection Methods	Organizational Role
Skalbeck (1991)	Qualitative (interpretive case study)	– 1 principal – 15 teachers – 2 VP's – 5 classified staff – 2 district administrators – 5 others – 10 parents, students, community members	– interview and observation – interviews – interviews – interviews – interviews – interviews – interviews	– principal
Smith (1989)	Quantitative	– 69 principals – 88 superintendents	– Survey (MLQ) – Survey (Educational Work Components Study)	– principals – superintendents
Vandenburghe & Staessens (1991)	Qualitative: case study	– 1 school	– questionnaire – interviews – observation – documents	– principal

Table 1 (contd.): Methodological Features of Studies of Transformational School Leadership

Dimensions of Transformational Leadership Relevant to School Settings

Twenty-one studies provided evidence about specific dimensions of transformational leadership relevant to school contexts: these included six qualitative and 15 quantitative studies. For each of these studies, the leadership dimensions explicitly referred to by the author(s) were identified and the effects reported. Table 2 summarizes the results of this analysis. The left column of this table indicates that a total of 12 dimensions of transformational leadership were inquired about in the 21 studies. All but two of these dimensions can be found in the research literature on transformational leadership in non-school settings. *Culture building* and *Structuring* are unique to school-based research: while these dimensions are found primarily in a series of studies carried out by Leithwood and his colleagues (Leithwood & Jantzi, 1990; Silins, 1994b; Leithwood & Steinbach, 1991), their relevance to leadership in schools is also reflected in the work of others. *Culture building* is prominent in studies by Sashkin and Sashkin (1990), Skalbeck (1991), Helm (1989). Vandenburghe and Staessens (1991), Darling (1990), and Hendrick (1988). *Structuring*, including the involvement of staff in decision making, for example, is identified as an important leadership practice by Helm (1989) and Roberts (1985).

Information in the second and third columns of Table 2 help assess the extent to which each leadership dimension has been found to be relevant to school settings. Using information in these columns, judgements of relevance depend on: the total number of studies providing data about the dimension (while there is no non-arbitrary way of establishing a minimum number, more studies add certainty to the judgement); the average number of significant positive relationships reported across studies between a leadership dimension and an outcome or dependent measure (many studies include multiple dependent measures); and the number of non-significant and significant negative relationships reported.

Clearly relevant to schools, given the evidence in Table 2, are leadership dimensions that have been the object of a relatively large number of studies, and in which an overwhelming proportion of significant positive relationships have been reported. Meeting this standard are: *transformational: composite (C)*, *charisma/inspiration/vision*, *intellectual stimulation*, and *individual consideration*. *Management-by-exception*, the object of many studies reporting a high proportion of significant negative relationships is the only leadership dimension

Leadership Dimension	# of Studies (Quant./Qual.)	# of Positive Outcomes	# of N.S. Outcomes	# of Neg. Outcomes
		Total M		
1. Transformational composite:	10 (8/2)	18 (1.8)	1	0
2. Transactional composite:	8 (8/0)	7 (.88)	11	0
3. Charisma/Inspiration/Vision	14 (2/12)	29 (2.07)	2	0
4. Goal Consensus	5 (4/1)	9 (1.5)	0	0
5. Individual Consideration	14 (12/2)	19 (1.36)	1	0
6. Intellectual Stimulation	14 (13/0)	20 (1.42)	2	0
7. Modelling	4 (3/1)	3 (0.6)	4	0
8. High Performance Expectations	4 (4/0)	4 (0.8)	4	0
9. Culture Building	4 (1/3)	5 (1.25)	1	0
10. Structuring	2 (0/2)	2 (1.0)	0	0
11. Management-by-Exception (Active/ Passive/Laissez-Faire)	9 (9/0)	1 (.1)	11	3
12. Contingent Reward	10 (10/0)	9 (.9)	5	2

Table 2: Dimensions of Transformational School Leadership Relevant to School Settings
(Total Number of Studies = 21)

clearly not relevant to schools. Of the remaining dimensions *contingent reward* and *transactional: composite (C)* have been relatively well-studied but results are conflicting, possibly suggesting that their effects are more contingent than are the effects of other dimensions. *Structuring* and *culture building* have been too little studied for a judgement of relevance to be made; the sparse results are promising, however. *High performance expectations* and *modelling* show signs of behaving like *contingent reward*, but the amount of evidence is sparse. And finally, *goal consensus* shows signs of being clearly relevant to schools, but more evidence is still needed to make that judgement with reasonable certainty.

The Theory and Practice of Individual Transformational School Leadership Dimensions

As Table 2 indicates, nine dimensions of transformational leadership are either clearly relevant to school settings, show promise of being relevant, or cannot yet be ruled out because of limited or ambiguous results. Excluded are *transformational C* and *transactional C* because they are a combination of other more specific dimensions; *management-by-exception* is ruled out on the grounds described above. For each of the nine dimensions, this section offers a definition and explains its contribution to the motivation of followers. Links with other relevant leadership theory are also made.

Based on a content analysis of findings of 21 studies, the specific behaviours or practices associated with each dimension are outlined. For quantitative studies, each item included in the survey scale measuring a leadership dimension was treated as a potential leadership behaviour or practice. Six survey instruments generated behaviours defined in this way, including: Bass's Multifactor Leadership Questionnaire (several different forms); Leithwood et al.'s Nature of School Leadership Survey, and a significant adaptation by Silins (1994b); Sashkin's (1985) Leader Behaviour Questionnaire; The Leadership Report (Darling, 1990); and the Leadership Posture Questionnaire (Kushner, 1982).

Charisma/Inspiration/Vision

Although treated as a single leadership dimension for this review, charismatic or inspirational practices and practices giving rise to shared school vision are distinct. Or at least they may be distinct, this uncertainty being a function of the data available. Evidence concerning charisma largely describes attributions made by 'followers' about the qualities of those believed to be charismatic. In contrast, evidence about vision building describes specific behaviours engaged in by leaders with their colleagues.

There is an extensively developed literature on charismatic leadership, in its own right, which substantially overlaps the literature on transformational leadership. For purposes of this chapter, transformational leadership is not considered to be synonymous with charisma but charisma is an important part of such leadership. Furthermore, efforts to inquire about charismatic leadership predate research about transformational concepts by many decades. For example, Weber's (1947) early work usefully distinguished alternative forms of power on which authority might be based. These include legal, traditional and personal forms, the latter being the form undergirding charismatic leadership. Personal power, Weber claimed, grows out of perceptions that leaders possess valuable expertise, as well as other unique attributes and characteristics. The term *perceived* is crucial to the concept of charisma. Most contemporary views stress the attributions of followers concerning their leaders (e.g., Conger & Kanungo, 1987). If followers do not 'feel' leadership, there isn't any. Such perceptions arise in the context of particular kinds of social relationships '... which, by virtue of both the extraordinary qualities that followers attribute to the leader and the latter's mission, the charismatic leader is regarded by his or her followers with a mixture of reverence, unflinching dedication and awe' (Bryman, 1992, p. 41).

Charismatic attributions are a consequence of what leaders do as well as the circumstances in which followers find themselves. Reflecting these different sources, Boal and Bryson (1988) argue that there are actually two types of charismatic leaders, 'visionary' and 'crisis-produced'. The power of visionary, charismatic leaders is to be found in the attractiveness of the missions which they espouse and the willingness of others to believe in those missions. From the perspective of motivational theory, then, visionary charismatics influence the nature of the personal goals motivating the behaviour of followers. Followers will aspire to more ambitious or perhaps even morally more defensible goals than would be the case in the absence of visionary charisma.

Crisis-produced charismatic leaders, on the other hand, are products of a set of circumstances which potential followers feel unable to cope with. Charisma is attributed to persons who are perceived to offer a way of at least beginning to deal with those circumstances. From a motivational perspective, crisis-produced charismatic leadership enhances followers' context beliefs; it increases followers' estimates of the likelihood of support for their change efforts through the actions of those awarded leadership status. Such attributions of charisma continue as long as those perceptions continue. Leadership attributions are not bi-polar, however. Charisma may vary in intensity and may be dispersed beyond single individuals to groups and even to whole organizations.

The experience of charisma, according to the 13 studies[3] of school leadership in which it was examined, generates increased optimism among colleagues about the future and generates enthusiasm about work. Charismatic school leaders are perceived to exercise power in socially positive ways. They create trust among colleagues in their ability to overcome any obstacle and are a source of pride to have as associates. Colleagues consider these leaders to be symbols of success and accomplishment, and to have unusual insights about what is really important to attend to; they are highly respected by colleagues.

A leader who assists his or her colleagues in identifying and articulating a vision, whether or not attributed charisma, engages in behaviours aimed 'at identifying new opportunities for his or her unit - and developing, articulating, and inspiring others with his or her vision of the future' (Podsakoff et al., 1990, p. 112). Such behaviour is not only central to theories of charisma, it is a critical part of the explanation for leaders' effects offered by Nanus (1992). To the extent that vision is required for planning, its roots can be found in classical theories of management developed by Barnard, Krech, and Crutchfield, among others, at least four decades ago (Bass, 1981).

Those studies which offered evidence about vision-building at the school level identified 8 associated behaviours:
- helping to provide colleagues with an overall sense of purpose;
- initiating processes (retreats, etc.) which engage staff in the collective development of a shared vision;
- espousing a vision for the school but not in a way that pre-empts others from expressing their vision;

- exciting colleagues with visions of what they may be able to accomplish if they work together to change their practices;
- helping clarify the meaning of the school's vision in terms of its practical implications for programs and instruction;
- assisting staff in understanding the relationship between external initiatives for change and the school's vision;
- assisting staff in understanding the larger social mission of which their vision of the school is a part, a social mission which may include such important end values as equality, justice and integrity;
- using all available opportunities to communicate the school's vision to staff, students, parents, and other members of the school community.

Vision-building behaviours identified primarily in studies of superintendents include:
- developing a district mission statement and constantly using it with staff in communication and decision making;
- creating a shared vision for the district in which most district members share;
- using research in decision making and planning;
- being sensitive to the views of the community, parents, board and staff about directions for the district;
- willing to take risks in order to bring about change;
- incorporating considerations of the district's past and present in developing plans for the future.

Goal Consensus

Vision building (the dimension of leadership discussed above) and the development of consensus about goals are closely related sets of leadership practices. The conceptual difference lies in the time frame and the scope of concern of the direction - setting activities that both sets of practices entail. Vision building is intended to create a fundamental, ambitious sense of purpose, one to be pursued over (likely) many years. Developing a consensus on goals focuses organizational members on what will need to be accomplished in the short run (e.g., this year), in order to move toward the vision.

This dimension of transformational leadership, then, includes behaviour 'aimed at promoting cooperation among employees and getting them to work together toward a common goal' (Podsakoff et al.,

1990, p. 112). Goal-setting activities fostered by the leader are motivational to the extent that they increase goal clarity and the perception of goals as challenging but achievable. The promotion of cooperative goals may positively influence teachers' context beliefs, as well.

Goal setting also is part of an approach to leadership, pursued vigorously in the 1950's and 60's, that focused on style or behaviour. This approach awarded substantial importance to the leader's 'initiation of structure' as a means to help define followers' tasks (e.g., Halpin, 1957; Yukl, 1989). Goal setting practices were pivotal to the initiation of structure, according to this approach. Furthermore the determination of objectives and the maintenance of goal direction were among the central functions of leadership identified even earlier by classical management and behavioural theorists (Bass, 1981). Contemporary social cognitive theories of leadership continue to ascribe substantial importance to goals and to goal setting (Sims & Lorenzi, 1992), awarding special attention to questions about how goals are set and what is the effect of variation in such processes.

Identified by the 5 studies[4] concerned with this dimension of leadership in schools were 10 specific behaviours:

- providing staff with a process through which to establish school goals and to regularly review those goals; this is likely to be a 'problem-solving' process and to include careful diagnosis of the school's context;
- expecting teams of teachers (e.g., departments) and individuals to regularly engage in goal setting and reviewing progress toward those goals;
- assisting staff in developing consistency between school visions and both group and individual goals;
- working toward the development of consensus about school and group goals and the priority to be awarded such goals;
- frequently referring to school goals and making explicit use of them when decisions are being made about changes in the school;
- encouraging teachers, as part of goal-setting, to establish and review individual professional growth goals;
- having ongoing discussion with individual teachers about their professional growth goals;
- clearly acknowledging the compatibility of teachers' and school's goals when such is the case;
- expressing one's own views about school goals and priorities;

- acting as an important resource in helping colleagues achieve their individual and school goals.

Three additional behaviours were identified in studies of superintendents:
- influencing others to accept district goals;
- focusing on intra-system development;
- empowering others through goal setting initiatives.

High Performance Expectations

This dimension of transformational school leadership consists of behaviour that 'demonstrates the leader's expectations for excellence, quality, and/or high performance on the part of followers' (Podsakoff et al., 1990, p. 112). Expectations of this sort by school leaders will be motivational as they help teachers see the challenging nature of the goals being pursued in their school. Such expectations may also sharpen teachers' perceptions of the gap between what the school aspires to and what is presently being accomplished. Done well, expressions of high expectations should also result in perceptions among teachers that what is being expected is also feasible.

Behaviour which demonstrates high performance expectations is also consistent with what House and his colleagues termed 'achievement-oriented leadership' in their path-goal theory. According to this theory, the effects of such expectations are contingent on both selected personal characteristics of followers and the environment in which they are working (e.g., House & Mitchell, 1974).

Four studies[5] in school settings inquiring about this dimension of leadership identified a total of six specific behaviours:
- expecting staff to be innovative, hard working and professional; these qualities are included among the criteria used in hiring staff;
- demonstrating an unflagging commitment to the welfare of students;
- often espousing norms of excellence and quality of service;
- not accepting second-rate performance from anyone;
- establishing flexible boundaries for what people do, thus permitting freedom of judgement and action within the context of overall school goals and plans;
- being clear about one's own views of what is right and good.

Studies of superintendents identified two additional practices:

- openly valuing justice, community, democracy, excellence and equality;
- expressing commitment to affective educational goals for students.

Individual Consideration

This dimension of transformational leadership encompasses behaviour indicating that the leader respects followers and is concerned about their personal feelings and needs (Podsakoff et al., 1990, p. 112). Such behaviour may be motivational through its influence on context beliefs, assuring teachers that the problems they are likely to encounter while changing their practices will be taken seriously by those in leadership roles and efforts will be made to help them through those problems.

This dimension of leadership closely parallels the central role of consideration in the 'style' approach to leadership: 'the extent to which leaders promote camaraderie, mutual trust, liking, and respect in the relationship between themselves and their subordinates' (Bryman, 1992, p. 5).

Fourteen studies[6] were sources of information for the twenty specific behaviours associated with this leadership dimension. These specific behaviours suggested several distinct facets of individualized support. One facet, involving the equitable, humane and considerate treatment of one's colleagues, included:

- treating everyone equally; not showing favouritism towards individuals or groups;
- having an 'open door' policy;
- being approachable, accessible and welcoming;
- protecting teachers from excessive intrusions on their classroom work;
- giving personal attention to colleagues who seem neglected by others;
- being thoughtful about the personal needs of staff.

A second facet of individual consideration is the provision of support for the personal, professional development of staff. This includes:

- encouraging individual staff members to try new practices consistent with their interests;

- as often as possible, responding positively to staff members' initiatives for change;
- as often as possible, providing money for professional development and other needed resources in support of changes agreed on by staff;
- providing coaching for those staff members who need it.

Individual consideration requires leaders to develop close knowledge of their individual colleagues. This is done by:
- getting to know individual teachers well enough to understand their problems and to be aware of their particular skills and interests; listening carefully to staff's ideas;
- having the 'pulse' of the school and building on the individual interests of teachers, often as the starting point for school change.

Consideration is also expressed through recognition of good work and effort. Transformational leaders:
- provide recognition for staff work in the form of individual praise or 'pats on the back';
- are specific about what is being praised as 'good work';
- offer personal encouragement to individuals for good performance;
- demonstrate confidence in colleagues' ability to perform at their best.

Finally, individual consideration is reflected in transformational leaders' approaches to change. These leaders:
- follow through on decisions made jointly with teachers;
- explicitly share teachers' legitimate cautions about proceeding quickly toward implementing new practices, thus demonstrating sensitivity to the real problems of implementation faced by teachers;
- take individual teachers' opinion into consideration when initiating actions that may effect their work;
- instill, in staff, a sense of belonging to the school.

Two studies of superintendents' individual support added nothing beyond those behaviours already described (Buck, 1989; Smith, 1989).

Intellectual Stimulation

Behaviour that 'challenges followers to re-examine some of their work and to rethink how it can be performed' (Podsakoff et al., 1990, p. 112) is the meaning of *intellectual stimulation*. This may consist of a type of feedback associated with verbal persuasion. Such stimulation also seems likely to draw teachers' attention to discrepancies between current and desired practices and to understand the truly challenging nature of school restructuring goals. To the extent that such stimulation creates perceptions of a dynamic and changing job for teachers, it should enhance emotional arousal processes, also.

Much of what organizational learning theorists have to say about leadership could be used to expand on the meaning of this dimension of leadership. Senge (1990), for example, argues that leaders' new work will require them 'to bring to the surface and challenge prevailing mental models, and to foster more systemic patterns of thinking - leaders are responsible for learning' (p. 9). Argyris and Schanted assumptions about their work, to engage in 'double loop' learning. To the extent that leaders' own intellectual resources have a bearing on their abilities to provide such intellectual stimulation, even cognitive resource theory (e.g., Fiedler & Garcia, 1987) may be helpful in better understanding the nature and effects of those practices included as part of this leadership dimension.

Transformational leaders, in the 14 studies[7] concerned with intellectual stimulation, used four basic strategies. One strategy was to change school norms that might constrain the thinking of staff. This was accomplished by:

- removing penalties for making mistakes as part of efforts toward professional and school improvement;
- embracing and sometimes generating conflict as a way of clarifying alternative courses of action available to the school;
- requiring colleagues to support opinions with good reasons;
- insisting on careful thought before action.

A second strategy used by transformational leaders was to challenge the status quo by:

- directly challenging staffs' basic assumptions about their work as well as unsubstantiated or questionable beliefs and practices;
- encouraging staff to evaluate their practices and refine them as needed;

- encouraging colleagues to re-examine some of their basic assumptions about their work; making problematic the way things are;
- stimulating colleagues to think more deeply about what they are doing for their students.

Encouraging new initiatives, a third strategy, entailed such behaviours as:
- encouraging staff to try new practices without using pressure;
- encouraging staff to pursue their own goals for professional learning;
- helping staff to make personal meaning of change;
- providing the necessary resources to support staff participation in change initiatives.

A fourth strategy used by transformational leaders for purposes of intellectual stimulation was to bring their colleagues into contact with new ideas. This was done by:
- stimulating the search for and discussion of new ideas and information relevant to school directions;
- seeking out new ideas by visiting other schools, attending conferences, and passing on these new ideas to staff;
- inviting teachers to share their expertise with their colleagues;
- consistently seeking out and communicating productive activities taking place within the school;
- providing information helpful to staff in thinking of ways to implement new practices.

Modelling

This dimension of transformational leadership encompasses behaviour on the part of the leader 'that sets an example for employees to follow that is consistent with the values the leader espouses' (Podsakoff et al., 1990, p. 112). Such behaviour may enhance teachers' beliefs about their own capacities, their sense of self-efficacy. Secondarily, such modelling may contribute to emotional arousal processes by creating perceptions of a dynamic and changing job.

Earlier trait theories of leadership (Bryman, 1992; Hunt et al., 1988), identified a handful of relatively robust personal characteristics of leaders, the impact of which can be explained, in part, through their modelling effects: for example, energy, honesty, integrity, self-confidence, initiative, and persistence.

Four studies[8] provided information about specific behaviours included in this dimension, all of which entail the leader acting as a role model, leading by doing rather than only by telling. Some of these behaviours model the transformational leader's general commitment to the school organization:

- becoming involved in all aspects of school activity;
- working alongside teachers to plan special events;
- displaying energy and enthusiasm for own work.

Other behaviours model commitment to professional growth:

- responding constructively to unrequested feedback about one's leadership practices;
- requesting feedback from staff about one's work;
- demonstrating a willingness to change one's practices in light of new understandings.

Yet other behaviours seem intended to enhance the quality of both group and individual problem solving processes:

- demonstrating, through school decision-making processes, the value of examining problems from multiple perspectives;
- modelling problem-solving techniques that others can adapt for their own work.

Finally, transformational school leaders also engage in behaviours intended to reinforce key values: the basic values of respect for others, trust in the judgement of one's colleagues, integrity, and even the instrumental value of punctuality.

Contingent Reward

As defined by Avolio and Bass (1988), contingent reward occurs when the leader 'is seen as frequently telling subordinates what to do to achieve a desired reward for their efforts' (p. 35). This leadership dimension typically is viewed, theoretically, as transactional. But the possibility of providing informative feedback about performance in order to enhance teachers' capacity beliefs as well as emotional arousal processes makes this behaviour potentially transforming, as well.

Contingent reward draws heavily on ideas central to path-goal theory (e.g., House & Mitchell, 1974) which itself draws extensively on behaviourist approaches to motivation.

Although ten studies[9] inquired about this dimension of leadership, only a small number of specific behaviours were identified. Those behaviours, largely based on survey items (in particular items from Bass's (1985) Multifactor Leadership Questionnaire) include:

- assuring staff members that they can get what they want personally in exchange for their efforts;
- paying personal compliments to staff when they do outstanding work;
- frequently acknowledging good performance;
- providing public recognition for good work.

Structuring

This dimension of transformational leadership includes behaviours aimed at providing opportunities for members of the school organization to participate in decision-making about issues which effect them and to which their knowledge is crucial. Also part of this dimension are behaviours which create discretion and autonomy for teachers to use their expertise to greatest effect. Empowering teachers in these ways contributes to the motivation to change by enhancing teachers' beliefs about the extent to which their working context will support their best efforts to implement new practices in their classrooms and schools.

Two studies provided descriptions of structuring behaviours (Helm, 1989; Leithwood & Jantzi, 1990) engaged in by school-level leaders. These behaviours included:

- distributing the responsibility and power for leadership widely throughout the school;
- sharing decision-making power with staff;
- allowing staff to manage their own decision-making committees;
- taking staff opinion into account when making own decisions;
- ensuring effective group problem solving during meetings of staff;
- providing autonomy for teachers (groups, individuals) in their decisions;
- altering working conditions so that staff have collaborative planning time and time to seek out information needed for planning and decision making;

- ensuring adequate involvement in decision-making related to new initiatives in the school;
- creating opportunities for staff development.

A number of structuring behaviours were observed as part of the repertoire of the transformational superintendent who was the subject of Roberts's (1985) case study. This female superintendent:

- designed an infrastructure in the district (formal and informal) to support change initiatives;
- hired and replaced staff to reflect changes in the district and the talent of district employees;
- developed joint expectations for the work of district and school staffs, and allowed considerable discretion in how these expedctations are achieved;
- employed participative management.

Culture Building

The culture of a school includes the norms, values, beliefs and assumptions shared by members of the school (Shein, 1985). Considerable evidence suggests that school culture, defined in this way, explains a large amount of the variation in school effects (e.g., Little, 1982; Nias, Southworth & Campbell, 1989). This explanation includes not only the *content* of the culture (e.g., student-focused norms are associated with 'effective' cultures), but its *strength* and *form* as well. The culture among professionals in schools is typically characterized as weak (little consensus) and isolated (Fieman-Nemser & Floden, 1986) whereas strong, collaborative school cultures contribute more substantially to school improvement initiatives. Recent research not specifically framed by concepts of transformational leadership have argued for the importance of culture building and described relevant leadership practices (Deal & Peterson, 1990; Cunningham & Gresso, 1993).

Culture-building by transformational leaders includes behaviours aimed at developing school norms, values, beliefs and assumptions that are student-centred and support continuing professional growth by teachers. Such behaviours also encourage collaborative problem solving when that is likely to be profitable: they have the potential to enhance teachers' motivation to change through their influence or context beliefs ('we're all in this together'); they may be motivational, as well, through enhanced self-efficacy resulting from the professional growth fostered by close working relations with peers.

Four studies provided descriptions of culture building behaviours (Helm, 1989; Leithwood, Dart, Jantzi & Steinbach, 1993b; Leithwood & Jantzi, 1990; Skalbeck, 1991) on the part of school leaders. Some of these behaviours aimed at *strengthening* the school culture by:

- clarifying the school's vision in relation to collaborative work and the care and respect with which students were to be treated;
- reinforcing, with staff, norms of excellence for their own work and the work of students;
- using every opportunity to focus attention on and to publicly communicate the school's vision and goals;
- using symbols and rituals to express cultural values in the context of social occasions in which most staff participate;
- confronting conflict openly and acting to resolve it through the use of shared values;
- using slogans and motivational phrases redundantly;
- using bureaucratic mechanisms to support cultural values and a collaborative form of culture (e.g., hiring staff who share school vision, norms and values);
- assisting staff to clarify shared beliefs and values and to act in accord with such beliefs and values;
- acting in a manner consistent with those beliefs and values shared within the school.

Other behaviours were aimed at the *form* of the school's culture, in particular the desire for it to be collaborative. These behaviours included:

- sharing power and responsibility with others;
- working to eliminate 'boundaries' between administrators and teachers and between other groups in the school;
- providing opportunities and resources for collaborative staff work (e.g., creating projects in which collaboration clearly is a useful method of working).

Summary

Evidence provided by twenty-one studies warrant continued attention, in school settings, to seven dimensions of transformational leadership originally proposed for non-school settings. This continuing attention is sometimes justified by substantial evidence of positive effects, as in the case of three dimensions: *charisma/inspiration/vision, intellectual stimulation, and individual consideration.* In the case of 4 dimensions, evidence is meagre but promising or ambiguous: *contingent reward, high performance expectations, goal consensus, and modelling,* and further inquiry is needed. One dimension, *management-by-exception* (attending to an aspect of the organization only when something exceptional or unusual occurs), clearly can be dismissed as having no productive contribution to make to school organizations. Two dimensions unique to school-based research on transformational leadership have been proposed: these are *culture building* and *structuring.* While there is only meagre direct evidence of their value in the 21 studies, substantial evidence is available outside the framework of transformational leadership theory.

Using survey items and qualitative descriptions, a synthesis of specific behaviours associated with each of nine leadership dimensions was described in this section. While most of these behaviours seem plausibly a part of the leadership dimensions in which they are classified, they are at best an eclectic 'starter set'. Considerably more research is necessary to approximate a comprehensive set of behaviours for each leadership dimension. More research also is needed to clarify the status of each behaviour's contribution to the effects anticipated for the leadership dimension of which it is a part. Is the behaviour a critical part of the dimension? Can other behaviours be substituted with no loss of effect? How contingent are these behaviours on the situation in which transformational leadership is being exercised? The 21 studies have nothing to say about these important questions.

EFFECTS OF TRANSFORMATIONAL SCHOOL LEADERSHIP

This section of the chapter takes up two matters concerning the effects of transformational school leadership. First, Bass's claim that transformational leadership is 'value-added' (Avolio & Bass, 1988, Bass & Avolio, 1993) is examined in the context of schools (8 studies). Then, evidence from 20 studies will be reviewed concerning the effects of transformational school leadership on the full array of outcomes used as dependent measures in these studies.

Extent of Support for a 'Two-Factor Theory' of Transformational Leadership in Schools

Only studies in schools which used either Bass's formulation of transformational leadership or modest adaptations of it were considered as evidence about the validity of the 'two-factor theory' in schools. This decision was made because the theory is largely attributable to Bass and his associates: according to their formulation transactional leadership (contingent reward, management-by-exception, and sometimes laissez-faire leadership) provides the essential requirements for organizational maintenance. Adding on transformational leadership (including charisma/inspiration, intellectual stimulation, and individualized consideration) produces change. These two forms of leadership are treated as composite, higher- or second-order factors in the empirical literature.

As a preliminary qualification to the following analysis, the Bass-related formulations of transactional leadership do not appear to adequately encompass the range of leadership practices legitimately conceptualized as "transactional". Subsequent discussions of the relative effects of transactional leadership are clearly limited in their value, as a consequence.

Eight studies were located which directly tested the two-factor theory in school settings. All but one of these studies relied on survey data and assumed Bass's five or six dimensional view of leadership practices.[10] These studies used data from Singapore (1 study), Australia (1), Canada (2), and the United States (4). One study (Buck, 1989) focused on the superintendent's role, another mixed elementary and secondary and higher education leadership roles (King, 1989). The remainder were studies of elementary and secondary school principal roles.

Two types of evidence are relevant to a test of transformational leadership as a 'two-factor' theory. One type of evidence concerns the *external validity* of the theory; this is evidence which confirms that each of the two higher-order factors in the theory has the consequences claimed for it. A second type of evidence bears on the *internal validity* of the theory. This is the claim that particular dimensions of leadership practice are related in the manner specified by theory: that is, charisma/inspiration/vision, intellectual stimulation and individual support form one related cluster of variables and contingent reward and management-by-exception form a second, different cluster.

Support for the external validity of the two-factor theory is to be found in evidence which demonstrates that transactional leadership practices are necessary to the maintenance of organizational routines, that they provide essential stability but do not, by themselves, stimulate much change. Only by 'adding on' transformational practices is change likely.[11] A quantitative test of this claim might use stepwise regression analyses, for example; measures of transactional leadership are entered in the regression equation first, in order to estimate how much variance in the dependent measure(s) is accounted for. When measures of transformational leadership, entered second into the regression equation, account for significant additional variation in the dependent measure(s), the external validity of the two-factor theory receives support.

The external validity of the two-factor theory could also be assessed using qualitative data. For example, case study data concerning the relative success of school improvement initiatives undertaken by school principals varying in the degrees to which they provided both transformational and transactional leadership practices would be relevant to a test of external validity.

Claims that the two-factor theory is internally valid require evidence demonstrating

    (a) very low correlations among those leadership dimensions conceptually defined as transactional and those defined as transformational and;

    (b) relatively high correlations among those dimensions within each leadership type. Factor analysis of responses to all items on a leadership survey is the most frequently used method of quantitatively testing the internal validity claim. Strongest support for the claim is provided by results in which all items load on only two factors. Those items considered part of transformational leadership, conceptually, load on one factor and all items consistent with the theoretical meaning of transactional leadership load on a second factor.

It is less obvious how this claim could be tested with qualitative evidence. However, teacher talk explicitly linking together, in terms of subjective meaning and perceived consequences, an array of practices theoretically considered to be transactional and yet another array considered to be transformational would assist with such a test.

Silins's (1992) study of Canadian school leaders provides evidence from 670 teachers bearing on both the internal and external validity of the two-factor theory. Confirmatory factor analysis strongly support an internal validity claim, but as Silins explains, '... these two [transactional] factors do not conform to Bass's hypothesized relationships' (1992, p. 326). Instead, *contingent reward* loaded on the factor which included transformational practices, leaving *management-by-exception* as the sole dimension defining transactional leadership. These data support the internal validity of a significantly modified theory of transformational leadership.

Evidence from Silins's (1992) study bearing indirectly on the external validity of transformational leadership theory was produced through a canonical correlation analysis of data using four different outcome measures, each based on teachers' perceptions. Although somewhat ambiguous for this purpose, results do not support external validity claims. *Management-by-exception*, the single dimension of practice empirically defining transactional leadership, had negative effects on school change, whereas at least neutral effects would be predicted by prior theory. Transformational practices, as a whole, had expected effects but one of the dimensions, *charisma/inspiration/ vision*, did not behave as predicted.

A second study by Silins (1994b) of Australian school leaders, using responses from 458 teachers, assessed the internal validity of the two-factor theory, as well as a more elaborate conception of transformational leadership theory influenced by work in both Australia and Canada. Confirmatory factor analysis provided weak support for the internal validity of a reformulated two-factor theory, as in the previous study. Leadership practices conceptualized as transformational all loaded on one factor along with practices associated with *contingent reward*. Items measuring the remaining transactional dimension, *management-by-exception*, loaded either negatively on the transformational factor or positively on a second factor.

In a third study based on responses from 679 teachers, again focused on Canadian school leaders, Silins (1994a) assessed both the internal and external validity of the two-factor theory using both canonical analysis and partial least squares path analysis with four different outcome measures. The path model resulting from canonical analysis supported the internal validity claims of a modified two-factor theory. In this study, *charisma/inspiration/vision* helped define, negatively, transactional leadership, whereas *contingent reward* contributed to the meaning of both transformational and transactional factors. The results provide strong direct support for external validity claims. Transformational leadership explained 55 percent of the variance in transactional leadership.

Results of Koh's (1990) study of Singapore principals do not support the internal validity of the two-factor theory. Exploratory factor analysis resulted in a unitary factor defined by three transformational leadership dimensions. However, transactional leadership practices loaded on three separate factors, factors best interpreted as *contingent reward, passive management-by-exception* and *active management-by-exception*. Had *contingent reward* loaded on the transformational factor, these results would not have been substantially different than those reported in the three Silins studies. This gives rise to the possibility that *contingent reward* can take several forms - one relatively inspirational in nature and focused on intrinsic rewards, and one that is more exchange-based and focused on extrinsic rewards.

Koh (1990) also conducted a hierarchical regression analysis with his data to directly test the external validity of the two-factor theory. Transactional practices added first to the regression analyses explained none of the variance in three aspects of a multidimensional outcome measure (organizational citizenship behaviour). When transformational practices were added, significant amounts of the variation in one aspect of this outcome measure was explained. More detailed analyses suggested the necessity of transactional leadership in producing transformational effects, thereby providing support for external validity claims.

King's (1989) data from 160 educators in K-12 and higher education settings was collected using a survey of transformational leadership practices and a measure of organizational climate. Analysis of these data provided a test of the external validity of the two-factor theory. The dependent measure, organizational climate, included perceptions of leader effectiveness, satisfaction with the leader and leadership style, developmental press, and control press. Using stepwise regression, transactional leadership measures were entered at a first stage to determine how much variance was accounted for in the dependent measure. Transformational leadership measures were entered next to estimate the amount of additional variation accounted for.

Results of the analysis support the claim that transformational leadership adds value to transactional leadership, but they also call into question the necessity of transactional leadership in relation to some dependent measures. With respect to perceptions of leader effectiveness, transactional leadership explained 19.6% of the variation, transformational leadership explained an additional 44.4%. With respect to satisfaction with the leader, the comparable figures were 20.8% and 54.6%. Both sets of results are consistent with predictions from the two-factor theory. Transformational leadership was the only significant predictor of developmental press, a result still consistent with theory. But control press (feeling constrained in one's actions by the leader), an outcome predicted for transactional leadership, behaved contrary to theory: transformational leadership predicted more variation in this outcome than did transactional leadership. Simple correlations were also higher between transformational leadership and control press ($r = .61$) than between this outcome and transactional leadership ($r = .40$).

Kirby, King, and Paradise (1991), using data from 103 educators mostly about K-12 school leaders, tested the external validity of the two-factor theory. Based on a stepwise regression procedure, they found that transactional leadership, entered first in the regression, explained significant variation in both satisfaction with the leader and perceptions of leader effectiveness. Transformational leadership, entered into the regression second, significantly increased the amount of explained variation on both dependent measures. This same study called into question the internal validity of the two-factor theory, however. Only *charisma/inspiration/vision* and *laissez-faire* dimensions of leadership were significant predictors of satisfaction, *charisma/inspiration/vision* and *intellectual stimulation* predicting perceptions of effectiveness. *Contingent reward* was related to transformational rather than transactional leadership dimensions.

Hoover's (1987) study provided unambiguous support for the internal validity of the two-factor theory. As with King's (1989) study, Hoover's data called into question the necessity of transactional leadership in relation to perceived leader effectiveness, and satisfaction with the leader. With respect to internal validity, a varimax rotation of first-order factor loadings resulted in two higher-order factors. One such factor was transformational (or active-proactive) leadership, including *charisma/inspiration/vision, individualized consideration* and *intellectual stimulation*. The second higher-order factor was transactional (or passive-reactive) leadership, including *contingent reward* and *management-by-exception*.

Correlations between the three first-order factors defining transformational leadership in this study and the two dependent measures were positive and significant in all but one case. In contrast, correlations between transactional leadership factors and the two dependent measures were non-significant, close to zero and, in half the cases, negative. These results, as with King's (1989), question the necessity of transactional leadership in relation to some outcomes. Indeed, the two outcomes for which transactional leadership did predict significant variation in King's study were the same two for which correlations with transactional leadership in Hoover's study approached zero. Such contradictory results, however, may be a function of different data analysis techniques.

Based on qualitative evidence collected from a reputationally effective sample of 51 Texas superintendents, Buck's (1989) study offers indirect evidence in support of the external validity of the two-factor theory. Superintendents varied widely in their use of both transactional and transformational practices: they believed transactional practices to be necessary and associated them with routine management, whereas transformational practices were associated with their change efforts.

Effects of Transformational School Leadership

Evidence about the effects of transformational school leadership was provided by a total of 20 studies, 5 of which were qualitative. These studies include estimates of the outcomes or effects of transformational and transactional higher-order factors considered separately; they also include estimates of the effects of each of the first-order dimensions of transformational leadership described in Table 2.

The 20 studies as a whole report evidence about 13 different types of effects (see Table 3). These are grouped into effects on perceptions of leaders, effects on the behaviour of followers, effects on followers' psychological states, organizational-level effects, and student effects. Table 3 describes: the number of studies in which evidence is reported about each effect; the number of positive relationships found between each outcome and the total set of transformational dimensions included in the studies; and the total number of relationships reported to be negative or not significant (in the case of the 15 quantitative studies, 'significant' means statistically significant). The remainder of this section examines evidence related to each effect, in turn: how the effect was defined and measured, the weight of the evidence in support of the effect, and those leadership dimensions which demonstrably contributed to the effect.

Types of Effects or Outcomes Measured	Number of Studies (N=20)	Total Posi-tive	Total N.S. or Nega-tive
Effects on Perceptions of Leader			
1. perceptions of leader effec-tiveness	3	15	4
2. satisfaction with leader(s) and style	5	16	5
Effects on Behavior of Followers			
3. extra effort	2	5	2
4. organizational citizenship behavior	1	1	3
Effects on Followers' Psychological States			
5. commitment	5	12	10
6. developmental press	4	12	6
7. control press	1	5	3
8. morale/job satisfaction	1	1	0
Organization-level Effects			
9. organizational learning	1	5	1
10. organizational improvement/ effectiveness	7	35	16
11. organizational climate and culture	7	14	1
Effects on Students			
12. teachers' perceptions of stu-dent effects	6	5	1
13. student participation and identification	2	0	2

Table 3: Effects of Transformational Leadership (Total Number of Studies = 20)

Effects on perceptions of leaders

Three studies, two carried out in the U.S. and one in New Zealand, examine transformational leadership effects on perceptions of leader effectiveness and satisfaction with the leader (King, 1989; Kirby, King & Paradise, 1991; Bass, 1985). Data from leaders at both school and district levels were collected in these studies, all of which used a version of Bass's (1988) Multifactor Leadership Questionnaire (MLQ). In addition to measuring aspects of transformational leadership, the MLQ includes a two-item scale measuring respondents' satisfaction with their leader and a four-item scale measuring perceptions of the leader's effectiveness.

These studies report largely consistent results in relation to both sets of effects. Positive relationships are reported between transformational and transactional higher-order factors. Among first-order leadership dimensions, these effects are most strongly related to *charisma/vision/ inspiration, intellectual stimulation, individual consideration* and *contingent reward*. Non-significant relationships are reported in respect to *management-by-exception. Laissez-faire* leadership was negatively related to both perceptions of leader effectiveness and satisfaction with the leader.

Two additional studies (Koh, 1990; Orr, 1990) report significant positive relationships between *transformational: C* and *transactional: C* (these are composite, higher-order factors) and satisfaction with the leader. Although Koh (1990) included Bass's MLQ among the instruments in his study of Singapore principals, he used a subscale of the Index of Organizational Reactions (Smith, 1976) to measure satisfaction with leaders. Orr (1990) developed two new instruments for his study of U.S. superintendents. Included in the instrument used to collect data from those working with superintendents was a two-item scale asking for a rating of the superintendent's performance.

Effect on behaviours of followers

Three studies (Bass, 1985; Koh, 1990; Orr, 1990) inquired about the effects of transformational leadership on two types of follower behaviours: the extent to which followers are prepared to engage in extra effort on behalf of their organization; and 'organizational citizenship behaviour'. Two of these studies were about superintendents (Orr's

U.S. study) or other central administrators (Bass's New Zealand study); Koh (1990) studied Singapore principals.

Bass (1985) assessed extra effort using responses of followers to a three-item scale included in the MLQ. These same three items were used by Orr (1990) to collect data from both superintendents and their immediate subordinates. Both studies report significant positive relationships between transformational leadership and followers' extra effort. In the Bass study, extra effort mostly was accounted for by *charisma/inspiration/vision, intellectual stimulation* and *individual consideration. Contingent reward* and *management-by-exception* had non-significant and negative correlations, respectively, with extra effort. Orr (1990) reported positive relations between extra effort and both transformational: C and transactional: C.

Organizational citizenship behaviour, one of the dependent variables in Koh's (1990) study, was measured using an adapted version of a questionnaire originally developed by Smith, Organ and Near (1983): sixteen items formed 3 sub-scales measuring altruism, compliance and non-compliance with leaders' suggestions. Transformational: C was significantly but negatively related to non-compliance This means, as Koh explains, 'The more the principals were perceived as transformational, the lower will be the teacher's tendency to take undeserved breaks, make unnecessary phone calls, and so forth' (1990, p. 113). Positively related to non-compliance were active and passive *management-by-exception*. No significant relations were evident with *contingent reward*.

Effect on followers' psychological states

There is evidence from 5 studies (4 quantitative) that transformational leadership influences four psychological states of those who experience such leadership: commitment, developmental press, control press, and satisfaction. Several forms of commitment served as dependent variables in these studies including teacher commitment to change (Leithwood, Jantzi, & Fernandez, 1993; Leithwood et al., 1993), and organizational commitment (Koh, 1990; Skalbeck, 1991). Considered to be part of this category of studies as well is Smith's (1989) study of teacher work motivation.

Evidence reported in the two studies by Leithwood and his colleagues were collected from 534 intermediate and secondary teachers in a large sample of schools in one Canadian province and from 168 teachers in nine secondary schools in a second province. Both of these studies used path analysis techniques to test a model in which transformational leadership, as well as sets of other in-school and out-of-school conditions were treated as independent variables. A multi-scale, multi-item survey of transformational school leadership, developed and refined in the earlier work of these researchers, was used to collect evidence about six dimensions of transformational leadership. Dependent variables, measured with items in the same survey, were four categories of psychological processes identified in the social-psychological literature as giving rise to teachers' commitment to change. Transformational: C had significant direct and indirect effects on teachers' commitment to change. These effects were accounted for most strongly by: *vision building, high performance expectations, developing consensus about group goals,* and *intellectual stimulation.*

Koh (1990) measured organizational commitment with the widely used, 15 item Organizational Commitment Questionnaire (OCQ) developed by Mowday, Steers, and Porter (1979). This instrument describes respondents' loyalty and attachment to an organization, their agreement with its purposes and values and their willingness to expend extra effort. Using hierarchical regression analyses, Koh found that transactional leadership explained a significant proportion of the variation in organizational commitment. Adding on transformational leadership explained a significant additional proportion of such variation, however, more than explained by transactional leadership, or any of several other variables measured in the study.

Skalbeck's (1991) qualitative study inquired about the transformational practices of one elementary school principal and the extent to which these practices influenced teachers' commitment to the school's mission and vision. Leadership practices accounting for such commitment can be classified as *individual support, culture building* and *contingent reward.*

Using Bass's MLQ as a measure of 100 superintendents' transformational leadership, Smith (1989) also collected evidence about the work motivation of about 100 principals associated with these superintendents. The questionnaire measuring such motivation was based on the work of Herzberg and others. Stepwise regression analyses of data from these samples of administrators identified *intellectual stimulation* as the dimension of transformational leadership best predicting principals' work motivation.

One quantitative (Leithwood, Jantzi, & Dart, 1991) and two qualitative (Skalbeck, 1991; Leithwood & Jantzi, 1990) studies reported effects of transformational leadership on the 'developmental press' created among those experiencing such leadership. Leithwood, Jantzi, and Dart (1991) measured transformational leadership using a version of the instrument described above: developmental press was defined as changes in teachers' attitudes and school or classroom behaviour. Data about both sets of variables were provided by 291 elementary school teachers and 43 principals in two Canadian provinces. Dimensions of transformational leadership significantly related to developmental press included: *vision building, developing consensus about group goals, individual consideration,* and *intellectual stimulation.* A dimension termed 'leadership pressure' had non-significant relationships with developmental press.

Skalbeck's (1991) study of a single principal suggested that the stimulus for growth among teachers (developmental press) was a function of the principal's *vision-building* initiatives and the *collegial culture* she was able to build among teaching staff. Interviews with 133 teachers from nine elementary and three secondary case schools provided the data for Leithwood and Jantzi's (1990) study. *Vision building, culture building, developing consensus about group goals, intellectual stimulation,* and *individual consideration* made substantial contributions to teachers' change initiatives in these schools; neither *modelling* nor *contingent reward* had such effects.

Only King's (1989) study provides evidence about the relationship between control press and transformational leadership (measured using Bass's MLQ). Control press, one of two higher-order factors measured in this study with the 80-item Organizational Climate Index (Stern & Steinhoff, 1965), is indicative of 'an organizational environment that emphasized high levels of orderliness and structure. The environment is work-oriented, rather than people oriented.' (King, 1989, p. 94). Contrary to expectation, King found that transformational leadership explained substantially more variation in control press than did transactional leadership. *Charisma/inspiration/vision, intellectual stimulation,* and *individual consideration* accounted for most of this variation.

Helm's (1989) qualitative study of principals' leadership in U.S. Catholic elementary schools was the only source of data about the effects of transformational leadership on teacher morale. Aspects of leadership contributing to teacher morale included warm, informal, positive relationships between principals and teachers (*individual consideration*) and the creation of opportunities for shared decision making and leadership (*structuring*).

Organization-level effects

Included among organization-level effects of transformational leadership that have been studied are organizational learning, organizational improvement and effectiveness, and organizational climate and culture. The effects of transformational leadership on organizational learning were examined by Leithwood and his colleagues (1993) in the context of secondary school improvement efforts. These efforts were partly in response to a major reform initiated in one Canadian province. Conditions giving rise to such learning were extracted from the literature. Both quantitative and qualitative data were collected from school staffs about the extent to which these conditions prevailed in their schools and whether and how school leaders influenced these conditions. Organizational learning was defined as an increase in the collective capacity of organizational members to better accomplish the purposes of the school. Transformational leadership practices were helpful in fostering organizational learning; in particular, *vision building, individual support, intellectual stimulation, modelling, culture building*, and *holding high performance expectations*.

Seven studies report more evidence about the relationship between transformational leadership and organizational improvement and effectiveness than any other set of outcomes. The majority of these studies come from one line of Canadian research (Leithwood et al., 1991, 1992, 1993; Silins, 1992a, 1992b, 1994a), the context for which was essentially the same as in the study of organizational learning described above. Both qualitative and quantitative evidence from these studies suggests that transformational leadership is a powerful stimulant to improvement. *Vision building, developing consensus about group goals, providing intellectual stimulation and individual support, culture building*, and *contingent reward* were the leadership dimensions that most accounted for this stimulation.

Two other studies also offer evidence relevant to transformational leadership and organizational effectiveness and improvement, Kendrick's (1988) case study of her own leadership in one school over a five year period makes a compelling case for the contribution of an evolving set of transformational leadership practices. Koh (1990), using evidence from the Index of Perceived Organizational Effectiveness (Mott, 1972), did not find support for the contribution of transformational over transactional leadership.

The contributions of transformational leadership to organizational climate and culture has been assessed in seven studies. Qualitative studies by Helm (1989), Kendrick (1988), Leithwood and Jantzi (1990), and Vandenburghe (1991) report generally positive contributions. In the case of culture, these studies provide extended descriptions of what it means to offer 'symbolic leadership': such practices help define the meaning of *culture building* as a distinct dimension of transformational leadership.

In three quantitative studies, measures used to describe climate and culture included the School Work Culture Profile (Darling, 1990), the Organizational Climate Index (King, 1989), and the Leader Behaviour Questionnaire (Sashkin & Sashkin, 1990). Each instrument measures something a bit different. Nevertheless, the studies all provide reasonably strong support for the claim that transformational leadership contributes to more desirable school cultures and climates.

Effects on Students

The effects on students of transformational school leadership are likely to be mediated by teachers and others. This may account for why so little evidence has been reported concerning such effects. The complexity of analyses required to determine the indirect effects of transformational leadership on students may also account for the limited evidence. Until the link between transformational leadership and student effects is explored in some depth, however, the utility of transformational leadership in schools will remain uncertain.

Leithwood and his colleagues offer the only evidence available about student effects. Six studies by this group inquire about the relationship between transformational school leadership and a construct they termed 'teacher-perceived student outcomes' (Leithwood, Cousins & G Steinbach, 1993a; Silins & Leithwood, 1994; Silins, 1992b; Silins, 1994a; Leithwood, Dart, Jantzi & Steinbach, 1991). This construct was measured through items on a survey which asked teachers to estimate the effects on students of various innovative practices being implemented in their classrooms. These practices were usually the product of school-wide initiatives, such initiatives often promoted (or at least supported) by those in formal school leader roles. While teacher perceptions offer indirect evidence of student effects, Leithwood et al. point to the substantial evidence of high correlations between such evidence and direct measures of student achievement such as those provided by standardized tests (Egan & Archer, 1985). Based on similar path analytic data analysis techniques, five of the six studies reported significant indirect effects of transformational school leadership on teacher-perceived student outcomes.

This same research group also report two studies inquiring about the effects of transformational school leadership on a construct they termed 'student participation in and identification with school' (Leithwood, Cousins & G3; Leithwood, Dart, Jantzi & Steinbach, 1993b). This construct is based on Finn's theory of factors explaining variation in student retention rates (Finn, 1989; Finn & Cox, 1992). Responses to the instrument developed for this research were provided by two samples of secondary school students (N = 3,557 and 2,045). Neither studies found significant direct or indirect effects of transformational school leadership on student participation in and identification with school.

Summary

This section of the chapter reviewed evidence concerning the internal and external validity of a conception of transformational leadership as a 'two factor' theory. Also reviewed was evidence of the effects of leadership on 13 types of outcomes.

Eight studies inquiring about this conception of transformational school leadership provided modest support for its internal validity but in an adapted form. Such an adaptation appears to be required largely because *contingent reward* is more often associated with transformational than transactional leadership. Modest support is also provided by these eight studies for the external validity of the two-factor theory. The sometimes ambiguous findings of the studies about external validity may be, at least in part, a function of the outcomes chosen as dependent measures. Transactional leadership may contribute little or nothing to some types of outcomes, although which outcomes is not yet clear.

Taken at face value, the twenty studies of transformational school leadership effects suggest that:

  - Transformational leadership, as a whole, is strongly related to satisfaction with the leader and positive perceptions of the leader's effectiveness.
  - Transformational leadership, as a whole, is strongly related to the willingness of organizational members to engage in extra effort but is weakly or negatively associated with most aspects of organizational citizenship behaviour.

- Psychological states of followers including their organizational commitment and perceptions of both a development and control press in the school environment are significantly and positively associated with transformational leadership.
- Organization-level effects are also positively associated with transformational leadership practices. Such practices explain significant variation in organizational learning, teachers' perceptions of school improvement and effectiveness, and productive school cultures and climate.
- Transformational leadership has significant indirect effects on teachers' perceptions of student effects but its effects on direct measures of student outcomes has yet to be demonstrated.
- The specific leadership dimensions most consistently explaining all transformational effects are charisma/vision/inspiration, intellectual stimulation, and individualized consideration. Less consistent in their effects, but still important are modelling and holding high performance expectations.
- The relatively little studied dimensions of culture building and structuring show promising effects but results, as yet, are extremely sparse.
- Contingent reward often has positive effects more consistent with predictions concerning transformational than transactional leadership.
- Management-by-exception (active or passive) typically has negative effects, whatever outcome is measured.

Twenty studies seems like a reasonably large number from which to draw inferences about the effects of transformational leadership However, the potential of the studies for this purpose is weakened considerably by their dispersion across 11 different outcomes. For six of these outcomes, there is evidence from only three or fewer studies. Indeed, the relatively large body of evidence available about organizational improvement and effectiveness (7 studies) and organizational climate and culture (7 studies) was created only because studies with loosely related but not identical outcomes were treated as comparable.

The twenty studies are overweighted in favour of those using quantitative methods (15). This suggests a 'hard edge' on the data with distinct advantages for the purpose of assessing effects of transformational leadership. Nevertheless, the hardness of that edge is partly compromised by the possibility of same-source bias. In most of the quantitative studies, data about both independent and dependent variables were collected using the same instruments and respondents. Studies by Koh (1990), Smith (1989), King (1989), Darling (1990), Leithwood, Cousins and Gérin-Lajoie (1993), and Leithwood, Dart, Jantzi and Steinbach (1993b) are exceptions to this general trend.

Problems of dispersed evidence and same-source bias preclude claims about the relative contribution of transformational leadership to specific types of outcomes. There is warrant for claiming that transformational school leadership has positive effects on schools but not for specifying what these effects are. Axiomatically, then, it is even more important to resist other than the most tentative conclusions about those specific leadership dimensions best explaining significant variation in different sets of outcomes.

CONCLUSION

A review of literature usually is carried out as a means of 'summing up' what is formally known about some phenomenon, issue or problem and assessing the degree of confidence that can be placed in that knowledge. The first part of this task (summing up) is much simpler to accomplish than is the second (assessing the resulting knowledge claims). When the evidence on which knowledge claims are based lend themselves to quantitative, meta-analytic techniques (e.g., Light & Pillemer, 1984; Rosenthal, 1984), probability theory can be used as one way of arriving at judgements of confidence (e.g., whether or not an 'effect size' is statistically significant).

When evidence being reviewed does not lend itself to quantitative meta-analysis, reviewers typically count the number of studies supporting and not supporting a knowledge claim (the so-called 'box score' method), as we have done to this point. This method, however, does not fully resolve the desire for an assessment of the robustness of the 'summed up' knowledge, since more than the quantity of evidence is entailed in such an assessment. Other relevant criteria include, for example, the methodological sophistication of individual studies reviewed, the extent to which results converge, and the adequacy of theory to which the data speak. But since those criteria are not easily combined, the problem the reviewer confronts in offering an overall assessment seems comparable to the task facing judges of athletic performances or artistic products. Based on sensitivities and impressions of such performances or products, these judges make comparisons with personal models of outstanding performances or products developed through extensive experience. They then express the outcome of this clearly private comparison in a publicly clear 'metric'.

What would these publicly clear metrics be in the case of a research review? As part of a review of research on knowledge about teaching, Fenstermacher (1994) surveys epistemological positions on the status of formal knowledge. Of particular value in providing readily understood ways of describing judgements about the robustness of knowledge claims are categories used by some epistemologists for this purpose and outlined by Fenstermacher. Thirteen categories are described, ranging from 'certainly false' through 'certain'. For purposes of this review, distinctions signified by three category labels seem most relevant. These categories are:

- *Evident*: in this review, knowledge claims will be judged as *Evident* when (a) there is a large amount of supporting research evidence, (b) there is very little or no disconfirming evidence, (c) supporting evidence is largely derived from research meeting conventional standards and (d) there are good theoretical arguments in support of the claims.
- *Beyond Reasonable Doubt*: this classification of knowledge claims will be used when (a) there is a substantial amount of evidence available, (b) a substantial minority of this evidence is split between non-confirmation and disconfirmation, (c) evidence is provided from a corpus of research ranging in quality from poor to excellent, and (d) there is a good theoretical argument in support of the claims.
- *Epistemically in the Clear*: this category will be used when, in Fenstermacher's terms, '... there are not better grounds for rejecting the [knowledge claim] than for accepting it' (1994, p. 24).

We conclude this chapter by revisiting the primary knowledge claims made or inferred by our review. In each case the status of the claim is classified using one of the three categories described above. Knowledge claims judged to be *epistemically in the clear* (and sometimes *beyond reasonable doubt*) are used as springboards for identifying useful foci for further research on transformational school leadership.

Status of Knowledge Claims About the Nature of Transformational School Leadership

That section of the review concerned with the nature of transformational leadership explained such leadership as a working theory for motivation. Evidence was examined about the relevance to schools of 10 dimensions of transformational leadership and specific behaviours associated with each were described. Of those 10 dimensions, we judge the claim that four are productive in school contexts to be *evident*: these dimensions include charisma/inspiration/vision, intellectual stimulation and contingent reward. Also *evident* is the claim that management-by-exception is unproductive in school contexts. Our confidence in these two claims is bolstered by the considerable body of unambiguous evidence available in the non-school transformational leadership literature.[12]

The claim that the remaining five dimensions are productive in school contexts is best judged as *epistemically in the clear*, a judgement consistent with the weak evidence reported in the non-school research about goal consensus, modelling and high performance expectations;[13] no evidence has been reported about structuring and culture building in the non-school literature. This judgement leans toward being conservative since there are good theoretical arguments in support of the five dimensions. These are compelling reasons for recommending subsequent research be conducted on the effects of these dimensions in general, as well as the conditions creating variability of effects. These dimensions may be highly contingent.

The same section of the review also described specific behaviours associated with each leadership dimension. The claim that such behaviours are a sufficient description of what is entailed in practice by each dimension is *epistemically in the clear*. But not even that level of confidence can be awarded the claim that they are necessary. A productive future inquiry aimed at teasing out the essential or necessary behaviours associated with each of the leadership dimensions in order to realize their theoretical effects would be productive. Such research ought to remain open to the possibility that alternative sets of behaviours within a single dimension are called for depending on the context in which leadership is exercised. We are not aware of any research in non-school settings which addresses either of these issues.

Status of Knowledge Claims About the Effects of Transformational School Leadership

The section of the review concerned with transformational school leadership effects examined the validity of a two-factor theory of transformational leadership in schools and assessed the contribution of transformational leadership to 13 different sets of outcomes. Claims for the internal and external validity of a two-factor conception of transformational school leadership are judged to be *beyond reasonable doubt*, if the theory is adapted; this adaptation entails reconceptualizing contingent reward as a transformational dimension, a view consistent with evidence from non-school settings. However, that leaves transactional leadership defined only by management-by-exception, a generally unhelpful if not actually destructive form of leadership in non-school as well as school contexts. Subsequent research ought to begin from a more adequate conception of transactional leadership than typically has been included in transformational leadership research in either school or non-school settings. It seems likely that there are important, as yet unidentified (in this body of research) managerial functions, for example, to which transformational practices add value. The failure to more adequately conceptualize and measure these functions is a significant limitation in the corpus of evidence about transformational leadership.

Thirteen outcomes have been used as dependent variables in studies of transformational school leadership. The claim that such leadership contributes to organizational improvement/effectiveness, teachers' perceptions of student outcomes, and organizational climate and culture, is *beyond reasonable doubt*. In concert with considerable evidence from non-school settings,[14] this same judgement is warranted about effects on perceptions of leader effectiveness and satisfaction with the leader. Claims about the effects of transformational leaders on the remaining outcomes are judged to be *epistemically in the clear*. An important contribution to knowledge about the effects of transformational school leadership would be a sustained program of research using the same set of dependent measures or outcomes: these outcomes ought to include not only selected student effects, but also those mediating variables which are both theoretically influenced by transformational leadership and demonstrably consequential in the production of student effects, for example teachers' sense of self-efficacy (Ross, 1994); Leithwood, Jantzi & Fernandez, 1994).

Many limitations of a theoretical and methodological nature remain in research on transformational school leadership carried out to date. Nonetheless, this evidence does provide a strong argument for expanding school leadership research in the direction of transformational perspectives. Such an expanded research base, however, should include studies which directly compare the power of competing conceptions of leadership to explain variation in important mediating and dependent variables. For example, the type of work recently reported by Heck and his colleagues (e.g., Heck, Marcoulides & Lang, 1991) exploring the effects of instructional leadership could be expanded with the same samples of school leaders also using measures of transformational leadership. Presently, there is evidence of quite positive effects of several forms of school leadership. But because of differences in the choice of dependent variables, research methods and the like in generating such evidence, the effects cannot be compared meaningfully. While the claim that 'leadership' is a critical variable in school improvement is *evident*, claims about the forms such leadership ought to take are weak, many based on no empirical evidence at all. An important project yet to be undertaken is a comparative analysis of the effects of alternative models of leadership in schools.

FOOTNOTES

1. Sometimes the term 'transformational leadership' is used as a superordinate term encompassing practices which are both transformational and transactional. On other occasions, the term signifies only dimensions of leadership assumed to have transformational effects.
2. Portions of this section are based on Leithwood, Jantzi & Fernandez (1994).
3. King (1989), Kirby, King & Paradise (1992), Bass (1985), Silins (1992), Leithwood, Dart, Jantzi & Steinbach (1993a,b, 1991), Leithwood, Jantzi, Silins & Dart (1993), Smith (1989), Skalback (1991), Leithwood, Jantzi & Fernandez (1994), Sashkin & Sashkin (1990), Vandenburghe & Staessens (1991).
4. Leithwood, Dart, Jantzi & Steinbach (1991, 1993a,b), Leithwood, Jantzi & Fernandez (1994), Vandenburghe & Staessens (1991).
5. Leithwood, Dart, Jantzi & Steinbach (1991, 1993a,b), Leithwood, Jantzi, Silins & Dart (1993).
6. King (1989), Kirby, King & Paradise (1992), Leithwood, Dart,

Jantzi & Steinbach (1991, 1993a,b), Leithwood, Jantzi, Silins & Dart (1993), Silins (1992, 1994b), Smith (1989), Skalbeck (1991), Leithwood, Jantzi & Fernandez (1994), Helm (1989), Bass (1985), Sashkin & Sashkin (1990).

7. Same studies as listed in note 6.

8. Leithwood, Dart, Jantzi & Steinbach (1991, 1993a,b), Skalbeck (1991).

9. King (1989), Kirby, King & Paradise (1992), Silins (1992), Silins (1994b), Leithwood, Dart, Jantzi & Steinbach (1991, 1993a,b), Leithwood, Jantzi, Silins & Dart (1993), Bass (1985), Smith (1989).

10. Sometimes 'management-by-exception' is considered to be two dimensions: 'active management-by-exception' and 'passive management-by-exception'.

11. This claim must, of course, acknowledge that factors other than leadership also give rise to change.

12. Howell & Higgins (1990), Podsakoff, MacKenzie, Moorman & Fetter (1990), Singer & Singer (1986), Tichy & Devanna (1986), Waldman, Bass & Einstein (1987), Waldman, Bass & Yammarino (1990), Bass, Waldman, Avolio & Babb (1987), Bass & Avolio (1989), Bennis & Nanus (1985), Deluga (1991), Hater & Bass (1988), Seltzer & Bass (1990), Singer (1985), Spangler & Braiotta (1990).

13. Podsakoff, MacKenzie, Moorman & Fetter (1990).

14. Seltzer & Bass (1990), Spangler & Braiotta (1990), Waldman, Bass & Yammarino (1990), Yammarino & Bass (1990), Deluga (1991), Hater & Bass (1988), Singer (1985), Podsakoff, Todor & Skov (1982), Podsakoff, MacKenzie, Moorman & Fetter (1990), Waldman, Bass & Einstein (1987).

REFERENCES

Argyris, C., & Schön, D.A. (1978). *Organizational learning: A theory of action perspective*. Reading, Mass.: Addison-Wesley.

Avolio, B.J., & Bass, B.M. (1988). Transformational leadership, charisma, and beyond. In J.G. Hunt, B.R. Baliga, H.P. Dachler, & C.A. Schriesheim (Eds.), *Emerging leadership vistas* (11-28). Lexington, Mass.: Lexington Books.

Bass, B.M. (1985). *Leadership and performance beyond expectations*. New York: The Free Press.

Bass, B.M. (1988). *The Multifactor Leadership Questionnaire, Form 5 (revised)*. Binghampton, NY: Centre for Leadership Studies, State University of New York @ Binghampton.

Bass, B.M. (Ed.) (1981). *Stogdill's handbook of leadership: A survey of theory and research*. London: Collier Macmillan Pub.

Bass, B.M., & Avolio, B.J. (1993). *Transformational leadership: A response to critiques. Leadership theory and research: Perspectives and directions* (49-80).

Bass, B.M., & Avolio, B.J. (Eds.) (1994). *Improving organizational effectiveness through transformational leadership*. Thousand Oaks, Cal.: Sage.

Bass, B.M., Waldman, D.A., Avolio, B.J., & Babb, M. (1987). Transformational leadership and the falling dominoes effect. *Group and Organizational Studies, 12*, 73-87.

Bennis, W.B., & Nanus, B. (1985). *Leaders: The strategies of taking charge*. New York: Harper & Row.

Boal, K.B., & Bryson, J.M. (1988). Charismatic leadership: A phenomenological and structural approach. In J.G. Hunt, B.R. Baliga, H.P. Dachler, & C.A. Schriesheim (Eds.), *Emerging leadership vistas* (11-28). Lexington, Mass.: Lexington Books.

Bossert, S., Dwyer, D., Rowan, B., & Lee, G. (1982). The instructional management role of the principal. *Educational Administration Quarterly, 18*(3), 34-63.

Bright, K.L. (1987). *Leadership behaviors of Ohio school superintendents: An examination of district situational demands and perceptions*. Ann Arbor, MI: UMI Dissertation Services.

Bryman, A. (1992). *Charisma and leadership in organizations*. Newbury Park, Cal.: Sage.

Buck, J.T. (1989). *Transformational leadership behaviors of exemplary Texas superintendents*. Ann Arbor, MI: UMI Dissertation Services.

Burns, J.M. (1978). *Leadership*. New York: Harper & Row.

Conger, J.A., & Kanungo, R.N. (1987). Towards a behavioural theory of charismatic leadership in organizational settings. *Academy of Management Review, 12*(4), 637-647.

Cunningham, W.G., & Gresso, D.W. (1993). *Cultural leadership*. Boston: Allyn & Bacon.

Darling, S.K. (1990). *A study to identify and analyse the relationship between (1) transformational leadership and collaboration, and (2) transactional leadership and collaboration in selected Minnesota elementary schools*. Ann Arbor, MI: UMI Dissertation Services.

Deal, T., & Peterson, K. (1990). *The principal's role in shaping school culture*. Washington, D.C.: U.S. Department of Education, Office of Educational Research and Improvement.

Deluga, R.J. (1991). The relationship of leader and subordinate influencing activity in naval environments. *Military Psychology, 3*(1), 25-39.

Downton, J.V. Jr. (1973). *Rebel leadership*. New York: Free Press.

Egan, O., & Archer, P. (1985). The accuracy of teachers' ratings of ability: A regression model. *American Educational Research Journal, 22*(1), 25-34.

Fenstermacher, G.D. (1994). The knower and the known: The nature of knowledge in research on teaching. In L. Darling-Hammond (Ed.), *Review of research in education, volume 20* (pp. 3-56). Washington, D.C.: American Educational Research Association.

Fiedler, F.E., & Garcia, E. (1987). *New approaches to leadership: Cognitive resources and organizational performance*. New York: Wiley.

Fieman-Nemser, S., & Floden, R.E. (1986). The cultures of teaching. In M.C. Wittrock (Ed.), *Handbook of research on teaching* (pp. 505-526). New York: Macmillan.

Finn, J.D. (1989). Withdrawing from school. *Review of Educational Research, 59*(2), 117-143.

Finn, J.D., & Cox, D. (1992). Participation and withdrawal among fourth-grade pupils. *American Educational Research Journal, 29*(1), 141-162.

Genge, M. (1993, June). *The development of transformational leaders: The journeys of male and female secondary school principals, alike or different?* Presented at the annual meeting of the Canadian Association for Studies in Educational Administration, Ottawa.

Halpin, A.W. (1957). The observed leader behaviour and ideal leader behaviour of aircraft commanders and school superintendents. In R.M. Stogdill & A.E. Coons (Eds.), *Leader behaviour: Its description and measurement*. Columbus: Ohio State University, Bureau of Business Research.

Hater, J.J., & Bass, B.M. (1988). Superiors' evaluations and subordinates' perceptions of transformational and transactional leadership. *Journal of Applied Psychology, 73*(4), 695-702.

Heck, R., Marcoulides, G., & Lang, P. (1991). Principal instructional leadership and school achievement: The application of discriminant techniques. *School Effectiveness and School Improvement, 2*(2), 115-135.

Helm, C.M. (1989). *Cultural and symbolic leadership in Catholic elementary schools: An ethnographic study*. Ann Arbor, MI: UMI Dissertation Services.

Hoover, N.R. (1987). *Transformational and transactional leadership: A test of the model*. Ann Arbor, MI: UMI Dissertation Services.

House, R.J., & Mitchell. T.R. (1974). Path-goal theory of leadership. *Journal of Contemporary Business, 3*(4), 81-97.

Howell, J.M., & Avolio, B.J. (1991). *Predicting consolidated unit performance: Leadership ratings, locus of control and support for innovation*. Paper presented at the 51st annual meeting of the Academy of Management, Miami, Florida.

Howell, J.M., & Higgins, C.A. (1990). Champions of technological innovation. *Administrative Science Quarterly, 35*, 317-341.

Hunt, J.G., Baliga, B.R., Dachler, H.P., & Schriesheim, C.A. (1988). *Emerging leadership vistas*. Lexington, MA: Lexington Books.

Jantzi, D., & Leithwood, K. (1994). *The role of gender and age in explaining transformational school leadership*. Toronto: Ontario Institute for Studies in Education, mimeo.

Kendrick, J.A. (1988). *The emergence of transformational leadership practice in a school improvement effort: A reflective study*. Ann Arbor, MI: UMI Dissertation Services.

King, M.I. (1989). *Extraordinary leadership in education: Transformational and transactional leadership as predictors of effectiveness, satisfaction and organizational climate in K-12 and higher education*. Ann Arbor, MI: UMI Dissertation Services.

Kirby, P.C., King, M.I., & Paradise, L.V. (1992). Extraordinary leaders in education: Understanding transformational leadership. *The Journal of Educational Research, 85*(5), 303-311.

Koh, W.L.K. (1990). *An empirical validation of the theory of transformational leadership in secondary schools in Singapore*. Ann Arbor, MI: UMI Dissertation Services.

Kushner, R. (1982). *Action theory congruence and the exercise of transformational leadership in Catholic elementary schools*. Ann Arbor, MI: UMI Dissertation Services.

Lehr, K.A. (1987). *A descriptive study of contemporary transformational leadership*. Ann Arbor, MI: UMI Dissertation Services.

Leithwood, K. (1992). The move towards transformational leadership. *Educational Leadership, 49*(5), 8-12.

Leithwood, K., & Jantzi, D. (1990). Transformational leadership: How principals can help reform school cultures. *School Effectiveness and School Improvement, 1*(4), 249-280.

Leithwood, K., & Steinbach, R. (1991). Indicators of transformational leadership in the everyday problem solving of school administrators. *Journal of Personnel Evaluation in Education, 4*(3), 221-244.

Leithwood, K., & Steinbach, R. (1993). Total quality leadership: Expert thinking plus transformational practice. *Journal of Personnel Evaluation in Education, 7*(4), 311-337.

Leithwood, K., & Steinbach, R. (1994). Expert problem solving: Evidence from school and district leaders. Albany, NY: SUNY Press.

Leithwood, K., Cousins, B., & Gérin-Lajoie, D. (1993). *Years of Transition, times for change: A review and analysis of pilot projects investigating issues in the Transition Years (Volume 2: Explaining Variations in Progress)*. Toronto: Final report of research to the Ontario Ministry of Education.

Leithwood, K., Dart, B., Jantzi, D., & Steinbach, R. (1991). *Building commitment for change: A focus on school leadership (Final report for year two of the research project: Implementing the primary program)*. Prepared for the British Columbia Ministry of Education.

Leithwood, K., Dart, B., Jantzi, D., & Steinbach, R. (1992). *Fostering organizational learning: A study of British Columbia's intermediate developmental site initiatives* (Final report). Victoria, BC: British Columbia Ministry of Education.

Leithwood, K., Dart, B., Jantzi, D., & Steinbach, R. (1993a). *Fostering organizational learning: A study in British Columbia's intermediate developmental sites, 1990-1992 (Final report for year three of the research project: Implementing the Year 2000 policies)*. Prepared for the British Columbia Ministry of Education.

Leithwood, K., Dart, B., Jantzi, D., & Steinbach, R. (1993b). *Building commitment for change and fostering organizational learning: Final report for phase four of the research project: Implementing British Columbia's education policy*. Prepared for the British Columbia Ministry of Education.

Leithwood, K., Jantzi, D., & Dart, B. (1991). *Toward a multi-level conception of policy implementation processes based on commitment strategies*. Paper presented at the Fourth International Congress on School Effectiveness, Cardiff, Wales.

Leithwood, K., Jantzi, D., & Fernandez, A. (1994). Transformational leadership and teachers' commitment to change. In J. Murphy & K. Louis (Eds.) (in press), *Reshaping the principalship*. Newbury Park, Cal.: Corwin Press.

Leithwood, K., Jantzi, D., Silins, H.C., & Dart. B. (1993). Using the appraisal of school leaders as an instrument for school restructuring. *Peabody Journal of Education, 68*(2), 85-109.

Light, R.J., & Pillemer, D.B. (1984). *Summing up: The science of reviewing research*. Cambridge, Mass.: Harvard University Press.

Little, J. (1982). Norms of collegiality and experimentation. *American Educational Research Journal, 19*(3), 325-340.

Mott, P.E. (1972). *The characteristics of effective organizations.* New York: Harper & Row.

Mowday, R., Steers, R., & Porter, L. (1979). The measurement of organizational commitment. *Journal of Vocational Behaviour, 14*, 224-247.

Nanus, B. (1992). *Visionary leadership.* San Francisco: Jossey-Bass.

Nias. J., Southworth, G., & Campbell, P. (1989). *Staff relationships in the primary school.* London: Cassell.

Orr, D.R. (1990). *An expectancy theory investigation of school superintendent job performance.* Ann Arbor, MI: UMI Dissertation Services.

Podsakoff, P.M., MacKenzie, S.B., Moorman, R.H., & Fetter, R. (1990). Transformational leaders' behaviors and their effects on followers' trust in leader, satisfaction, and organizational citizenship behaviors. *Leadership Quarterly, 1*(2), 107-142.

Podsakoff, P.M., Todor, W.D., & Skov, R. (1982). Effect of leader contingent and non-contingent reward and punishment behaviors on subordinate performance and satisfaction. *Academy of Management Journal, 25*(4), 810-821.

Roberts, N.C. (1985). Transforming leadership: A process of collective action. *Human Relations, 38*(11), 1023-1046.

Rosenthal, R. (1984). *Meta-analytic procedures for social research.* Beverly Hills: Sage.

Ross, J. (1994). *A review of research on teacher self-efficacy.* Toronto: Ontario Institute for Studies in Education, mimeo.

Sashkin, M. (1985). *Trainer guide: Leader behavior questionnaire.* Bryn Mawr, PA: Organization Design and Development.

Sashkin, M., & Sashkin, M. (1990, April). *Leadership and culture-building in schools: Quantitative and qualitative understandings.* Paper presented at the annual meeting of the American Educational Research Association, Boston.

Schein, E.H. (1985). *Leadership and organizational culture.* San Francisco: Jossey-Bass.

Seltzer, J., & Bass, B.M. (1990). Transformational leadership: Beyond initiation and consideration. *Journal of Management, 16*(4), 693-703.

Senge, P. (1990). *The fifth discipline: The art and practice of the learning organization.* London: Doubleday.

Silins, H.C. (1992). Effective leadership for school reform. *The Alberta Journal of Educational Research, 4*, 317-334.

Silins, H.C. (1994a). *The relationship between transformational and transactional leadership and school improvement outcomes.* Adelaide: The Flinders University of South Australia.

Silins, H.C. (1994b). *Analysing leadership and its components: What makes the difference?* Adelaide: The Flinders University of South Australia.

Silins, H.C., & Leithwood, K. (1994). *The relative impact of factors influencing student outcomes in the transition years.* Adelaide: The Flinders University of South Australia.

Sims Jr., H.P., & Lorenzi, P. (1992). *The new leadership paradigm: Social learning and cognition in organizations.* Newbury Park, Cal.: Sage.

Singer, M.S. (1985). Transformational vs. transactional leadership: A study of New Zealand company managers. *Psychological Reports, 57*, 143-146.

Singer, M.S., & Singer, A.E. (1986). Relation between transformational vs. transactional leadership preference and subordinates' personality: An exploratory study. *Perceptual and Motor Skills, 62,* 775-780.

Skalbeck, K.L. (1991). *Profile of a transformational leader: A sacred mission.* Ann Arbor, MI: UMI Dissertation Services.

Smith, C.A., Organ, D.W., & Near, J.P. (1983). Organizational citizenship behavior: Its nature and antecedents. *Journal of Applied Psychology, 68,* 653-663.

Smith, F.J. (1976). The index of organizational reaction (IOR). *JSAS catalogue of selected documents in psychology: Volume 6, M.S. No. 1265.*

Smith, J.G. (1989). *The effect of superintendent leader behavior on principal work motivation.* Ann Arbor, MI: UMI Dissertation Services.

Spangler, W.D., & Braiotta, L. (1990). Leadership and corporate audit committee effectiveness. *Group and Organizational Studies, 15*(2), 134-157.

Tichy, N.M., & Devanna, M.A. (1986). *The transformational leader.* New York: John Wiley & Sons.

Vandenburghe, R., & Staessens, K. (1991, April). *Vision as a core component in school culture.* Paper presented at the annual meeting of the American Educational Research Association, Chicago.

Waldman, D.A., Bass, B.M., & Einstein, W.O. (1987). Leadership and outcomes of performance appraisal processes. *Journal of Occupational Psychology, 60*(3), 177-186.

Waldman, D.A., Bass, B.M., & Yammarino, F.J. (1990). Adding to contingent reward behavior: The augmenting effect of charismatic leadership. *Group and Organizational Studies, 15*(4), 381-394.

Weber, M. (1947). *The theory of social and economic organization* (A.M. Henderson & T. Parsons, translators). T. Parsons (Ed.). New York: Free Press.

Webster's Seventh New Collegiate Dictionary (1971). Toronto: Thomas Allen & Sons.

Yammarino, F.J., & Bass, B.M. (1990). Transformational leadership and multiple levels of analysis. *Human Relations, 43*(10), 975-995.

Yukl, G. (1989). *Leadership in organizations* (2nd edition). Englewood Cliffs, N.J.: Prentice-Hall.

Chapter 23: Perception, Prescription, and the Future of School Leadership

DANIEL L. DUKE
University of Virginia

The dilemma is familiar to anyone engaged in the preparation of professionals. Should preparation programs focus on current or anticipated expectations? In many ways, the safer course involves concentrating on what practitioners currently are expected to do. Trying to anticipate future needs invariably entails untested assumptions, inferences, and the risk of error. Continuing to base preparation programs on *current* expectations when those expectations have been found inadequate, of course, is not without risk either. Those in educational administration often deal with the dilemma by hedging their bets and trying to prepare school leaders for today *and* tomorrow, a strategy that sounds far easier than it actually is.

This chapter does not promise a foolproof approach to designing educational administration programs. Rather, it aims

1) to clarify how we try to understand leadership in general and school leadership in particular and
2) to identify a promising alternative conception of future school leadership to guide educational administration programs.

The assumption is that there exist multiple ways for educational administration specialists to make sense of the leadership needs of schools and that how we do so is not always as productive as it could be.

The opening section presents the basic argument – that the conventional tendency to treat leadership as a descriptive concept can be limiting. A case is made for considering the perceptual and prescriptive aspects of leadership. Perceptual aspects entail the perceived need for leadership and the conditions that are offered to justify the perceived need for leadership. Prescriptive aspects involve the expectations associated with addressing the conditions perceived to necessitate leadership.

K. Leithwood et al. (eds.), International Handbook of Educational Leadership and Administration, 841-872.
© 1996 Kluwer Academic Publishers, Printed in the Netherlands.

Subsequent sections apply this alternative perspective to recent reform literature in education and business. Three questions guide the review and analysis:

1. To what extent do reformers agree on the conditions necessitating organizational change?
2. To what extent do reformers agree on the organizational changes to address these conditions?
3. To what extent do reformers agree on the leadership needs of organizations occasioned by these changes?

The chapter closes with a discussion of the implications of the review and analysis for the preparation of school leaders.

UNDERSTANDING LEADERSHIP

How we think about leadership influences how we design and conduct leadership preparation programs. Until recently, leadership has been treated by scholars primarily as a descriptive term (Immegart, 1988). Efforts to understand leadership focused on identifying observable aspects of the phenomenon. Presumed exemplars of leadership, nominated by peers or chosen by researchers using various criteria, were studied in order to isolate key behaviours, functions, and related characteristics. The results of these studies were converted into lists of competencies, proficiencies, and performance standards, which, in turn, guided the preparation, selection, and evaluation of school leaders.

The last few decades have witnessed a modest effort to balance the emphasis on describing leadership with greater understanding of the meanings associated with leadership (Duke, 1986; Leinberger and Tucker, 1991). This effort has been characterized by an interest in leadership as a *perception* (Immegart, 1988, p. 264). Treating leadership as a perception shifted focus from leaders and what they do to observers, including followers, and how they make sense of what leaders do. The frustrating lack of consensus regarding the definition of leadership came to be seen as a natural consequence of the fact that perceptions vary according to individuals' past experiences, current circumstances, and future aspirations. Academic descriptions of leadership seemed to ignore or downplay the variability which characterizes perceptions of leadership in everyday circumstances.

Recently an attempt to extend this thinking has been made by the author (Duke, 1994). The guiding premise is that leadership constitutes a perceived *need* for many, if not most, people. Unlike the needs identified by theorists such as Alderfer (1972), Maslow (1970), and McClelland (1975), however, the focus of the need for leadership resides outside the individual. The need for leadership is associated with external situations and sets of circumstances. As a construct, the *perceived need for leadership* is assumed to vary within and across individuals. For some, the need may be relatively high and relatively constant. Others may perceive a high need for leadership episodically. When direction is clear and commitment is high, for example, the perceived need for leadership may be relatively low (Duke, 1994).

The last observation indicates that the perceived need for leadership requires a companion construct, which might be referred to as *the conditions perceived to necessitate leadership,* or *perceived leadership conditions* for short. A case can be made that leadership cannot be fully understood until the specific conditions under which leadership is perceived to be needed are determined. The perceived need for leadership and perceived leadership conditions make up the *perceptual dimension* of leadership. Studying this dimension of leadership calls for a shift of focus from leaders to followers. This shift is consistent with other recent developments in leadership theory (Rost, 1991, pp. 97-128) and the general increase in interest in symbolic interactionism, constructivism, and critical theory (Schwandt, 1994). Leadership ceases to be solely a matter of mastering a set of general standards or manifesting certain descriptive criteria. Nor does it mean much for leaders themselves to assert that their performance constitutes leadership. Instead, what those in need of or subject to leadership perceive it to be is pertinent. In order to better understand these perceptions of leadership, researchers must identify when individuals perceive the need for leadership to be relatively high or low and determine the specific conditions characterizing these occasions.

To illustrate how the perceptual dimension of leadership can be applied, a review of selected books on education and business reform is undertaken in this chapter. The books were chosen in part because they specified conditions that reformers felt necessitated new forms of organizational leadership. Other selection criteria will be discussed in the next section.

A focus of inquiry in this chapter concerns the extent to which reformers in education and business agree on the conditions that necessitate changes in organizational leadership. If agreement is extensive, those involved in preparing future school leaders would be wise to attend closely to calls for reform. On the other hand, if perceptions of the need for new leadership and leadership conditions vary widely, a more cautious response might be better.

Deborah Stone (1989) offers a useful way to think about any set of conditions invoked to justify action. Advocates for action, she maintains, develop *causal stories* based on attributions of cause, blame, and responsibility. The conditions cited to necessitate action possess no inherent properties that make them 'more or less likely to be seen as problems' (p. 282). Advocates, in other words, deliberately portray conditions in ways calculated to generate support for their position.

How have advocates of new types of school and business leadership constructed their causal stories? Have they deliberately focused on certain conditions and ignored others? Are the conditions predicted to face tomorrow's schools similar to those for tomorrow's businesses? Some tentative answers to these and related questions will be found in the next section.

The second major aspect of leadership that will guide this review and analysis concerns prescriptions for future leaders. Once education and business reformers identify conditions perceived to be problematic, they typically prescribe changes in organizations and organizational leadership.

The prescriptive aspect of leadership embodies speculation, dreams, values, and sometimes a dose of pragmatism. There can be no such thing as certainty, of course, when individuals a set of predicted conditions. Only time will tell whether particular prescriptions are valid. For present purposes, the task is to assess the extent to which prescriptions for changes in organizations and organizational leadership are similar across selected examples of education and business reform literature. It is possible, for example, that reformers agree on the conditions necessitating change, but not on the prescribed changes themselves. Conversely, they may disagree on leadership conditions, but concur on prescriptions for leadership.

Before beginning the review, a few words about the selection of reform documents are in order. First, only books published since the beginning of 1990 were examined. Second, each book had to include

1) a set of conditions perceived by the author or authors to necessitate changes in organizational structure and leadership and

2) specific recommendations for organizational change and changes in organizational leadership.

A list of books was compiled through nominations by professors of education and business and an extensive search of the literature.[1] The books listed below represent, in the author's judgment, a representative sample of recent books dealing with the reform of education and business:

Educational Reform Books
- Brian J. Caldwell and Jim M. Spinks, *Leading the Self-Managing School.* London: Falmer, 1992.
- Louis V. Gerstner, Jr., *Reinventing Education.* New York: Dutton, 1994.
- Ray Marshall and Marc Tucker. *Thinking for a Living: Education and the Wealth of Nations.* New York: Basic Books, 1992.
- David Osborne and Ted Gaebler, *Reinventing Government.* New York: Plume, 1993.
- Theodore R. Sizer, *Horace's School.* Boston: Houghton Mifflin, 1992.

Business Reform Books
- Joseph H. Boyett and Henry P. Conn, *Workplace 2000: The Revolution Reshaping American Business.* New York: Plume, 1992.
- Peter R. Drucker, *Management for the Future.* New York: Penguin Books, 1992.
- Charles Handy, *The Age of Unreason.* Boston: Harvard Business School Press, 1990.
- Paul Leinberger and Bruce Tucker, *The New Individualists.* New York: Harper Collins, 1991.
- Peter M. Senge, *The Fifth Discipline.* New York: Doubleday Currency, 1990.

The books share other similarities besides those associated with the original selection criteria. With the exception of *The New Individualists*, none is based on systematic empirical investigation. Most of the books combine secondary analysis of current literature, descriptions of promising innovations, and straightforward reform advocacy. Another similarity is that the authors tend to be outsiders. In other words, at the time of writing they were not practitioners in the organizations they sought to reform. The authors represent business and education professors, consultants, and researchers. Louis Gerstner, the chairman and

CEO of IBM, writes about reforming public schools, not private industry. Only Jim Spinks is the head of a school.

THE NEED FOR CHANGE

The prescriptions for new schools and businesses contained in the ten recent reform books are premised on perceptions of changing conditions. These perceptions are woven into causal stories which, for the most part, are strikingly similar. Not surprisingly, economic changes serve to justify recommendations for reform in business. Less predictably, all but one of the educational reform authors construct causal stories based, in part, on changes in the economy. Sizer, alone of all the reformers, chooses to justify the need for educational change without directly invoking economic reasons.

This section highlights several general conditions perceived by most of the authors to warrant new organizations and forms of organizational leadership. Where differences in perceptions of precipitating conditions arise, they are noted. The section closes with a consideration of whether or not a 'standard' causal story currently exists to legitimize the need for changes in schools and business.

A case can be made that most of the ten books on business and education reform would not have been written if Americans still enjoyed the relatively high standard of living that characterized the fifties and sixties. The primary impetus for the five business reform books and three of the five education reform books are the twin perceptions that the economic base for Americans already has slipped and that it will continue to erode unless efforts are made to adjust to new economic realities.[2]

A variety of reasons are offered for why the economy slipped in the first place. Drucker (1992, p. 29) blames the basic assumptions undergirding prevailing economic theory. Marshall and Tucker (1992, pp. xiv-xv) observe that productivity began to level off and was surpassed by consumption. Boyett and Conn (1992, pp. 12-16) contend that the quality of goods and services deteriorated. Most of the authors devote relatively little space, however, to past problems, preferring to concentrate on current conditions that demand new thinking about organizations.

The advent of global competition is cited by every author except Sizer. Drucker (1992, p. 95), Handy (1990, pp. 52-53), and Leinberger and Tucker, 1991, p. 334) note a basic shift from manufacturing to service, a shift which increases the importance of information. As the number of jobs requiring relatively menial skills shrinks, workers must be more adept at acquiring and processing knowledge (Caldwell and Spinks, 1992, pp. 7-8; Drucker, 1992, pp. 131-133; Handy, 1990, p. 34). Handy (1990, pp. 87-115) further points out that the character of the workforce itself is changing, as full-time employment and job security declines and part-time employment increases.

While most of the authors perceive that changing economic conditions constitute the primary justification for changes in organizations and organizational leadership, they vary somewhat in their emphases concerning secondary conditions. For example, Leinberger and Tucker (1991) conclude, after investigating the offspring of William H. White's 'organization men,' that today's workers are less disposed to follow organizational leaders (p. 410), owe their loyalty to an organization (p. 398), or derive their primary identity from their job (p. 350). They also find that workers desire more individual responsibility than did their predecessors (p. 404).

Several authors argue that changing beliefs in society-at-large have influenced economic changes. Drucker (1992, p. 21) cites the relatively recent idea, bolstered by the courts, that a job is a property right. Marshall and Tucker (1992, p. xiii) maintain that society no longer believes that only a few people need to know a lot in order for all to do relatively well.

Most authors link economic change with new technology, including the widespread use of computers (Boyett and Conn, 1992, p. 2; Gerstner, 1993, p. 4), telecommunications (Caldwell and Spinks, 1992, pp. 7-8; Handy, 1990, p. 104), and advances in other forms of information processing (Leinberger and Tucker, 1991, p. 332). Among other things, these changes are forcing people to rethink the definition of an organization. Work and study, for example, no longer must be confined to a workplace or school.

Public schools are blamed for contributing to economic slippage at the same time they are perceived to be keys to economic growth. Boyett and Conn (1992, pp. 273-275), Caldwell and Spinks (1992), and Osborne and Gaebler (1992, p. 1) maintain that most schools are not matched to the needs of the new economy. Educational expectations are indicted for being too modest (Gerstner, 1994, p. 8; Marshall and Tucker, 1992, p. 82; Sizer, 1992, p. 144). The issue is not whether large numbers of underachieving students can be helped to meet current expectations, but how to raise expectations – and subsequently achievement – for *all* students. Schools are perceived to have placed the economy at risk because they fail to meet the diverse needs of young people, particularly those from poor backgrounds (Gerstner, 1994, p. 6). The fault may not rest with the schools alone, though. Several authors point to the abundance of government regulations that constrain educators and frustrate local initiative (Gerstner, 1994, p. 19; Marshall and Tucker, 1992, p. 86; Osborne and Gaebler, 1992, pp. 314-319).

What, then, can be said about the conditions perceived by reformers to justify the need for organizational change? Is there agreement on a modal causal story? Do reformers writing about the needs of business and education share similar perspectives?

All of the authors, with the exception of Sizer, agree on the broad conditions necessitating change. Their causal stories recognize that the world economy is changing and that schools in the U.S. have been slow to adjust. Furthermore, they assume that schools *should* adjust – that a key function of schools, in other words, is to support economic development. Mass production – in business and education – may have been sufficient in the past, but this strategy is incapable of coping with the rapid changes and diverse needs characterizing today's world. The convergence of perceptions concerning the need for change suggests that the lines separating the private and public sectors may be blurring. This idea will be explored again in the upcoming sections on prescriptions for change.

Alone of the ten books, Sizer's *Horace's School* justifies the need for change solely on non-economic grounds. The basis of Sizer's argument is that schools can be better than they are. Among the reasons for their lack of success is confusion regarding purpose, a problem that permits means – such as tests – to become ends (p. 11). Sizer also indicts the inefficient bureaucracies that run schools, adults' underestimation of the abilities of most students, and rampant mistrust at all levels.

In one regard, interestingly, all ten accounts agree on one condition justifying change. Inadequate or misguided leadership is noted by every author as a key to problems in business and education. Of equal interest is the fact, to be examined later, that leadership is prescribed by all authors as one of, if not the, key to resolving these problems. The abiding faith that answers to major social, educational, and economic problems rest with leadership remains a hallmark, it seems, of Western thought.

Before concluding this analysis of the perceptual dimension of leadership, it may be useful to consider some of the conditions that the authors do not address. Most of the authors say little or nothing about crime, school violence, unethical conduct by leaders, escalating racism, or social unrest in general. They neither stress that these conditions are currently important or suggest that they are likely to continue. Are the reformers naive, misinformed, or simply confident that economic and educational improvements will restore civility and order? They may need to consider the possibility that improvements in schools and businesses actually are contingent on increased public safety, interpersonal sensitivity, ethical behaviour, and social justice, rather than prerequisites.

R$_X$ FOR NEW SCHOOLS AND BUSINESSES

Each of the ten books offer recommendations on how to reform, restructure, and reinvent schools and businesses. In this section, these prescriptions are reviewed to determine whether agreement exists concerning the desired characteristics of tomorrow's organizations. Specific recommendations are clustered into seven areas:
  – Greater focus and direction
  – Greater market sensitivity
  – Reduced size and scale of operations
  – Flatter structure
  – Greater participation
  – Reduced control orientation
  – Increased complexity of relationships

Greater focus and direction

Although the suggestion is made in different ways, each reformer insists that tomorrow's organization, to be successful, must possess a clear mission. All point out that one organization cannot be all things to all people. Lack of focus and clear direction is stressed particularly by those urging school reform. Marshall and Tucker (1992, p. 118) point out, for example, that most school systems are not mission-driven because they 'are managed to respond to ever-changing pressures from an endless round of unanticipated quarters, in no particular order.' Gerstner (1994, p. 67) adds that, except 'in the most vague and inconclusive way, public schools have failed to specify their goals.'

In some cases it is difficult to determine whether the reformers are more disturbed by the schools' lack of focus or their particular focus. Marshall and Tucker (1992, p. 144) observe, in this regard, that American schools have standards for student achievement, but that the standards are too low. Later, they contend that the real problem concerns the fact that schools are guided by input rather than outcome standards (p. 144). Most of the reformers agree that the mission of schools should be linked directly to student outcomes.

Consensus regarding how student outcomes should be determined does not exist. Gerstner (1994, p. 67) maintains that the 'most important decision a school community makes is what to teach.' Marshall and Tucker (1992, p. 112) echo this view when they indicate that the first step in school restructuring involves communities achieving clarity about what students are expected to know and be able to do when they graduate from high school. Caldwell and Spinks (1992, p. 7), on the other hand, see goals and standards increasingly set by 'central authorities.' Osborne and Gaebler (1993, p. 316) contend that state governments and school boards will 'steer the system but let others row.' They explain that these bodies will set minimum standards, measure performance, and enforce broad goals related to racial integration and social equity.

Greater market sensitivity

Business and education reformers agree that sensitivity to customers' needs is critical to the success of tomorrow's organization, be it public or private. Except for Sizer, who does not address the issue, all the reformers invest faith in the market as the most appropriate mechanism for protecting consumer interests. They tend to oppose government regulations that interfere with the ability of organizations to respond to the market, though the education reformers, again with the exception of Sizer, acknowledge that some protections are needed for traditionally disadvantaged groups.

Markets, in their purest form, offer customers a variety of choices. Most of the reformers endorse the idea of choice, arguing in the case of schools that parents should be able to choose where children attend and their programs of study. They believe that most parents will choose wisely, opting for schools with successful track records rather than those that merely are conveniently located. Gerstner (1994, p. 46) points out that 'customer satisfaction' is the ultimate criterion for judging accountability. He then proceeds to list as customers of schools students, parents, employers, and taxpayers in general. The IBM executive fails to indicate how schools should proceed when some customers are satisfied and others are not. Employers and taxpayers, after all, do not choose schools in the same sense that parents and students do.

In order for parents to make sound choices, they must have access to timely and accurate information concerning school outcomes. The reformers are split, however, on the matter of who should collect and distribute this information. Some believe these tasks best can be undertaken by individual schools. Others argue for government involvement to ensure that data are accurate and accessible to all.

Taken literally, these recommendations may mean the end of the comprehensive school. Schools are unlikely to develop a clear and focused mission and also address all the needs of a diverse constituency. Osborne and Gaebler (1993, p. 131) recognize this dilemma when they state:

> Public organizations work best when they have *one* clear mission. Unfortunately, governments tend to load several different – and often conflicting – missions on each agency as the years go by.

The only possible course of action, they contend, is to break up large organizations into smaller ones, thereby allowing each to specialize and develop a market 'niche.' This suggestion leads to the third area of organizational change.

Reduced size and scale of operations

Business and education reformers agree that the era of large organizations is coming to an end. In the private sector, serious questions have been raised about the efficiency of vertical integration (Handy, 1990, p. 117; Leinberger and Tucker, 1991, p. 343). Productivity and quality can be increased and costs lowered through outsourcing and sub-contracting (Boyett and Conn, 1992, p. 2; Drucker, 1992, p. 127; Handy, 1990, p. 213). Handy (1990, p. 117) sees the huge corporation of the past being replaced by federal-style alliances of smaller, more specialized organizations, while Leinberger and Tucker (1991, p. 334) note the rise of 'network' organizations.

Education reformers voice concern over size as well. Sizer (1992, p. 4), for instance, points out that schools cannot be as effective when teachers and administrators do not know all their students. Smaller schools make it easier for teachers and students to feel a sense of 'ownership' and responsibility. Caldwell and Spinks (1992, pp. 7-8), along with Sizer (1992, p. 187), envision more outsourcing and sub-contracting as schools scale back on services. Smaller schools mean smaller staffs, thereby reducing the supervisory load for administrators and enhancing coordination.

Flatter structure

The 'downsizing' of organizations is accompanied by flatter organizational structures. Multiple layers of supervisors and managers are less necessary. Boyett and Conn (1992, p. 3) observe that this 'thinning' process eliminates many opportunities for career advancement. Those who used to seek job improvement through promotion to administrative positions increasingly will advance only by starting their own businesses, either as adjuncts to existing organizations or apart from them. This return to 'entrepreneurialism' is not limited to the private sector, either. Witness the current interest in charter schools and schools-within-schools (Gerstner, 1994, pp.54-55).

As organizations shrink, role structure changes. The lines traditionally separating workers and managers blur (Sizer, 1992, p. 208). Flattened hierarchies mean that status is less likely to derive from an individual's position in the hierarchy (Boyett and Conn, 1992, p. 5; Leinberger and Tucker, 1991, p. 404). Leinberger and Tucker (1991, p. 350) conclude that 'one's identity is defined less by a job description, as in the old bureaucratic ideal, than by one's relation at any given moment to groups and people inside and outside the organization whose identities are similarly shifting.'

School districts, of course, rarely are as hierarchical as large private corporations, but the prescription to reduce bureaucratic layers nonetheless is being applied to them as well. As central office managers and supervisors disappear, teachers and building administrators are expected to assume greater leadership. These new expectations extend to decision making and governance.

Greater participation

Decentralization of authority is one of the hallmarks of recent reform in business and education. It means that individuals who used to have little to say about organizational goals, governance, and policies now are expected to share their feelings.

Every reformer supports shared decision making, though they do not always specify exactly which individuals and groups should be involved or the specific types of decisions to be shared. The education reformers for the most part prescribe greater teacher and community participation, but student involvement is not stressed. Marshall and Tucker (1992, p. 112) and Gerstner (1993, p. 85) believe the community should help determine what students learn. They do not indicate what role teachers should play in the process. Osborne and Gaebler (1993, p. 3) are insistent that budget decisions be pushed down to the lowest levels, but they fail to state who should make them or how.

A resounding rejection of most centrally dictated policies appears to be the point about which the reformers are most clear. They express faith that the people in the 'front lines' are more likely than central bureaucrats to understand resource needs and how to resolve operating problems. What the reformers neglect is the possibility that those in the front lines may disagree. For example, little is written about what to do when parents and/or professionals disagree over instructional decisions and resource issues. In a pure market, service providers make decisions of this kind and customers either accept or reject the consequences. Most of the education reformers, however, admit that public education cannot become a pure market, since certain safeguards for particular groups of at-risk students are likely to be necessary.

Reduced control orientation

The traditional approach to organizations held that control mechanisms were necessary to prevent employees from neglecting organization goals and concentrating on their own self-interest. Reformers in business and education agree that too heavy an emphasis on control can be counter-productive. Senge (1990, p. 290) suggests that the very idea of any central leader being 'in control' is – and has been – more illusion than reality. Sizer (1992, p. 89) poses a blunt question:

> Could there be an American education policy founded on the idea that everyone meant well and could be counted on? Continuing to assume the opposite will surely be costly. Everyone will be testing everyone else. The prospect is ugly. Schools filled with such distrust – such disrespect – are hardly places in which to educate decent, thoughtful adolescents.

In place of classical control mechanisms such as direct supervision and evaluation based on compliance with rules and regulations, Gerstner (1993, pp. 84-87), Marshall and Tucker (1992, pp. 126-127) and Osborne and Gaebler (1993, p. 111) see greater emphasis on outcomes, including linking incentives to outcomes. Gerstner also specifies that failure to achieve outcomes should be penalized. In a sense, though, penalties may be redundant in the market model advocated by most reformers. Schools that fail to satisfy their customers, after all, would face the prospect of going out of business.

Giving up traditional forms of supervision and evaluation does not mean that tomorrow's organizations will be free of feedback. Boyett and Conn (1992, pp. 4-5), for example, indicate that sharing information on performance is critical to success. Senge (1990, pp. 139-173) adds that organizations improve only to the extent that individuals within them are provided opportunities to reflect on and improve performance.

While new organizations will be characterized by less managerial control, they may not be entirely free of control. Boyett and Conn (1992, pp. 6-7) see employees exercising more peer control and self-control. Sizer (1992, p. 188) anticipates professional cultures where teachers engage in various forms of collective accountability. Handy (1990, p. 214) predicts that every student (or parent) will sign a contract, specifying learning outcomes and strategies for achieving them, with his or her school.

Increased complexity of relationships

Relationships are always complicated, but in the past organizations attempted to reduce complexity through such mechanisms as job descriptions, organization charts with clear lines of authority, specialization, and standardization. The watchwords of the new organization, however, are flexibility, team work, and networks. Complexity of relationships is accepted as part of the territory.

Leinberger and Tucker (1991, p. 334) observe that organizational life increasingly means 'the dissolving of departments in favour of teams across functions, and the ad hoc creation of small, flexible groups to accomplish specific tasks.' They go on to point out that the emerging model of the organization resembles a network with 'constantly shifting nodes of power and influence, often geographically distant from each other, but tightly linked by communications.' Handy (1990, pp. 90-101) describes this new model as a 'shamrock organization' made up of a small, core group of mostly professional workers employed on a full-time basis, a flexible labour force of part-time and temporary workers, and various sub-contractors to whom much of the organization's work is outsourced.

New organizational configurations require that people relate to each other in new ways (Marshall and Tucker, 1992, p. 111). Information cannot be jealously guarded as a source of power, as it tended to be in the past. Instead, information must be shared in ways that promote the mission of the organization and foster collaboration (Boyett and Conn, 1992, pp. 4-5). When necessary information is missing, members of organizations will be expected to discover it. Emphasis on team learning is increasing (Senge, 1990, pp. 233-269). Most of the reformers insist that a major focus of activity in the new organization will be group inquiry and collaborative professional development (Boyett and Conn, 1992, p. 8; Drucker, 1992, pp. 335-336; Gerstner, 1994, pp. 126-127; Handy, 1990, pp. 55-76; Marshall and Tucker, 1992, pp. 126-127). Traditional hierarchical relations are regarded as incompatible with organizational learning.

Relations are changing not only within organizations, but between organizations and their external environments. Once again, greater complexity characterizes the change. Organizations are forming partnerships, informal networks, and temporary alliances (Drucker, 1992, p. 16; Handy, 1990, p. 117; Leinberger and Tucker, 1991, p. 347). For schools, the most important partnerships will continue to be those with parents. Gerstner (1994, p. 80) maintains that 'the well-run school will find that parents are frequently in classrooms, just as teachers are in homes.' Teachers who have grown accustomed to relating primarily to students and fellow teachers must learn to collaborate with parents. The key to the new and more complex relationships will be trust (Sizer, 1992, p. 188). If satisfying customers is the driving force behind tomorrow's school, educators must stop acting as if pleasing politicians and policy makers is their highest priority (Osborne and Gaebler, 1993, p. 20).

THE CHANGING CONCEPT OF ORGANIZATIONAL LEADERSHIP

The preceding prescriptions for new organizations necessitate a new type of leadership, claim the reformers. This section examines their leadership recommendations to determine if some agreement exists across the business and education literature. If actual changes in school leadership result from the current ferment, they are most likely to be those on which reformers tend to agree. That thinking about school leadership may be shaped by people outside the educational administration community, of course, is not a new development. Funk and Brown (1993), Murphy (1992), and Tyack and Hansot (1982) make the case that non-educators long have influenced prevailing notions of school leadership.

While each of the ten reform documents envisions organizational leadership in a somewhat different way, they share many similarities. These common features have been clustered into five dimensions of emerging organizational leadership: accountability, entrepreneurship, empowerment, organization culture, and development. Each dimension will be described and its implications for school leadership discussed.

The accountability dimension

The link between leadership and accountability is hardly new. What is changing, however, is the basis upon which judgments of accountability are made. Organizational leaders have been criticized for holding employees accountable for compliance with rules and regulations rather than customer satisfaction and product quality. Oversight concentrated on inputs instead of outcomes (Osborne and Gaebler, 1993, p. 316). Business and education reformers agree that tomorrow's leaders will be held accountable for 'results' and that they, in turn, will hold employees accountable for 'results.' Desired results will be embodied in mission statements, performance standards, and lists of goals and objectives.

The first obligation of future school leaders will be to see that intended outcomes are specified. They will not begin from scratch, however. President Clinton's Goals 2000 initiative and efforts by states and subject matter groups to identify what all students should know are providing parameters within which to work. Some reformers insist that the local community also must play a role in determining intended learning outcomes. Sizer (1992, p. 166) sees a clear role for teachers as well. With various groups becoming involved in setting the direction for schools, school leaders likely will have to ensure that disagreements are resolved and consensus regarding outcomes is forged and maintained.

Consensus in public education frequently is achieved through the politics of accommodation. To ensure the broadest base of support, efforts are made to address everyone's preferences. Schools have been criticized for being overly-accommodating – for undertaking too many goals and trying to please too many people. Osborne and Gaebler (1993, p. 131) insist that public organizations function best when they have a single mission. School leaders will be expected to ensure that intended outcomes are focused and compatible. This task may become somewhat easier as schools downsize and opportunities for parents to choose schools expand. Whether a meaningful commitment to diversity can be sustained in the face of choice, downsizing, and mission narrowing is unclear.

While school outcomes should be realistic, they also should be challenging. Marshall and Tucker (1992, p. 109) contend that a 'truly good school would be one that graduated students who are more successful than would be predicted by their social class.' Low expectations are offered as an explanation for the disappointing school experiences of poor and minority students. Raising expectations to the levels to which middle class students are held accountable no longer is sufficient, however. Marshall and Tucker (1992, p. 101) maintain that schools must follow the example of business and set 'benchmarks' based on the outcomes of the most successful schools. This process may require looking abroad at the achievement of students in high-performing school systems. School leaders will be expected to monitor the best schools and adjust their own schools' outcome targets accordingly.

Mission statements, performance standards, goals, and outcomes are of little value, of course, if stakeholders are unaware of them. Consequently, school leaders will be expected to apprise teachers, other staff members, parents, and students of what they are expected to accomplish. Such a task cannot be undertaken episodically. Schools, after all, receive a steady flow of newcomers. These individuals should not have to wait to discover what they are expected to know and do. Awareness of intended outcomes requires the continuous sharing of information.

Outcomes also are of little benefit if stakeholders do not know the extent to which they are being achieved. As Gerstner (1994, p. 103) argues,

By itself, however, the process of setting goals can become an empty exercise, unless it is backed up by an explicit plan for action, a set of benchmarks of progress, and a system of measuring progress toward these goals.

Recommendations concerning the best ways to assess progress vary among reformers as well as within the educational research community. The role of high-stakes standardized testing continues to be debated. Sizer (1992, pp. 82-101) makes the case that the application of knowledge is the ultimate manifestation of learning. He advocates the use of school-based exhibitions requiring students to integrate knowledge from various subject matter areas as they tackle projects and problems. Reaching agreement concerning how best to determine student progress may be one of the greatest challenges facing future school leaders.

One aspect of the accountability dimension about which most of the reformers agree involves rewards. It is assumed that an effective way to ensure that designated outcomes are achieved is through the use of performance incentives. School leaders will be expected to manage these incentives, determining which staff members hit the target and which do not (Gerstner, 1994, pp. 84-87; Marshall and Tucker, 1992, pp. 110-111). Reformers do not agree about how to handle those who miss the mark.

The implications of the accountability dimension for the role of principal are substantial. Much more time will have to be spent dealing with school mission, standards, goals, and outcomes than currently is the case in many schools. Some of this time can be purchased with savings from the areas of conventional supervision and evaluation. None of the education reformers suggest that the current emphasis on classroom observations, pre- and post-observation conferences, and end-of-the-year evaluation write-ups should continue. What teachers do on a day-to-day basis in classrooms is displaced in importance by what their students achieve. Emphasis on instructional leadership is shifting to assessment leadership. Tomorrow's principal will concentrate on ends rather than means.

The entrepreneurial dimension

It comes as no surprise that business reformers are calling on executives to recapture the spirit of entrepreneurship that presumably led to economic greatness in the first place. What is unexpected is the call by education reformers for school leaders to become more entrepreneurial. This recommendation is based on the assumption, acknowledged by all the education reformers except Sizer, that competition increasingly will characterize public schooling. Osborne and Gaebler (1993, p. 19), in fact, see governments actually encouraging competition throughout the public sector in order to provide citizens with greater choice and promote better quality at a lower price. Gerstner (1994, p. 48) insists that the 'poor and dispossessed, no less than their more fortunate neighbours, should have a moral right to choose....'

What will it mean for school leaders to conduct themselves in a more entrepreneurial manner? First of all, they must make it their business to know their customers, particularly parents and students. No longer will school leaders be able to survive by focusing on the wants of politicians and policy makers. Since it is unlikely that a knowledge of customers' wants can be obtained simply by remaining at school, school leaders must spend more time in their communities, getting to know parents and other patrons. They must adopt a new mindset, one that recognizes that growing numbers of customers have a choice.

Schools leaders also must know their competition. No longer blessed with a largely captive clientele, future school leaders will need to monitor enrolment patterns and programs in nearby schools. Like tuition-driven private schools, public schools increasingly will depend on attracting students to generate operating revenue.

It is likely that much of the responsibility for student recruitment will be assumed by school leaders. They must acquire marketing skills and learn to develop school plans. Programs will have to be developed from time to time to attract new groups of students. While school leaders may not actually draft plans for these new programs, they undoubtedly will have to coordinate program development and implementation. Programs that fail to meet the needs of students will have to be revised or replaced.

Most of the reformers admit that no one program can be expected to meet the needs of all students. In some cases programs may be well-conceived, but poorly matched to particular students. Ensuring that students are placed in appropriate programs will be one of the most important functions of tomorrow's school leader (Caldwell and Spinks, 1992, p. 201). Monitoring placements will necessitate sensitivity to customer needs on the part of all school employees. When information on inappropriate placements is concealed to protect program enrolment, everyone eventually suffers.

Earlier it was indicated that schools increasingly will employ outside service providers to handle highly specialized needs. School leaders must be able to identify and evaluate service providers and promote competition among them. Developing and monitoring contracts for services doubtless will become part of the new leader's duties as well.

To say that the emerging entrepreneurial dimension of school leadership represents a change for principals is to risk understatement. Traditionally principals were not expected to, nor did they need to, 'sell' their school. Assured of students, they were free to focus on matters other than recruitment and monitoring the competition. Declining enrolment and fiscal retrenchment in the seventies and eighties gave some principals, particularly those in urban school systems, a taste of what to expect. The advent of open enrolment plans, magnet schools, charter schools, and modified voucher plans is increasing competition both within public school systems and between public and private schools. With increased competition comes the necessity of anticipating student needs and preventing problems before they arise. School choice means that parents no longer have to wait for problems to be resolved.

It is only fair to point out that entrepreneurialism entails risks as well as benefits. While the reformers largely are silent on this issue, school leaders must recognize that anticipating student needs and preventing problems before they arise are hardly foolproof endeavours. Leaders may anticipate needs incorrectly or raise anxieties unnecessarily by trying to deal with problems before they arise. In addition, customers rarely share the same needs and desires. In some instances, efforts to please certain parents may guarantee the displeasure of other parents. School leaders in large urban areas may enjoy the luxury of specializing in meeting the needs of particular students, but such a strategy could be disastrous in a small town or rural area.

The empowerment dimension

In the downsized and decentralized world of organizations envisioned by the reformers, organization leaders will not be subject to the micromanagerial whims of chief executives and their lieutenants. They will not be completely free, however, to run their organizations as they wish. The reformers all see a growing demand on the part of employees, customers, and patrons to be involved in organizational decision making.

Caldwell and Spinks (1992, p. 203) predict the expansion of 'self-managing schools' in which principals become leaders of leaders. In their view, the key to empowerment is revising 'structures' and 'processes' in order to disperse leadership throughout the school. Gerstner (1994, pp. 134-135) likewise regards teacher leaders as an important element of tomorrow's schools. These individuals, in his view, will model the philosophies and techniques embodied in the school's mission. High schools will be sub-divided into houses, according to Sizer (1992, pp. 164-165). Each house will consist of a team of teachers and a teacher leader who together handle decisions concerning scheduling, student assignments, and how to meet curriculum standards. Osborne and Gaebler (1993, p. 316) expect a growing number of alternative schools to be created and run by small groups of teachers.

Teachers are not the only beneficiaries of empowerment. Most of the education reformers call for a greater role in school decision making for parents. School leaders are expected to provide opportunities for involvement and make sure parents are notified of such opportunities.

For the most part the education reformers fail to specify the kinds of decisions that will be made by teachers and parents or whether principals will have veto power. Opportunities for shared decision making, of course, also are opportunities for conflict and disagreement, a point virtually ignored in the reform literature. What should school leaders do when teachers and parents are unable to agree on school mission, learning outcomes, personnel matters, or the allocation of resources? As was the case with the entrepreneurial dimension, the assumption seems to be that the market will resolve problems. When shared decision making produces dissensus, individuals presumably will be free to choose other schools, form their own, or engage in internal competition within schools. Boyd (1992, p. 521) warns, though, that competition within organizations may be inferior to collaboration as a basis for activity. The market, in other words, has its limits.

Little in the current training of principals prepares them to promote empowerment, manage conflict, or cultivate staff leaders. Furthermore, as teacher leadership expands, the lines between principals and teachers are expected to blur. Questions may be raised, therefore, about the source of authority for tomorrow's principals. If they cannot rely as heavily on their instructional expertise, power to command and control, and decision making responsibilities, upon what bases is their leadership to rest? Will principals continue to be held personally accountable for school performance or will new forms of collective accountability – more compatible with the spirit of empowerment – be developed?

The cultural dimension

A growing number of students of organizations are recognizing that organizations encompass distinctive cultures characterized by norms, shared beliefs, and collective aspirations. Most of the reformers address the part leaders play in shaping organizational culture. Specifically, they see a need for tomorrow's leaders to nourish cultures that promote teamwork and continuous improvement.

Handy (1990, p. 143), for example, explains that a 'collegiate culture of colleagues' is necessary because organizations no longer can rely on command-and-control. Shared understanding is the only way to make things happen, he maintains. In the past, organizational leaders may have talked as if teamwork were important, but too often individual loyalty and seniority were the primary bases for rewards. Teamwork thrives, however, in organizations where employees perceive that cooperation is truly valued.

Teamwork also is more likely to be found where leaders inspire employees to commit to causes greater than their own self-interest. Vision can be a powerful tool in this regard. Of vision, Boyett and Conn (1992, p. 147) note that it must be 'so inspirational [that] followers will voluntarily suspend rational judgement about the probability of success.' Vision keeps people focused on the horizon, rather than on the next step, thereby reducing the likelihood that they become mired in day-to-day problems. Vision also may help people maintain a sense of the 'whole' amidst the increasing decentralization likely to characterize future organizations (Handy, 1990, p. 113).

A vision, no matter how potent, is unlikely to inspire if followers distrust leaders. Boyett and Conn (1992, p. 154) believe that the new organizational leader must devote time and energy to trust-building, a process combining the talents of the magician and the preacher. That vision development and the promotion of teamwork can be daunting tasks is captured in the following observation by Leinberger and Tucker (1991, p. 397):

> As difficult as it is to understand changes in market forces, effectively track demographic and social trends, manage fast-track product cycles and incorporate the latest in technological

advances, it is far more difficult to inspire commitment, create a sustainable vision, and encourage self-management and autonomous work teams.

School cultures, of course, have not always been known to stress the importance of teamwork. The common image of a school is of individual teachers isolated in classrooms, scheduled too tightly to collaborate or function in teams. In their speculation on the school of the future, the education reformers envision that teacher isolation will be reduced partly as a result of greater emphasis on continuous improvement. They see professional and organizational development becoming basic expectations. More will be said of these matters in the next section.

Traditionally school cultures emphasized rules and regulations. There was a right and a wrong way to do just about everything. The school of the future will focus, instead, on teaching and learning. To reinforce the importance of teaching and learning, school leaders will be expected to employ rituals, recognition, and informal incentives. Building new cultures also may require changing people's attitudes, values, and ways of relating to each other (Marshall and Tucker, 1992, p. 111). It is probably safe to conclude that many of today's school leaders have received little or no training in how to effect such changes.

The developmental dimension

As organizational cultures inculcate the expectation of continuous improvement, leaders will need to play an active role coordinating growth activities. Most of the reformers point out the importance of linking these activities to organizational mission. Where schools are concerned, such linkages will mean a merging of organizational development and professional development. The shift in focus from compliance with rules and regulations to performance and outcomes is expected to encourage employees to take risks, generally regarded as a key element in growth.

Risk-taking may be a key to growth, but support is vital to risk-taking. School leaders will need to function less as supervisors and more as facilitators and teachers (Sizer, 1992, p. 166). If they expect teachers to commit to continuous improvement, school leaders also must make a similar commitment. By modelling openness to performance feedback, curiosity concerning ways to increase personal and organizational effectiveness, and a willingness to listen to and learn from others, school leaders can help create a climate conducive to growth. The ability to challenge 'sacred' assumptions without demeaning those who hold them also can be an important spur to professional and organizational development.

Senge (1990, p. 345) contends that the developmental dimension of organizational leadership entails a design function:

> In essence, the leaders' task is designing the learning processes whereby people throughout the organization can deal productively with the critical issues they face, and develop their mastery in the learning disciplines.

Senge goes on to explain that today's leaders may not be well-equipped for this task, since they probably were chosen for leadership roles for reasons other than their 'skills in mentoring, coaching, and helping others learn.'

Another aspect of the developmental dimension involves resources. Employee growth requires time, training, and materials. Securing resources for growth is not always easy, particularly in financially strapped public school systems. School leaders may have to undertake advocacy for growth resources in the community and elsewhere. Marshall and Tucker (1992, p. 127) recommend that an amount equal to four percent of annual salaries and wages be reserved for the continuing education of school staff members. Few school systems currently have access to such resources.

As in the case of the other four dimensions, the developmental dimension will require many school leaders to think about their work differently. School leaders typically have concerned themselves with in-service education when new mandates have been passed down or when teacher supervision and evaluation revealed deficiencies in the practice of individuals. The idea of continuous improvement based on regular monitoring of intended outcomes necessitates a new way of approaching individual and organizational development. Principals and teachers must be willing to examine their roles in student learning and forego the temptation to blame low achievement on factors outside the school. Principals must institutionalize the same openness to trial-and-error experimentation that presumably characterizes scientific communities.

The beginnings of consensus

A review of ten recent books on the reform of schools and businesses suggests a number of areas of agreement concerning the perceived need for new organizations and new leadership. In addition, the prescriptions for organizational change and changes in the role of organizational leader also reflect considerable agreement. It is important to remember the sources of this emerging consensus, however. The authors of the ten reform documents include business leaders, management consultants, social scientists, and former public officials. Only three authors are involved in the education field at the present time – Theodore Sizer is a professor of education at Brown University, Brian Caldwell is a reader in education at the University of Melbourne, and Jim Spinks is a high school principal in Tasmania.

The fact that educators, particularly specialists in educational administration, are under-represented among this particular group of reformers may cause some readers to regard the prescriptions for schools and the school leaders with suspicion. It may be productive, therefore, to compare the perceptions and prescriptions in the ten reform documents with those contained in *Leaders for America's Schools: The Report of the National Commission on Excellence in Educational Administration*. This report, published in 1987, constitutes one of the most recent and broad-based efforts by members of the educational administration community to envision the future of schools and school leaders. If the recommendations in this report correspond in significant ways with those contained in the selections from the education and business reform literatures, there may be reason to hope that an era of meaningful school improvement can commence.

One additional comment about the ten reform documents is in order. The prescriptions offered by the reformers are not solely the product of armchair speculation, logical analysis, and creative imagination. In the case of the five education reform books, the authors draw on actual examples of innovative schools in the United States and abroad. That the proposals for new schools and new school leaders are *possible*, therefore, is not in question. The only issue is whether or not the proposals will be widely adopted.

A VISION FROM THE EDUCATIONAL ADMINISTRATION COMMUNITY

Leaders for America's Schools devotes relatively little space to a causal story or justification for new school leadership. The post-*A Nation at Risk* ferment in public education is acknowledged in the Preface. The need for school reform is premised in passing on the advent of global economic competition and other 'forces over which this country has little control' (p. xv). The authors of the report take for granted, it seems, that economic factors are a prime justification for educational change.

After the Preface, the report presents a 'vision of school leadership' in the form of a day-in-the-life of the principal of innovative Jefferson School. The vignette concludes with a list of four 'musts' for tomorrow's schools. Schools are exhorted to

1) demonstrate that they are learning communities,
2) foster collegiality,
3) individualize instruction, and
4) encourage involvement (pp. 4-5).

The first recommendation mirrors the reduced control orientation and emphasis on development found in the preceding reform reports. The need for greater focus and direction, also a feature of the other reform reports, is addressed in the statement that standards need to be high and clearly understood by students and staff.

The need to foster collegiality reflects both the increasing complexity of relationships predicted in the reform reports and their call for cultures that value teamwork and collaboration. *Leaders for America's Schools* stresses that administrators and teachers must share in leadership functions such as planning and evaluation. The leader's obligation to match needs with resources also is noted, as it was in many of the reform reports.

The fourth recommendation, involving the encouragement of greater community involvement in schools, also is echoed in the reform reports. *Leaders for America's Schools* endorses broad-based participation in setting school standards, reviewing school progress, and developing programs. Similarly, the reform reports call for the empowerment of parents and other citizens and the cultivation of greater ownership in school decisions.

Only the recommendation for the individualization of instruction receives relatively little attention in the reform reports. The closest a reformer comes to a similar suggestion is Gerstner's call for schools to develop learning contracts for every student. It is safe to say that the education reformers as a group do not see a compelling need to redesign the delivery of instruction. Sizer (1992) is an exception in this regard.

If the ten reform reports are indicative of feelings outside the educational administration community and if *Leaders for America's Schools* accurately captures feelings within this group, consensus appears to exist that the new school leader must be able to promote continuing professional growth, collaboration, and widespread participation in school decision making. Many school leaders may say that this prescription is hardly revolutionary. Effective principals presumably have been doing these things for many years. Why, then, have large numbers of contemporary school leaders been unable to devote sufficient time and energy to professional development, collegiality, and empowerment? Answering this question would be a worthy undertaking for educational administration researchers.

Two dimensions of the new leadership which receive little or no attention in *Leaders for America's Schools* are the accountability and entrepreneurial dimensions. Whether these dimensions were discussed and rejected or not discussed at all during the deliberations of the National Commission on Excellence in Educational Administration is unclear. What is apparent, though, is that concepts perceived to be closely associated with business – concepts like incentives, consumer choice, and marketing – have not been embraced widely by many members of the educational administration community. These individuals often prefer to stress the differences between schools and businesses rather than their similarities. Those who see the world from a 'political frame' may speculate on what is to be gained from such a position.

The time has come to correct the myopia which limits the vision of educational administration reformers. The reform reports strongly suggest that concepts once discussed only in the context of the private sector are receiving careful attention from public sector spokespersons. The movement to expand parental choice, promote competition among schools, and revise the bases for school accountability no longer can be ignored. Such matters deserve to be confronted constructively by the best minds in educational administration.

REQUIEM FOR INSTRUCTIONAL LEADERSHIP

A review of ten recent books on the reform of schools and businesses reveals substantial agreement regarding the need for change and prescriptions for new organizations and new organizational leadership. If such agreement does not erode, what will it mean for the educational administration community?

The major implication of the current reform movement, in this author's judgment, is the retirement of instructional leadership as a guiding concept in the preparation of school leaders. Instructional leadership had its critics in the Eighties, to be sure, but many of them argued, not that instructional leadership was unimportant, but that most school administrators were in no position to exercise it. The leadership prescriptions of contemporary reformers, on the other hand, suggest that leaders' time can be better spent on other pursuits. Instead of investing energy in supervision, teacher evaluation, and instructional improvement, tomorrow's principal is urged to concentrate on student outcomes and monitor progress toward school goals. Assessment replaces instruction as a primary focus for school leadership.

Assessment leadership also is apparent in the insistence by reformers that school leaders become more entrepreneurial. Principals are exhorted to assess the needs of customers, track the success of competitors, and establish performance benchmarks based on the most successful programs. Much of what was regarded as instructional leadership a decade ago is likely to become the responsibility of teachers, newly empowered as a result of greater decentralization and shared decision making. Teachers, not principals, will decide how best to achieve intended learning outcomes. Principals, on the other hand, will make sure that learning outcomes are established, that stakeholders are aware of them, that outcomes are continuously assessed, and that lack of progress is analysed and corrected.

If the reformers' current prescriptions for school leadership gain a foothold, it will be hard to resist noting the irony. The rise of instructional leadership in the Eighties, ably traced by Hallinger (1992), marked one of the rare occasions when members of the educational administration community actually played a leading role in shaping the desired image of the school leader. Funk and Brown (1994, p. 767) claim that the 'business paradigm' previously dominated thinking about schools and school leadership. Furthermore, they contend that 'this business orientation... got education into its current mess in the first place.' Interestingly, none of the reformers chose in their causal stories to indict American business for the perceived failings of public education.

Is there currently a home-grown successor to instructional leadership, one with the potential to compete with business-based leadership prescriptions for the hearts and minds of educational administration specialists? Transformational leadership (see Ken Leithwood's chapter) probably comes closest to a competing prescription, though it derives from the work of political scientist James MacGregor Burns. To date, however, relatively few educational administration programs actually have been influenced directly by transformational leadership. Since transformational leadership and the leadership prescription outlined in this chapter share a number of similar emphases, an integration of the two eventually may be attempted.

If educational administration programs return to business-based prescriptions for school leadership, after instructional leadership's brief interlude, it could indicate that many people still think of schools as businesses. Despite business's sorry track record in the Seventies and Eighties, there is hope, however, that ideas from the private sector can help educators. As business reformers point out, business, too, is changing. If members of the educational administration community hang onto old prejudices against business and ignore these changes, they are likely to be the losers. The important areas of convergence in thinking about organizational leadership – described in the preceding section – need to be exploited. Other, more controversial, aspects of leadership such as entrepreneurship, knowing the competition, benchmarking, and marketing, should not be rejected simply because they derive from the private sector. We in the learning business still have much to learn.

REFLECTIONS ON PERCEPTIONS AND PRESCRIPTIONS

The case made in the preceding pages is straightforward – to understand prescriptions for leadership, it is important to study perceptions of the need for leadership and the conditions that necessitate it. Such an approach can be of particular value to those engaged in the redesign of leader preparation programs. These individuals invariably are exposed to various sets of recommendations regarding leadership. Studying the perceptual underpinnings of the recommendations can help to reveal the causal stories that justify calls for new leadership and key assumptions concerning the context in which leadership is and will be exercised. This information provides a useful basis for the systematic comparison of competing sets of recommendations.

To demonstrate how the approach can be applied, sample prescriptions from recent literature on the reform of education and business were examined. The results of this examination, in turn, were compared to the recommendations of the National Commission on Excellence in Educational Administration. Comparisons of this kind permit judgments to be made regarding the extent to which a 'shared vision' of leadership exists among reformers. Based on the reformers reviewed in this chapter, substantial agreement on the leadership needs of public schools exists. Furthermore, their visions of leadership derived, to a large extent, from emerging and anticipated conditions rather than the status quo. Those presently engaged in the redesign of educational administration programs must determine whether efforts to accommodate the perceived leadership needs of today's schools preclude or interfere with efforts to address the needs of tomorrow's schools. My own view is that the reformers fail to confront such pressing contemporary issues as school violence and racial isolation. They seem to imply, naively, that social problems will evaporate as economic concerns are resolved.

The perceptual dimension of leadership provides a basis for studying how ordinary citizens, as well as reformers, think about leadership. Blase (1993) and McDade (1995), for example, have investigated teachers' perceptions of school leadership. The latter study revealed that teachers vary in the perceived frequency of the need for leadership and the particular conditions associated with the need for leadership. Studies of this kind are invaluable, given the growing interest in teacher empowerment, site-based management, and shared decision making. It appears that teachers may not be of one mind in their understandings of leadership.

How people think about and make sense of leadership is a promising new direction in leadership studies. Until fairly recently, scholars tended to concentrate on how leaders thought. By recognizing that leadership is as much a perception as a descriptive research construct, a small, but growing number of leadership theorists are forcing a shift in the force of inquiry from leaders to followers, critics, and reformers. By understanding how these 'consumers' and students of leadership think, it may be possible to discover the roots of ambivalence regarding leadership. Such ambivalence is illustrated by the fact that those who criticize leadership tend to prescribe leadership as a corrective mechanism.

FOOTNOTES

1. The author would like to thank his graduate assistant, Abra Feuerstein, and all those who recommended books for consideration.
2. The reform book by Sizer, as indicated earlier, does not cite economic reasons to justify school reform. Caldwell and Spinks recognize economic reasons as one of several impetuses to change, but they include other industrialized nations besides the United States. It is interesting that the only authors to be directly involved in the operation of schools or the preparation of educators are also the only ones who do not perceive economic reasons as *the* key to the need for change

REFERENCES

Alderfer, C. P. *Existence, Relatedness, and Growth.* New York: Free Press, 1972.
Blase, J. 'The Micropolitics of Effective School-Based Leadership: Teachers' Perspectives,' *Educational Administration Quarterly*, 29-2 (May 1993), pp. 142-163.
Boyd, W.L. 'The Power of Paradigms: Reconceptualizing Educational Policy and Management,' *Educational Administration Quarterly*, 28:4 (November 1992), pp. 504-528.
Boyett, J. H. & Conn, H. P. *Workplace 200: The Revolution Reshaping American Business.* New York: Plume, 1992.
Caldwell, B. J. & Spinks, J. M. *Leading the Self-Managing School.* London: Falmer, 1992.
Drucker, P. L. *Managing for the Future.* New York: Dutton, 1992.
Duke, Daniel L. 'The Aesthetics of Leadership,' *Educational Administration Quarterly*, 21:2 (Winter 1986), pp. 7-27.
Duke D.L. 'Drift, Detachment, and the Need for Teacher Leadership.' In Donovan R. Walling (ed.), *Teachers As Leaders: Perspectives on the Professional Development of Teachers.* Bloomington, Indiana: Phi Delta Kappa, 1994.
Funk, G. & Brown, D. 'Reaching a Business/Education Equilibrium,' *Phi Delta Kappan*, 75:10 (June 1993), pp. 766-769.
Gerstner, L. V., Jr. *Reinventing Education: Entrepreneurship in America's Public Schools.* New York: Dutton, 1994.
Hallinger, P. 'The Evolving Role of American Principals: From Managerial to Instructional to Transformational Leaders,' *Journal of Educational Administration*, 30:3 (1992), pp. 35-48.
Handy, C. *The Age of Unreason.* Boston: Harvard Business School Press, 1990.
Immegart, G. L. 'Leadership and Leader Behaviour.' In Norman J. Boyan (ed.), *Handbook of Research on Educational Administration.* New York: Longman, 1988.
Leaders for America's Schools, The Report of the National Commission on Excellence in Educational Administration. University Council for Educational Administration, 1987.
Leinberger, P. & Tucker, B. *The New Individualists.* New York: Harper Collins, 1991.

Marshall, R. & Tucker, M. *Thinking for a Living.* New York: Harper & Row, 1970.

Maslow, A. H. *Motivation and Personality,* rev. ed. New York: Harper & Row, 1970.

McClelland, D. C. *Power: The Inner Experience.* New York: Irvington Publishers, 1975.

McDade, B. *Teacher Perceptions of School Leadership.* Doctoral dissertation, University of Virginia, 1995.

Murphy, J. *The Landscape of Leadership Preparation.* Newbury Park, Calif.: Corwin Press, 1992).

Osborne, D. & Gaebler, T. *Reinventing Government.* New York: Plume, 1993.

Rost, J. C. *Leadership for the Twenty-first Century.* New York: Praeger, 1991.

Schwandt, T. A. 'Constructivist, Interpretivist Approaches to Human Inquiry.' In Norman K. Denzin and Yvonna S. Lincoln (eds.), *Handbook of Qualitative Research* (Thousand Oaks, CA: Sage, 1994), pp. 118-137.

Senge, P. M. *The Fifth Discipline.* New York: Doubleday Currency, 1990.

Sizer, T. R. *Horace's School: Redesigning the American High School.* Boston: Houghton Mifflin, 1992.

Stone, D. A. 'Causal Stories and the Formation of Policy Agendas,' Political Science Quarterly, 104:2 (Summer 1989), pp. 281-300.

Tyack, D. & Hansot, E. *Managers of Virtue.* New York: Basic Books, 1982.

Chapter 24: Gender, Organizations, and Leadership

CAROLYN RIEHL AND VALERIE E. LEE
University of Michigan

Sex and gender are among the most fundamental of human attributes. Of all physical traits, a person's biologically-determined sex is noticed first and recalled most easily by other persons. Being female or male predisposes an individual towards a complex array of behaviors known as a gender role, but persons socially construct their own gender identities by accepting, resisting, or transforming their assigned gender roles (Epstein, 1988; Lorber, 1994; Oakley, 1972). Gender identity is both a cause and an effect: it structures how individuals encounter the world and is itself a product of that encounter (Epstein, 1988; Goffman, 1967). Since social patterns of power and domination are often closely associated with gender, it can be understood as a fundamental political category within society as well (Burrell & Hearn, 1989). In short, gender is writ large on the narrative of individual character and collective social life.

Although gender is ubiquitous, it is not always recognized as important. Thus it is that in a decade when most school principals in the United States were male, Harry Wolcott (1973) could write an ethnography entitled *The Man in the Principal's Office* and describe his subject, Ed Bell, as a 'typical' school principal, paying almost no attention to gender as a contributor to the principal's role performance. As an anthropologist, Wolcott was careful to qualify the degree to which his description of one school principal might be generalizable, but he did not suggest that gender might cloud the issue. Gender was not salient in Wolcott's study because women were inconspicuous in the domain of human activity that the study addressed. This is only one example of how school leadership has been construed from a male perspective and infused, however subtly, with elements derived from men's experience. Researchers have documented the androcentric nature of much research in educational administration, in both the United States (Epp, Sackney, & Kustaski, 1994; Shakeshaft, 1989; Shakeshaft & Hanson, 1986), and in Britain (Hough, 1986).

Over the past thirty years, however, as more women have become both educational leaders and educational researchers, the issue of gender has received increased attention. The discourse about school lead-

K. Leithwood et al. (eds.), International Handbook of Educational Leadership and Administration, 873-919.
© *1996 Kluwer Academic Publishers, Printed in the Netherlands.*

ership has thus begun to change in at least three ways. First, and most obviously, the research base has grown to include more comparisons between women and men leaders. Do men and women enter school administration with comparable levels of preparation? Are they equally likely to be selected for leadership positions, and are the types of leadership opportunities available to men and women similar? How alike or different are the leadership behaviors of women and men, and how are women and men leaders perceived and responded to by those with whom they work? Such questions are seen as legitimate because they point to important issues of equity and representation, but they also have the potential to shed light on previously hidden dimensions of leadership.

A second way in which the examination of school leadership changes as gender becomes salient is that it draws out other issues. For example, sexuality becomes problematic, and questions are raised about the relationship between leadership and sexuality, the explicit sexual behavior of leaders (including sexual harrassment), and the more general issue of the connections between public and private selves within organizational contexts (e.g., Burrell, 1992; Collinson & Collinson, 1989; Gutek, 1989; Marshall & Mitchell, 1989; Morgan, 1986). Because gender relations are often about power, power differentials become more apparent when gender is discussed. Indeed, the very nature of power is often questioned more closely. Other aspects of interpersonal behavior, such as communication patterns, take on new interest when gender is a focal concern. Shining a 'gender lens' on school leadership not only highlights issues regarding women, but also sheds light on masculinity and the concerns of men (e.g., Hearn & Morgan, 1990; Kimnel, 1987; Skelton, 1993). Other forms of difference also come into focus, including differences based on race, ethnicity, social class, or national culture. Indeed, not only do such categories begin to stand out in relief, but the very process of categorizing and labeling becomes problematic.

When conversations about leadership incorporate gender, they change in a third way. The evidentiary bases for empirical observations and the logical bases for theoretical conclusions come under scrutiny. If there are potential differences between women and men that are relevant to an understanding of leadership, then gender must be accounted for in research designs that seek to describe or analyze leadership. It is no longer possible to warrant generalizations about leadership from studies based on only male leaders, nor is it possible to provide credible evidence of how women and men differ if either gender is inadequately represented in a corpus of research literature. In fact, women may not divulge truths about their experience unless the research process itself explicitly considers women's realities rather than treating women as the 'other' category (Strachan, 1993). Feminist research methods in the social sciences have called into question long-held tenets of epistemology and methodology, with one result being that research findings are more contextualized, more relativistic and less static, and often reflect less distance between knower and known (Nielsen, 1990; Thibault, 1988). These trends are beginning to be reflected in research on gender issues in school leadership (e.g., Dunlap & Schmuck, 1995).

In these and other ways, introducing gender into the study of leadership has a transformative effect, not simply an additive one. It is by no means the only route by which leadership studies have been enlivened in recent years, but it clearly has the potential for moving work on leadership in new directions, much as feminist scholarship has transformed other areas of the social and behavioral sciences and humanities.

In this chapter, we approach the topic of gender and educational leadership with these changes in mind. We first broaden the discussion by exploring a key topic that comes into view when a gender focus is introduced: how gender affects the school organization. Gender issues, woven into the interstices of organizational life, present a variety of problems and opportunities for leaders. Second, we narrow our focus on gender and leadership by looking more closely at the nature of leadership itself. We ask how normative and descriptive perspectives on leaders are shaped by women's contributions to the conversation. What are women themselves saying about leadership and about phenomena that may be related to leadership? How does this discourse alter the direction of leadership theory and practice within education?

There are several reasons why gender issues are especially pertinent in education. First, using the United States as an example, the pre-collegiate educational system has a unique gender structure − or, more accurately, two unique structures. Elementary schools are dominated by women teachers and have a predominantly male-controlled administrative hierarchy, but women are obtaining many new leadership positions at this level. Secondary schools, on the other hand, have more gender balance in the ranks of teachers but a far more male-dominated administrative structure which has been more resistant to change over time. Thus, elementary and secondary schools are dynamic contexts in which to examine issues of gender representation and gender relations. Gender-relevant aspects of school structure and process need to be described and analyzed in much greater detail. Another reason for the special salience of gender is a crisis in the educational system (in the United States, at least), with declining public confidence and increasing pressures not only to reform existing schools but also to experiment with the creation of entirely new institutional forms such as charter schools and privatized instructional delivery systems. Amid the cacophony of voices calling for change, one hears the frequent refrain that new approaches to leadership are needed. As the present volume indicates, school leadership is undergoing major transformations in both practice and theory, and there is considerable curiosity about how issues of gender intersect with these new directions.

Finally, gender issues are salient to school leadership because they are an overlay on a central mission of schooling, namely the socialization and education of young people. Although public schools were initially designed to serve the needs of young males preparing to enter the public workforce (Shakeshaft, 1993), they quickly adopted as their mission the education of both males and females (Tyack & Hansot, 1990). However, there is evidence that neither are boys and girls having equitable educational experiences in schools, nor are they being helped by their schooling to make good transitions to adult roles (Hansot & Tyack, 1988; Sadker & Sadker, 1994). School leaders must understand the salient gender issues for children under their charge. This, in turn, requires that school leaders have a full understanding of the gender issues facing the adults in their institutions.

In essence, this chapter presents a gendered perspective on leadership within the gendered context of schools. This gender lens, we argue, adds both complexity and clarity to understandings of schooling. It is an important addition to the school administrator's conceptual toolkit. Although rarely acknowledged by school leaders (Kempner, 1989), responsible attention to gender issues is a vital element of good administrative practice.

GENDER AND ORGANIZATIONAL THEORY

For most of its history, organizational theory has been dominated by managerial concerns for effectiveness, efficiency, and control, with the personal attributes of workers important only in terms of their impact on organizational functioning. The major theories of organizational behavior have mostly been gender-blind, assuming either that most workers (at least the important ones) are male or that the gender of workers in organizations does not matter (Mills & Tancred, 1992; Shakeshaft, 1993). Weber explicitly formulated his theory of bureaucracy around attributes of positions, not the individuals who fill them; work follows "calculable rules and 'without regard for persons'" (Gerth & Mills, 1946, p.215). Similarly, Taylor's *Principles of Scientific Management* (1915) deliberately focused on work tasks, independent of the workers who perform them. The theorists associated with the 'human relations' school sought to reintroduce informal groups and interpersonal relationships as important factors in organizational processes. They focused on general notions of human needs and desires, however, without specific reference to gender. Although not all of the classic organizational theories were developed by men, even those developed by women (e.g., Follett, 1924; Woodward, 1965) reinforced mainstream concerns about productivity and the relation between organizational structure, task performance, and personal attributes of workers.

Social and organizational theories from the 1950s and 1960s at least acknowledged women as present in organizations. Their attempts to account for women's experiences were subsumed, however, under the more general structural-functionalist project of justifying existing organizational forms (Hearn & Parkin, 1992). These theories typically adopted the Parsonian distinction between the instrumental roles of men and the expressive roles of women (e.g., Parsons, Bales, & Shils, 1951). Such a distinction provided a functionalist rationale for women's subordinate positions within organizations and for occupational sex distributions by which women were relegated to tasks consistent with gender stereotypes. In this vein, Simpson and Simpson (1969) suggested that women's occupational choices (especially nursing, teaching, and social work) were related to their natural roles and personality dispositions. In formulations such as these, gender divisions at work which had beforehand been invisible were now reified as proper and inevitable.

The concern with managerial issues so dominates organizational thinking that women as well as men have had difficulty traversing its boundaries (Sheriff & Campbell, 1992). Moreover, although mainstream organizational ideologies have been challenged from interpretive or critical theory quarters where the subjectivities of individual and group identity are recognized, gender did not make an appearance as a key subjectivity until feminist approaches underscored its importance (Acker, 1990; Hearn & Parkin, 1992). Nonetheless, recent work in organizational theory has highlighted the experiences of women in organizations. Almost inevitably, by making the invisible category of women explicit, this work has also focused attention on the invisible – because – ubiquitous category of men. Thus, out of feminist or women-centered research has grown a more expansive category of gender research, which encompasses masculinity in organizational life as also problematic (Hearn, 1987).

This burgeoning field of study has explored the organizational impact of gender in at least four new ways, by providing new perspectives on gender and occupations, on gender relations and organizational power, on gender and organizational culture, and – partly as a means of integrating all the others – on gender and the basic logic of organization. We provide brief discussions of each of these streams of work, and consider their implications for educational leadership.

Gender and occupations

Although research on sex stratification in work and occupations has developed independently of organizational theory (Yeakey, Johnston, & Adkison, 1986), it has much relevance to organizations, which are usually structured around constellations of individuals in related occupational categories. Thus, a key element of a gendered theory of organizations is an analysis of the gender structure of occupations. In this section, we draw most heavily on evidence from the United States, although many of the trends we note are evident in international data as well (Kauppinen – Toropainen & Lammi, 1993).

The occupational structure in the United States is heavily segregated by sex and has been so throughout the twentieth century (Reskin & Roos, 1990). Men not only tend to be employed in higher-status occupations (a pattern known as horizontal segregation) but are also found disproportionately in the top posts in all occupational classifications (the pattern of vertical segregation) (Bradley, 1993). During the 1970s, when women's overall participation in the paid workforce increased dramatically, their representation in some traditionally male-dominated occupations increased, but the overall degree of sex segregation changed very little. By 1980, half of all workers, both men and women, still were employed in sex-segregated occupations; i.e., those in which over eighty percent of the workers were of one gender (Jacobs, 1993; Reskin & Roos, 1990).

When occupational positions are held primarily by members of one sex, that occupation is considered to be sex-typed (Epstein, 1970). A prime research question in work on occupations is how occupations become sex-typed (e.g., Baron & Bielby, 1985; Reskin & Roos, 1990). One explanation is that the characteristics of jobs – for example, whether they involve heavy labor or tending small children – make them more suitable for one sex or the other, in the minds of both employers who hire workers and the men and women who seek jobs. But a counter-argument is that many supposedly natural proclivities of males and females, which might incline them towards certain jobs, are in fact socially constructed, in part by men's and women's experiences in the work they do. Thus, this argument goes, sex-typing creates and reinforces gender roles, not vice versa (Epstein, 1988).

Another explanation for the gendered division of labor is presented by Kanter (1977), who suggests that structural conditions in organizations – including power resources and the proportional gender composition of different job levels – affect the mobility of individuals within organizations, thus ultimately influencing occupational sex distributions. Others, however, claim that differential attitudes towards and treatment of women and men have stronger effects than structural conditions (cf., Martin, 1981, cited in Hearn & Parkin, 1992; Sheppard, 1992; Wolff, 1977; Zimmer, 1988).

Some occupations have changed their sex-typing over time. Women tend to make advances into a male-dominated occupation when there is a shortage of male workers, either because the demand for workers exceeds the supply of desirable men, or, more often, because some change in the job itself or in the context of the job makes the job less attractive to men. The most salient changes are when the pay for jobs declines, or when changes in the task or technology of the job make it more routine, less autonomous, or otherwise less appealing (Jacobs, 1993; Reskin & Roos, 1990). Occasionally, women post gains in occupational categories for reasons pertaining specifically to their attractiveness to employers. Employers often make judgments on the basis of stereotyped notions, for example that women tend to perform well in situations where relating to others is a priority (Reskin & Roos, 1990). Affirmative action and the influence of social forces such as the women's movement are other reasons why employers may change their hiring practices (Epstein, 1988). There is some evidence that when women enter occupational fields, those fields are devalued, although experimental studies have not consistently shown this as a causal relationship (Gutek & Cohen, 1992).

It is very rare for men to surpass women in jobs that traditionally are female-dominated. No occupation shifted away from being mostly female during the 1970s. Over the past century, the chief example is the work of tending to childbirth, which changed because men directly sought to define this activity as health care and to gain control of and professionalize it. Men have entered female-dominated occupations during times of economic stress, and occasionally women's jobs have been ceded to immigrant men, but in general, men have little incentive to enter women's fields: the pay and status are lower, and since there are relatively few female-dominated jobs, they do not substantially expand employment opportunities for men. Moreover, men also frequently suffer a heightened gender-role disparity, loss of self-esteem, and anxiety about their 'damaged masculinity' when they work in traditionally female occupations (Bradley, 1993; Carmichael, 1992; Jacobs, 1993).

Organizations often benefit from and help perpetuate occupational sex-typing (Acker, 1990). Hiring workers of the same gender, who may share many attributes and behavioral styles, can increase levels of trust and reduce overall levels of uncertainty surrounding jobs (Kanter, 1977; Mills, 1992). Other benefits seem to pertain mostly to female sex-typed jobs. Women-dominated jobs historically have been relatively manageable with bureaucratic control mechanisms such as hierarchical lines of authority and externally-imposed rules (Simpson & Simpson, 1969). Women are more likely than men to work in jobs where working hours are flexibly scheduled and part-time work is possible. This benefits organizations because part-time workers are unlikely to challenge organizational management or to form powerful coalitions or subcultures. The lower pay structures associated with women's work are of course advantageous for organizations. When a female-dominated secondary labor market exists within an organization, the workers in higher-level occupational categories often are buffered from disruptions such as economic downturns (Morgan, 1986). These patterns can sometimes backfire for organizations, as in the case of organizations dominated by women that cannot shake the low social status associated with their workers. Moreover, sex segregation can mean that potentially useful alternative approaches that might be proposed by members of the opposite sex are not introduced into the work context – a kind of gender – based groupthink.

These issues are especially germane to elementary and secondary education. In the United States and much of the world, men and women are distributed quite differently in the occupational categories of teaching and school administration. These distributions are associated with particular organizational trends that have important ramifications for educational leaders.

Teaching in the United States has been an occupation dominated by women almost since the inception of common schooling in the nineteenth century. At first, men often took teaching jobs during the winter months when farm work was scarce, or while they waited for better opportunities to come along. But school officials soon displayed a preference for hiring women as teachers. Women could be paid much less than men. It was believed that women were more naturally fitted to instruct the young. Women were also considered more docile, thus more likely to carry out directions from school governing bodies (Tyack & Hansot, 1982). Gradually, male teachers were replaced by women. By 1920, 86 percent of the teaching force was female. As a result, school teaching has been associated since its early days with women – and correspondingly with low status, low pay, and limited autonomy.

The gender distribution of secondary school teaching had somewhat different origins. High schools, which first appeared in larger urban areas around the turn of the century, were designed to prepare students for the world of work or higher education. Because adult roles for males and females differed, male and female students often took different classes and were taught by different teachers (Hansot & Tyack, 1988; Tyack & Hansot, 1988). Men comprised the majority of early high school teachers. Although women were hired to teach some subjects, they were constrained from full and equal participation in the occupation. They were paid less than men teachers, and they were required to resign when they got married, thus ensuring a transient workforce with low job investment.

Teaching still reflects these initial gender distinctions. In 1990, 83 percent of public elementary school teachers in the United States were female, while 53 percent of public secondary school teachers were female (National Center for Education Statistics [NCES], 1994). Although secondary school teaching is nearly evenly balanced by gender, there is considerable sex segregation within the field. Women are overrepresented as teachers in the subject areas of language arts, reading, and special education, but are underrepresented in social studies, health and physical education, music, vocational education, and classes for the gifted. Segregation extends within subject area fields as well. For example, while mathematics and science have nearly equal proportions of men and women teachers, women science teachers are much less likely to teach earth science and chemistry than to teach biology.

Despite the considerable growth in career opportunities for women in other fields, the proportion of women in the teaching profession has changed little since 1970. In fact, teaching in the United States may be growing slightly more feminized. In 1982, 68 percent of all teachers were female, compared to 73 percent in 1990. All of the increase occurred at the secondary level (deMarrais & LeCompte, 1995). This may be because teaching continues to be highly compatible with women's responsibilities in the domestic sphere, as wives and parents. Gender role and occupational stereotypes may continue to exert pressures on women to choose school teaching as an occupation. Or it may be that men more than women shun the occupational conditions of teaching – relatively low pay, low autonomy, low mobility, and low status.

An altogether different pattern is observed in school administration. School superintendents in the largely rural America of the 1800s were sometimes women. Phyliss Stock (1978) quotes a committee report on the hiring of a superintendent: 'as there is neither honor nor profit connected with this position, we see no reason why it should not be filled by a woman' (cited in Nicholson, 1994). But the ideological, normative, and practical foundations of modern school administration clearly have masculine roots. These were based in the scientific management initiatives in business and industry sweeping the United States in the early 1900s. The 'professional experts' who became school administrators sought to enhance their legitimacy by adopting management techniques that would meet the approval of the business leaders and others who held the public pursestrings and controlled local school boards (Callahan, 1962). Male professors taught in the university programs where these new administrators were trained. They also controlled far-reaching employment networks and quickly dominated professional associations for school administrators. Although women fought for leadership positions in schools, as administrators gained more power, prestige, and rewards in burgeoning school bureaucracies, the jobs went to men (Tyack & Hansot, 1982).

By 1940, men held the majority of elementary school principalships, as well as continuing to dominate secondary school administration. Since the late 1970s, however, the number of women in school administration has increased. We have examined data on new administrators, using nationally-representative data from the Schools and Staffing Survey, collected by the National Center for Education Statistics (Riehl & Byrd, 1995). Our research indicates that women are making numerical gains at the elementary level, but somewhat fewer gains at the secondary level. In 1988, 29 percent of the teachers who had become new school administrators (as principals or assistant principals) were women (including 67 percent at the elementary level and 17 percent at the secondary level). Some of the increase is attributable to women obtaining relevant qualifications, specifically advanced degrees in educational administration and recent part-time administrative experience. These indicators of women's preparation for administration do not fully account for women's progress, however. Family context (being married and having children) is negatively associated with women becoming administrators. Other factors, such as sponsorship by influential others, district selection procedures, and affirmative action policies (which were not examined in our analysis), explain even more about women's access to school administration.

Although women are making gains, school administration is still heavily dominated by men. In 1990, 70 percent of all public school principals in the United States were male (64 percent at the elementary level and 89 percent at the secondary level), a five percent drop from 1987 figures (NCES, 1994). Other leadership positions in education also have skewed gender distributions. At the beginning of the 1990s, only a third of local school board members were women, and only 9 out of 50 chief state school officers (18 percent) were women (deMarrais & LeCompte, 1995).

In most developed countries, women dominate teaching. In many developing countries, men are the majority of teachers, especially as the age of students increases (Davies, 1990). Low rates of women's participation in administration is a global phenomenon, however. The sparse representation of women in school administration has been documented in Austria (Epstein & Coser, 1981), Canada (Baudoux, 1988; Tabin & Coleman, 1991), Finland (Gordon, 1991), India (Varghese, 1990), Malaysia (Karim, 1983), Mexico (Cortina, 1989), New Zealand (Strachan, 1993), and the former Soviet Union (Epstein & Coser, 1981). In Britain, although women have been the majority of headteachers in primary schools, there are proportionately fewer women heads than women teachers, and women are underrepresented as heads in larger schools. Moreover, there is some speculation that women's role in school leadership in Britain will decline, since the national government's Education Reform Act of 1988 reconstituted the position of head as more a managerial than an instructional role (Darley & Lomax, 1995).

The gender distribution of teaching raises several issues for school leaders. The first concerns employment trends. If school officials intend to promote equity in hiring, they must make efforts to recruit men into teaching at the lower grades, but without showing preferences that alienate women. At the secondary level, school leaders should continue to seek a gender-balanced teaching force, and should keep close watch over the gender distribution of teachers in departments and subject areas that tend to be sex-typed.

The second issue is even more crucial. Teaching's semi-professional roots have been well documented. Teachers have some autonomy in their work, but only within the context of much external control over the conditions of their employment, the availability of resources, and both broad goals and narrow prescriptions for how they will apply their knowledge and skills. Numerous scholars (e.g., Apple, 1986; deMarrais & LeCompte, 1995; Simpson & Simpson, 1969; Skelton, 1991) have suggested that this is directly linked to the fact that teaching is a feminized profession, associated not only with subordinated workers (women) but also with powerless clients (children). Founding conditions of organizations are difficult to overcome; the same may be true for occupations within organizations (Stinchcombe, 1965). This raises a question: if teaching remains a female-dominated occupation and cannot escape its feminized, powerless roots, how can teaching be seen as a legitimate profession? Recent work on teacher professionalism has had little impact on how the occupation is perceived in its wider environment; teaching continues to be viewed by the general public as a low-status occupation (deMarrais & LeCompte, 1995). Simply hiring more men teachers is not the solution. Educators, including school leaders, must continue to examine the political, economic, and ideological modes of control under which teaching operates and to critique both the gender relations that underly them and to suggest alternatives that can enable teachers to garner the professional recognition they deserve.

A third issue, which we examine more closely in the next section, is that power relations often follow gender relations. The gender distribution of teachers between elementary and secondary schools, as well as between departments in secondary schools, has implications for how power and influence are distributed within schools. Male teachers and male-dominated departments have access to more resources of prestige, money, and influence, while female-dominated sectors have access to more emotional power and effort from teachers themselves (Riehl & Sipple, 1995). School leaders need to be cognizant of such disparities.

A fourth issue is how gendered hiring patterns in teaching directly affect children's socialization in schools. The absence of men as teachers of young children, or their dominant presence in secondary subject areas like physical education and chemistry, strongly reinforces social constructions of female and male gender roles. School leaders concerned to eliminate gender biases in students' educational experiences must be cognizant of how those biases are introduced by the hiring patterns in teaching.

A major problem confronting school leaders is how to redress the imbalance of a male-dominated leadership structure in charge of a female-dominated teaching workforce. Policies to alter this situation should include efforts in two directions: first, to restructure the work of school administration so that women find it interesting and compatible with their other responsibilities; and second, to help women obtain relevant educational preparation and job experience (Riehl & Byrd, 1995). Increasing women's representation in school administration must not, however, parallel other experiences of occupational feminization. Education is not immune to such problems; school administration in Israel is an interesting case in point. Within the past twenty years, women's representation as school principals in Israel has more than tripled (Goldring & Chen, 1993). Yet during the same period, the occupational prestige of the principalship has declined markedly, as has the power and influence of the principalship in the national educational bureaucracy. In the United States, as federal and state governments and business leaders take more interest in education, women school administrators may find that they have obtained positions that are more powerless and bureaucratic than when male principals were in charge and were left alone.

Gender and power

Power is a key aspect of organizational life. It is important for organizational members, including leaders, to understand how to generate and use power (Pfeffer, 1981). People want power themselves, and they want to work for powerful people (Kanter, 1977). In a later section, we discuss different conceptions about power that may be held by women. Here we want to look at how gender relations within organizations interact with power dynamics. Again, our goal is to suggest how this issue concerns educational leaders.

Some theorists argue that gender relations within organizations are always about power. In its more militant form, this argument suggests that men are always seeking to maintain their long-held hegemony and to reproduce the power relations of the domestic sphere in the public sphere. In its less militant form, the argument is that since men tend overwhelmingly to occupy positions that are more powerful than women's, power and control inevitably are part of gender interactions. As Etzioni (1969) noted, relations between nurses and doctors, social workers and their supervisors, and members of other organizational hierarchies probably would be quite different if these were not also relations between women and men. To ignore gender dynamics, then, would be to miss some fundamental dimensions of power in organizational life.

A very interesting example of this problem concerns one of the most famous studies of workplace behavior, the Hawthorne experiments. Classic analyses of the Hawthorne results have highlighted the impact of informal work groups and positive work climates on worker morale and performance (Perrow, 1986; Roethlisberger & Dickson, 1939). But in one of the earliest analyses of gender issues in organizations, Acker and Van Houten (1974) argued that the Hawthorne studies demonstrate more importantly that organizations rely on sex-based hierarchies and exert social control through what they call the sex power differential. In the Hawthorne studies, the work group that altered its performance under experimental conditions (the Relay Assembly Test Room) was all female, while the work group that did not improve was all male (the Bank Wiring Observation Room). Most analysts conclude that the Relay Assembly Test Room workers responded to the attention they got from supervisors and researchers, but Acker and Van Houten argue that the women responded to the exercise of power – or at least the threat of it – from their male superiors. When two women in the Relay Assembly Test Room resisted some components of the study (specifically, the physical exam), they were removed from the team and replaced by women (both recent immigrants) who were even more susceptible to the sex power differential as it was manifested through paternalistic treatment, special rewards, and coercion. The male work group, on the other hand, experienced neither individual contact with superiors nor the scrutiny and control that was exercised with the women's work group. Thus, argue Acker and Van Houten, the treatment effect, usually thought to be benign attention from superiors, may really have been gender-differentiated social control.

Power has been a gendered issue in schooling since the days when women were able to become powerless rural school superintendents but were not hired as secondary school principals where they could have authority over male teachers. Has the situation changed much in contemporary times? In this section, we discuss two of our own empirical studies that bear on the issue of gender and power.

The first study, described more fully by Lee, Smith, and Cioci (1993), poses two research questions. First, how are individual teachers' perceptions of the effectiveness of their principals' leadership affected by gender (both that of the teacher and the principal)? And second, how does gender affect teachers' perceptions of their own power within the school?

The data for this study are drawn from the 1984 Administrator and Teacher Survey, a supplement of the High School and Beyond Study (Moles, 1988), with a random sample of 8,894 teachers nested within 377 high schools. The large majority of schools are public (82 percent), and most of the private schools are Catholic (69 percent). The size and representativeness of the sample allow us to generalize results to American secondary schools, teachers, and principals in the mid-1980s. While the teacher sample is nearly evenly balanced by gender (44 percent are females), the school principals are not (only 10 percent are women).

The study employs a highly reliable composite indicator of teachers' perceptions of effective leadership, based on eleven individual measures. We use several composite measures to tap the construct of teacher power, which we separate into three different levels: personal power (self-efficacy and locus of control); interpersonal power (staff collegiality and support); and organizational power (teacher control over classroom practice and staff influence over school policy). All of the outcomes are presented in a common standardized metric known as an 'effect size.' All results include adjustment for teachers' years of teaching experience and salary, factors that differ by gender and are related to perceptions of power. Although several other characteristics of schools and teachers were potentially confounding variables, only these two are related to our outcomes and/or teacher or principal gender. We use two-way analysis of variance (ANOVA) to analyze the data, a method which is very useful for identifying interaction effects. We display the study's results in a series of graphs (Figures 1 through 6), which present the adjusted mean values of each dependent measure for male and female teachers who work in schools led by male and female principals.

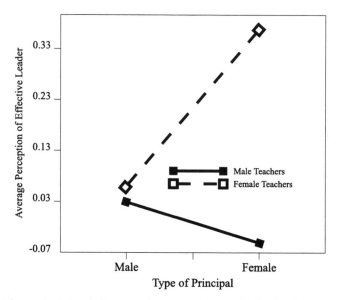

Figure 1: Adjusted means for perceptions of effective leadership

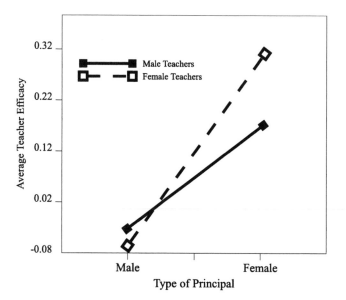

Figure 2: Adjusted means for teacher efficacy

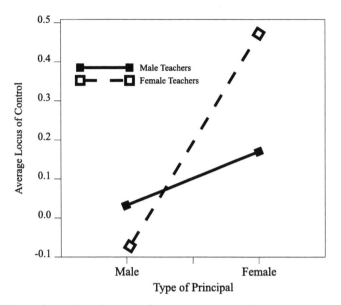

Figure 3: Adjusted means for teacher locus of control

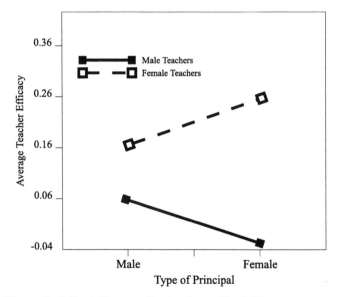

Figure 4: Adjusted means for teacher collegiality

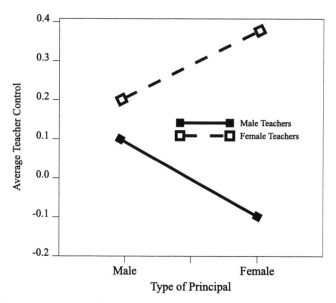

Figure 5: Adjusted means for teacher control over classroom practice

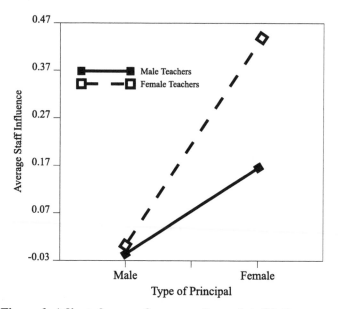

Figure 6: Adjusted means for perceptions of staff influence over school policy

Figure 1 shows the results of the analysis of teachers' perceptions of effective leadership. These results suggest that although male and female teachers who work in high schools with male principals perceive their leaders' effectiveness rather similarly, the teachers who work in high schools with women principals do not. Female teachers consider the women principals under whom they serve to be very effective leaders, whereas men working for women principals assess that leadership more negatively. The effect size difference here is large (close to one-half of a standard deviation difference between men and women teachers). These results suggest that women and men working for the same women principals respond differently in assessing their leaders' effectiveness.

The next two figures display the results of our analyses of teachers' perceptions of personal power, measured in terms of efficacy (Figure 2) and locus of control (Figure 3). These analyses control for teachers' perceptions of the effectiveness of their principal as a leader (the outcome variable in Figure 1), as well as for the effects of teacher experience and salary. Once teachers' opinions about leadership are accounted for (on which there was a large interaction of teacher gender by principal gender, as Figure 1 shows), teachers' assessments of personal power show two quite different patterns. First, both male and female teachers experience higher levels of personal power in schools headed by women than men. And second, men show larger differences in this type of empowerment than women when compared across the gender of their principal. That is, the *increase* in personal power felt under women principals, compared to men principals, is higher for male teachers than for female teachers. Although the two patterns are rather similar for the two outcome measures, the effect is larger for locus of control than for self-efficacy.

We next turn to interpersonal power, measured in terms of teachers' perceptions of collegiality and support among fellow teachers in their schools. Figure 4 displays differences between male and female teachers' responses, again shown separately for schools headed by men and women. Two different patterns emerge here, again after adjusting for teachers' assessments of the effectiveness of leadership in their schools. First, women teachers generally rate collegiality in their schools higher than do their male counterparts, whatever the gender of their principals. Second, again male and female teachers make very different assessments of collegiality and support in schools headed by women. Whereas women see such schools as especially collegial and supportive environments, men rate the same schools as low in terms of interpersonal power (a moderate effect, about .3 SD).

Figures 5 and 6 show the results for teachers' perceptions of organizational power. The patterns are rather different for the two types of organizational power we measure. The pattern for teachers' perceptions of power over classroom practice (Figure 5) is quite similar to the pattern for perceptions of effective leadership (Figure 1). In general, men see themselves as having less control than women over conditions in their classrooms, and this is particularly the case for men working in schools headed by women. In those same schools, women teachers see themselves as particularly empowered over classroom conditions. For staff influence over school policy (Figure 6), both men and women rate this type of power lower in schools headed by men than in schools with female principals. This perception of power over policy is particularly marked for women teachers (again, a moderate difference of .3 SD).

It is clear that the daily practices of principals are seen quite differently by men and women teachers, and those differences are magnified when we consider the principal's gender. A strong and consistent finding from the study is that women teachers feel empowered when working in environments where their direction comes from women leaders, and male teachers do not. The consistency of results across several levels of power (individual, interpersonal, and organizational), with female teachers' perceptions of their own power increasing as a result of working for women principals, is quite persuasive. Female leadership seems to have positive effects on female teachers. Moreover, on two measures of teacher power, personal locus of control and staff influence over policy, the adjusted means for both men and women teachers were higher in schools headed by women. This suggests some real differences in organizational conditions generated by the leadership styles of women principals, relative to men principals.

On the other hand, men seem to be uncomfortable working for women. Why do men who teach in secondary schools not appreciate or feel supported by the leadership of women? One explanation may be that they resist what is unfamiliar. Men have little experience with women leaders. Though women, too, have less experience with women leaders, they may be more familiar and comfortable with the ways women do things. The adjustment necessary when serving under a female leader is less extreme for women teachers. Another explanation may be that women principals do not correspond to the bureaucratic model of leadership that teachers have come to expect. Women are less often distant managers than active participants in the daily business of schools. The participatory management style of women may threaten the autonomy that teachers (especially male teachers) have come to expect as an integral part of their jobs. Participatory management suggests that teachers are expected to take part in school decisions, a process that begins to blur traditional lines of authority. Such a style could open to group scrutiny decisions that some teachers have jealously guarded for themselves, particularly those governing daily life inside classrooms. An in-group bias might also prejudice men against women leaders. Men have been well served in a system where their own gender dominates the principalship, and they could harbor some fear that when women occupy leadership positions, men will lose certain advantages.

Another of our empirical studies also focuses on gender differences in teachers' perceptions of power. In this study, the contrasts are not between men and women *teachers* who work with male or female principals, but between men and women teachers who work in schools with different gender distributions of *students*, that is, single-sex or coeducational. Research has suggested that single-sex secondary schools have particular benefits for students, especially females, (Bryk, Lee, & Holland, 1993; Lee & Bryk, 1986; Lee & Marks, 1990), and it is possible that benefits may extend to teachers as well. Since virtually all public high schools are coeducational by law, this study uses data from a random sample of independent schools in the United States. Independent schools are free from most forms of external control, so teachers within them may experience a greater range of power and control than teachers in public schools do. Here we focus only on organizational power, i.e., the teachers' control over school policy and/or their classrooms. We are again particularly interested in the possibility of gender matching, whereby teacher gender and school gender composition may combine to produce particularly empowered teachers. Thus, we again pose an interaction question: are gender effects on teachers' control over school and classroom policy different, depending on the gender grouping of the school in which teachers work?

The study is based on survey data from the entire population of mathematics and English teachers (n=629) in 60 independent secondary schools during the 1988-89 academic year. Included are 20 girls' schools, 20 boys' schools, and 20 coeducational schools. The study design is fully specified by Lee, Loeb, and Marks (1995). Teacher and school gender are reasonably well matched in these schools: 73 percent of girls' school teachers are female, whereas only 14 percent of the teachers in boys' school and 43 percent of the teachers in coeducational schools are women. Few teachers had attended private schools themselves, and many have teaching experience in public schools.

The two outcomes – control over classroom and school policies – are constructed from questionnaire items identical to those in the study just described, again combined into highly reliable composites and scaled in a standardized (effect-size) metric. We control for the effects of teacher experience and school characteristics (selective enrollment policies, finishing-school status, and school size); other possibly confounding factors were considered but dropped from the final analysis. Because this study's central focus is on schools and the teachers in them, we employ hierarchical linear modeling (HLM), a statistical method appropriate for multilevel research designs. Although we confirmed the HLM results with a more common methodology, ordinary least squares (OLS) regression, the results we present are from HLM analyses.

The results of the study are summarized graphically in Figures 7 and 8. They show several striking patterns. One strong finding is that male teachers in single-sex schools (either boys' or girls' schools) see themselves as disenfranchised in these settings, at least in comparison to their counterparts in coeducational schools. This comparison is especially evident in teachers' assessments of control over school policies (Figure 8). A second notable finding concerns women teachers, who see themselves with considerable control over classroom policies but with very little control over school policy, regardless of the type of school in which they teach (Figure 7 vs. 8). It is also striking (but not surprising) that the small proportion of women teaching in boys' schools feel they have very little control over policy in these settings (Figure 8).

In the supposedly gender-neutral coeducational school environments, teachers' assessments of control over classroom policy vary little by gender. However, male teachers see themselves with considerable control over school policy in mixed-gender settings, while female teachers feel somewhat disenfranchised in these schools. The latter is a large effect (close to .5 SD). Even larger are the gender differences in teachers' assessments of control over their classrooms in girls' schools (an effect size of .6 SD), where male teachers feel they have very little control and female teachers report that they have considerable control. As in the previous study, these results are particularly striking, in that teachers in the same schools are likely to report such differences.

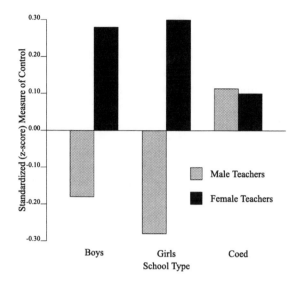

Figure 7: Teachers' Perceived Control over Classroom Policies
Based on Full HLM Model

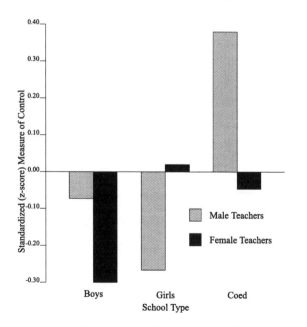

Figure 8: Teachers' Perceived Control over School Policies
Based on Full HLM Model

Thus, we find that women teaching in girls' schools see themselves with more control over school policies than men teaching in girls' schools, the reverse of the pattern in boys' and coeducational schools. This suggests that some organizational properties of girls' schools may lead women teachers to feel empowered to participate in policy decisions. Important in this context is the fact that most girls' schools have women heads, while boys' and coeducational independent schools are led almost entirely by men. Another factor is, rather obviously, that an all-female student body may allow a school to focus on special issues for women. The research literature suggests that a single-sex student body may facilitate the empowerment of female teachers by de-emphasizing traditional sex roles (Chafetz, 1990; Tyack & Hansot, 1990). Geile (1978) points out that sex differentiation in a male-dominated culture inherently leads to the relative devaluation of the female. These factors suggest something special about the environments of girls' schools.

These two studies focus on gender differences in teachers' perceptions of power in the secondary school organizations in which they work. The disenfranchisement (actual or perceived) of workers in any organization is problematic because of the potential benefits for the organization of empowered workers, including increased worker satisfaction and productivity (Alutto & Belasco, 1973; Bronfenbrenner, 1976; Corcoran, 1990). At least one set of findings is quite consistent across the two studies: women teachers feel more empowered when they work in educational environments that are either led by women or are directed to the concerns of women. But, of course, most public schools in the United States are headed by men and are coeducational.

These results have several implications for educational leaders. First, strategies must be identified that will empower women teachers in all schools, not just those headed by women or populated with mostly female students. Disenfranchised female teachers provide weak role models for students, and thus reinforce sex-differentiated social and professional roles in students' minds. Moreover, gender equity in teachers' empowerment and organizational control is especially relevant in view of the current reform efforts to provide teachers with input into organizational decisions (Shedd & Bacharach, 1991). As teachers gain more say in school decisions, differences in influence between men and women could actually widen, increasing gender stratification and providing even poorer role models for students. Second, men teachers must be helped to feel more comfortable working with female principals, but not at the women's expense. Men's resistance to women's leadership in schools may reflect nothing more than resentment and an attempt to retain power and advantage, and catering blindly to these tendencies would sustain the traditional power imbalance, even if women had access to formal positions of power. On the other hand, both genders may need to learn slowly how to deal with altered power dynamics.

Gender and organizational culture

Current approaches to organizational analysis place great importance on culture as a defining characteristic of organizations and a determinant of organizational performance (Bolman & Deal, 1992; Deal & Kennedy, 1982). The culture of an organization embodies shared meanings and understandings which are socially constructed. Culture is manifested symbolically through ceremonies, rituals, myths and stories of heroes, and slogans, and through such social processes as norms governing participation and processes to socialize newcomers. Even the symbolic components of such seemingly rational-technical aspects of organizations as rules, standard operating procedures, and formal organizational charts can provide an 'interpretive lens' pointing to key elements of organizational culture (Morgan, 1986). Organizational cultures are often less monolithic than supposed and are open to multiple interpretations (Martin, 1992). Organizational subcultures may also exist, because not all individuals are connected to organizations in exactly the same way, and because people are located at different positions on continua of power, status, and role. A key task of the organizational leader is to help manage the organization's culture.

Social understandings of gender are clearly part of organizational cultures. Indeed, there is a 'dialectical relationship' between organizational constructions of gender and the broader value system within society. Meanings about gender developed within the organizational context may reflect and reinforce wider social meanings (Mills, 1992, p. 99). These meanings can vary across organizations and even across national cultures. Masculine gender characteristics may be prized in the formal organizations of one country, such as Japan, but much less salient in another, such as Sweden (Bass, 1990). In the organizational context, gender meanings are made manifest in many ways. The sexual division of labor is one example, where sex-typed occupations reflect organizational norms about men's and women's abilities and interests. Dominant metaphors are another aspect of organizational culture which can be gendered, as when organizational performance is referred to as a 'game' or a 'battle' and leaders are likened to coaches, players, or generals. Another source of organizational values about gender is an organization's folklore about its great women or men. But myths or hero-stories may reflect the gender bias often inherent in social attributions. That is, when women succeed, their success is often attributed to luck, while men's success is attributed to ability (Epstein, 1988; Lips, 1991).

Cultural values about gender are also reflected in organizational approaches to the expression of emotion. Rational models of organization have typically treated emotion – and women, as the primary bearers of emotion – as extraneous to core organizational processes (Adkison, 1981). But in reality, organizations rely heavily on the management of the emotions of both clients and workers, and the responsibility for this is often institutionalized in women's work, for example in the position of secretary in an office or flight attendant on an airline crew, because women are seen stereotypically as more attuned to emotion than are men (Calas & Smircich, 1993; Hochschild, 1983). Similarly, organizational approaches to sexuality and workers' bodies reflect values about gender. Since the days of the medieval Catholic church – one of the first formal organizations – organizations have sought to exert control over workers' sexuality (Burrell, 1992; Morgan, 1986). In general, women have been subject to more control than men; women's sexuality is considered antithetical to work in the public realm, while men's sexuality – and related characteristics such as aggressiveness and strength – is often incorporated into organizational life (Gutek & Cohen, 1992). Men can use their sexuality to manage their images, dominate others, and gain power (Collinson & Collinson, 1989). But women must learn to downplay their sexuality in order to resolve the contradictions of being female and a worker, especially in occupations traditionally defined with regard to male roles. For women, gender becomes a 'managed status' within an organization (Sheppard, 1992), and women adopt strategies regarding dress, language, and relationships so that they blend into prevailing organizational norms about gender and sexuality.

Although it is widely acknowledged that for children, school culture is quite gendered, there is little research evidence on the gendered nature of school cultures for the adults who work in them. Certainly the sexual division of labor in education is value-laden, but does this create highly feminized or masculinized cultures (or subcultures) within schools? How dependent is school culture on the culture of teaching versus the culture of administration? Are these various cultures relatively stable across elementary schooling or secondary schooling as institutional forms, or do they vary considerably school by school, or district by district? What are the effects of gender-biased cultures in schools?

Men who become teachers provide useful perspectives on gender in schools and on the culture of teaching. For example, male elementary teachers in Iowa (Allan, 1993) reported that they felt valued and needed during the hiring process, but then were not always fully accepted by female teachers. In this study, two respondents experienced conflict with their male principal, who seemed accustomed to being the 'rooster in the hen house' (p. 120). The teachers were expected to be atypical, 'nurturing' males of young children, but they were also expected to behave in stereotypically masculine ways (e.g., by doing tasks that involved physical labor). Thus, the men teachers experienced a variety of gender contradictions and had to construct new notions of masculinity on the job. They were sometimes hired to be 'role models,' but then did not know what this meant within the school context; they were feared if they acted like men, but they also could not act like women.

These experiences can be stressful for men. Male teachers are hampered by societal attitudes about men and children; the fear of being accused of sexual misconduct often restricts men's behavior with children (Skelton, 1993). Men report that they miss working with other men, and that they feel caught in a double bind of identity, treated as strangers by other men and as men by women teachers (Kauppinen – Toropainen & Lammi, 1993). Men teachers tend to seek out other men, even at different levels of the hierarchy, for companionship at work. But this can breed resentment among female peers. In any case, whether male teachers form alliances with male principals or female teacher-colleagues, they present 'an implicit challenge to institutionalized relationships between men and women' in schools (Allan, 1993, p.121). There is evidence that male kindergarten teachers are more likely than women to move out of the profession (Robinson, 1979, cited in Kauppinen – Toropainen & Lammi, 1993), as are men in other female-dominated jobs (Jacobs, 1993).

These findings do not lead to an inevitable conclusion that teaching cultures are hostile environments for men. On the contrary, Skelton (1993) describes how the informal curriculum of a preservice educational program in physical education in Britain reinforced a 'hegemonic masculinity' among physical education teachers. He suggests that physical education teachers help to generate the perception of themselves as hypermasculine, in part as a defensive reaction against their marginalization within an academic curriculum. Moreover, there is some evidence that when men enter female occupations, they tend to be treated well by the women, who hope they might bring added prestige and pay to the occupation. The positive treatment men receive might also be due to the less competitive environment of female-dominated jobs or to the facr that women frequently defer to men (Kauppinen – Toropainen & Lammi, 1993).

The culture of school administration presents a different face. At the secondary level, at least, it appears to be the product of strong, regularized patterns of administrator socialization and of enduring features of the bureaucratic organization of schools (Marshall & Mitchell, 1989). Male images of discipline and power often pervade school administration, along with a devaluation of reflection (Kempner, 1989). Administrative culture is dominated by norms such as a prohibition against risk-taking, the need to remake policy quietly and avoid moral dilemmas, and an official intolerance for divergent values. These norms can create an inhospitable context for outsiders or newcomers such as women (Marshall & Mitchell, 1991). A variety of 'gender filters' in the administrative culture of schools silence newcomers and maintain the privilege of the dominant role incumbent, who is often a white male (Rusch & Marshall, 1995). These filters include a tendency toward anger with challengers, the denial of privilege or oppression, intellectualizing the problem of equity, and only going partways to advocate fairness.

Blackmore (1993) reports that the culture of school administration in Australia is masculine and hegemonic, based on such familiar images as the benevolent patriarch and the rational man. She argues that when women first entered teaching, they violated the traditional dichotomy between men's public lives and women's private lives. This contradiction was resolved by assigning to women the emotional tasks associated with teaching and nurturing, while men displayed discipline, authority, and rationality as administrators. Blackmore finds it ironic that newer visions of school administration incorporate 'feminine' values such as empathy and interpersonal skill, but use these to further the goals of the organization, not necessarily to enhance the condition of workers as persons.

Although these studies suggest the existence of gendered teacher and administrative subcultures within schools, there has been little scrutiny of the positive and negative effects of such cultures, or about how school leaders should work to influence these cultures. If female-dominated elementary teacher cultures favor norms of congeniality over conflict, how can administrators help teachers to accept conflict as an inevitable part of collaborative decision making? How can male elementary teachers be helped to find a comfortable role, without resorting to placing them in higher-status positions within the school such as teaching older grade levels or more talented students? If male-dominated subcultures within secondary schools promote particular images of masculinity and sexuality to both staff and students, how can (primarily male) administrators help resist or transform them? How can pensive school administrators survive in a culture that has traditionally favored action over reflection? Understanding both the nature and effects of gendered cultures within schools is an important step in creating effective, and equitable, school environments.

Gender and the logic of organization

Examining gender themes in occupations, in organizational power, or in organizational culture may not completely uncover the role of gender in organizational life. It is also necessary to consider how gendered roles and gender relations are written into the very logic of bureaucratic organizations. Wolff (1977), one of the earliest critics of organizations from this perspective, describes formal organizations as predicated on an ostensibly gender-neutral distinction between public and private life which invariably works to exclude women. Within this logic, jobs are abstract categories designed to be filled by disembodied workers who have no other 'imperatives of existence' that might interfere with their work (Acker, 1990, p. 149). Organizations structured along such a fundamental separation between work life and home life can only find room (at the top, expecially) for those who choose to accept this dichotomy. Most women, however, do not have the luxury of such a choice.

Formal, bureaucratic organizations are a product of modernity and the impulse to rationalize – an impulse which has been felt in the private sphere but which has found much more fertile ground in the public sphere. As industrial capitalism developed, organizations took on a hyperrational, unemotional, and authoritative logic (Reiger, 1993). This logic is traditionally associated with masculinity and, when combined with men's numerical dominance in organizations, has reinforced and reproduced gendered patterns of advantage, control, and distinctions between action and emotion (Acker, 1990). Secretaries are the exception that prove the rule. Women in this position stand in opposition to the degendered (but, in effect, male-gendered) bureaucracy; they bring the private into the public sphere, performing a role akin to wife or mother which embodies emotionality and links instrumental and expressive domains (Calas & Smircich, 1993; Pringle, 1989).

The bureaucratic logic of modern organizations, which separates public and private lives and values rationality over emotion, is increasingly criticized as creating societies in which people suffer from unconnectedness and anonymous social relations (Bellah, 1985). Ferguson (1984) argues this point from a feminist perspective that has parallels from other standpoints as well. By robbing workers of control over their productive labor, organizations treat all workers – not just women – as the 'second sex.' This process, claims Ferguson, parallels the historic subjugation of women. It occurs through worker isolation, deskilling (even in the guise of specialization), the promotion of an official discourse which prohibits critical scrutiny and social criticism, and the obscuring of visible targets of opposition. When women enter organizational life and critically encounter bureaucracy, she argues, they can reveal these patterns of power and domination that affect all workers, although it is not inevitable that women will do so.

Ferguson and others have suggested that there can be alternatives to bureaucracy which reconstruct notions of public and private life and rely more on collaboration and community and less on domination. Indeed, such new organizational forms have also been proposed by managerialist theorists concerned more with productivity than with gender equity. But the problems and pressures facing such alternatives have been described by several authors (e.g., Acker, 1990; Martin, 1990; Sirianni, 1984). Moreover, it is important to remember that bureaucracy's reliance on non-personalistic job attributes has enabled qualified women to obtain positions once available only to men, especially in larger, more egalitarian organizational settings (Epstein, 1988). There may also be a functional rationality to bureaucracy which can be separated from a structure based on domination (Ramsay & Barker, 1992). These debates are ongoing. Overall, it appears that a gender-related critique has become part of a widespread reexamination of the logic of bureaucratic organization.

This issue has a particular relevance to the organization of schooling and school leadership. Schools rely heavily on female labor in teaching, and they connect in unique ways with children and family life.

Thus, although the fundamental logic of schools is quite bureaucratic, they have also been organized in ways that acknowledge the private lives of both workers and clients. Specifically, work hours generally permit teachers to be at home when their own children are out of school and need tending. Thus, one might conclude that schools are a model for reconnecting public and private lives. Yet this comes at a cost. Teachers spend most of their time in school working directly with students, and there are not many regular work hours allotted to interaction with colleagues away from students. To add work hours for such activity would most likely alter the ways in which teachers can balance their public and private responsibilities. However, the many initiatives for school improvement, including school-based management, collaborative teaching, and teacher leadership, require increased time for teachers to work together. Thus, school leaders face a dilemma – how to reform schooling while retaining those elements of the basic organizational logic which transcend male-normed bureaucratic notions. If school officials expected that all work be performed on site (many teachers currently spend considerable hours at home on work-related tasks), then they would be less responsive to workers' private needs. The gender distribution of teaching might change, with a concomitant shift in power relationships between teachers and administrators, as well as a change in expressions of organizational culture. Thus, while administrators may rarely consider the gender biases built into school organizational logics, they encounter the effects of these logics all the time.

GENDER AND LEADERSHIP

We have presented theoretical and empirical evidence to support the notion that gender impacts on many dimensions of organizational life, and that successful leaders need to understand and manage these gender issues. We have further argued that these issues are pertinent to school leaders, both because of the unique patterns of gender relations in school organizations and because children are attentive witnesses to how adults produce and reproduce gender within schools. Because gender colors our encounters with organizations, it also colors our conceptions of leadership and administrative practice. People believe that women and men have important differences, and they extend this contrast to stereotypes about leaders as well. Accordingly, a full treatment of gender issues in organizational leadership must include an examination of leadership itself, and to that we now turn.

The rise of women in school administration has led to many studies describing women's experiences and contributions as school leaders, and comparing women leaders with men. This research has been summarized several times over the past few years (e.g., Adkison, 1981; Eagly, Karau, & Johnson, 1992; Fishel & Pottker, 1979; Gross & Trask, 1976; Jones, 1990; Shakeshaft, 1989). In these reviews and meta-analyses, some persistent gender differences emerge. For example, women principals have been demonstrated to have greater interest than men principals in the social and emotional development of students, to be more able and willing to help beginning teachers, and to be more effective at working with parents (Fishel & Pottker, 1979). Women elementary school principals tend to be more involved with faculty matters, to be more involved in instructional issues, and to deal with student matters more (Charters & Jovick, 1981). Eagly, Karau, and Johnson (1992) reviewed 50 studies (most conducted at the elementary school level) and found that women principals tend to be more democratic and less autocratic, and to be more task-oriented than their male counterparts. This latter, somewhat counter-stereotypic, finding may be explained by the more general finding that people are more task-oriented in positions that are congenial to their gender. Some studies have shown that women principals are more positive communicators (e.g., Gougeon, 1991) and place more emphasis on parent and community involvement in the school (Adkison, 1981; Fishel & Pottker, 1979). Women principals have demonstrated greater ability to resolve conflicts and to be somewhat less likely to invoke hierarchy and dominance in solving conflicts with students (Marshall & Mitchell, 1989). At least one study (Adler, Laney, & Packer, 1993) suggests that women may display different leadership styles because more behavioral options are open to them. For example, women are not seen as violating gender stereotypes if they display warmth and approachability.

In general, however, summary reviews and meta-analyses have concluded that male and female school administrators are far more similar than different. For example, Jones (1990) reviewed 147 tests of gender differences among school administrators and found only six statistically significant differences. The possible reasons for the lack of strong evidence about gender differences are many. Some studies may lack adequate samples, methodological rigor, or sensitivity to leadership dimensions along which real gender differences might exist (Hearn & Parkin, 1992; Jones, 1990). Structural conditions in schools may force men and women leaders to behave similarly. Training and selection processes might produce men and women leaders who think and behave in similar, even predictable, ways. Women (and men too, for that matter) who might act differently may simply be rejecting school leadership in favor of other pursuits. Thus, while efforts to compare men's and women's leadership in schools have led to some potentially interesting contrasts, this line of inquiry has yet to produce definitive results.

Another approach to an examination of leadership from a gendered perspective is to listen to the voices of women, not to compare them with men but simply to let women claim some of the discourse space about leadership in general and school leadership in particular. As Eccles and Nohria (1992) state, 'Managers live in a rhetorical universe – a universe where language is constantly used not only to communicate but also to persuade, and even to create' (p.9). The incursion of scientific management into the educational system of America in the early 1900s created a new rhetoric about leadership. It was an ideological and prescriptive approach, not just a technical development, and it had significant effects. As a form of rhetoric, it framed school administrators' understandings of their work and mobilized leaders to specific kinds of action. Similarly, women's theorizing about leadership and their empirical examination of it can be seen as a form of rhetorical expression, as much as their actual leadership behavior is rhetorical practice. Thus, by looking at leadership from women's perspectives, we can begin to identify the content and themes of their approaches toward leadership and how they might like to see leadership evolve. The question is not whether all women lead in particular ways, or even whether women tend to lead in ways that differ from men. Rather, the question is whether women promote, through their practice and research, a particular rhetoric about leadership that can contribute to more effective leadership and more successful schools.

Descriptions by women of how women lead provide one source of information about the rhetoric of leadership. For example, Helgesen (1990) observed four women who were successful leaders in diverse organizations, and found several common patterns in their leadership styles. The women placed a high priority on maintaining positive relationships among workers, and they were likely to find ways to share information with others in their organizations and beyond. In addition, the women had 'complex and multifaceted' identities; they valued both their work roles and family roles and worked hard to integrate them rather than compartmentalize them as separate responsibilities.

Helgesen describes the women's approaches to organizational structure as promoting a web-like structure, with many interconnections,
and with the leader in the middle of things rather than at the top.

Astin and Leland (1991) studied over seventy women who had made
significant contributions in a variety of pursuits, especially on behalf of
women. These researchers conclude that central to the women's success and effectiveness as leaders was a passion for justice and social
change. The leaders' deeply held beliefs motivated risk-taking to promote their values. Also, these influential women relied on networks of
relationships developed carefully through listening to and empowering
others, and they paid careful attention to details and nuances in bringing about change.

Some researchers who examine women's leadership have focused
specifically on issues of power. Women, who have traditionally held
little power, often express ambivalent feelings about it. They dislike
and mistrust power, especially when it is associated with unilateral
domination (Adler, Laney, & Packer, 1993). When women do hold
power, primarily in their roles as mothers or teachers, it is only temporary, because children grow up and students move on, whereas men
typically have access to more permanent expressions of power (Lather,
1994). Thus, it is not surprising that women have struggled to find
ways to accommodate power comfortably and effectively within leadership positions.

Women researchers and theorists have written of power as capacity,
energy, or potential, rather than as force or the ability to dominate. In
this vein, Hurty (1995) studied seventeen women elementary school
principals and found that they saw themselves as having power *with*
others, not power *over* others, echoing a theme introduced many years
earlier by Follett (1924). Hurty characterizes the women leaders as
developing power through five dimensions of leadership. The women
used a full range of emotional energy in their work with others, and
they nurtured all kinds of growth in others. They engaged in 'reciprocal
talk' – talking with others, not at others, as a key element of leadership.
They practiced 'pondered mutuality,' or keeping others in mind when
making decisions; and they focused on collaborative change. These
dimensions fostered a constant connectedness with others, and led to a
form of leadership that Hurty calls 'coactive power.'

Not all women are feminists, and some women administrators have
found it necessary to eschew any connections to feminism in order to
succeed (Bell, 1995). Nonetheless, another source of rhetoric about
women and leadership is feminist theory. There are many different

approaches to feminism, but it is generally agreed that they share at least four common elements: the perspective that gender is socially constructed, that gender relations are unequal, that gender is a key explanatory variable for many social phenomena, and that part of the project of explicating the issue of gender necessarily involves taking a proactive stance toward social change and gender equity. Feminists do not simply study women, but instead consider the world from women's perspective (Ferguson, 1984). These themes are echoed by pro-feminist men; they, too, focus on difference and display a willingness to confront inequality actively. Both feminists and pro-feminists examine the dominant culture from an 'outsider' perspective and seek to find – and critique – the fault lines within society (Smith, 1987, cited in Gosseti & Rusch, 1995).

Feminist values can inform leadership practice with specific perspectives and purposes. Under the rubric of feminism, leadership is seen as responsibility to others and empowerment of others; it allows people to identify and activate connections among themselves (Blackmore, 1989). Feminist leadership theory advocates a form of practice which Grundy (1993) calls 'emancipatory praxis.' Emancipatory praxis stands in contrast to technical action-rational forms of planning, assessment, and other activities that are often embedded in a bureaucratic, hierarchical structure, and to practical action, which may be more reflective, democratic, and interactive, but which may often be based on hegemonically determined ideals. Emancipatory praxis incorporates efforts that seek freedom, are critical in nature, and that oppose inequality and injustice. Its practitioners negotiate goals and purposes with others and embrace conflict as a legitimate aspect of working together. Emancipatory leaders engage in continual evaluation and critical self-reflection. They provide others with the tools needed to share in critical reflection. They ensure symmetric communication to facilitate that reflection, and help their group to be cognizant of its institutional and social context (Grundy, 1993).

These feminist themes are embodied in practical suggestions for women in leadership. Gosetti and Rusch (1995) stress the importance of maintaining an 'outsider within' stance and resisting the 'privileged perspectives' that status-quo leaders often adopt. Meyerson and Scully (1994) suggest an approach of 'tempered radicalism,' whereby women maintain a dual identity within their organizations, at once committed to their work and productive in it, but also serving as vital sources of resistance, alternative ideas, and transformation. These authors play with the nuanced meaning of 'tempered, ' which suggests paradoxes such as calm rage and permanent ambivalence. Calas and Smircich (1993) also invoke alternative images for feminists working within organizations, including the frugal housewife who wastes no resources available to her, the earth mother who pays much more than lip service to ecological issues, and the hysterical woman who expresses righteous outrage about real injustice.

Martin (1993) argues that women will resist the 'normative masculinity of management' only if they can organize, take political action, and force organizations to change. She advocates a form of 'feminist practice' to promote social change, which is based on feminist legal practice. Martin describes eight components of feminist practice: asking the woman question (how does a situation affect women or other disadvantaged groups?); using feminist practical reasoning (responding to concrete dilemmas rather than choosing between abstract perspectives); consciousness-raising (using dialogue about personal experiences to gain understandings and promote multiple perspectives); promoting community and cooperation; promoting democracy and participation; promoting subordinate empowerment; promoting nurturance and caring; and striving for transformational outcomes.

Some women researchers and theorists have examined approaches to leadership that are specifically ethical in nature. Noddings (1984, 1990) argues that a central theme in women's historical experience has been the role of caregiver – particularly of young children – and that this can provide a strong grounding for the practice of school teaching, and leadership as well. In this vein, caring is seen as a relationship with particular dimensions of reciprocity between the caring – for individual and the cared – for individual. More accurately, persons who care form concentric circles of relationships, and it is their tending to these relationships which gives rise to actions that can be construed as highly moral. For Noddings, placing a value on the caring in which teachers engage with their students would generate a completely different version of teacher professionalism, one that rejects the notion that those who are able to move farther from direct work with children are viewed as more professional. Thus, Noddings also implies a different vision of school leadership, one in which practitioners remain actively involved in caring for students and their lives.

Beck (1994) argues for an approach to educational leadership as a 'caring profession' that is grounded more firmly in philosophical ethics than in women's tradition, although the two certainly are not antithetical. That is, there are both deontological and consequentialist justifications for why educational administrators ought to pursue caring as a core value, with caring conceived as promoting human development and responding to human needs. Too often, Beck argues, educational administrators have acted in a reactive fashion, taking their cues for action from political events or cultural pressures. Instead, if administrators focus explicitly on the three aspects of caring she describes as 'receiving, responding, and remaining,' they will more effectively meet the challenges of improving academic performance, addressing social problems, and rethinking school structures.

There are, to be sure, many barriers to caring in schools; these include the increase of externally-imposed mandates for standardization and uniformity, as well as structural relationships among students, teachers, and administrators in schools that are based upon distance and inequality (McCall, 1995). Moreover, not all conceptions of caring are transformative in the sense of developing a critical self-consciousness or awareness of injustice and exclusion. But the image retains considerable potency, especially in light of growing evidence that more communal school organizations with more personalized relationships among students, teachers, and administrators may be more effective than bureaucratically-organized schools (e.g., Bryk, Lee, & Holland, 1993).

Many of these images of leadership echo themes in other forms of rhetoric about leadership that are not derived so explicitly from a gendered or feminist perspective. For example, Dunlap and Goldman's (1991) conception of facilitative power presents power as an act of relationship between equals, with power being enacted through increasing the capacity of others and providng support and facilitation of others' knowledge, talent, and expertise. Leithwood's (1994) characterization of transformational leadership also resonates with the images of leadership conveyed through women's rhetoric, including striving to develop a common vision, continual evaluation and self-assessment, and working to enhance the performance of others. Foster's (1989) formulation of the administrator as a 'transformative intellectual' who uses moral language – 'a languge of critique and hope' – to transform social structures is consistent with feminist approaches as well. Feminism has a tradition of being aligned with other inclusive or emancipatory efforts towards social transformation, and the power of ideas about leadership derived from women's perspectives only grows if they are corroborated from other perspectives such as these. Consistent with the espoused values of feminism, feminist theory is best viewed as connected with other approaches, not standing above them.

There is room for caution here, however. Gosetti and Rusch (1995) suggest that some new approaches to leadership pay inadequate attention to the full range of women's perspectives, including their concerns about equity and justice as well as their good ideas about leadership practice. This, they argue, may result in an appropriation of some ideas from women and an ostensibly pro-woman stance, while also ignoring women's issues of access and equity. Calas and Smircich (1993) have a related perspective. They examine the trend towards the feminization of management within business and conclude that women are being called in, with all of their interpersonal skills and empathy, to manage painful conditions of decline and downsizing in firms, while the real action has moved to the level of international management, where men predominate in positions of power. By providing a kindler and gentler approach to management, women can soften the blows inflicted by impersonal, bottom-line-driven organizational hierarchies, allowing them to go unchallenged. In a similar vein, it is somewhat ironic that nontraditional, 'feminine' leadership styles and collaborative forms of organization are being advocated within education (in the United States, at least) at the same time that policy-making and accountability are moving increasingly away from local school agencies toward the state and federal levels. Is this another example of women being permitted to manage only within relatively constrained and powerless contexts?

It would violate much of women's rhetoric about leadership as participation, collaboration, and empowerment if we focused only on positions of formal leadership within schools. Thus, we conclude this section with a brief look at scholarship on teacher leadership. As with administrative leadership, not all of the work in this area is particularly feminist or has a gendered perspective. However, much of it embodies a rhetoric that is consistent with many ideas we have presented here, by suggesting that teachers can themselves practice leadership, both within the classroom and within the school organization, in ways that are collaborative, caring, and emancipatory (e.g., Weiler, 1988). The teacher leadership literature recognizes many ways in which teachers have been accustomed to working independently, even while under the supervisory and administrative control of a principal. Merely shifting leadership from principal to peers will not necessarily change teachers' preference for autonomy, especially if teacher-leaders are 'empowered' by the traditional administrative hierarchy (Cooper, 1988; Wasley, 1991). However, teachers may be willing to accept leadership from a colleague if that leadership is exercised in ways that are respectful of other teachers and that build on collaborative activity for reviewing and reflecting on teacher practice (Little, 1988). Principals are sometimes reluctant to embrace the notion of teacher leadership; their concerns range from worrying that the community will perceive that no-one is in charge to feeling that their own role is threatened. This is especially a problem when leadership is seen as a zero-sum game; the more someone has of it, the less someone else has (Troen & Boles, 1995). Nonetheless, some administrators have found that their own influence over classroom teaching has been enhanced by involving teachers in decision-making (Little, 1988). And administrators may have more success accommodating to teachers' exercise of leadership if norms of caring are extended toward everyone involved in decision-making, including those whose decision-making power is reduced (Hollingsworth, 1994). Work on teacher leadership is at an early stage; as it incorporates more explicitly an examination of power relations and gender relations among school professionals at all levels, it may provide additional support for the approaches to leadership that women administrators and scholars have been developing.

CONCLUSION

We introduced this chapter by asserting that gender is typically invisible unless two genders are present. In schools, as women step out of their traditional roles as teachers and move into leadership positions, they not only increase their own visibility but also highlight the salience of gender as both problem and possibility. We have presented a variety of gender issues that fall under the purview of school leaders, along with some examples of rhetorical positions that women are taking in shaping new approaches to leadership. As our review of the literature suggests, much more research in these areas is needed, including documentation of how gender issues emerge in educational settings and how school leaders work to resolve them.

Gender issues are not just women's issues, but they are often seen that way, and so it is frequently the case that women must shoulder the primary responsibility for identifying gender-related concerns and seeking equitable resolutions. A more permanent and appropriate stance, however, is that all educational leaders should be good stewards of gender and should be committed to creating positive school environments that are gender-inclusive, not simply gender-neutral. New conceptualizations of educational leadership, therefore, should

912

embody the recognition that effective leaders are activists about gender.

REFERENCES

Acker, J., & Van Houten, D. R. (1974). Differential recruitment and control: The sex structuring of organizations. *Administrative Science Quarterly, 19*(2), 152 – 163.

Acker, J. (1990). Hierarchies, jobs, bodies: A theory of gendered organizations. *Gender and Society, 4*(2), 139 – 158.

Adkison, J. A. (1981). Women in school administration: A review of the research. *Review of Educational Research, 51*(3), 311 – 343.

Adler, S., Laney, J., & Parker, M. (1993). *Managing women: Feminism and power in educational management.* Buckingham, England: Open University Press.

Allan, J. (1993). Male elementary teachers: Experiences and perspectives. In C. L. Williams (Ed.), *Doing 'women's work': Men in nontraditional occupations* (pp. 113 – 127). Newbury Park, CA: Sage Publications.

Alutto, J. A., & Belasco, J. A. (1973). Patterns of teacher participation in school system decision making. *Educational Administration Quarterly, 9*(1), 27 – 41.

Apple, M. W. (1986). *Teachers and texts: A political economy of class and gender relations in education.* New York: Methuen.

Astin, H. S., & Leland, C. (1991). *Women of influence, women of vision.* San Francisco: Jossey – Bass.

Baron, J. N., & Bielby, W. T. (1985). Organizational barriers to gender equality: Sex segregation of jobs and opportunities. In A. S. Rossi (Ed.), *Gender and the life course* (pp. 233 – 251). New York: Aldine.

Bass, B. M. (1990). *Bass & Stogdill's handbook of leadership* (3rd ed.). New York: The Free Press.

Baudoux, C. (1988). The female being and the management of school establishments in Quebec. *Resources for Feminist Research, 17*(4), 12 – 18.

Beck, L. G. (1994). *Reclaiming educational administration as a caring profession.* New York: Teachers College Press.

Bell, C. S. (1995). 'If I weren't involved with schools, I might be radical': Gender consciousness in context. In D. M. Dunlap & P. A. Schmuck (Eds.), *Women leading in education* (pp. 288 – 312). Albany: State University of New York Press.

Bellah, R. N. (1985). *Habits of the heart: Individualism and commitment in American life.* Berkeley, CA: University of California Press.

Blackmore, J. (1993). 'In the shadow of men': The historical construction of educational administration as a masculinist enterprise. In J. Blackmore & J. Kenway (Eds.), *Gender matters in educational administration and policy: A feminist introduction* (pp. 27 – 48). London: Falmer Press.

Blackmore, J. (1989). Changing from within: Feminist educators and administrative leadership. *Peabody Journal of Education, 66*(3), 19 – 40.

Bolman, L. G., & Deal, T. E. (1992). Leading and managing: Effects of context, culture, and gender. *Educational Administration Quarterly, 28*(3), 314 – 329.

Bradley, H. (1993). Across the great divide: The entry of men into 'women's jobs.' In C. L. Williams (Ed.), *Doing 'women's work': Men in nontraditional occupations* (pp. 10 – 27). Newbury Park, CA: Sage Publications.

Bronfenbrenner, U. (1976). The experimental ecology of education. *Educational Researcher, 5,* 5 – 15.

Bryk, A.S, Lee, V. E., & Holland, P. B. (1993). *Catholic schools and the common good.* Cambridge, MA: Harvard University Press.

Burrell, G. (1992). Sex and organizational analysis. In A. J. Mills & P. Tancred (Eds.), *Gendering organizational analysis* (pp. 71 – 92). Newbury Park, CA: Sage Publications.

Burrell, G., & Hearn, J. (1989). The sexuality of organization. In J. Hearn, D. L. Sheppard, P. Tancred – Sheriff, & G. Burrell (Eds.), *The sexuality of organization* (pp. 1 – 28). London: Sage Publications.

Calas, M. B., & Smircich, L. (1993). Dangerous liaisons: The 'ferminine in management' meets 'globalization.' *Business Horizons,* 73 – 83.

Callahan, R. E. (1962). *Education and the cult of efficiency.* Chicago: University of Chicago Press.

Carmichael, J. V., Jr. (1992). The male librarian and the feminine image: A survey of stereotype, status, and gender perceptions. *Library and Information Science Research, 14*(4), 411 – 446.

Charters, W. W., Jr., & Jovick, T. D. (1981). The gender of principals and principal/teacher relations in elementary schools. In P. A. Schmuck, W. W. Charters, Jr., & R. O. Carlson (Eds.), *Educational policy and management: Sex differentials* (pp. 307 – 331). New York: Academic Press.

Chafetz, J. S. (1990). *Gender equity: An integrated theory of stability and change.* Newbury Park, CA: Sage Publications.

Collinson, D. L., & Collinson, M. (1989). Sexuality in the workplace: The domination of men's sexuality. In J. Hearn, D. L. Sheppard, P. Tancred – Sheriff, & G. Burrell (Eds.), *The sexuality of organization* (pp. 91 – 110). London: Sage Publications.

Cooper, M. (1988). Whose culture is it, anyway? In A. Lieberman (Ed.), *Building a professional culture in schools* (pp. 45 – 54). New York: Teachers College Press.

Corcoran, T. B. (1990). School workplace: Perspectives on workplace reforms in public schools. In M. W. McLaughlin, J. E. Talbert, & N. Bascia (Eds.), *Contexts of teaching in secondary schools: Teachers' realities* (pp. 142 – 166). New York: Teachers College Press.

Cortina, R. (1989). Women as leaders in Mexican education. *Comparative Education Review, 33*(3), 357 – 376.

Darley, J., & Lomax, P. (1995, April). *The continuing role of women as primary school headteachers in the transformed British school system.* Paper presented at the annual meeting of the American Educational Research Association, San Francisco.

Davies, L. (1990). *Equity and efficiency? School management in an international context.* London: Falmer Press.

Deal, T. E., & Kennedy, A. A. (1982). *Corporate cultures.* Reading, MA: Addison – Wesley.

deMarrais, K. B., & LeCompte, M. D. (1995). *The way schools work: A sociological analysis of education* (2nd ed.). White Plains, NY: Longman Publishers.

Dunlap, D. M., & Goldman, P. (1991). Rethinking power in schools. *Educational Administration Quarterly, 27*(1), 5 – 29.

Dunlap, D. M., & Schmuck, P. A. (Eds.). (1995). *Women leading in education.* Albany: State University of New York Press.

914

Eagly, A. H., Karau, S. J., & Johnson, B. T. (1992). Gender and leadership style among school principals: A meta – analysis. *Educational Administration Quarterly, 28*(1), 76 – 102.

Eccles, R. G., & Nohria, N. (1992). *Beyond the hype: Rediscovering the essence of management.* Cambridge: Harvard Business School Press.

Epp, J. R., Sackney, L. E., & Kustaski, J. M. (1994). Reassessing levels of androcentric bias in Educational Administration Quarterly. *Educational Administration Quarterly, 30*(4), 451 – 471.

Epstein, C. F. (1970). *Woman's place: Options and limits in professional careers.* Berkeley: University of California Press.

Epstein, C. F. (1988). *Deceptive distinctions: Sex, gender, and the social order.* New Haven: Yale University Press.

Epstein, C.F., & Coser, R. L. (1981). *Access to power: Cross – national studies of women and elites.* London: George Allen & Unwin.

Etzioni, A. (Ed.). (1969). *The Semi – professions and their organization.* New York: The Free Press.

Ferguson, K. E. (1984). *The feminist case against bureaucracy.* Philadelphia: Temple University Press.

Fishel, A., & Pottker, J. (1979). Performance of women principals: A review of behavioral and attitudinal studies. In M. C. Berry (Ed.), *Women in educational administration* (pp. 24 – 31). Washington, DC: National Association for Women Deans, Administrators, and Counselors.

Follett, M. P. (1924). *Creative experience.* New York: Longmans, Green and Co.

Foster, W. (1989). The administrator as a transformative intellectual. *Peabody Journal of Education, 66*(3), 5 – 18.

Geile, J. Z. (1978). *Women and the future: Changing sex roles in modern America.* New York: The Free Press.

Gerth, H. H., & Mills, C. W. (1946). *From Max Weber: Essays in sociology.* New York: Oxford University Press.

Goffman, E. (1967). *Interaction ritual: Essays in face – to – face behavior.* Chicago: Aldine Publishing Company.

Goldring, E., & Chen, M. (1993). The feminization of the principalship in Israel: The trade – off between political power and cooperative leadership. In C. Marshall (Ed.), *The new politics of race and gender* (pp. 175 – 182). Washington, DC: The Falmer Press.

Gordon, T. (1991). Is education 'controlled by women'?; Onko kasvatus 'naisten kasissa'? *Kasvatus, 22*(3), 205 – 211.

Gosetti, P. P., & Rusch, E. (1995). Reexamining educational leadership: Challenging assumptions. In D. M. Dunlap, & P. A. Schmuck (Eds.), *Women leading in education* (pp. 11 – 35). Albany: State University of New York Press.

Gougeon, T. D. (1991, June). *Principal – teacher cross gender communication: A replication study.* Paper presented at the annual meeting of the Canadian Association for the Study of Educational Administration, Kingston, Ontario.

Gross, N. C., & Trask, A. E. (1976). *The sex factor and the management of schools.* New York: John Wiley and Sons.

Grundy, S. (1993). Educational leadership as emancipatory praxis. In J. Blackmore & J. Kenway (Eds.), *Gender matters in educational administration and policy: A feminist introduction* (pp. 165 – 177). London: Falmer Press.

Gutek, B. A. (1989). Sexuality in the workplace: Key issues in social research and organizational practice. In J. Hearn, D. L. Sheppard, P. Tancred – Sheriff, & G. Burrell (Eds.), *The sexuality of organization* (pp. 56 – 70). London: Sage Publications.

Gutek, B. A., & Cohen, A. G. (1992). Sex ratios, sex role spillover, and sex at work: A comparison of men's and women's experiences. In A. J. Mills & P. Tancred (Eds.), *Gendering organizational analysis* (pp. 133 – 150). Newbury Park, CA: Sage Publications.

Hansot, E., & Tyack, D. (1988). Gender in American public schools: Thinking institutionally. *Signs: Journal of women in culture and society, 13*(4), 741 – 760.

Hearn, J. (1987). *The gender of oppression: Men, masculinity, and the critique of Marxism.* Brighton: Wheatsheaf Books.

Hearn, J. and Morgan, D. H .J. (1990). *Men, masculinities and social theory.* London: Unwin Hyman.

Hearn, J,, & Parkin, P. W. (1992). Gender and organizations: A selective review and a critique of a neglected area. In A. J. Mills & P. Tancred (Eds.), *Gendering organizational analysis* (pp. 46 – 66). Newbury Park, CA: Sage Publications.

Helgesen, S. (1990). *The female advantage: Women's ways of leadership.* New York: Doubleday Currency.

Hochschild, A. R. (1983). *The managed heart.* Berkeley: University of California Press.

Hollingsworth, S. (1994). *Teacher research and urban literacy education: Lessons and conversations in a feminist key.* New York: Teachers College Press.

Hough, J. (1986). Gender bias in educational management and administration. *Educational Management and Administration, 16,* 69 – 74.

Hurty, K. S. (1995). Women principals – leading with power. In D. M. Dunlap, & P. A. Schmuck (Eds.), *Women leading in education* (pp. 380 – 406). Albany: State University of New York Press.

Jacobs, J. A. (1993). Men in female – dominated fields: trends and turnover. In C. L. Williams (Ed.), *Doing 'women's work': Men in nontraditional occupations* (pp. 49 – 63). Newbury Park, CA: Sage Publications.

Jones, K. (1990). The gender difference hypothesis: A synthesis of findings. *Educational Administration Quarterly, 26*(1), 5 – 37.

Kanter, R. M. 1977. *Men and women of the corporation.* New York: Basic Books.

Karim, W. J. (1983). Malay women's movements: Leadership and processes of change. *International Social Science Journal, 35*(4), 719 – 731.

Kauppinen – Toropainen, K., & Lammi, J. (1993). Men in female – dominated occupations: A cross – cultural comparison. In C. L. Williams (Ed.), *Doing 'women's work': Men in nontraditional occupations* (pp. 91 – 112). Newbury Park, CA: Sage Publications.

Kempner, Ken. (1989). Getting into the castle of educational administration. *Peabody Journal of Education, 66*(3), 104 – 123.

Kimnel, M.S. (1987). *Changing men: New directions in research on men and masculinity.* London: Sage.

Lather, P. (1994). The absent presence: Patriarchy, capitalism, and the nature of teacher work. In L. Stone (Ed.), *The education feminism reader* (pp. 242 – 251). New York: Routledge.

Lee, V. E., & Bryk, A. S. (1986). Effects of single – sex secondary schools on student achievement and attitudes. *Journal of Educational Psychology, 78,* 381 – 395.

916

Lee, V. E., & Marks, H. M. (1990). Sustained effects of the single – sex secondary school experience on attitudes, behaviors, and values in college. *Journal of Educational Psychology, 82,* 578 – 592.

Lee, V. E., Smith, J. B., & Cioci, M. (1993). Teachers and principals: Gender – related perceptions of leadership and power in secondary schools. *Educational Evaluation and Policy Analysis, 15*(2), 153 – 180.

Lee, V.E., Loeb, S., & Marks, H.M. (1995). Gender differences in secondary school teachers' control over classroom and school policy. *American Journal of Education, 103*(3), 259 – 301.

Leithwood, K. (1994). Leadership for school restructuring. *Educational Administration Quarterly, 30*(4), 498 – 518.

Lips, H. M. (1991). *Women, men, and power.* Mountain View, CA: Mayfield Publishing Company.

Little, J. W. (1988). Assessing the prospects for teacher leadership. In A. Lieberman (Ed.), *Building a professional culture in schools* (pp. 78 – 106). New York: Teachers College Press.

Lorber, J. (1994). *Paradoxes of gender.* New Haven: Yale University Press.

Marshall, C., & Mitchell, B. A. (1991). The assumptive worlds of fledgling administrators. *Education and Urban Society, 23*(4), 396 – 415.

Marshall, C., & Mitchell, B. A. (1989, March). *Women's careers as a critique of the administrative culture.* Paper presented at the annual meeting of the American Educational Research Association, San Francisco.

Martin, J. (1992). *Cultures in organizations: Three perspectives.* New York: Oxford University Press.

Martin, P. Y. (1993). Feminist practice in organizations: Implications for management. In E. A. Fagenson (Ed.), *Women in management: Trends, issues, and challenges in managerial diversity* (pp. 274 – 296). Newbury Park: Sage Publications.

Martin, P. Y. (1990). Rethinking feminist organizations. *Gender & Society, 4,* 182 – 206.

Martin, P. Y. (1981). Women, labour markets, and employing organizations: A critical analysis. In D. Dunkerley & G. Salaman (Eds.), *The International Yearbook of Organization Studies.* London: Routledge & Kegan Paul.

McCall, A. L. (1995). The bureaucratic restraints to caring in schools. In D. M. Dunlap, & P. A. Schmuck (Eds.), *Women leading in education* (pp. 180 – 196). Albany: State University of New York Press.

Meyerson, D., & Scully, M. (1994). *Tempered radicalism and the politics of ambivalence and change.* Unpublished manuscript, University of Michigan, Ann Arbor.

Mills, A. J. (1992). Organization, gender, and culture. In A. J. Mills & P. Tancred (Eds.), *Gendering organizational analysis* (pp. 93 – 111). Newbury Park, CA: Sage Publications.

Mills, A. J., & Tancred, P. (Eds.). (1992). *Gendering organizational analysis.* Newbury Park, CA: Sage Publications.

Moles, O. (1988). *High school and beyond: Administrator and teacher survey.* Washington, D.C.: U.S. Department of Education, Office of Educational Research and Improvement.

Morgan, G. (1986). *Images of organization.* Beverly Hills, CA: Sage Publications.

National Center for Education Statistics. (1994). *Public and private school principals: Are there too few women?* (Issue Brief). Washington, D.C.: U.S. Department of Education, Office of Educational Research and Improvement.

Nicholson, L. J. (1994). Women and schooling. In L. Stone (Ed.), *The education feminism reader* (pp. 73 – 83). New York: Routledge.

Nielsen, J. M. (Ed.). (1990). *Feminist research methods: Exemplary readings in the social sciences.* Boulder, CO: Westview Press.

Noddings, N. (1990). Feminist critiques in the professions. In C. B. Cazden (Ed.), *Review of Research in Education (Vol. 16)* (pp. 393 – 424).

Noddings, N. (1984). *Caring: A feminine approach to ethics and moral education.* Berkeley: University of California Press.

Oakley, A. (1972). *Sex, gender and society.* London: Temple Smith.

Parsons, T., Bales, R. F., & Shils, E. A. (1951). *Working papers in the theory of action.* Glencoe, IL: Free Press.

Perrow, C. (1986). *Complex organizations: A critical essay.* (3rd ed.). New York: Random House.

Pfeffer, J. (1981). *Power in organizations.* Marshfield, MA: Pitman.

Pringle, R. (1989). Bureaucracy, rationality and sexuality: The case of secretaries. In J. Hearn, D. L. Sheppard, P. Tancred – Sheriff, & G. Burrell (Eds.), *The sexuality of organization* (pp.158 – 177). London: Sage Publications.

Ramsay, K., & Barker, M. (1992). Gender, bureaucracy, and organizational culture. In M. Savage & A. Witz (Eds.), *Gender and bureaucracy* (pp. 253 – 276). Oxford: Blackwell Publishers.

Reiger, K. (1993). The gender dynamics of organizations: A historical account. In J. Blackmore & J. Kenway (Eds.), *Gender matters in educational administration and policy: A feminist introduction* (pp. 17 – 26). London: Falmer Press.

Reskin, B. F., & Roos, P. A. (1990). *Job queues, gender queues.* Philadelphia: Temple University Press.

Riehl, C., & Byrd, M. A. (1995). *Gender differences among new recruits to school administration: Cautionary footnotes to an optimistic tale.* Manuscript submitted for publication.

Riehl, C., & Sipple, J. W. (1995, April). *Scheduling time and talent: The impact of secondary school organizational conditions and teachers' work assignments on teachers' perceptions of efficacy and professional commitment.* Paper presented at the annual meeting of the American Educational Research Association, San Francisco.

Robinson, B. E. (1979). A two – year followup study of male and female caregivers. *Child Care, 8*(4), 279 – 294.

Roethlisberger, F. J., & Dickson, W. J. (1939). *Management and the worker.* Cambridge, MA: Harvard University Press.

Rosenthal, R., & Rosnow, R. L. (1984). *Essentials of behavioral research: Methods and data analysis.* New York: McGraw – Hill.

Rusch, E. A., & Marshall, C. (1995, April). *Gender filters at work in the administrative culture.* Paper presented at the annual meeting of the American Educational Research Association, San Francisco.

Sadker, D., & Sadker, M. (1994). *Failing at fairness: How America's schools cheat girls.* New York: Charles Scribner's Sons.

Shakeshaft, C. (1993). Gender equity in schools. In C. A. Capper (Ed.), *Educational administration in a pluralistic society* (pp. 86 – 109). Albany: State University of New York Press.

Shakeshaft, C. (1989). *Women in educational administration.* Newbury Park, CA: Sage.

918

Shakeshaft, C., & Hanson, M. (1986). Androcentric bias in the Educational Administration Quarterly. *Educational Administration Quarterly, 22*(1), 68 – 92.

Shedd, J. B., & Bacharach, S. B. (1991). *Tangled hierarchies: Teachers as professionals and the management of schools.* San Francisco: Jossey – Bass.

Sheppard, D. (1992). Women managers' perceptions of gender and organizational life. In A. J. Mills & P. Tancred (Eds.), *Gendering organizational analysis* (pp. 151 – 166). Newbury Park, CA: Sage Publications.

Sheriff, P. [Tancred –], & Campbell, E. J. (1992). Room for women: A case study in the sociology of organizations. In A. J. Mills & P. Tancred (Eds.), *Gendering organizational analysis* (pp. 31 – 45). Newbury Park, CA: Sage Publications.

Simpson, R. L., & Simpson, I.H. (1969). Women and bureaucracy in the semi – professions. In A. Etzioni (Ed.), *The semi – professions and their organization* (pp. 196 – 265). New York: The Free Press.

Sirianni, C. (1984). Learning pluralism: Democracy and diversity in feminist organizations. In F. Fischer & C. Sirianni (Eds.), *Critical studies in organization and bureaucracy* (2nd ed.) (pp. 554 – 576). Philadelphia: Temple University Press.

Skelton, A. (1993). On becoming a male physical education teacher: The informal culture of students and the construction of hegemonic masculinity. *Gender and Education, 5*(3), 289 – 303.

Skelton, C. (1991). A study of the career perspectives of male teachers of young children. *Gender and Education, 3*(3), 279 – 289.

Smith, D. E. (1987). *The everyday world as problematic.* Boston: Northeastern University Press.

Stinchcombe, A. L. (1965). Social structure and organizations. In J. G. March (Ed.), *Handbook of organizations* (pp. 142 – 193). Chicago: Rand McNally & Company.

Stock, P. H. (1978). *Better than rubies: A history of women's education.* New York: G. P. Putnam's Sons.

Strachan, J. (1993). Including the personal and the professional: researching women in educational leadership. *Gender and Education, 5*(1), 71 – 80.

Tabin, Y., & Coleman, P. (1991, April). *Joining the old boys' club? Women's careers as school principals in British Columbia, Canada, 1980 to 1990.* Paper presented at the annual meeting of the American Educational Research Association, Chicago.

Taylor, F. W. (1915). *The principles of scientific management.* New York: Harper & Brothers Publishers.

Thibault, G. (1988). Women and education: On being female in male places. In W. Tomm & G. Hamilton (Eds.), *Gender bias in scholarship: The pervasive prejudice* (pp.63 – 98). Waterloo, Canada: Wilfrid Laurier University Press.

Troen, V., & Boles, K. C. (1995). Leadership from the classroom: Women teachers as a key to school reform. In D. M. Dunlap, & P. A. Schmuck (Eds.), *Women leading in education* (pp. 358 – 379). Albany: State University of New York Press.

Tyack, D., & Hansot, E. (1990). *Learning together: A history of coeducation in American public schools.* New Haven: Yale University Press.

Tyack, D., & Hansot, E. (1982). *Managers of virtue: Public school leadership in America, 1820 – 1980.* New York: Basic Books.

Varghese, M. A. (1990). Women administrators in education. New Delhi, India: Har – Anand Publishers in association with Vikas Publishing House.

Wasley, P. A. (1991). *Teachers who lead: The rhetoric of reform and the realities of practice.* New York: Teachers College Press.

Weiler, K. (1988). *Women teaching for change: Gender, class and power.* New York: Bergin & Garvey Publishers.

Wolcott, H. F. (1973). *The man in the principal's office.* New York: Holt, Rinehart and Winston.

Wolff, J. (1977). Women in organizations. In S. Clegg & D. Dunkerly (Eds.), *Critical issues in organizations* (pp. 7 – 20). London: Routledge & Kegan Paul.

Woodward, J. (1965). *Industrial organization: Theory and practice.* London: Oxford University Press.

Yeakey, C. C., Johnson, G. S., & Adkison, J. A. (1986). In pursuit of equity: A review of research on minorities and women in educational administration. *Educational Administration Quarterly, 22*(3), 110 – 149.

Zimmer, L. (1988). Tokenism and women in the workplace: The limits of gender – neutral theory. *Social Problems, 35*(1), 64 – 77.

Chapter 25: Decentralization, Collaboration, and Normative Leadership: Implications for Central Office Practice and Research

DICKSON CORBETT, BRUCE WILSON AND JACI WEBB-DEMPSEY

Research for Better Schools, Philadelphia; and Centre for the Renewal of Professional Preparation and Practice, West Virginia University

The preparation of this chapter was supported by funds from the United States Department of Education, Office of Educational Research and Improvement (OERI). The opinions expressed do not necessarily reflect the position of OERI, and no official endorsement should be inferred.

> 'A sociological writer cannot, in the present state of our science, hope to get very far ahead of common sense, and he is usually fortunate if he does not fall behind it.' (Waller, 1932:3)

Waller could have been speaking about the current relationship between central office research and practice as well. For example, scholarly cautions about the modest classroom effects of site-based management (Fullan, 1991; Murphy & Beck, 1995) and academic misgivings about the ultimate efficacy of many broad-based visioning processes (Barth, 1993) have done little to slow widespread acceptance and partial implementation of such initiatives in a host of school systems. Rightly or wrongly, the references districts use to determine whether they should change are more likely to be the experiences of other school systems than empirical studies.

Many reasons for the lack of synchronization between practical experience and central office research come to mind: researchers' insufficient attention to issues of importance to practitioners; practitioners' overestimation of the applicability of practices from another setting to theirs; an unhelpful preponderance of negative (i.e., what not to do) findings; practitioner impatience; the imperative to act built into policy mandates; turgid prose; and recommendations weak because of many qualifiers. But the foremost reason resides in the fact that central

K. Leithwood et al. (eds.), International Handbook of Educational Leadership and Administration, 921-946.

office research results travel poorly through time and space, which requires educators to carefully and thoughtfully adjust and adapt the research to fit their particular situations. Unfortunately, the political and economic exigencies of the central office environment seriously constrain the mental and physical resources that they can allocate to such activity.

Thus, facing uncertainty, the researched have little luxury to wait for researchers to ponder daily school life and issue sage advice; the former can only bemoan the irrelevance of the latter's products when an occasional pause for reflection reveals the help to be too far behind. Conversely, finding interesting issues and situations to examine along the way, researchers have little time to reflect on what they are seeing because they perceive that only reasoned speculation can travel fast enough to keep up with practitioners' reflective *and* reflexive actions, relegating the actual research to a Jurassic Park of outdated recommendations.

This situation is analogous to taking a field trip with elementary students. As the students disembark from their yellow school buses, teachers herd them into tight lines, admonishing the children to stay close together. But inevitably – as the group sets out for the library, museum, or picnic grounds – an untied shoestring, a dropped pencil, or a deliberate tripping of a classmate causes the spacing among the students to become uneven. The teacher then stops the front of the line to wait for the back to catch up. Repeated interminably over the course of the day, this process results in those in the front becoming frustrated and increasingly unruly because of the incessant delays while those in the back become tired and fed up with continually having to hurry without ever getting to rest.

Neither the elementary field trip nor the gap between the need to act and the availability of research assistance will become less troublesome in the foreseeable future. The latter poses a particular problem for reviews such as this because past lessons learned do not really fit the circumstances in which district people currently work. Indeed, the patterns of control, coordination, and communication that typify the organizational world of the central office today bear little resemblance to the one that most of them faced even five years ago. Decision making has steadily devolved to school administrators and teachers; school boards resolutely micro-manage; and community stakeholders leap into strategic planning activities, invited or uninvited – to name a few of the complications for central office personnel. The world of the local school system is intense, fluid, keenly visible, and fraught with demands (Conley, 1993). Moreover, the very relevance of having a central office is in dispute. Some view the central office as the key to reform: 'In the long run, therefore, who the superintendent is, what the superintendent values, and the style of operation supported by the superintendent will be manifest throughout the school system' (Schlechty, 1990;128); others wonder about the need for one: 'I...ultimately leave open the question of whether we should have school districts at all' (Fullan, 1993:143).

With these demands and the ambivalence about the future of the district office in mind, this chapter explores salient features of the local district landscape, discusses what research (and, more prevalently, some reasoned speculation) has to say about the implications of this environment for the role of the central office, and suggests some ways that research and practice might better accommodate one another in the future. The chapter is divided into three sections, one lengthy and two brief. The first concentrates on three organizational developments – facts of life, really – that have forced central office educators to act far ahead of any empirical guidance: site-based management (SBM) or *decentralization*; external and internal *collaboration*, or partnering; and visioning and the necessity for exercising *normative leadership.* Each is a significant influence on the types of roles that central office staff members might be reasonably expected to perform if they are to remain vital players in local educational systems, and therefore this section looks closely at these roles as well. Although we treat the three topics separately for analytical reasons, they are inextricably intertwined with each other in reality. Indeed, underlying these developments is a central cultural theme – the need for establishing a norm of reciprocity in order for school systems, indeed all organizations, to become as effective as they can be. The second section of this chapter develops this idea further and uses it as a springboard to the third section, which discuss how research on these critical central office issues might better inform central office practice and get everyday common sense back into view.

We use the terms 'district office' and 'central office' interchangeably and include as occupants of them all extra-school professional personnel, such as curriculum supervisors who do not have school-based teaching responsibilities, directors, assistant superintendents, and superintendents. Of course, in some rural systems the superintendent is the central office; whereas, in large urban areas the systems are sometimes partialed into subdistricts with each effectively having its own superintendent and a host of other staff.

The 'research' we constantly refer to is that which specifically addresses decentralization, collaboration, and normative leadership in local school systems, with most attention given to information and ideas that point the way to possible important roles for central office people to play as these trends evolve over time. For the most part, we have shied away from research more tangential to education. But we should add that the literature on educational change offers considerable general support for the three developments as potentially significant and positive factors in enabling school systems to alter their operations. This literature has received excellent treatment at length from Fullan (1991) and more succinctly in Fullan and Miles (1992). While the tone of this chapter implies that central office research per se is ambiguous about (1) the effects of initiatives related to these topics on instruction and students' learning and (2) concrete implications for district officials' behaviour, there is no question that involving the people affected by change in decision making, sharing human and other resources with entities outside and inside the system, and promoting shared views of purpose and practice are central components to creating a continuous learning organization for adults (Burbach & Crockett, 1994). Remaining to be answered are what effective, day-to-day central office actions look like in the context of decentralization, collaboration, and normatively based leadership, and what research can do to better inform this action.

THREE DEVELOPMENTS AFFECTING THE CENTRAL OFFICE

The most common theme in the literature on the central office role in school improvement is the recognition that there is not much research about that role (Crowson & Morris, 1992; Murphy, Peterson, & Hallinger, 1986). Indeed, with the exception of five studies summarized in two recent issues of the journal *School Effectiveness and School Improvement* (Leithwood, 1992), there is no unified, coherent body of research. The limited empirical work that is available focuses attention almost exclusively on the role of the superintendent, ignoring the significant variety of role groups who provide instructional support and reside somewhere in district organizational charts between the superintendent and building principals (see, e.g., Pajak, 1989).

Two strands of research on superintendents dot this meagre landscape. The first is historical and is best exemplified by the work of Tyack and Hansot (1982) and Cuban (1988). They offer compelling evidence about why superintendents have not had more influence in changing the core activities of schooling – teaching and learning. As Cuban so ably points out, superintendents managed rather than led because (a) their positions were originally conceived of as administrative, (b) they were socialized and trained to perform a management function, (c) it was more convenient to manage, (d) management helped reduce conflict, and (e) education had such ambiguous effectiveness indicators. And as Tyack and Hansot note (1982: 252): 'Public school leaders in the past have mostly been able to absorb the demands for change by accretion, without changing much the central core of instruction. As a result, American education has been both faddish in particulars and resistant to change in its basic mode of operation.'

The other strand of research has involved in-depth qualitative studies of the behaviour of superintendents, typically the more successful ones (see, e.g., Crowson & Morris, 1992), probing the meaning of leadership. These scattered research efforts document the varied leadership roles of superintendents including evaluation (Dimmock & Wildy, 1992), support and consultation (Hord, Jolley, & Mendez-Morse, 1992; Murphy & Beck, 1995), agenda setting (Hallinger & Edwards, 1992), and modelling of valued behaviour (Peterson, Murphy, & Hallinger, 1987). What is beginning to emerge from this research is an acknowledgment of the need to focus attention on instruction, not withstanding all the pressures to deal with managerial and political demands (Cuban, 1989). The more successful central offices are those where shared norms about accountability and program operations defined by student learning are what keep instruction at the forefront (Coleman & LaRocque, 1990).

The whole thrust of this previous district office research, sketchy as it is, is how district personnel, primarily superintendents, managed those inside the system and created buffers against external intruders so as to preserve and protect the core technology of schooling – instruction – in its existing form (see, e.g., Hallinger & Murphy, 1987 and Peterson, 1987). Control, coordination, and communication were found to be decidedly one-way and mostly top-down phenomena. Today, these organizational processes have changed decidedly in most school districts. Control has become intentionally decentralized; communication about school district operation occurs through elaborate and extensive collaborative activities; and coordination seems to be more normatively driven by shared values than bureaucratically driven by formal rules. The stimuli for these changes have been many, ranging from the application of ideas from the business management literature to pressure from a dissatisfied public. The changes are significant in that, as Leithwood (1992) argues, such external influences play a considerable role in shaping the leadership practices of the central office. And, indeed, the effects of the three have been an incredible opening up of school district functioning to the purview and influence of many citizens and educators alike and a considerable challenge for those who traditionally 'ran' these systems.

Decentralization

> ...Others say that when school officials reach out to parents, they are trying to co-opt them into a school-reform process that is proceeding on a narrow path. 'I don't buy the strategic-planning committees,' Penny L. Sisson told the Ohio state board. 'I don't buy any of it because I see the work is all done.' (Pitsch, 1994:21)

Informally, school districts have always been somewhat decentralized. As Corwin and Borman (1988:212) claim:

> The dilemma of administrative control is that central office administrators are officially in charge of school districts, but actually many policies are determined by the actions of local schools. Consequently, in effect, district administrators are held accountable for things they cannot always control. This condition is a product of decentralization processes within formally centralized school districts.

As a consequence, according to Hannaway (1989:91-92), superintendents operate 'with only limited and perhaps biased information about what is going on in their organization.' The defining characteristic of recent changes in control has been to more formally devolve decision making to other groups. The road has been bumpy, as power once held is not easily relinquished – to the consternation of people such as the one quoted at the beginning of this section. Nevertheless, the momentum to distribute authority widely is strong, and more than likely the current era benchmarks a transition period to even greater decentralization.

Matters of 'control' have historically been central issues in district office studies. Recently, however, the argument has been advanced that this should no longer be the primary focus. Instead, what is needed to insure effective and coordinated activity in a school district is to build up the commitment of other participants to furthering the organization's mission (Rowan, 1990). In other words, the drive to excel should be internal rather than external; self-regulation is much more efficient than supervision or monitoring (Sykes & Elmore, 1989). This view appears to have taken hold universally; school people cannot escape the ground swell of support for site-based management (SBM) and other forms of decentralization as the means to increased empowerment and, thereby, ownership of the actions decided on (Murphy & Beck, 1995).

'SBM is generally associated with plans to delegate decision making authority to the school level and to distribute that authority among clusters of site actors, usually principals, teachers, and parents' (Malen, 1994:263). The simplicity of abstract definition belies the complexity in concrete practice. Indeed, many different arrangements have appeared under the guise of SBM, raising questions about what 'it' is exactly. Is it increased representation of previously under-represented groups on existing committees and councils? Is it a broader range of advisors to those who traditionally have made most of the decisions? Is it relocating decisionmaking in several well-defined areas, such as instruction, to subordinate positions? Is it relinquishing super ordinate control over most decisions, including resource allocation, to others? Is it obliterating the super ordinate-subordinate distinction completely? All of the above have been proposed and/or tried.

This makes any research on the topic difficult to synthesize because one has to be very careful to take note of discontinuities in practice across sites, and that information is not always available. Murphy and Beck (1995) propose that types of SBM can be identified in terms of the role/group that has responsibility for decisionmaking (administrators, professionals, or community members) and the functions about which they make decisions (goals, budgets, personnel, curriculum, and structure). Describing different incarnations of SBM in this way at least avoids the obvious, hopeless confusion associated with trying to compare the community-controlled teams in Chicago that hire staff members with the more prevalent school-level, principal-run groups in which a few others supply occasional advice on matters such as scheduling and time use.

Needless to say, given the multiplicity of conceivable SBM types and the relative thinness of the research, acceptance of SBM-like initiatives is far ahead of research on their effects. Even the cynical do not have the basis for judging whether their criticisms rest on poor implementation of a good idea or just a bad idea. Certainly it is unclear whether pushing decisions closer to those working with students actually has benefited students in any way (e.g., Taylor & Bogotch, 1994; Meister, 1994), and others have already concluded that '...reforms that devolved decisionmaking to schools may have altered governance procedures, but did not affect the teaching-learning core of schools' (Fullan, 1991:201). Apart from students and classroom instruction, there is evidence that SBM has political utility in managing conflict (e.g., diffusing it, averting it, and/or mediating it) and creating greater legitimacy for the system (Malen, 1994) by 'evok[ing] widespread positive reactions to policy actions and policy systems' (Elder & Cobb, 1983:66). However, other evidence reveals that SBM can be a source of conflict itself (Weiss & Cambone, 1994). Moreover, such strategies sometimes come across to participants as being manipulative (Conley, 1991) – a thinly disguised way of shifting the burden of work (Carnoy, 1990). Predictably, the research gives little guidance as to when one side of the Janus face is more likely to appear than the other (Malen, 1994).

Just inviting people in is not enough to achieve positive effects. Decentralized decisionmaking places a much greater burden on practice than that, as Mirel (1994:516) so clearly points out:

> The question of who controls the schools or in this case who sets the reform agenda directly confronts issues of power, resources, and prestige. Reformers cannot expect that these deeply political issues will always, or even often, be resolved by appeals for consensus.... large-scale educational change will not succeed unless reformers address the material and political dimensions of reform well before embarking on a campaign of change. They must face the power-brokering reality of the reform process, clearly recognizing which issues strike deeply at vested interests. From the beginning and throughout the project, they must be as well versed in strategic negotiation and alliance building as they are in devising breakthrough educational programs. In the process, they must also become competent in judging when to compromise, redesign, or stand fast. Reformers will have to recognize that the process of change involves not just building constituencies but also maintaining them, not just gaining power but also exercising it wisely.

Thus, decentralization requires considerable social and political adeptness.

Power, then, is not the only resource that needs to be decentralized (Weiss & Cambone, 1994; Wohlstetter, Smyer, & Mohrman, 1994). In fact, a report from the Rand Corporation (1994) suggests that the only way for any decentralization attempt to truly support school self-governance is for every decision to be made at that level, including staffing and budgeting. This finding means that core technical knowledge and the human resources available to do the work must also become widely distributed. In that light, Crowson and Morris (1992:85) argue that there must be a balancing of district office 'oversight' and school autonomy and that there are still some centralized functions that a district office should play: risk-management, keeping an eye on the 'big picture,' and nurturing external relationships.

Thus, SBM seems to be more likely to yield beneficial results when combined with a curriculum and instruction initiative that also includes training both in process and content knowledge/skills. In fact, Murphy and Beck (1995) conclude that many of the problems associated with SBM's being a 'weak' intervention is probably because the focus is too much on structure and governance and not enough on education and community.

Fullan (1993:146) notes three conclusions to be drawn from central office research on this topic:

1. Centralization does not work.
2. Decentralization does not work.
3. Simultaneous uncoordinated centralization-decentralization does not work. The answer, I believe, lies in some form of 'coordinated co-development of schools and the district.'

Louis (1989: 161) also supports this perspective when she writes: '...the picture is one of co-management, with coordination and joint planning through the development of consensus between staff members at all levels about desired goals for education.'

Thus, although a perceived loss of control may be a singularly threatening development to central office staff members, in reality decentralization may actually magnify the importance of their work. But that work would take on an entirely different character than that which they currently perform. Regardless, this decisive change in control feeds directly into the other developments that are radically shaping the leadership role that central office personnel must play.

Collaboration

> In more than thirty years as a self-styled school reformer and critic of the educational status quo, I have learned one lesson over and over from observing or being involved in many, many failed reform attempts and a few wonderful successes. Significant changes at the school level are most likely to happen when there is consumer demand for change and when the reform effort includes families and communities in partnership with educators. Such a simple lesson. But so hard for educators, administrators, and political leaders to learn. (Davies, 1994:44)

> School improvement is a multi-level process. Thus, it typically requires the cooperation of actors at different levels in the educational system, ranging from teachers, students, administrators, and parents up through policymakers and key educational constituencies. (Louis, 1989:146)

Even district leaders who have learned this lesson and welcomed new partners find that the road is not always smooth. Nowhere has that been more poignant than in Littleton, Colorado where a collaborative effort around constructing new outcome-based graduation requirements collapsed and the ten-year superintendent lost her job over it.

> It's popular to say that the Littleton schools didn't do a good job of informing the public about their reforms, leaving the door open for suspicion and rumours to flourish. Karen Laplan, a 15-year board member, says the district did reach out. 'But we reached out once,' she says, 'and sometimes you forget – I know I did – that the stakeholders change.'... 'The major issue for us, underneath all this stuff is that there are major philosophical differences in the community,' she adds, 'and we don't know how to address them and talk about them with each other.' (Bradley, 1994:25)

Still, leadership and support for school reform take shape in the context of relationships with others wherein information and opinions about important issues are shared. Once one-way and at the instigation of the schools, communication has become much more intensive through collaboration, both externally and internally.

External Collaboration

Stone and Wehlage (1992:9) propose at least three distinct forms of external collaboration that serve to 'create an information flow and maintain norms that help establish a trustworthy, predictable context for organized activity.' The first is an expanded notion of parental participation, which means the active engagement of parents, not only with educators (e.g. instruction, classroom assistance, governance, and their own educational improvement), but also in personal interaction with their children about school work and larger educational issues. Stone and Wehlage hypothesize that when parents have a more clearly defined role in a school several positive benefits emerge:

1. a more meaningful two-way flow of information blossoms between parents and schools,
2. this information articulates more clearly for all the parties involved (parents, students, and teachers) what the norms and expectations are for appropriate behaviour, and
3. organizational skills on the part of the school are fostered, which in turn create a more trustworthy context for action.

The second type of external collaboration is between educators and the business community. A whole plethora of school-business partnerships emerged in the 1980s, many of which operated on the assumption that educational outcomes and economic productivity are tightly coupled. In these models, schools were viewed as being primarily responsible for creating productivity problems and that the solutions rest in reforming education. A more sophisticated view is emerging in the new wave of school-business relationships where the relationship between school and employment is seen as much more complex. Schooling must be viewed by business as more than the acquisition of knowledge and skills; it must also include the development of social capital. Any collaboration between educators and the private sector must build on '...a consensus about the importance of education, training, and a reasonable promise of future opportunities as a way of developing a work force capable of participating in high performance work organizations (Stone & Wehlage, 1992: 21).' As Bruner (1991) points out, such collaboration lends greater visibility to child issues, provides additional legitimacy to policy reform claims, provides extra funding for new or innovative approaches, and offers a cadre of volunteers to provide guidance, support and role models for students and their families.

The final category of external collaboration is with human service organizations, those agencies that offer services typically beyond the reach of schools (e.g. housing, health care, and income support), but which are viewed as integrally affecting the learning of students. The primary problem with the current state of these services is the fragmentation and isolation of most forms of assistance. One agency does not know about, and in some cases even contradicts, the services of another. Yet, the solution has to be more than simply increasing integration and coordination. For all the agencies to work more effectively they must view the problem as organizations needing to:

> ... empower families to respond to the common problems of their neighbourhoods and communities. This approach implies that social services treat people less as clients in need of direct services and more as people with resources who can respond to the human problems created by deteriorated neighbourhoods. The goal of collaboration for human services is to work with other institutions to rebuild the social and economic infrastructure of communities. (Stone & Wehlage, 1992:24)

If instruction is ultimately to be more effective with parental and community involvement, then systems need to develop a structure that brings them in wholeheartedly rather than one that measures their entry like an intravenous drip line. Essentially, the task has changed from figuring out how to keep external people out to how to work with them productively. 'A systematic, symbiotic relationship is required between schools and local agencies' (Fullan, 1993:162-163).

Internal Collaboration

The professional culture of teaching puts the view of 'my classroom as my castle' center stage. In other words, each classroom is the teacher's fiefdom where individual adults make their own decisions about how best to work with the students under their charge. A strong norm of individual autonomy (Lortie, 1975) makes it very difficult for staff to work toward some larger collective good. Moreover, job demands make it difficult for administrators to supervise in the way that they should in order to be instructionally relevant and credible. Creating a true collaborative atmosphere in schools is obviously extremely difficult to do (Newmann, 1994). Thus, Fullan (1993:146) observes: 'What is especially missing and needed in the research on districts is not research on districts qua districts but on the changing role relationships between schools and districts.' That is, what are the internal collaborative roles that are analogous to the external ones described above?

Given the complexity of school operation and reform, such roles will have to be more than local change facilitation, which was a redefined role called for in more limited improvement reforms in the 1980s (see Cox, 1983). But establishing different relationships will also have to avoid going down a path that leads to 'impossible work' (Sykes & Elmore, 1989:81) – that is requiring people to work together in ways that are contradictory to the means available to them. What needs to take place is a mutual sharing of strengths among internal staff members, as Stoll and Fink (1992: 34) point out in their study of new collaborative bonds established in one Canadian district:

> The reorganization of central office support staff requires people in positions of responsibility to think and behave as service providers to teachers in schools, as opposed to deliverers of policy and procedure.

The district role is to work with school staff to develop a vision, provide development support in implementing that vision, and encourage school-level change efforts, thereby creating a 'collaborative culture' (Stoll & Fink, 1992:26). Clark (1991) echoes this view.

This new way of thinking about the central office relationship to schools is further clarified by a description of the Vancouver, Washington school district:

> The implicit assumptions in Vancouver's reorganization is that the central office functions more as a support agency staffed by facilitators and resource coordinators. The district office continues to do those things it can do most efficiently, notably strategic planning, curriculum coordination, transportation, legal services, accountability and research, payroll, and food services, while emphasizing new and expanded roles at the building level. (Parsley, 1991:14)

Collaboration, whether between educators and outsiders or just among educators, may also have an additional benefit in an age in which school financing becomes increasingly problematic – and that is as a vehicle for building social capital. Borrowing from Coleman (1988), social capital refers to the social and organizational relationships among people that facilitate collective action. Put another way, social capital becomes the structure of obligations and expectations that define and direct organizational behaviour. Thus, it can become a resource, a 'currency' even, that can be invested in the future of the organization and therein be a means of widening the stake that people have in its healthy operation. As with decentralization, such collaboration also represents a threat in that the work of schools will become more visible to those who may criticize it. Nevertheless, that risk may well be worth the potential benefit of heightened psychic and actual investment on the part of a wider cast of people and agencies.

Normative Leadership

> Leadership only manifests itself in the context of change (Leithwood, 1994:499).

For work to get done in a coordinated and coherent fashion, people must have clues about how to act appropriately. These clues might derive from formal rules codified in policy manuals and job descriptions as they do in bureaucratic organizations, or from more informal norms or values as they do in professional organizations (Schlechty, 1975). Regardless, the concern is with how to enhance the probability that the system will operate in the way that it should. Change, of course, poses a challenge to coordinated activity, and thus the road to improvement may first travel through a period of worsened performance (Fullan and Miles, 1992). Nevertheless, it is the job of leaders (whatever position they may occupy) to see to it that this period does not become permanent and that ultimately the system once again runs effectively.

It is a little unfair to imply that there was ever an emphasis in the research on technical or instructional leadership by the central office. Generally, superintendents seemed to be treated as leaders by virtue of their position, but whether they were really leading (getting others to behave in ways they would not ordinarily) or managing (enabling people to continue to do the jobs they are assigned in the way they currently do the job) is unclear. Wimpleberg (1987) claims that the instructional leadership aspect of the district office has never really been fully explored. Most studies on the superintendent illustrate that their attention gets pulled from instructional matters (Hannaway &

Sproull, 1978-1979), and little research has been done on the other denizens of the district office. The effective schools movement, of course, gave a distinct boost to the importance of principals being instructional leaders (Leithwood, 1994), but this coupled with SBM initiatives generally caused people to wonder if district offices were really needed.

In response, several authors tried to stake out an instructional leadership role for central office people, such as providing important cultural and political linkages between schools and the rest of the district (Wimpleberg, 1987; Pajak, 1989). But it is clear that there is no rational basis for assuming that the effects of central administration on students can ever be anything more than a mediated effect at best. As Crowson and Morris (1992:70) observe,

> The superintendent is oriented to interaction with outsiders, to policy questions rather than direct management responsibilities, and to daily tasks that distance the incumbent from the basic activities (teaching and learning) of the organization. Given these conditions of the job, how does leadership reveal itself in the ongoing life of a school system?

Our sense is that the kind of leadership that is becoming increasingly required in school districts is more normative than technical. That is, with increased decentralization and greater collaboration, coordination by insuring adherence to formal rules is unwieldy and contradictory. Instead, this process is much more likely to occur through the sharing of common values. As people try to figure out what actions are appropriate, they then refer to those principles, visions, goals, or missions that they highly value. The task of leadership is to encourage the sharing of what is valued and to continually signal what these are. Fullan (1993:162) notes:

> In most restructuring reforms, structure attempts to push cultural change, and mostly fails. Clearly, there is a reciprocal relationship required between the two, but it might be more effective if the conceptual and normative changes being attempted accumulate to drive structural changes conducive to new ways of working. It is much more powerful and meaningful when teachers and administrators begin working in new ways only to discover that school structures must be altered than the reverse situation in which rapidly implemented new

structures create confusion, ambiguity, and conflict ultimately leading to retrenchment.

In other words, there has to be an accommodation between the way the school system is organized and new beliefs and behaviours brought on in reform, and the preference is to derive organization from the beliefs and behaviours. The new rules, roles, and relationships inherent in decentralization and collaboration are unlikely to be reinforced by those that fit with more centralized and isolated actions.

So, which will win? The new or the old norms? It partially depends on which ones people perceive to be most valued in the system and these perceptions, in large measure, derive from symbolic signals from leaders.

> Actors at the school site seek signals from the district office to assess the commitment of the superintendent and district staff to the implementation of a particular innovation. (Hallinger & Murphy, 1987:185).

The type of support flowing from the central office is one major signal. That is, what activities and people receive the most resources, training, technical assistance, information, or authority? Other signals can be the content of the interactions that people have with one another and whether central office people have a consistent message about what the important goals and activities in the system are (Corbett & Wilson, 1992).

The danger of mixed signals is confusion, and often leaders are unaware that their words and deeds contradict one another. As an example, consider the following two quotes, one from a central office administrator and one from a teacher in the same district (Webb, 1991:15):

> I think you could say we are really becoming a central office for students...We're reorganizing around the needs of our students; we're, all of us, working to keep the focus on student results...You can see that mission statement all over the building.

> We don't really see the central office as involved in the changes we're making. They're still so invested in rules and regulations. They still get in the way of us being able to do

some of the things we know are important, that our kids need so much.

Nevertheless, consistent symbolic signalling, by itself, is not enough to achieve widespread, unified purposeful activity. Also necessary, and more important, are shared agreements about the overall mission of a school system – and presumably this mission should center around students. However, there is considerable angst over what students should get out of school. Succeed at what? Learn what? This concern has led to the claim that vision-building around results for students is also a critical step in reculturing (Wilson, Webb, & Corbett, 1995). Much different from instructional leadership, this requires normative leadership that targets values and beliefs rather than technical skills. Unfortunately, the task is fraught with difficulty. Says Newmann (1994:2):

> School-wide consensus on clear and focused educational goals eludes many schools. For one thing, staff members – and parents as well – can find themselves divided by differences between traditional and progressive educational philosophies. Also, academic specialization tends to compartmentalize teaching into such different subjects that common threads are hard to find. And by trying to respond to the diverse needs, abilities and interests of students, schools create distinct programs that are often unconnected by specific common goals. Escalating diversity in the student population continues to magnify this issue.

Schools, more than almost any formal organization in fact, have difficulty in articulating a set of clear and focused goals, as Hodgkinson notes (1991: 62):

> A crucial difference between educational and other subsets of administration such as hospital, police, industry, trade and commerce is a lack of goal specificity. All of the latter know with some clarity what determines an effective organization and the evaluative criteria are built in through rational measures of health care, law and order, or profit. Balance sheets and statements of profit and loss can be drawn up and are overtly meaningful. In education, however, no such clarity of ends and means exists and, while financial statements of a sort can be ingeniously contrived, there are really meaningful only

in showing discrepancies between budgeted and actual expenditures. To relate the budget itself to either the underlying educational philosophy or to ultimate educational outcomes is a task which is by no means overt or explicit and in general is of the utmost difficulty. To put it very bluntly, the educational enterprise does not always know where it is going, or what it is actually accomplishing, or even how to do what is supposed to be its primary task – the teaching-learning process.

Corbett, Wilson, & Webb (1995) discuss how cultural, social, economic, and political diversity among teachers and community members, can become a barrier to recognizing whatever commonalties may exist. These commonalties typically emerge around what stakeholder adults believe about the kinds of people students should become. Once surfaced, the commonalties provide the framework for a vision, while the process of surfacing shared ground builds the basis for more meaningful and supportive relationships among previously disenfranchised groups. They note (1995:23), '...equally important (as the resulting vision) would be that in the course of discussion, recognition would emerge of potential coalitions bridging the visible differences between the two groups... Teachers and community members alike would discover allies in their advocacy of a better education for students.'

The culture of schools generally does not promote reflection, analysis, or dialogue around the issue of success for all students (Lortie, 1975). Whether it is the schedule that keeps teachers so preoccupied with the day-to-day concerns, the students they work with, or the larger professional climate that discourages more global thinking about educational matters, the bigger picture of meeting the needs of all students is rarely discussed. Normatively oriented leaders need to structure time so that dialogue can occur, assist decisionmaking about what success means and how to document it, and encourage use of those agreements in practice.

The implications for central office leadership of the above would be that cookie-cutter models of 'vision building' do not work. What does work is flexibility, meaningful representation, real participation, respectful dialogue, recognition of differences and commonalties, and a clear, easily articulated, shared vision. Rather than the application of a model (e.g. the tenets of effective schools), this requires the exercise of context-intelligent leadership.

There is another consideration as well. According to Sykes and Elmore (1989:87), 'Structures should be flexible enough to capitalize on leadership where and when it occurs. This means uncoupling leadership from formal roles.' Wood (1992:235-236) elaborates:

> There is no getting around the fact that in the schools we have visited there has been a person or persons who began the process of developing a school vision. Most often it was the principal, but it didn't have to be. But this individual or groups of individuals was always able to lead democratically by sharing and developing the vision of what the school should be.

From this perspective, normative leadership becomes not the responsibility of a preordained position but of people who are occupy the best roles to influence the behaviour of others.

So, it is unwise to stake a de facto claim for central office people as being the key leaders. Instead, they should probably look at themselves as much as leadership developers who recognize and encourage attempts to move the district in desired directions wherever and whenever they occur, welcoming leadership efforts in support of the district's vision rather than being jealous of them.

RECIPROCITY: THE UNDERLYING THEME

The previous section of this chapter examined decentralization, collaboration, and normative leadership as three developments that, to varying degrees, are already taking hold, intended or not, in many school districts. Reading between the lines, the reader has likely detected that we see these developments as improvements, not just changes, and that people who have traditionally occupied positions in the central office have important roles to play in promoting the continued growth of these developments.

But the three do not comprise a list of discrete organizational changes that a school district might want to partially plan for and implement; they are too interconnected to be as separated in practice as they were in our analysis. For example, decentralization without collaboration and normative leadership could evolve into each school's becoming its own fiefdom, having little continuity with the other buildings; collaboration without the other two would improve every one's knowledge about each others' work, but people would have great difficulty acting on that knowledge in a concerted way; and normative leadership attempts, in the other two's absence, would ring very hollow.

We reiterate, however, that the literature contains little evidence that these developments have had significant effects in school systems. Instead, they presently have more the 'appearance of reform' (LeCompte & Wierelak, 1993). We feel there is a reason for this lack of evidence. It stems from missing the thread that binds the developments together, and that thread is *the establishment of reciprocal relationships among citizens, educators, and students.* Reciprocal relationships are ones in which all parties have contributions to make to each other and all have needs that the others can meet. Their hallmark is equality, fairness, and an 'others' orientation. They allow for mutual construction of meaning and maximizing the best interests of all. Maintaining unequal and one-sided working relationships in the context of democratizing changes, then, would be a powerful antidote to the realization of reform intentions.

Stated differently, decentralization, collaboration, and normative leadership are means to an end. The end is the purposeful pursuit of the school district's mission in a way that is personally meaningful and collectively worthwhile for citizens, educators, and students alike; and our 'bet' is that the creation of reciprocal relationships is what makes these changes powerful, engendering deep commitment to action and a keen sense of responsibility for the system's overall health.

This norm of reciprocity as a characteristic of effective working relationships is similar to the point that Block (1993:xx-xxi) makes in the preface to his book *Stewardship*:

> Stewardship is defined in this book as the willingness to be accountable for the well-being of the larger organization by operating in service, rather than in control, of those around us...Stated simply, it is accountability without control or compliance.

> The underlying value is about deepening our commitment to service...Authentic service is experienced when there is a balance of power...The primary commitment is to the larger community...Each person joins in defining purpose and deciding what kind of culture the organization will become...[And] There is a balanced and equitable distribution of rewards.

The topics of the previous section, then, are simply examples of strategies that, when taken together, create and support reciprocal, others-oriented relationships in school systems that want to become effective service-based organizations. It is such relationships that enable individuals to view themselves as effective, capable, and nurtured; and it is such relationships that, in the aggregate, enable the system to become effective, capable, and nurturing with students.

Indeed, it may be helpful to look 'upward' at a reciprocal system through the eyes of students:

> Students told us 'the way teachers treat you as a student – or as a person actually,' counted more than any other factor in the school setting in determining their attachment to the school, their commitment to the school's goals and, by extension, the academic future they imagined for themselves. Without a sense of visibility at school, students who weren't attached to conventional academic goals, or who weren't motivated by college competition, too often tuned out or dropped out. One Latina on the verge of dropping out told us, 'They didn't really care if you were in the classroom, they didn't care what you were doing. I could have done anything. They had no idea who I was'. (McLaughlin, 1994:9)

In this instance, ''restructuring practices' make a difference in student achievement and engagement when they support personal and sustained connections between students and adults in the school setting, and when they facilitate the sharing of knowledge about students as individuals and learners' (McLaughlin, 1994:9). In other words, the relationships between teachers and students tend to mirror those among the adults. Sharing among the adults will carry over to their relationships with students.

To assert that promoting reciprocity in a school system is the ultimate lesson toward which the previous discussion is moving is to say that current trends are likely to lead to central office people having to relinquish the traditional bases of their influence: the authority to control others' behaviour and the expectation that others will comply. Such relinquishing is the logical and natural conclusion of the journey on which decentralization, collaboration, and normatively-based leadership are stops. Obviously such a trip will not be easily made. But the risk in not following it through to its ultimate destination is to render as superficial and unimportant all of the prior efforts.

RECIPROCITY AND IMPLICATIONS FOR RESEARCH

We have construed the research and reasoned speculation which we have drawn on in this chapter to support the view that central office people can be integral to directions that school systems are moving in, primarily by viewing themselves as serving citizens, educators, and students and establishing more equitable relationships in the process. Make no mistake. The research does not 'say' this; we do. We have engaged in the same 'ahead of the studies' sense making that Waller says tends to keep common sense in front of research.

Is research doomed to forever lag common sense or at least the everyday experiences of educators? People often speak of a gap between research and practice. Perhaps this image of a chasm between the two leads to imagining improbable solutions concerned with bridging the distance. In other words, the notion that research and practice reside in separate locales puts a great emphasis on how to communicate across the divide. It might be better to discard this metaphor and adopt another – that research and practice should be reciprocally-based activities carried out in the context of mutually-constructed relationships among practitioners and researchers. What separates the two currently, then, is neither intellectual nor actual distance but the lack of opportunities to interact. Working together, they could jointly assist each other in constructing mutual meaning from events – in real time.

For example, Senge, Ross, Smith, Roberts, and Kleiner (1994) argue that organizational learning occurs in a continuing cycle of public reflection, shared meaning, joint planning, and coordinated action. Both 'hard' and 'soft' data have a considerable role to play in organizational reflection as people wrestle with what each other believes represents 'reality' in their setting and as people create shared insights into the problems and prospects of their work. This interpretative activity sets the stage for the group's subsequent planning and actions. Research activity that is integrated into the learning cycle can play an obvious role during the reflective phase and can be significantly informed itself by the meaning, or lack there of, that the group attaches to data provided. This enables the researchers to springboard concomitantly into a parallel learning cycle for the project. The consequence is that both researchers and practitioners become better informed about their work than they would be if they carried out these processes independently of one another.

The downside, obviously, is that both the setting and the research become 'contaminated,' such that neither evolves as it would in the absence of the other. We dismiss this as a weakness of such an approach; instead we view this commingling of thought and action as a powerful advancement in the context-dependent and highly interpretative arena of school reform and as an extremely promising way of bringing research and practice meaningfully together.

REFERENCES

Barth, R. (1993). Coming to a vision. *Journal of Staff Development, 14*(1), 6-11.

Block, P. (1993). *Stewardship: Choosing service over self-interest.* San Francisco: Berrett-Koehler Publishers.

Bruner, C. (1991). *Thinking collaboratively: Ten questions and answers to help policymakers improve children's services.* Washington, DC: Institute for Educational Leadership.

Burbach, H., & Crockett, M. (1994). The learning organization as a prototype for the next generation of schools. *Planning and Changing, 25*(3/4), 173-179.

Carnoy, M. (November 7, 1990). Restructuring has a down side, too. *Education Week,* 24, 32.

Clark, T. (1991). *Collaboration to build competence: The urban superintendents' perspective.* Washington, DC: U. S. Department of Education.

Coleman, J. (1988). Social capital and the creation of human capital. *American Journal of Sociology, 94,* 95-120.

Coleman. P., & LaRocque, L., (1990). *Struggling to be 'good enough': Administrative practices and school district ethos.* London: Falmer Press.

Conley, D. (1993). *Roadmap to restructuring: Policies, practices and the emerging visions of schooling.* Eugene, OR: ERIC Clearinghouse on Educational Management.

Conley, S. (1991). Review of research on teacher participation in school decision making. In G. Grant (ed.), *Review of research in education.* Washington, DC: American Educational Research Association.

Corbett, D., Wilson, B., & Webb, J. (1995). Visible differences and unseen commonalties: Viewing students as the connections between schools and communities. In J. Chibulka & W. Kritek (eds.), *Coordination among school, families, and communities.* Albany, NY: State University of New York Press.

Corbett, H. D., & Wilson, B. L. (1992). The central office role in instructional improvement. *School Effectiveness and School Improvement, 3*(1), 45-68.

Corwin, R., & Borman, K. (1988). School as workplace: Structural constraints on administration. In N. Boyan (ed.), *Handbook of research on educational administration.* New York: Longman.

Cox, P. (1983). Complementary roles in successful change. *Educational Leadership, 41*(3), 10-13.

Crowson, R. L., & Morris, V. C. (1992). The superintendency and school effectiveness: An organizational hierarchy perspective. *School Effectiveness and School Improvement, 3*(1), 69-88.

Cuban, L. (1988). *The managerial imperative and the practice of leadership in schools.* Albany, NY: SUNY Press.

944

Cuban, L. (1989). The district superintendent and the restructuring of schools: A realistic appraisal. In T. J. Sergiovanni & J. H. Moore (eds.), *Schooling for tomorrow: Directing reforms to issues that count*. Boston: Allyn & Bacon.

Davies, D. (October 6, 1994). Partnerships for reform: Change happens at the local level, and must link family, community, school. *Education Week*, 44, 34.

Dimmock, C., & Wildy, H. (1992). The district superintendent and school improvement: A Western Australia perspective. *School Effectiveness and School Improvement, 3*(2), 150-172.

Bradley, A. (June 1, 1994). Requiem for a reform. *Education Week*, 21-25.

Elder, C. D., & Cobb, R. W. (1983). *The political uses of symbols*. New York: Longman.

Fullan, M. (1993). Coordinating school and district development in restructuring. In J. Murphy & P. Hallinger (eds.), *Restructuring schooling: Learning from ongoing efforts*. Newbury Park, CA: Corwin.

Fullan, M. (1991). *The new meaning of educational change*. New York: Teachers College Press.

Fullan, M., & Miles, M. (1992). Getting reform right: What works and what doesn't. *Phi Delta Kappan, 73*(10), 745-752.

Hallinger, P., & Edwards, M. A. (1992). The paradox of superintendent leadership in school restructuring. *School Effectiveness and School Improvement, 3*(2), 131-149.

Hallinger, P., & Murphy, J. (1987). Instructional leadership in the school context. In W. Greenfield (ed.), *Instructional leadership: Concepts, issues, and controversies*. Boston: Allyn and Bacon.

Hannaway, J. (1989). *Managers managing: The working of an administrative system*. New York: Oxford University Press.

Hannaway, J., & Sproull, L. S. (1978-1979). Who's running the show? Coordination and control in educational organizations. *Administrator's Notebook, 27*, 1-4.

Hodgkinson, C. (1991). *Educational leadership: The moral art*. Albany, NY: SUNY Press.

Hord, S. M., Jolley, D. V., & Mendez-Morse, S. E. (1992), The superintendent's leadership in school improvement: A rural perspective. *School Effectiveness and School Improvement, 3*(2), 110-130.

LeCompte, M., & Wierelak, M. E. (1993). *Constructing the appearance of reform: Using chaos theory to analyze site-based management, restructuring, and shared decision-making*. Boulder, CO: University of Colorado.

Leithwood, K. (1992). Editor's conclusion: What have we learned and where do we go from here? *School Effectiveness and School Improvement, 3*(2), 173-184.

Leithwood, K. (1994). Leadership for school restructuring. *Educational Administration Quarterly, 30*(4), 498-518.

Lortie, D. (1975). *Schoolteacher*. Chicago: University of Chicago Press.

Louis, K. (1989). The role of the school district in school improvement. In M. Holmes, K. Leithwood, & D. Musella (eds.), *Educational policy for effective schools*. Toronto: OISE Press.

Malen, B. (1994). Enacting school-based management: A political utilities analysis. *Educational Evaluation and Policy Analysis, 16*(3), 249-267.

McLaughlin, M. (1994). Somebody knows my name. *Issues in Restructuring Schools*, (Fall, 7), 9-11.

Meister, G. (1994). *'The way it's supposed to be': A report on school-based instructional decisionmaking and the regional centres in Maryland.* Philadelphia: Research for Better Schools.

Mirel, J. (1994). School reform unplugged: The Bensenville New American School Project, 1991-93. *American Educational Research Journal, 31*(3), 481-518.

Murphy, J., & Beck, L. (1995). *School-based management as school reform: Taking stock.* Thousand Oaks, CA: Corwin Press.

Murphy, J., Peterson, K., & Hallinger, P. (1986). The administrative control of principals in effective school districts: The supervision and evaluation functions. *The Urban Review, 18*(3), 149-175.

Newmann, F. (1994). School-wide professional community. *Issues in Restructuring Schools.* (Spring, 6), 1-2.

Pajak, E. (1989). *The central office supervisor of curriculum and instruction: Setting the stage for success.* Boston: Allyn and Bacon.

Parsley, J. (1991). Reshaping student learning. *School Administrator, 48*(7), 9, 11, 13-14.

Peterson, K. D. (1987). Administrative control and instructional leadership. In W. Greenfield (ed.), *Instructional leadership: Concepts, issues, and controversies.* Boston: Allyn and Bacon.

Peterson, K., Murphy, J., & Hallinger, P. (1987). Superintendents' perceptions of the control and coordination of the technical core in effective school districts. *Educational Administration Quarterly, 23*(1), 79-95.

Pitsch, M. (October 19, 1994). Critics target Goals 2000 in schools 'war': Groups rally to decry Clinton reform agenda. *Education Week*, 1,21.

Rand Corporation. (1994). *The decentralization mirage: Comparing decisionmaking arrangements in four high schools.* Santa Monica, CA: The author.

Rowan, B. (1990). Commitment and control: Alternative strategies for the organizational design of schools. *Review of Research in Education, 16*, 353-392.

Schlechty, P. (1990). *Schools for the twenty-first century: Leadership imperatives for educational reform.* San Francisco: Jossey-Bass.

Schlechty, P. (1975). *Teaching and social behaviour.* Boston: Allyn & Bacon.

Senge, P. M., Roberts, C., Ross, R. B., Smith, B. J., & Kleiner, A. (1994). *The fifth discipline fieldbook: Strategies and tools for building a learning organization.* New York: Currency-Doubleday.

Stoll, L., & Fink, D. (1992). Effecting school change: The Halton approach. *School Effectiveness and School Improvement, 3*(1), 19-41.

Stone, C., & Wehlage, G. (1992). *Community collaboration and the restructuring of schools.* Madison, WI: Center on Organization and Restructuring of Schools.

Sykes, G., & Elmore, R. F. (1989). Making schools manageable: Policy and administration for tomorrow's schools. In J. Hannaway and R. Crowson (eds.), *The politics of reforming school administration.* New York: Falmer Press.

Taylor, D. L., & Bogotch, I. E. (1994). School-level effects of teachers' participation in decision making. *Educational Evaluation and Policy Analysis, 16*(3), 302-319.

Tyack, D., & Hansot, E. (1982). *Managers of virtue: Public school leadership in America, 1820-1980.* Mew York: Basic Books.

Waller, W. (1932). *The sociology of teaching*, New York: Wiley.

Webb, J. (1991). *Regulatory flexibility and restructuring in North Carolina: Is it really happening.* Paper presented at the Annual Meeting of the American Educational Research Association, Chicago, IL.

Weiss, C. H., & Cambone J. (1994). Principals, shared decision making, and school reform. *Educational Evaluation and Policy Analysis, 16*(3), 287-301.

Wilson, B. L., Webb, J., & Corbett, H. D. (1995). Restructuring and policy research: Connecting adults to students. In W. T. Pink & G. W. Noblit (eds.), *Continuity and contradiction: The futures of the sociology of education.* Cresskill, NJ: Hampton Press.

Wimpleberg, R. (1987). The dilemma of instructional leadership and a central role for central office. In W. Greenfield (ed.), *Instructional leadership: Concepts, issues, and controversies.* Boston: Allyn and Bacon.

Wohlstetter, P., Smyer, R., & Mohrman, S. A. (1994). New boundaries for school-based management: The high involvement model. *Educational Evaluation and Policy Analysis, 16*(3), 268-286.

Wood, G. H. (1992). *Schools that work: America's most innovative public education programs.* New York: Plume.

Section 5

**Critical Perspectives on Educational Leadership and
Administration**

David Corson – Section Editor

Chapter 26: The Cultural Politics of Schools: Implications for Leadership

GARY L. ANDERSON
The University of New Mexico

> In low-income public high schools organized around control through silence, the student, parent, teacher, or paraprofessional who talks, tells, or wants to speak transforms rapidly into the subversive, the troublemaker. (Fine, 1992, p. 132)

There is an increasing interest among educational researchers in the ways resistance occurs in schools and how schools systematically silence the voices of students, teachers, and disenfranchised communities. The literature on institutional resistance and silencing is part of a broader literature that addresses the cultural politics of schools (Kanpol, 1992; Quantz, Rogers, and Dantley, 1991). 'Cultural politics' refers to the ways schools (a.) silence 'disruptive' voices, (b.) serve as sites in which student identities are negotiated within contexts that reflect the complex and interactive dynamics of class, race, gender, disability, and sexual orientation, and (c.) embed power relations in the structures, practices, curriculum, and everyday life of schools (Cherryholmes, 1988)[1].

In this chapter I will, first, discuss why the dominant paradigm in the field of educational administration has ignored and/or been unable to meaningfully incorporate the research on cultural politics, including a discussion of how notions of 'culture' and 'politics' have been constructed within the field. Second, I will briefly review the literature on school cultural politics and discuss how it might inform current work in the area of school leadership, concentrating specifically on the cultural politics associated with inequality, control, resistance, and identity. Finally, I will argue that the question of who school administrators ultimately work for has not been seriously theorized in the field of educational politics. In spite of a thick cloud of empowerment rhetoric, the present commitment of most appears to be to the legitimation of a non-democratic and unequal status quo, rather than to the creation of democratic school cultures in which multiple voices and ways of being in schools and society are legitimated.

K. Leithwood et al. (eds.), International Handbook of Educational Leadership and Administration, 947-966.
© 1996 Kluwer Academic Publishers, Printed in the Netherlands.

CONFLICTING PARADIGMS, DISCOURSES, AND INTERESTS: TOWARD A
CRITICAL CONCEPTION OF CULTURE AND POLITICS

Much has been written about the paradigm debates within the field of
educational administration. From the Greenfield – Griffiths debates of
the 1970's to more recent attention to alternative paradigms (Griffiths,
1991) and multiparadigmatic approach (Capper, 1993) some scholars
have wrestled theoretically with what a challenge to the dominance of
structural – functionalism might mean for the field of educational
administration. While debates about alternative paradigms are carried
on around the margins of the field, the structural – functionalist mainstream continues to remain dominant by absorbing these new perspectives into its discourse. Perhaps the most remarkable example of
functionalist administrative discourse absorbing radical critique is the
oxymoron described in the title of Tom Peters' (1993) recent book *Liberation Management*. These appropriations of alternative discourses
are not necessarily cynical attempts to co-opt opposing views. They
rather reflect the tendency of the management paradigm of the administrative sciences to assimilate any new idea into the technical rationality and management bias that dominates the field.

Ferguson (1984) in her feminist critique of bureaucracy argues that
the debates that take place in the administrative sciences center on
'small questions, questions that beg the larger issues of coercion and
control.' She argues that those who train administrators and engage in
research in the administrative sciences seldom deal critically with
issues of power and control, because they constitute an organizational
elite who benefit from current organizational arrangements. 'To put the
matter crudely,' she asserts, 'they know who they work for.' (Ferguson, 1984, p. 81)

This question of who we work for in the administrative sciences is
one that has lead many to point out the 'managerial bias' of fields like
public administration, business administration, and educational administration. In official discourse, administrators will claim that their clients, consumers, or students are their central concern. Any educational
administrator will recognize the 'kids come first' mantra that is obliga-
tory in all public school discourse. However, decades of research concludes that schools and classrooms tend to be highly bureaucratized
and teacher-centered rather than student-centered. An area superintendent of a large school district indicates that,

a review of the agenda for board meetings, the superintendent's cabinet, principal's meetings, and even school faculty
meetings indicates that the recurrent topics are finance, state
policies, contract management, student performance (i.e. test
scores and drop-out rates), record keeping, new programs,
personnel issues, school planning, discipline policy, new
assessment programs, and so on. But we never talk about who
the kids are and why they are not more enthusiastic about
going to school (Lytle, 1992, p. 128)

This gap between discourse and practice is often explained in organizational theory texts as 'goal displacement'. However, one of the reasons
that espoused client-centered, egalitarian goals are displaced by ones
that serve the maintenance of the status quo is that administrative discourse lacks a language appropriate to the nurturance and empowerment of human beings. Steeped in Neo-Taylorism, behavioural and
industrial psychology, and, more recently, neo-liberal economics,
administrative discourse,

    ...rebuffs the project of social criticism and political change.
    There are discourses of resistance...and they are found in the
    language of the oppressed, the excluded, the renegades, the
    critics and the 'losers.' These are discourses that are full of
    struggle and vision, but they are not welcome in an arena
    dominated by administrative discourse. (Ferguson, 1984,
    p. 82)

These 'discourses of resistance' form what Fine & Weiss (1993) call a
'discursive underground' consisting of counter discourses that challenge the official administrative discourse of schooling. There is considerable evidence that the field of educational administration has
appropriated some of the language of critique (i.e., empowerment, participatory decision-making, etc.) without its content or goals as a strategic move in the cultural politics of legitimating educational
institutions that are in crisis (Anderson and Dixon, 1993)
  My point here is that schools cannot be understood in functionalist
terms wherein they pursue a mythical set of interests and values that
are shared by 'society.' Instead they must be viewed as arenas of cultural politics in which the outcomes of schools are always contingent
on the daily political struggles that take place both within them and
without. In the following section I will briefly describe how the con-

structs of 'culture' and 'politics' have been appropriated by the management paradigm of the field in ways that mask the conflicts of interest that exist within educational institutions.

The Construction of 'Culture' in Educational Administration

The notion of culture in the field of educational administration has been appropriated largely by structural – functionalists who view it as something to be managed in order to build coherence and consensus within school sites. While adding some important dimensions to our understanding of organizational life, the organizational cultures literature is generally viewed as useful only to the extent that it promotes 'healthier' organizational climates and serves to enhance human resource development (Sergiovanni, 1984). A major appeal of organizational culture is its potential as a vehicle for tightening up control in loosely coupled systems through the adept manipulation of myth and symbol (Firestone and Wilson, 1985)

Providing a different view of culture, Quantz (1992) argues that,

> culture is not so much the area of social life where people share understandings as that area of social life where people struggle over understandings. Culture is a contested terrain with multiple voices expressed though constitutive power relations. (p. 487)

The constitutive power relations that Quantz refers too are asymmetrical, meaning that some people and groups have more power to influence the outcomes of cultural politics than others.

For this reason the shift from a structuralist – functionalist view of leadership to a critical one involves shifting the discourse of 'school cultures' to one of the 'cultural politics of schools.'

Elsewhere, I have developed the notion of the management of school culture as both a form of institutional legitimation (Anderson, 1990) and of ideological control (Anderson, 1991). This emphasis on the ways administrators manage meaning through the manipulation of language and other symbol systems holds great promise for understanding how the status quo is maintained in schools and whose interests school administrators ultimately work for (Bates, 1986; Lee, 1993). The notion of cultural politics in this chapter assumes a definition of culture that views schools as arenas of cultural and political struggle, in which the goal is investigating and understanding these struggles rather than merely managing them. This type of cultural and political literacy is a necessary first step toward creating democratic schools.

The Construction of 'Politics' in Educational Administration

Recently attention in educational administration has turned to 'micro-politics' or the study of less visible, behind the scenes, negotiations of power, what Hoyle (1982) calls 'the dark side of organizational life' (p. 87). This work has provided the study of educational politics with accounts of the daily subtle negotiations that occur within the under-world of educational institutions (Ball, 1987, Blase, 1991). In the hands of management oriented researchers, however, studies of micro-politics are often little more than a listing of strategies that various organizational stakeholders engage in to get what they want. Neverthe-less, micro-political research has played an important role in opening up and legitimating a closer analysis of issues previously ignored in educational administration. Some of these issues are: the relationship between leadership and organizational micropolitics (Blase and Ander-son, in press), the ways administrators manage the meaning of the organization through the manipulation of organizational discourses and symbol systems (Anderson, 1991; Smircich and Morgan, 1982), the contrived nature of much of what passes as collaboration and participa-tory decision-making (Hargreaves, 1991; Malen and Ogawa, 1988), and the political negotiations that occur at the classroom level (Bloome and Willett, 1991)

The effects of important shifts in political and feminist theory regarding the concept of power are also being reflected in research in educational administration. Dunlap and Goldman (1991), Gronn (1986), Lukes (1974) and others have argued for new definitions of power. Lukes (1974) builds on Bachrach and Baratz (1963) notion that power is exercised not only through decisions made in formal decision-making arenas, but also through keeping decisions out of those arenas. Lukes (1974) extends this to the notion that we can also be kept una-ware that we have interests and needs that require decisions:

'A' may exercise power over 'B' by getting him to do what he does not want to do, but he also exercises power over him by influencing, shaping or determining his very wants...One does not have to go to the lengths of talking about *Brave New World*, or the world of B.F. Skinner, to see this: thought control takes many less total and more mundane forms, through the control of information, through the mass media, and through the processes of socialization. (p. 23)

Through these processes the dominant culture legitimates the values, norms, perceptions, beliefs, sentiments, and prejudices that support and define the existing distribution of goods, the institutions that decide how this distribution occurs, and the permissible range of disagreement about those processes. This legitimation is, however, never complete, and as Gramsci (1971) pointed out through his discussions of 'cultural hegemony' power is not only political and economic, but is also exercised in the realm of culture.

The notion that power in educational institutions is exercised in far more complex ways than previously acknowledged and that control is not total but must be constantly achieved, leads to a new view of school politics. Seen through this political lens, schools are cites of constant political and cultural struggle: Teachers, parents, and administrators struggle with each other over the meaning of the school. Students struggle with teachers over control and struggle with each other and the dominant culture over identity and status. These struggles, cannot be understood without understanding how power is mediated by culture, but the construction of culture and politics supplied by the field of educational administration is one that masks rather than illuminates these struggles.

THE CULTURAL POLITICS OF INEQUALITY

There is an unprecedented interest among educational researchers and practitioners in issues of social inequality, school failure, and the influence of race, class, and gender on student achievement and identity development. Movements such as full inclusion of special education students, de-tracking schools at all levels through heterogeneous grouping and cooperative learning, and gender-fair instruction have gained momentum in schools. These innovations are the result of cultural politics at national and local levels and their success or failure will also be largely the result of cultural politics, both nationally and locally.

In spite of this groundswell of interest in issues of equality, such issues are still marginal in the major journals and conferences in educational administration. This is partly because of the well documented dominance in the field of technical rationality and narrow empiricism, pushing issues of justice, morality and ethics to the margins. (Schon, 1983; Smith and Blase, 1989)

In fact, with rare exceptions, researchers in educational administration tend to study schools as black boxes in which students barely exist except as producers of test scores or carriers of social pathologies that label them 'at-risk'. Since the 1960's social inequality has been linked to deficit notions of a culture of poverty or culturally disadvantaged students, notions that continue today in much of the literature about 'at-risk' students.

Many of our attitudes in the field of educational administration have been influenced by these views. With regard to issues of equality, the task of administrators has traditionally been limited to obtaining and managing the various 'compensatory' funds available to provide programs that help to make up some of the deficit that poor and minority parents and communities allegedly impose on their children. Textbooks that are used for administrator training are unlikely to contain anything about social inequality and schools' role in either its reproduction or amelioration. Only recently, and with much internal dissension, did the University Council on Educational Administration add 'social and cultural influences on schooling' to its knowledge base in the field.

It is not the purpose of this chapter to review the massive research on social inequality and schooling. There is, however, increasing evidence that complex institutional dynamics which administrators often set in motion are implicated in the social reproduction of unequal student outcomes related to class, race, gender, disability, and sexual orientation. With few exceptions, this research is being done outside the field of educational administration.

In the following sections I will discuss several interrelated themes from this research that relate to schools as sites of cultural and political struggle. The first is the dynamic relationship between schools' role in *social reproduction* and the ways some students, parents, teachers, and occasionally administrators *resist* institutional practices that sustain it (Kanpol, 1992; Willis, 1977) The second is the theme of *institutional silencing* which, constitutes a process of institutionalized policies and practices which obscure the very social, economic, and therefore experiential conditions of students' daily lives, and which expel from written, oral, and non-verbal expression substantive and critical 'talk' about these conditions. (Fine, 1987, p. 157)

The third is the theme of *identity politics* and the recognition that educational institutions provide contexts in which identities are daily constructed by students (Wexler, Crichlow, Kern, & Martusewicz, 1992). The last theme concerns the *cultural politics of leadership* and the role that administrators of educational institutions are expected to play in sustaining these practices in order to maintain the legitimacy of existing social arrangements (Anderson, 1990). As we will see, however, some administrators also find ways to subvert practices that lead to school failure and inequality. In the following sections, I will discuss each of these four themes, the ways they reflect institutional cultural politics and implications for institutional policies and practices.

The Cultural Politics of Control and Resistance

Educational institutions are characterized by a complex dynamic among teachers, students, parents, and administrators of control, resistance, accommodation, compliance, and withdrawal. More than three decades of qualitative investigation has provided a wealth of data on how these dynamics too often result in school failure, social stratification and dropping out for students, burn out and despair for teachers, and an increasing demand on administrators to effectively manage the legitimation crisis created by an increasingly stratified school system and society.

Many of the earlier studies were attempts to peer into the black box of schooling as it related to the social reproduction of inequality. Both Marxist and non-Marxist scholars had attempted to document the structural imperatives that led to the social reproduction of inequality. (Bowles and Gintis, 1976; Jencks, 1972) Although the educational system was implicated in these accounts, it took a series of critical ethnographies to show how social reproduction was mediated in complex and often contradictory ways by the cultural forms produced within the school setting. (Rist, 1970: Willis, 1977) These theories of cultural production suggested that culture was not merely reproduced by students absorbing the dominant ideology, but rather was culturally *produced* through a series of complex negotiations between students struggling to construct an identity and the values represented by the dominant culture. Many of these studies emphasized the influence of popular culture, working class values, racism and sexism. Willis (1977) emphasized that many of the working class 'lads' he studied had decoded the school system and could have perhaps worked it successfully had they so chosen. However, their adherence to a culture of resistance, tied to, for example, their allegiance to working class cultural norms that saw manual labour as more masculine than mental labour, caused them to ultimately follow their fathers' into the factories. Similarly, Fordham and Ogbu (1986), focusing on the cultural politics of race, describe the dilemmas of African-American students for whom 'acting white' often means success in school but rejection by peers. Like Willis's lads, the cultural politics of schooling constantly place them in situations in which the price of conforming is not worth the perceived costs.

These studies and many that followed demonstrated that school *failure* had less to do with a failure to learn than with a *refusal* to learn based on complex social and cultural factors (Kohl, 1992; Ogbu, 1989; Suarez – Orozco, 1987). Even more relevant to the field of educational administration, many studies began to suggest that the institutional arrangements that administrators promoted and maintained contributed in significant ways to inequality and school failure (Fraatz, 1987; McNeil, 1986; Metz, 1978; Oakes, 1985; Sapon – Shevon, 1994) A common theme that runs through all of this qualitative research is that school failure should not be blamed on the student's linguistic code, family arrangements, or cultural practices. The implications for educational practice are that schools are themselves in deficit and must adapt the classroom learning environment and school culture in ways that promote school success for low-income, minority, and female students rather than merely expecting them and their families to adapt.

Several qualitative researchers have made this institutional context the focus of their work (Cusick, 1973, 1983; Mehan, 1992; McNeil, 1986) For example, Mehan (1992), working from a social constructionist view, argues for a 'constitutive theory' of schools which sees them as producing student identities and careers through internal bureaucratic decision-making:

> I am distinguishing between the view of human action in resistance theory and the view of human action in constitutive theory. Correctives of reproduction theory have cast people as

active agents by introducing human agency into explanations of inequality. Social actors in resistance theory make choices in the face of structurally provided possibilities. However, the practices and procedures by which people acting together assemble social structures which then stand independently of their means of production is not the same as people making choices among predetermined options. Our understanding of the reproduction of social inequality will be more complete when we include in our theories the routine bureaucratic practices which structure students' educational careers. (p. 11)

While clearly the same social constructionist argument can be made for the 'structurally provided possibilities' that exist at more macro-social levels, the immediate organizational environment is more amenable to short term change (Robinson, 1994).

Mehan (1992) provides an example of constitutive theory drawn from special education. He points to Mercer's (1974) finding that there were no special education students in Catholic schools even though the IQ distribution was roughly equivalent in Catholic and public schools. The Catholic school students were not mentally retarded because the catholic schools neither had this category nor the mechanisms (IQ test, school psychologists, special education committees) for classifying students. 'Without a socially constructed lens through which to see the students, their behaviour was not viewed as retarded; unusual, to be sure, but not retarded.' (Mehan, 1992, p.12)

The above example stands social reproduction theory on its head. Rather than elite social actors at macro-structural levels imposing practices that lead to social stratification on schools, we find social actors at institutional levels constituting student identities and careers which in turn constitute the aggregate patterns of stratification at broader levels. According to Mehan (1992),

> a macro structure, the aggregate number of students in various educational programs and the students' identities as 'special' or 'regular' students is generated in a sequence of organizationally predictable 'micro events' (classroom, testing session, committee meetings)' (p. 12)

Mehan (1992) does not include in his analysis the constitutive actions at macro-policy levels that produced the special education legislation that spawned many of the micro events he describes. Moreover, as

Weatherley and Lipsky (1977) have documented, mandates at macro-policy levels take on a life of their own as they are filtered through the policy chain and ultimately implemented by street level bureaucrats. Thus, the micro-macro relationship more closely resembles Giddens' (1984) theory of structuration in which structure is both the medium and the product of action, and in which all of social life is being reconstructed at all times in a multiplicity of circumstances and social systems at all levels of society. One also feels compelled to add here a lesson from critical theory; some social actors and coalitions of social actors have more power and resources to influence social constructions than do others. In spite of these limitations, Mehan's theory of constitutive action helps us to explain how well-meaning educators who are genuinely concerned with the well-being of their students can collude in creating the stratified structure of opportunities available to their students.

Socially constructed structural limitations like unequal funding for high and low income schools place severe resource limitations on what schools in low-income neighbourhoods can do. Moreover, it is naive to think these socially constituted arrangements can be deconstructed without challenging the power that maintains privilege and class interests. Nevertheless, many arenas have been identified wherein schools can deconstruct current opportunity structures and replace them with new ones.

One of the primary findings of recent studies is that school failure has much to do with a student's relationship to the dominant culture. (Cummins, 1986; Ogbu, 1989) Since schools and classrooms tend to reflect the dominant culture, these studies provide valuable suggestions for institutional and classroom restructuring.

The Cultural Politics of Institutional Silencing

Fine's (1988) research on institutional silencing was prompted by a study she did comparing characteristics of 'dropouts' and 'persisters' in an urban high school. Her findings surprised her:

> The dropout profile was of a student relatively nondepressed, critical of social injustice, willing to take initiative, and unwilling to conform mindlessly. 'Good students,' those who persisted, were relatively depressed, self-blaming, teacher-dependent, unwilling to take initiative in response to an unfair

grade, and endlessly willing to conform. So much for the stereotype of the helpless dropout; and, perhaps as tragic, so much for the image of the assertive, well-socialized, good student. (p.90)

Fine goes on to wonder who is served by the popular image of dropouts as losers. She asks, 'what is obscured if dropouts are themselves presumed to be *deficient* in a *fair* system, rather than *challengers* of an *inequitable* one?' (p. 90) These questions are not unlike those being asked by Native Americans who wonder who is served by celebrating America's 'discovery' by Europeans. Cultural politics is linked to the myriad ways that social institutions maintain a status quo that benefits some while silencing, marginalizing, and pathologizing those voices that challenge its legitimacy.

According to Fine (1992), there are two important moments in research on silencing. The first involves unpacking the dynamics of power and privilege in universities and schools that nurture, maintain, and legitimate silencing. This involves documenting and ultimately subverting those policies, practices, and discourses that silence. The second moment in research on silencing means seeking policies, discourses and practices that elicit the voices of those who have been silenced.

Eliciting voice, however, too often naively assumes that the institution wants to hear the voices. This is unfortunately seldom the case since voices tend to be silenced in order to protect the powerful and privileged interests that institutions protect (Anderson and Herr, 1993; Apple, 1993). Without an understanding of who administrators ultimately work for in social institutions, the notion that administrators will hear, much less work to elicit, subordinates' voices may be naive.

The Cultural Politics of Identity

Hopkins (1994) has recently called for a shift in the root metaphor of schooling. He argues that both mechanistic and systems metaphors support the control orientation of organizations by viewing students as products or outputs. This results, he argues, in 'the purposeful manipulation of students toward predetermined ends and ignores the experience of the students themselves, viewing it as contaminating the process.' (p. 23) Hopkins argues for narrative as an alternative root metaphor for schooling. By narrative Hopkins refers to the experiences that clients – in this case students – bring to the organization. According to Hopkins,

> To attend to the experience of people is to empower them, give them a voice, challenge and disrupt established arrangements, to engage in dialogue and thus to evoke what Paulo Freire (1970) called 'generative themes' that point to change and reconstruction, whether in a classroom or in a society. (p.17)

What makes this shift to narrative so important is the recent acknowledgment that students construct identities within educational institutions. This politics of self is present on a daily basis in schools and is closely related to students' achievement, self-esteem, and persistence in school. Mikhail Bakhtin's (1981) notion of inner voice has aided educators in theorizing the importance of schools as organizations in the identity politics of students.

Briefly, Bakhtin argues that our identity is a product of multiple inner voices that struggle for legitimacy. Our social environments serve to legitimate some voices and not others. Legitimated voices are strengthened and articulated. Non-legitimated voices are weakened and ultimately silenced. Brown and Gilligan (1992) have also elaborated a theory of voice based on the struggle of early adolescent girls to maintain an authentic voice developed within relationship.

Wexler, Crichlow, Kern & Martusewicz (1992) describe how schools are characterized by students' daily struggle to construct an identity, or what the students in their study refer to as 'becoming somebody.' Wexler found that,

> Becoming somebody was an organizationally patterned process of production that used cultural resources deeply ingrained in more pervasive societal structures of inequality and difference. (p. 7)

The 'Product' of this production process that schools provide is 'identity, selfhood, the 'somebody' which the students work to attain through their interactions in school' (p. 8) The cultural resources or 'capital' that students bring to the interaction and the structures and images that the school provides as raw material for identity production vary by class, ethnicity, race, and gender. The significance of Wexler, et al.'s findings for administrators is the extent to which administrative practices serve to empty the school of the kinds of genuine relation-ships within which identities are traditionally constructed. Absent these relationships, students are left to seek compensatory identities in the facile images presented by the media and readily available school roles, such as 'jock', 'rad', 'nerd', etc. Wexler, Crichlow, Kern & Mar-tusewicz (1992) describe how students who adopt the 'rad' role are constituted by a complex combination of school disciplinary practices and images provided by popular culture:

> The immediate cause of the rad identity, for example, is the combination of encounter with the disciplinary apparatus and its vicious circle of escalating social extrusion with mass cul-turally inspired peer models. The deeper cause is that forma-tion of identity in relation to this apparatus...is a derivative, compensatory mode of identity formation. These institutional methods... are substitutes for authentic committed relations in which identity is the result of more deeply rooted emotional commitment, commingling of selves, and caring. (p. 34)

A common theme emerges in research centered in the cultural politics of schooling: Administrative practices grounded in concerns with legit-imation, tracking, control, and efficiency turn schools and classrooms into ineffective, uninspiring, and inequitable environments for those who work and study in them (Fraatz, 1987; Lytle, 1992; McNeil, 1986)

The Cultural Politics of Leadership

Few current proposals for school leadership are compatible with a view of schools as a site of cultural and political struggle. In most leadership theory, either leaders are encouraged to impose their moral authority or vision on a school (Greenfield, 1987), or they are encouraged to step back and 'empower' teachers to make decisions (Barth, 1990). This latter 'empowering' leadership strategy seldom empowers students or communities since the interests of teachers are often more akin to those of administrators than to their students and communities.

Both the moral authority and teacher empowerment models call themselves 'transformative' approaches to leadership. However, they both define leadership in terms of an individual who is located within a hierarchical structure, has formal power, and is willing to share it, but only at the leader's discretion. Another way of saying this is that current transformative models of leadership retain a 'power over' or 'power through' approach. That is, either they seek to use their power to get others to share their view of the world or they attempt to use power to accomplish externally determined goals *through* the efforts of other organizational actors (Maxcy, 1991). Feminists and critical theorists are currently attempting to develop a democratic theory of power that leads to a 'power with' model of leadership in which leadership and followership is a fluid and interactive process (Foster, 1986; Marshall and Anderson, in press).

Leadership theory which acknowledges the cultural politics of silencing described above, must confront several challenges. First, a new discourse is needed within the field of educational administration to replace 'power over' and 'power through' discourses. As previously discussed the managerial bias of the field has appropriated even those 'alternative' administrative discourses based on cultural, cognitive, or critical theory. As Giroux (1992) points out:

> Administrators and teachers in schools of education and leadership programs need...a language that is interdisciplinary, that moves skilfully among theory, practice, and politics. This is a language that makes issues of culture, power, and ethics primary to understanding how schools construct knowledge, identities, and ways of life that promote nurturing and empowering relations. We need a language in our leadership programs that defends schools as democratic public spheres... (p. 8)

This new administrative discourse must not only critique current practices, but also provide a vision of what a democratic school culture would look like. Unlike current notions of school culture, democratic cultures are not about managed consent, but rather cultures in which multiple voices are allowed to be expressed and in which a variety of possible ways of being in organization are legitimated.

Second, since change is not merely cognitive, but also behavioural, we must find ways to make sure that a new discourse is put into practice in ways that do not distort or subvert institutional democracy. Drawing on the work of Argyris, et al. (1985), Robinson (1994) argues that it is possible to achieve critical dialogue grounded in both critical theory and organizational learning which can provide methods for testing whether actors' 'theories-in-use' are consistent with democratic discourses grounded in a 'power with' approach to institutional cultural politics.

CONCLUSION

Rather than focus on this rich literature that describes the cultural politics of schooling, the field of educational administration continues to speak in narrow functionalist and prescriptive terms of managing conflict, managing 'negative' employees and 'difficult' parents, and my current favourite, 'managing diversity'. The field of educational administration manages critique by marginalizing and pathologizing the messengers.

Perhaps the most credible insight into why school cultural politics is ignored when possible and 'managed' when it cannot be ignored, comes from the area superintendent of a large urban school district quoted above:

> In order to survive, urban school districts must invest an enormous amount of energy and political capital in maintaining a public image of legitimacy. In part, urban districts must do this because the public knows or suspects how poorly a majority of the clients are performing and how resistant many of them are...My hypothesis is that the pressures, or perceived pressures on urban school districts to be 'legitimate institutions' so preoccupy them that they are ultimately unable to be responsive to their clients – because to do so they would need to restructure or reconfigure their ways of delivering services so radically that they would no longer be considered school districts. (Lytle, 1992, p. 127)

Through a better understanding of cultural politics and shifting our commitment to currently silenced groups in schools, the field of educational administration could support an emerging critical restructuring movement. This movement, currently being led by marginalized groups of teachers, parents, and students could result in transforming schools into democratic public spheres (Anderson, Herr, and Nihlen, 1994; Gitlin, et al., 1992; Lee, 1992; Miller, 1990). But first, each of us who works in the administrative sciences must ultimately struggle to answer a key question, one that has been kept off our agenda through cultural politics: 'Who do we work for?

FOOTNOTES

1. Although we refer to 'schools' throughout this chapter, the issues raised are valid for all educational institutions, including universities.

REFERENCES

Anderson, G.L. (1990). Toward a critical constructivist approach to school administration: Invisibility, legitimation, and the study of non – events. *Educational Administration Quarterly*, 26(1), 38 – 59.

Anderson, G.L. (1991). Cognitive politics of principals and teachers. Ideological control in an elementary school. In J. Blase (Ed.). *The politics of life in schools.* (pp. 120 – 138) Newbury Park: Sage.

Anderson, G.L. and Dixon, A. (1993). Paradigm shifts and site – based management in the United States: Toward a paradigm of social empowerment. In J. Smyth (Ed.) *A socially critical view of the self – managing school* (pp. 49 – 61) London: Falmer Press.

Anderson, G.L. and Herr, K. (1993). The micropolitics of student voices: Moving from diversity of bodies to diversity of voices in schools. In C. Marshall (Ed.) *The new politics of race and gender: The 1992 yearbook of the Politics of Education Association.* (pp. 58 – 68) Washington, D.C.: Falmer Press.

Anderson, G.L., Herr, K., and Nihlen, A. (1994). *Studying your own school: An educator's guide to qualitative, site – based research.* Newbury Park: Corwin Press.

Apple, M. (1993). *Official knowledge: Democratic education in a conservative age.* New York: Routledge.

Argyris, C., Putnam, R. and McLain – Smith, D. (1985). *Action science.* San Francisco: Jossey – Bass.

Bachrach, P. and Baratz, M. (1963). Decisions and non decisions: an analytical framework. *American Political Science Review*, 56, 947 – 52.

Bakhtin, M. (1981). *The dialogic imagination.* Austin: University of Texas Press.

Ball, S. (1987). *The micro – politics of the school: Towards a theory of school organization.* New York: Methuen.

Barth, R.S. (1990). *Improving schools from within.* San Francisco: Jossey – Bass.

Bates, R. (1986). *The management of knowledge and culture.* Geelong: Deakin University Press.

Blase, J. (Ed.) (1991). *The politics of life in schools.* Newbury Park, CA: Sage.

Blase, J. and Anderson, G. (in press). *The micro – politics of school leadership: From social control to social empowerment.* London: Cassell.

Bloome, D. and Willett, J. (1991). Toward a micropolitics of classroom interaction. In J. Blase (Ed.) *The politics of life in schools* (pp. 207 – 236) Newbury Park, CA: Sage.

Bowles, S. and Gintis, H. (1976). *Schooling in capitalist America.* New York: Basic Books.

Brown & Gilligan (1992). *Meeting at the crossroads: Women's psychology and girls' development.* Cambridge: Harvard University Press.

Capper, C. (1993). Educational Administration in a pluralistic society: A multipara-digm approach. In C. Capper (Ed.). *Educational administration in a pluralistic society* (pp. 7 – 35) Albany: SUNY Press.

Cheryholmes, C. (1988). *Power and criticism: Poststructural investigations in education.* New York: Teachers College Press.

Cummins, J. (1986). Empowering minority students: A framework for intervention. *Harvard Educational Review*, 56, 58 – 72.

Cusick, P. (1973). *Inside high school: The student's world.* New York: Holt, Rinehart & Winston.

Cusick, P. (1983). *The egalitarian ideal and the American high school.* New York: Longman.

Dunlap, D.M. & Goldman, P. (1991). Rethinking power in schools. *Educational Administration Quarterly*, 27, 5 – 29

Ferguson, K. (1984). *The feminist case against bureaucracy.* Philadelphia: Temple University Press.

Fine, M. (1987). Silencing in public schools. *Language arts*, 64(2), 157 – 174.

Fine, M. (1988). De – institutionalizing educational inequity: contexts that constrict and construct the lives and minds of public school adolescents. In Council of Chief State School Officers, *School success for students at risk.* (pp. 89 – 119) Orlando: Harcourt Brace Jovanovich.

Fine, M. (1992). *Disruptive voices: the possibilities of feminist research.* Ann Arbor: The University of Michigan Press.

Fine, M. and Weiss, L. (1993). Introduction. In L. Weiss and M. Fine (Eds.) *Beyond silenced voices: Class, race, and gender in United States schools.* (pp. 1 – 6) Albany: SUNY Press.

Firestone, W. and Wilson, B. (1985). Using bureaucratic and cultural linkages to improve instruction: the principal's contribution. *Educational Administration Quarterly*, 21(2), 7 – 30.

Fordham, S. and Ogbu, J. (1986). Black students' school success: Coping with the 'burden of acting white.' *Urban Review*, 18(3), 176 – 206.

Foster, W. (1986). *Paradigms and promises.* Buffalo, NY: Prometheus Books.

Fraatz, J.M.B. (1987). *The politics of reading: Power, opportunity, and prospects for change in America's public schools.* New York: Teachers College Press.

Freire, P. (1970). *Pedagogy of the Oppressed.* New York: Seabury Press.

Giddens, A. (1984). *The constitution of society.* Berkeley, CA: University of California Press.

Giroux, H. (1992). Educational leadership and the crisis of democratic government. *Educational Researcher*, 21(4), 4 – 11.

Gitlin, A., Bringhurst, K., Burns, M., Cooley, V., Myers, B., Price, K., Russell, R., and Tiess, P. (1992). *Teachers' voices for school change: An introduction to educative research.* New York: Teachers College Press.

Gramsci, A. (1971). *Selections from prison notebooks.* London: Lawrence and Wishart.

Greenfield, W.D. (1987). Moral imagination and interpersonal competence: Antecedents to instructional leadership. In W.D. Greenfield (Ed.) *Instructional leadership* (pp. 56 – 73) Boston: Allyn and Bacon

Griffiths, D. (1991). Introduction: Non traditional theory and research. *Educational Administration Quarterly*, 27(3), 262 – 264.

Gronn, P. (1986). Politics, power, and management of schools. In E. Hoyle (Ed.) *The world yearbook of education 1986: The management of schools* (pp. 45 – 54) London: Kegan Paul.

Hargreaves, A. (1991). Contrived collegiality: The micropolitics of teacher collaboration. In J. Blase (Ed.) *The politics of life in schools.* (pp. 46 – 72) Newbury Park, CA: Sage.

Hopkins, R. (1994). *Narrative schooling: Experiential learning and the transformation of American education.* New York: Teachers College Press.

Hoyle, E. (1982). Micropolitics of educational organizations. *Educational Management and Administration,* 10, 87 – 98.

Jencks, C. et al. (1972). *Inequality.* New York: Basic books.

Kanpol, B. (1992). *Towards a theory and practice of teacher cultural politics.* Norwood, NJ: Ablex.

Kohl, H. (1992). I won't learn from you!: Thoughts on the role of assent in learning. *Rethinking Schools,* 7(1), 16 – 19.

Lee, E. (1992). The crisis in education: Forging an anti – racist response. *Rethinking schools,* 7(1), 4 – 5.

Lee, S. (1993). *Hegemony in an elementary school: The principal as headless horseman.* Paper presented at the Annual Meeting of the American Educational Research Association, Atlanta.

Lytle, J. (1992). Prospects for reforming urban schools. *Urban Education.* 27(2), 109 – 131.

Lukes, S. (1974). *Power: A radical view.* London: Macmillan.

Malen, B. and Ogawa, R. (1988). Professional – patron influence on site – based governance councils: A confounding case study. *Educational Evaluation and Policy Analysis,* 10(4), 215 – 70.

Marshall, C. and Anderson, G.L. (in press). Rethinking the public and private spheres: Feminist and cultural studies perspectives on the politics of education. In J. Scribner and D. Layton (Eds.) *The 1994 politics of education association yearbook.* London: Falmer Press.

Maxcy, S.J. (1991). *Educational leadership: A critical pragmatic perspective.* New York: Bergin & Garvey.

McNeil, L. (1986). *Contradictions of control: School structure and school knowledge.* New York: Routledge.

Mehan, H. (1992). *Understanding inequality in schools: the contribution of interpretive studies.* Sociology of Education, 65(1), 1 – 20

Mercer, J. (1974). *Labelling the mentally retarded.* Berkeley: the University of California Press.

Metz, M. (1978). *Classrooms and corridors: The crisis of authority in desegregated secondary schools.* Berkeley: University of California Press.

Miller, J. (1990). *Creating spaces and finding voices: Teachers collaborating for empowerment.* Albany: SUNY Press.

Oakes, J. (1985). *Keeping track: How schools structure inequality.* New Haven: Yale University Press.

Ogbu, J. (1989). The individual in collective adaptation: A framework for focusing on academic under performance and dropping out among involuntary minorities. In L. Weiss, E. Farrar, and H. Petrie (Eds.). *Dropouts from school: Issues, dilemmas, and solutions.* (pp. 181 – 204) Albany: SUNY Press.

Peters, T. (1993). *Liberation management.*

Quantz, R. (1993). On critical ethnography (with some postmodern considerations). In M. LeCompte, W. Millroy, and J. Preissle (Eds.) *The handbook of qualitative research in education*. San Diego: Academic Press.

Quantz, R., Rogers, J. & Dantley, M. (1991). Rethinking transformative leadership: Toward democratic reform of schools. *Journal of Education*, 173(3), 96 – 118.

Rist, R.C. (1970). Student social class and teacher expectations: The self – fulfilling prophecy in ghetto education. *Harvard Educational Review*, 40, 411 – 451.

Robinson, V. (1994). The practical promise of critical research in educational administration. *Educational Administration Quarterly*, 30(1), 56 – 76.

Sapon – Shevin, M. (1994). *Playing favourites: Gifted education and the disruption of community*. Albany: SUNY Press.

Schon, D.A. (1983). *The reflective practitioner*. New York: Basic Books.

Sergiovanni, T. (1984). Cultural and competing perspectives in administrative theory and practice. In T. Sergiovanni & J.Corbally Eds.) *Leadership and organizational culture* (pp. 1 – 13) Urbana – Champagn: University of Illinois Press.)

Smircich, L. and Morgan, G. (1982). Leadership: *The management of meaning. The journal of applied behavioural science*, 18(3), 257 – 273.

Smith, J. and Blase, J. (January, 1989). You can run but you cannot hide: Hermeneutics and its challenge to the field of educational leadership. *Organizational Theory Dialogue*, 1 – 7.

Suarez – Orozco, M. (1987). 'Becoming somebody': Central American immigrants in U.S. Inner – City Schools. *Anthropology and Education Quarterly*, 18, 287 – 299.

Weatherley, R. and Lipsky, M. (1977). Street – level bureaucrats and institutional innovation: Implementing special education reform. *Harvard Educational Review*, 47(2), 171 – 97.

Wexler, P., Crichlow, W., Kern, J. & Martusewicz, R. (1992). *Becoming somebody: Toward a social psychology of school*. London: Falmer Press.

Willis, P. (1977). *Learning to Labour: How working class kids get working class jobs*. New York: Columbia University Press.

Chapter 27: Cultural Dynamics and Organizational Analysis: Leadership, Administration and the Management of Meaning in Schools

LAWRENCE ANGUS

Monash University

In this chapter my focus is upon ways in which the cultural dynamics of schooling are conceptualized. Our conceptions of such things as school culture are not simply individualistic or voluntarist constructs. They are influenced in various ways by the social and cultural context within which education, and discourses of educational administration and leadership, are located. My essential argument is that our conceptions of such matters not only reflect our understanding of how educational organizations work, but also constrain and/or enable us as participants in the ongoing process of institutional life, and in shaping the organizational values to which we might aspire. Therefore, conceptions such as 'organizational culture', which frequently appear in the educational administration literature as part of an attempt to explain and, often, control cultural dynamics, act as ideologies.

Within current educational administration literature, it could be argued that the cultural perspective that is generally articulated is one in which the social context of school dynamics is largely overlooked. Administrators are typically expected to become symbolic managers of schools and their cultures (Bates 1987). Indeed, current management theory explicitly constructs administrators as manipulators of culture and belief, who, if they are good at their jobs, should be able to construct or impose corporate control within their institutions in the increasingly decentralized organizational form which is considered necessary for organizational efficiency and, most importantly, legitimacy, in the increasingly complex post-industrial society (Parker, 1992).

My general argument is that the predominant perspective misconceives organizational dynamics as sets of behaviours that can largely be predicted and contained within school cultures, and which can largely be controlled by administrators. This is because culture is considered, by and large, as an organizational variable. It is represented in the prevailing literature as an internal aspect of institutions, one that

967

K. Leithwood et al. (eds.), *International Handbook of Educational Leadership and Administration*, 967-996.
© 1996 Kluwer Academic Publishers, Printed in the Netherlands.

may be manipulated by management in order to enhance subordinates' organizational commitment and efficiency. That is, the organization and its leadership are conceptualized as generators of particular cultural values, practices and attributes that are associated with corporate solidarity and a sense of mission or corporate vision (Deal & Kennedy, 1982).

I shall argue that such a perspective on organizational dynamics fails to acknowledge that culture is shifting and contested, and is continually being constructed and reconstructed. Instead, the emphasis in the prevailing literature is upon managerial intervention in organizational culture to shape it in ways that are thought to be conducive to the realization of organizational goals. This conception, in which management is privileged, betrays significant misappropriations from anthropology and cultural theory. Not only is there a lack of appreciation of the importance and complexity of cultural dynamics, but also there is a taken-for-granted assumption that organizational culture will reflect unproblematically norms and goals which are internalized to form stable, integrated organizational structures. A more complex notion of organizational dynamics, in which organizational culture is linked with subjectivity, cultural politics and social context, is advocated in this chapter.

LEADERSHIP AND CULTURAL CONTROL

Traditionally, educational administration and leadership have been presented in the literature largely in technical and managerial terms. The mainstream literature, historically, has been concerned with equipping educational administrators, especially school principals, with the necessary tools of the trade. These usually amount to techniques of management, planning, decision making, motivation, delegation, communication and, especially, leadership. From the traditional perspective, the definition of problems and solutions in educational administration is relatively narrow because they are generally conceptualized as management problems that can be solved by technical means. The literature is directed particularly at educational administrators, and at other scholars who see their work as the preparation of school managers. Most of the commonly used textbooks in the field of educational administration, including such standards as Hoy and Miskel's (1987 [see especially their preface and opening chapters]), fit comfortably within this tradition. The orientation is towards efficient, effective, goal-oriented and neutral management.

Alternative conceptualizations of educational administration are much less likely to be found in the standard text books or in the minds of practising administrators. Indeed, research that has been conducted on practising administrators (e.g. Kempner 1992) consistently shows that they tend to see their work in a technical way, that they generally believe that specialist managerial traits and skills are required, and that they have little time for 'theory'. As a result, although the language of management is external (not natural) to administrators, they have taken it on board as part of the necessary learning they must do. If Kempner (1992) is correct, administrators, typically, largely accept the technical, managerial discourse of administration without examining it in relation to their lived experience. As a result, such discourse increasingly shapes definitions of administrators' work so that they see administration and leadership as being concerned with straight-forward technical and managerial matters.

The combination of a narrowly functionalist orientation and an obsession with the practicalities of administrative leadership constructs educational administration as a technology of control (Bates 1987). The effect of this particular combination is that organizational dynamics are reduced to a functionalist notion of 'organizational culture' that is regarded virtually as a 'controllable variable' in the hands of the leader (Killman et al., 1985). In what the editors claim represents the 'state of the art' in the still-burgeoning literature on corporate culture, Killman and colleagues' (1985) *Gaining Control of the Corporate Culture* urges leaders to 'take charge' and manage the culture. In the various chapters of this influential book, leading authors in the field emphasize that strong cultures can be created by management (Schein, 1985); that strong cultures emanate from the beliefs, values and philosophies of senior management and serve to unite lower level workers (Lorsch, 1985; Martin, 1985); and that workers, through the age-old combination of rewards and sanctions offered by management, can be brought to internalize management wishes and directions and so do what managers want without having to be told (Allen, 1985). A similar argument is advanced in educational administration by Smith and Peterson (1988) in their influential text on *Leadership, Organizations and Culture*. These authors clearly regard organizational culture as a dependent variable of leadership. For corporate leaders to gain control of the corporate culture, therefore, organizational culture needs to be defined, as and constructed as, 'the major beliefs and values as expressed by top management that provide organizational members with a frame of reference for action' (Goll & Zeitz, 1991, p. 191). Leaders, from this perspective, create their own organizational environments (Kirby et al., 1992, p. 303). The leader's values, in other words, virtually *are* the organization; or, as Bottery (1988, p. 342) puts it:

> whoever is in charge of the organization has the right to dictate its aims;

> these aims can be relatively easily decided upon and implemented;

> as the organization's aims are more important than those of individuals within the organization, it is perfectly acceptable to treat people as means to the organization's ends.

Mainstream authors, of course, are rarely as blunt as Bottery. However, the managerial orientation he identifies seems quite explicit in many of the works cited above.

Sleezer and Swanson (1992), who recommend 'culture surveys' as a 'tool' that managers can use when they 'are faced with the challenge of changing the organizational culture to support new ways of accomplishing work' (p. 22), provide another example of this orientation. These authors advise that 'because time is money, the longer it takes a manager to solve a problem, the greater the cost to the organization' (p.22). Therefore, in order to move quickly and get the culture right as efficiently and cost-effectively as possible, 'management can use culture surveys to communicate its vision of the organization's culture and the performance expectations that operationalize the vision' (Sleezer & Swanson, 1992, pp. 23-24). Subordinates, it appears, are expected simply to accept this communication, adopt the new vision, and blithely alter their organizational values and practices to suit the new culture that management has articulated. This vision of compliance and tranquillity on the part of workers in response to imposed change, however, seems to fly in the face of just about everyone's experience of organizational life. For most of us, as Meek (1988, p. 461) puts it, 'organizations are often arenas for dispute and conflict... Organizations are not one homogeneous culture, but are 'multi-cultural', and culture can be a source of conflict'.

In educational administration, scholars have been joining with their colleagues in the field of business administration in the common pursuit of cultural leadership techniques. Notions of appropriate school leadership have been heavily influenced by culture concepts in United States management literature such as *In Search of Excellence* (Peters & Waterman, 1982). Similar ideas have been picked up in the school effectiveness literature (e.g. Purkey & Smith, 1985). Scholars such as Caldwell and Spinks (1988) combine these literatures and give special attention to the so-called 'higher-order attributes of leadership, namely the capacity to articulate and win commitment to a vision for the school and ensure that vision is institutionalized in the structures, processes and procedures which shape everyday activities' (p. 21). These literatures follow the trend of assuming that appropriate cultural expectations for all of those associated with a school are rightfully embodied in the particular values and vision of the leader. The view seems to incorporate the dangerously elitist implication that leaders have superior values to, and are more visionary than, anyone else. The general approach seems totally consistent with the long historical tradition of managerial reforms in which management has attempted to secure the consent of subordinates and build it into otherwise unchanged forms of management control (Wood, 1985).

Good leaders, in this approach, are expected to shrewdly manipulate culture, people and situations so that their own 'vision' will be willingly shared by followers. For this to happen, the desires and needs of followers must be incorporated into a corporate agenda that is set by the leader. The approach draws heavily on the work of such scholars as Weick (1976), Burns (1978), Vaill (1984), Bennis and Nanus (1985) and Deal and Kennedy (1982). It is believed that leaders of vision will be pro-active in bringing about a negotiated order – an organizational culture – which accords with their own definitions and purposes and ensures that any change is directed into reasonable, predictable channels by their own overriding moral force. Teachers, parents, students and other organizational participants are rarely mentioned at all, and if they *are* mentioned, they are generally viewed as essentially passive recipients of the leader's vision. By asserting and defending particular values, leaders so strongly articulate and endorse their own vision that it becomes also the vision of followers and so bonds leader and followers together in a shared covenant which then informs the non-negotiable core beliefs and values of the organization.

According to Caldwell and Spinks (1988, pp. 174-5) the process is argued to work in schools as follows: the leader (principal) articulates a vision for the school which becomes shared by other school members; the vision then 'illuminates' the ordinary activities of school members and invests them with 'dramatic significance'; at this point the leader 'implants the vision in structures and processes of the organization, so that people experience the vision in the various patterned activities of the organization'; this leads to the happy situation in which day-to-day decisions are made 'in the light of the vision' which by then has become 'the heart of the culture of the organization'; one can recognize that the leader's vision has been institutionalized in this way when 'all members of the organization celebrate the vision in rituals, ceremonies and art forms'.

This approach clearly places extraordinary demands on the leader. This is not especially surprising since most would agree that organizational 'leaders', such as principals, rightly seek, and are generally expected, to influence organizational arrangements. Moreover, they are generally in a better position than most other organizational participants to do so. As such, they cannot escape being, at least to some extent, 'managers of organizational meaning, the custodians of organizational legitimacy, and the definers of organizational and social reality' (Anderson, 1990, p. 43) – just as the corporate culture theorists advocate. However the prevailing view goes further and assumes that 'leaders' have virtually unlimited management power. But this assumption would appear to be untenable because, although those with power are able to influence organizations in various ways, particularly because of their access to resources and information, leaders have no monopoly on the development of organizational meaning (Smircich, 1983, p. 161). Everyone, whether they like it or not, is a participant in this process (Angus & Rizvi, 1989). Moreover, there is a range of cultural influences on an organization such as a school over which a 'leader' can have little if any control. The list would include history, national culture, international cultures, professional cultures, gender cultures, class cultures, the economy and many more.

This realization might lead us to consider that organizational meaning and culture are perhaps created not by management but are perhaps constantly emerging, being made, in the context of the total organization and all that influences it. If this is so, then we must accept that the making of meaning is a highly problematic and uncertain process in which meanings have to be asserted, contested and learned. Only when such learning results in the acceptance of meanings that are largely taken for granted, can they become institutionalized as formal or informal 'rules' (Clegg, 1981) which 'guide people in appropriate or relevant behaviour, help them to know how things are done, what is expected of them, how to achieve certain things, etc.' (Mills, 1988, p. 360). But even learning of this type is not simply soaked up by people without question. Meaning is mediated by structures, both organizational and social, and is therefore the result of contested social practices in arenas of unequal power relations.

Where meaning in the form of rules for organizational practice is widely accepted, and where organizational legitimacy seems to prevail, therefore, such agreement is less likely to be the result of natural consensus than the product of 'the control of those resources which render meanings and identities seemingly unproblematical for the practical, historically conditioned, purposes of particular individuals and groups' (Coombs et al., 1992, p. 69). Meaning produced in this way always remains part of 'the competitive struggles over material and symbolic resources whose asymmetrical distribution routinely privileges the claims of some agents (and especially managers) in their exercise of control' (Coombs et al., 1992, p. 69). Drawing on the work of Willis, Apple (1992, p. 138) explains this point nicely:

> making meaning is not only an individual act, but a profoundly social act, one structured by location and situation. However, locations and situations are not only to be understood as determinations. They are also, and profoundly, 'relations and resources to be discovered, explored and experienced' As Willis goes on to say, race, class, gender, age and membership are not simply learned; they are lived and experimented with, even if only by pushing up against the oppressive limits of established order and power.

The conclusion to be drawn here is that the making of meaning requires agency, energy and struggle. Meaning is made against other meanings, possibly dominant meanings. This is a critical point because, given that schools have generally promoted the interests of capital and of dominant social groups, as Giroux (1984) argues, then educational administrators should turn their attention to the way in which 'the issue of how teachers, students and representatives from the wider society generate meaning tends to be obscured in favour of how people can master someone else's meaning, thus depoliticizing both the notion of school culture and the notion of classroom pedagogy' (Giroux, 1984, p. 37). In other words, meanings that are embodied or negotiated or contested within school culture, pervade school life, including its informal and formal arrangements, and give legitimacy to particular cultural, social and educational values. The contingency and indeterminacy of such cultural dynamics ensures that organizational culture, while powerful at any moment, is always provisional. The meaning of organizational culture is therefore extraordinarily complex and dynamic.

THE MEANING OF ORGANIZATIONAL CULTURE

According to Meek (1988, p. 463), who draws upon the work of Smircich (1983), theories of organizational culture can be divided into two groups. The first treats culture as a variable – as something 'the organization has' which is able to be manipulated and controlled. The second regards culture as something 'the organization is' – as 'the product of negotiated and shared symbols and meanings; it is produced from human action'. The first way of seeing culture (as something the organization 'has') is broadly consistent with functionalist accounts of organizations and society. This is the view that I have generally discussed so far. The second way of seeing culture (as something an organization 'is') draws upon interpretive accounts in which reality is thought to be socially constructed. Literature employing the second way of seeing is likely to be more analytical and to employ the notion of culture as a 'root metaphor' (Smircich 1983) for understanding the social construction of organizational life. In this literature, culture is typically regarded as 'the pattern of basic assumptions that the group has invented, discovered or developed in learning to cope with external adaptation and internal integration' (Schein, 1986, p. 9).

The interesting point about much of the literature that is directed at managers, including a number of the works cited above, is that it adopts a largely interpretive account in its description and discussion of culture as a concept, yet switches to the functionalist perspective – the view that culture can be manipulated and controlled – when advocating or prescribing managerial action. For instance, in the educational administration literature, school culture – which is said to include values, symbols, beliefs, shared meanings, customs and traditions, legends and sagas, stated and unstated understandings, habits, norms and expectations, common meanings and shared assumptions – is thought to enable the unified school to become 'effective' and achieve its objectives (Sergiovanni & Corbally, 1984, p. viii). The best way in which this can happen, it is argued, is if school culture can be aligned with a vision of 'excellence'. Such a culture, strongly asserted by a visionary leader, provides a source of common meaning and significance for school participants, and so creates common values and a common direction (Sergiovanni, 1984, p. 10). By providing the necessary 'vision', administrators can control the culture.

It seems odd that so much management literature can start out embracing the notion of shared values, interpretations, meanings, and culture, yet end up taking a contradictory position by claiming that such sharing is the result of organizational participants bending their wills in order to accept the values, interpretations, meanings and culture that have been defined for them by a leader. It would surely seem ludicrous to an anthropologist to suggest that a leader could define the culture of a group in what is a complex interactive process. In terms of cultural politics, also, management can be only a part of the total organizational culture. The fact that much educational administration literature can seemingly accommodate such a startling contradiction is perhaps partly due to the long-standing concern in school management for order and regularity (Bates, 1980, 1987).

To be sure, culture is an extraordinarily complex concept and one that is extremely difficult to define. However, despite the variability and complexity of different definitions, a particular view of organizational culture, with its particular misconceptions and misappropriations, seems now to have been asserted within management theory and to have been generally accepted as largely non-controversial despite being somewhat problematic. There is now general agreement, according to Mitchell and Willower (1992, p. 6), that organizational culture is typically taken to be 'the way of life of a given collectivity (or organization) particularly as reflected in shared values, norms, symbols and traditions'.

While there is some agreement at this level of generality, however, when it comes to cultural dynamics, it is probably correct to say that 'there is no single comprehensive theory that fully explains the complexity of the school as an organization' (Shaw, 1992, p. 295). What is lacking in both the ways of understanding organizational culture mentioned above (whether it is regarded as something an organization 'has' or something an organization 'is') is any account of the relationship between the organization and other organizations, social spheres and social experiences. This point is critical. The focus in both cases is internal to the specific organization within which it is assumed that there is a natural tendency towards consensus and harmony – either because that is natural and functional (something the organization 'has'), or because it is the assumed outcome of group negotiation (something the organization 'is'). In both cases, social conflict and the external cultural, social and economic context in which organizations are embedded, are generally excluded from the analysis. Therefore, while there are problems with various traditions, both mainstream conceptions of organizational culture (which have been enthusiastically and uncritically appropriated into educational administration) reduce the complexity of culture to an almost absurd level of simplicity by emphasizing only that culture creates consensus.

Management writers seem to assume without question that sharing of beliefs, values and culture in fact exists, and to overlook the capacity of individuals to challenge and ignore, as well adapt to, organizational rules. The functionalist perspective, in particular, seems to dismisses even the capacity of organization members to comment critically on their situation (Golden, 1992, pp. 1-2). As Golden (1992, p. 2) points out, 'the majority of writers... systematically overlook this aspect of culture, focusing instead on the ways in which individuals adapt to, and reinforce, the organization's rules for action'. There is presumed to be a unitary ('the') organizational culture rather than a complex of subcultures within an organization. This presumption is directly contradicted, however, in ethnographic traditions of cultural work in education which indicate that pupils and teachers comprise somewhat different sub-cultures. Indeed, from the perspective of cultural politics, such work indicates that organization members would probably switch back and forth among many sub-cultures during the school day (Schultz, 1991).

Social and cultural practices are explained in the prevailing functionalist literature mainly in terms of their supposed contribution to a stable and coherent organization. Much of the literature therefore presumes that 'there exists in a real and tangible sense a collective organizational culture that can be created, measured and manipulated in order to enhance organizational effectiveness' (Meek, 1988, p. 454). Meek regards this situation as a serious oversimplification of culture and as an illustration of the...

> danger that, when one area of study borrows from another discipline, the concepts become either stereotyped or distorted in the transfer. Also... they may not be borrowed in toto: that is, rather than accepting an entire 'package' – which may include the historical debates surrounding the 'proper' use of the concepts – people only select aspects of the concepts that suit

their interests and thinking at a particular time. (Meek, 1988, p. 454)

Most importantly, Meek (1988) argues, misappropriation from the structural functionalist theoretical tradition, without the accompanying debates and criticisms, has resulted in a notion of organizational culture which is narrowly stereotyped. The interests that are served by this are, most directly, those of management, but also, as I shall argue later, the dominant social and economic interests in the society. These interests are served partly by the privileging of leadership within organization literature and partly by a fascination with business management. Indeed, business has become the dominant metaphor in educational administration (Kempner, 1992; Mitchell & Willower, 1992). This is illustrated by, for example, the fascination with, and space devoted to, works such as Peters and Waterman's *In Search of Excellence* in a number of standard educational administration texts (e.g. Caldwell & Spinks, 1988). The 'adoration of business' in educational administration has led to the situation in which 'business operations, management, and leadership are often used by administrators and scholars in education as models of success' (Kempner, 1992, p. 110).

As Bates (1987) and others (Anderson, 1990; Angus, 1993; Meek, 1988) have pointed out, the kind of managerial shift that is advocated in much recent management literature is from strictly bureaucratic control to ideological control under the guise of a celebration of organizational culture. In the educational sphere, this logic would imply that, regardless of popular rhetoric of devolution and decentralization, current literature on the local management of schools, and the emphasis on 'corporate culture' in their administration, may have much less to do with democratic governance than with traditional managerial concerns with organizational control (see, for example, management texts by Beare et al., 1989; Caldwell & Spinks, 1988; and critiques of these by Angus, 1993; Smyth, 1993). The predominance of these traditional concerns would partly explain why, in many current educational contexts, management, leadership and cultural control have become so significant. The emphasis on control, of course, is hardly new (Callahan, 1968), but it has been asserted in such a way as to renovate earlier managerial traditions and to marginalize alternative traditions of cultural work within educational administration.

EDUCATION AND CULTURE

There is a long-held popular wisdom among teachers and administrators that when you walk into a school you almost immediately pick up a 'feel' for whether it is a 'good' school with a distinctive character or 'climate'. The notion of 'school climate' links with a particular tradition of administrative theory – that of the human relations school of scientific management. This group of theorists revised the classical model of organization by emphasizing the need for the motivation of, rather than the control of, subordinates. They argued that organizational success depends on the 'social integration' of an organization (see Perrow, 1979, for an overview).

From the human relations point of view, managers are encouraged to understand the human condition in order to influence it in organizations. Although the needs of employees were to be taken into account, these theorists held that 'to the extent that personal sentiments, values, and goals are in conflict with formal regulations and organizational objectives, the job of managers is to reconcile individual and organizational needs' (Werlin, 1988, p. 52). Therefore, although regarding organization participants as humans rather than machines, as had largely been the case in classical scientific management (Wood, 1985), managers did need to divest themselves of any direct control. It could therefore be argued that the strongly pro-management position of the human relations school 'resulted in biased research that studied the 'irrational' behaviour of lower ranking personnel and supported unquestioningly the 'rational manager' model' (Gregory, 1983. p. 361). The objective of human relations management was to diagnose and control the organization and its culture, and therefore control subordinates. Current literature on school culture and corporate culture generally takes a similar stance and, although it rarely acknowledges it, fits squarely into the human relations tradition.

Notions of rational management such as those ingrained in the human relations school were challenged in educational administration some time ago by Greenfield (1973, 1983), who regarded organization merely as a process of people organizing themselves. From this perspective, organizations such as schools 'have no ontological reality beyond the specifications of individuals whose attitudes, values and motivations define organization' (Greenfield, 1983, p. 50). Organizations, therefore, as Greenfield put it in an early paper which launched his sustained critique of the prevailing functionalist perspective in educational administration, are sites of cultural negotiation among those people who have a stake in them:

> what many people seem to want from schools is that schools reflect the values that are central and meaningful in their lives. If this view is correct, schools are cultural artifacts that people struggle to shape in their own image. Only in such form do they have faith in them; only in such form can they participate fully in them. (Greenfield, 1973, p. 570)

Greenfield's important insight is that, in attempting to understand schools as organizations, the focus of attention should be on ordinary participants and their day-to-day social interaction rather than on management, techniques of management control, or universal laws of administration. This seemingly simple point posed a serious challenge to the prevailing orthodox or traditional approach to organizational analysis.

Greenfield's emphasis on the social construction of organizations directly contradicted the 'core idea' (Benson 1977) of the rational model of organizational analysis – the idea that the organization *is* indeed 'rational' and, as if it has a will of its own, seeks to achieve its goals in the most effective and efficient manner. Goal-achievement, within this rational model, is assumed to be what organizations are all about. Therefore, questions about organizational structure, authority relations, rules and regulations, would be examined in terms of their contribution to the organization achieving its goals. The rational model, with its emphasis on technical, managerial management, embraced a fairly simplistic form of positivism that amounted to a way of looking at the world which is concerned with 'the facts of the matter' – with measuring and recording organizational 'reality' with a view to identifying laws of organizational behaviour. Not only is there an obsession with measuring the relationships between organizational variables in this technical approach, but also, once relationships are 'discovered', there is an emphasis on devising ways in which these can be used to predict and control organizational behaviour. This means that 'organizational reality' is likely to be taken for granted as unproblematic. The politics of organizational life that lead to the production of the 'reality' being measured are therefore likely to be ignored. So is the idea that there may be multiple perceptions of organizational 'reality' depending on one's location in the organizational structure. Instead, the perspective of management tends to be regarded as the correct and universal perspective. Therefore, the concerns of the organizational analyst are the managerial, or 'administrative-technical' (Benson 1977), concerns of management, and it is assumed that administrative devices for controlling the organization in line with these concerns are necessary. That is, the emphasis is on finding administrative ways or techniques for improving organizational effectiveness – which amounts to the realization of specified goals.

The main features of conventional organizational analysis discussed above – the rational model, positivist methodology, and the dominance of administrative-technical concerns – are regarded by Benson (1977) as the 'three features of othodoxy'. Collectively, as he points out, they amount to 'an uncritical stance towards the organizational world' (Benson 1977, p. 40). My argument in this chapter has so far been that prevailing notions of organizational culture continue to reflect an uncritical and largely unexamined view of organizations and leaders. In the literature on educational administration, even where, following Greenfield, scholars have been interested in understanding organizational participants' values and experiences (e.g. Sergiovanni 1991; Starratt 1986, the realization that organizations are sites of cultural interaction has not generally led to analysis of broader questions about cultural dynamics in schools, the nature of social interaction, the politics of administration, educational change, and the relationship between schools and society. This is largely because, even in this relatively progressive literature, the reduction of organizations to collections of voluntarist individuals largely ignores, or at least oversimplifies and underestimates, the influence on organizations of power, history and the social, economic and cultural structures within which schools and all organizations are embedded. In other words, as I now want to argue, school culture is not simply the creation of, or the property of, individual school members. Organizational participants operate within social constraints. If this is the case, then educational administration is intimately connected with power and politics and is itself a dynamic political process.

The point here is not so much that the 'orthodox' perspective totally ignores the question of power. It is that in this perspective power is regarded as part of the organizational framework and is usually associated with a top-down authority structure that is thought to be functional in achieving organizational goals. As I have already emphasized, such a view takes the status quo as normal and natural rather than as the product of political human action. As Benson (1977, p. 43) points out, if power analysis is conducted 'it leads to the recognition that the organization's needs, goals, and essential outputs are based on an underlying power distribution'. In other words, the existing arrangements are *already* the result of power having been exerted and possibly entrenched in organizational structures. The organization therefore needs to be understood as a social formation structured by power relationships. Attempts to bring about future change, or to resist change, require the use of power. As Benson (1977, p. 43) goes on to explain, 'the organization as we encounter it – its goals, technology, division of labour, etc. – can be understood as the expression of the power of certain interests inside and outside the organization's boundaries'.

This means that many aspects of organizational life, structure, culture and apparent order are likely to be the results of power relationships and of attempts to exert organizational control. There is no such thing as a neutral, apolitical set of cause and effect relationships which can be explained simply in terms of organizational rationality or efficiency. However, as organizational actors we may take for granted organizational rules and expectations that are the product of such power relations, but which are manifested in benign notions of 'organizational culture'. In other words, we may not recognize the power relations we are immersed in because, through our socialization and familiarity with the organization and its structure, we have come to regard certain organizational arrangements as normal and natural. We need to understand also that organizations are caught up in power relations that extend beyond the institution and into the society at large.

The implication of the above is that educational control is therefore linked to broader social control. And the most significant aspect of educational administration in this process of control is likely to be its capacity for enhancing or challenging institutionalized power. The essential point is summed up in Bates' claim that educational administration typically amounts to the management of culture and knowledge (see, for example, Bates, 1980, 1987). As such, educational administration, Bates argues, provides ideological and cultural legitimation to prevailing power relations in society. In short, it generally confirms the status quo but could, if a critical perspective were adopted, contribute instead to greater social justice, liberty and equity.

Bates pursues these concerns by investigating the role of administration in legitimating structures of knowledge and providing differential access to 'what counts' as culture and knowledge to children of different social backgrounds. As Anderson (1990, p. 43) points out, by emphasizing the issue of 'what counts' as legitimate culture and knowledge, Bates particularly draws attention to the contested nature of meaning in educational organizations. In other words, as Anderson (1990, p. 43) puts it, 'meaning is the result of intersubjective negotiation within organizations, but what 'counts' as meaning is determined within contexts – both organizational and social – of unequal power relations'. This point has also been recognized by some recent researchers into teacher culture and pupil culture (e.g. Erickson, 1987).

While the notion that power relations are unequal implies that culture may be constructed and experienced differently from different social positions within the school, one point on which there is general agreement is that teacher and pupil cultures intersect at least in their common perception that the essential role of the teacher is to control pupils. This commonality, however, may be due largely to the social conditions which shape the practices and expectations of both teachers and pupils. As Britzman (1986, p. 444) explains, 'What dominates the perceptions of both teachers and students is the individual teacher's ability to control the class'. In other words, teacher and pupil cultures influence each other in complex ways such that each shapes, enculturates and socializes the other:

> Years of classroom experience allow students to have very specific expectations of how teachers should act in the classroom. Students, for example, expect the teacher to maintain classroom control, enforce rules and present the curriculum. Students expect teachers to be certain in both their behaviour and their knowledge, and students articulate these expectations if the teacher in any way deviates from this traditional image. In this sense students do coach their teachers in ways which reinforce school structure and, as such, constitute an immediate source of teacher socialization. (Britzman, 1986, pp. 445-446)

Britzman raises two points here that are especially important in conceptualizing school culture. The first is that students and teachers are not simply passively socialized by schools, nor are they inert victims of cultural reproduction in schools. They are active agents in the process. Teacher and pupil cultures act on each other. Despite such interaction, however, teachers are typically highly individualized while being subject to the general demands of bureaucratic control and school structures. The research generally concludes that teacher culture is 'practical in its orientation, largely uncritical and unreflective, and is concerned more with means rather than ends' (Sachs & Smith, 1988, p. 425).

The second point raised by Britzman is one that few researchers into teacher culture seem to have taken into account, but it is one that is vital for understanding the complexity of school culture. For Britzman, the research findings that teacher culture is characterized by such things as individualism and practicality merely identify cultural myths. The point is to look behind the myths at how teachers' work is influenced by institutional practicalities and school structures. When this is done, Britzman (1986, p. 448) argues, we can begin to see how the myths of teacher culture 'valorize the individual and make inconsequential the institutional constraints which frame the teacher's work. [In the research] the teacher is depicted as a self-contained world. [But] such myths transform the teacher's actual isolation into a valued autonomy which, in turn, promotes the larger social value of rugged individualism'. According to this argument:

> Teaching style, then, turns out to be not so much an individually determined product as it is a complex movement between the teacher, the students, the curriculum and the school culture. The myth that teachers are self-made serves to cloak the social relationships and the context of school structure by exaggerating personal autonomy. (Britzman, 1986, p. 452)

This sort of analysis is particularly useful because it connects student and teacher cultures with school structures, power relationships and the social context of schooling-elements which are often overlooked in interpretive and interactionist, as well as managerial and functionalist, descriptions of culture. All of these are interrelated in complex ways and are relevant to the important and varied body of work on cultural reproduction in education. Scholars in this tradition, influenced by a number of Weberian, neo-marxist and critical theoretical perspectives, reject the implicit assumption of mainstream approaches to educational administration that schools are socially and politically neutral institutions simply to be managed in the most efficient manner. Instead, schools are regarded in this tradition as social and cultural institutions, sites of power relationships, in which schooling serves the interests of dominant groups largely through the production and reproduction of meaning and of relations of class, race and gender.

While the variety of specific positions within this tradition makes generalization difficult, this socially critical perspective generally focuses upon 'macro-structural relationships and how these relations in the form of structural determinations shape, as well as limit, the actions of human beings, (Giroux, 1981, p.13). Scholars within this tradition, therefore, reject consensus as the normative glue of the social system; instead, they focus on the way in which dominant classes are able to reproduce existing power relations in an unjust and unequal society' (Giroux, 1981, p. 13). Work on cultural reproduction in schools, especially analyses of the so-called 'hidden curriculum', opened the way for sophisticated analysis and theorizing about the nature of schools as organizations, the complexity of their cultures, and the problematic relationship between schools and society. These insights, although they may have been expressed in a somewhat crude and reductionist manner in some cases, helped us to understand schooling as a social, political and cultural process that is far from neutral. It is precisely this fundamental lesson that is ignored in the currently dominant perspective on school culture. It is to particular elements of this critical tradition, especially its critique of the normalization of meaning in organizational contexts, that I now turn.

CULTURE, CONTEXT AND ORGANIZATIONAL POWER

Context issues, which grapple with both cultural dynamics and the social and political location of schooling, provide the essential problematic in critical approaches to educational administration (Anderson, 1990; Bates, 1987). These see organizations as manifestations of cultural forms (Smircich, 1983) or rules (Clegg, 1981) and also as sites of cultural contestation (Benson, 1977). In critical perspectives, in institutions such as schools, rather than a uniform concept of organizational culture simply being imposed from above, or bequeathed from the past, contest occurs over the construction and assertion of cultural forms. Organization members are regarded as active and knowing agents who are assumed to have the capacity to influence organizational culture and structure. They simultaneously adapt to, and influence to some extent, strongly institutionalized cultural expectations, both within institutions and in society more broadly. That is, cultural dynamics are part and parcel of the ongoing dialectic of agency and structure in the construction of organizational and social meanings.

In education, Giroux (e.g. 1984) and other critical scholars have long argued that the bland discourse of management, with its emphasis on control, regularity and predictability, leads both administrators and other organizational participants to be caught up in the 'culture of administration' in which, 'though they downplay it and whether they want it or not, principals, for example, typically have more power than teachers, students, parents, and others' (Sergiovanni, 1991, p. 43). Therefore, 'despite commitments to empowering and shared decision making, relationships between school administrators and others are often inherently unequal' (Sergiovanni, 1991, p. 43). However, the domination of managers in organizational settings, or any other form of domination for that matter, is by no means automatic.

A focus on power relationships can help organization researchers to illuminate the dynamics of organizational culture in action and the ways in which domination occurs in practice. And since power relationships extend beyond any single organization, such a focus also encourages us to connect organizations in dynamic ways with other, larger social contexts and to explore relations between them. Seeing educational institutions in a broad social and political context means seeing the relationship between education and other institutions in a dynamic way. The relationship is more than a connection. It is an *interaction* that is multi-dimensional because it is part of a web of interactions. The extent of interactions is too complex ever to pin down completely. Therefore, while recognizing the impossibility of ever creating any sort of map of the social and political context and its multiple relationships, it *is* important to adopt a 'way of seeing' that accepts multi-dimensionality, multiple causes and effects, and which recognizes that causes and effects occur in complex ways at various levels. For instance, adopting an interactive relationship between education, schools and society would mean theorizing the embeddedness of schooling, and schools as institutions, within wider social dynamics and power relationships. This point is particularly important for the critical social science perspective on organizational culture. In short, as Detz and Kerston concisely explain:

> The critical school views organizations as constructed realities but stresses the fact that this construction is not a free, voluntary process. The critical school view the system of meanings that exist at the surface or participant level as resulting from deep social and material forces. Creation of meaning is not an arbitrary process that occurs through friendly negotiation and talk. The social reality legitimizes particular social relations, structures and conditions, and it is explained by the deep social and material forces. To understand organizational real-

ity, then, is to ascertain why a particular meaning system exists by examining the conditions that necessitate its social construction and the advantages afforded to certain interests. (Deetz & Kerston, in Anderson 1990, p. 44)

In organizations, and in social life more generally, it seems that cultural forms become hegemonic when understandings are so strongly entrenched that they become internalized as guides for appropriate action. But this does not mean that an organizational culture simply bears down upon individuals in an institution so that a monolithic sense of organization is unproblematically sustained. Organizational culture, like the rest of the social world, must be continuously constituted. It is therefore always imperfectly reconstructed amongst contested meanings, discourses and subjectivities. Institutions like schools should therefore be seen as sites in which culture is constructed, contested and enacted (Willis, 1977; Giroux, 1984). In the process, entrenched expectations and hegemonic understandings act as background rules which influence the actions of organizational participants (Clegg, 1981; Giddens, 1976,1984). And while a particular organizational culture may be associated with specific institutions, these institutions are also influenced by, and partly mediate, broader social structures and societal cultures.

Socially constructed organizational 'rules' (Clegg, 1981) can take the form of informal meanings, institutionalized expectations and entrenched organizational features such as bureaucratic rationality. When taken for granted they amount to pervasive, but unrecognized, structures of power (Angus & Rizvi, 1989). However, they need not be hard and fast rules, and they may be mediated or broken, without much thought or quite deliberately, in different ways in different situations involving different people. Rules, then, largely in the form of institutionalized meanings, expectations and values, influence the nature and quality of individual and group participation in organizational life in complex and variable ways. Such 'rules' may be messy and confusing, indeterminate, partially understood, or understood in contradictory ways. According to Giddens (1976, p. 121), rules of this kind may still amount to structures which are 'both constituted *by* human agency and yet at the same time are the very *medium* of this constitution'. Giddens emphasizes both the dynamic relationship between structure and agency and the important point that structures do not merely constrain but also *enable* meaningful choices that may lead to action. A gender regime in a particular organization could be seen as an illustration of such influence (see Angus, 1993).

Mills makes the relevant and obvious point here that 'people do not leave their cultural perspectives at the gates of organizations' (1988, p. 355). They bring their beliefs, values, social conditioning and location within wider social and cultural dynamics and power relationships with them. This means that:

> schools must be seen as institutions marked by the same complex of contradictory cultures that characterize the dominant society. Schools are social sites constituted by a complex of dominant and subordinate cultures, each characterized by the power they have to define and legitimate a specific view of reality. Teachers and others interested in education must come to understand how the dominant culture functions at all levels of schooling to disconfirm the cultural experiences of the 'excluded majorities'. (Giroux, 1984, p. 37)

Schools therefore influence and are influenced by the cultural milieu of the society in which they are embedded. From this perspective, they are simultaneously sites in which cultural negotiation and contestation occurs, sites of cultural dominance, and sites which, actually as well as potentially, wield power in society.

Some institutional theorists (e.g. Meyer & Rowan, 1977) argue that, in the process of cultural construction, organizations such as schools may tend to reflect the dominant society because they need to be seen to conform with, and to adopt strategies that are consistent with, their cultural environments in order to maintain legitimacy and survive within them. However, this does not rule out the potential of schools to challenge and comment critically on social norms and practices. Galbraith, as Meek (1988, p. 461) points out, argues that it is through 'persuasion, education or the social commitment to what seems natural, proper or right' that institutions like the corporation, school, church and state 'cause the individual to submit to the will of another or of others' (in Meek, 1988, p. 461). Such conditioning is fundamental to the functioning of modern, complex society and so we may conclude, with Meek, that while we should understand the modern organization as a form of social control, we also need to recognize that 'it is not a form of social control created by management, but a process in which management, workers and the community at large are participants alike' (Meek, 1988, p. 462).

Schools, because they are expressly intended to reinforce what counts as knowledge, are, along with the media perhaps, particularly well placed to contribute to the making of social meaning and, indeed, the production of macro-culture. Although they certainly possess a degree of autonomy, schools and the education system 'must still articulate with other sectors of the social formation' (Johnston, 1991, p. 32). This articulation is, of course, accepted without question in the functionalist tradition in which schools are seen as being necessarily functional in socializing the young to take their place in society and the economy. Functionalist scholars are therefore unlikely to be troubled about the way in which many current educational reforms, largely informed by New Right thinking (Angus, 1992) which has become pervasive in social, political and educational debates, are directed at 'providing educational conditions believed necessary for increasing profit and capital accumulation' (Apple, 1991, p. 22). A similar logic promotes 'programs of choice to make schools like the idealized free-market economy' (Apple, 1991, p. 23).

The current use of business metaphors, especially the analogy of the market, in educational administration can therefore be seen to have profound cultural significance. As Bowles (1991, p. 11) argues, 'markets are as much political and cultural institutions as they are economic'. This is because markets 'not only allocate resources and distribute income, they also shape our culture, foster or thwart desirable forms of human development, and support a well defined structure of power' (Bowles, 1991, p. 11). This is what all cultural institutions do. As Bowles (1991, p. 12) reminds us, 'anthropologists have long stressed [that] how we regulate our exchanges and coordinate our disparate economic activities influences what kind of people we become'. Because of current obsession with 'the market' and the insidiousness of market arrangements throughout society, 'we learn to function in these environments, and in so doing become someone we might not have become in a different setting' (Bowles, 1991. p. 13).

The influence in educational administration of the notion of 'the market', which in recent education policy has been strongly asserted as the appropriate cultural metaphor for both the competitive relationship between schools and the relationship of schools to their communities, is becoming increasingly apparent. It is significant, for instance, that a number of well-regarded scholars in educational administration have recently closely linked organizational culture, leadership, market and school effectiveness (e.g. Caldwell & Spinks, 1988; Beare et al., 1989). For some, school culture seems to amount to little more than market image. In this case, managing the culture is managing the appropriate image so that a commodified package that is acceptable to consumers is presented to the market (Beare, 1982; Millikan, 1984). Such importation into education of business management methods directly influences educational practices and school culture. Market rationality, therefore, is but one example of how various elements of culture serve particular interests over others and connect with broader forms of social power and control. Indeed, the institutionalization of market thinking as right and proper for school management and organization provides an excellent illustration of the relationship between culture and power that I have been discussing.

CONCLUSION: CRITICAL CULTURAL ANALYSIS

I began this chapter by emphasizing that orthodox or traditional perspectives in educational policy and administration, by and large, imply conservative social positions on the nature and purpose of organizations and educational institutions within society, and conservative positions on social change. The general perspective is well illustrated by complementary aspects of functionalist social science and logical positivism, both of which have been extraordinarily influential not just in the literature on management and organizational analysis, but on social thinking more generally. This perspective is accommodated, I have argued, in prevailing notions of organizational culture in the literature on educational administration and leadership. This literature encourages scholars and administrators to think in managerial terms and to have in mind notions of systematic organization, prediction and managerial control, reliable and effective techniques, and a concern with the means of achieving particular goals.

There are a number of significant limitations of the functionalist position itself, and I have commented on some of these throughout the chapter. I have particularly discussed the consequences of the legacy of the orthodox approach on current perspectives on organizational culture in educational administration and leadership. As Ozga (1992), in reviewing recent education management texts, says of the literature in the field:

Most striking, and most significant, is the absence of any reflection in these texts of the origins and dimensions of the field of study they seek to expound. The impression that this is an area of teaching, research and publication without a sense of itself, of its intellectual origins and characteristics, is very strong. And this is a very significant absence, as self-consciousness in the area might generate self-criticism. At the moment the 'how to' texts create a false and unreliable impression that, if the correct procedures are followed, education is manageable. This both exaggerates the impact of tidy systems, and distracts managers from their obligation to establish direction and purpose as a preliminary to efficient system operation. (Ozga 1992, p.279)

I have indicated broad agreement with Ozga's criticism of many such texts, and specific points made in the above quotation have been taken up in this chapter. In particular, I have stressed that in such technical and managerial approaches, context is regarded largely as a backdrop to school organization, as part of the environment beyond the boundary of the school or as a source of inputs to which the school must respond by appropriate managerial action. This a point of direct contrast with critical approaches in which schools and education are seen as being in a state of constant interaction with multiple contexts as both causes and effects of social and educational concerns. This means that, in a socially critical approach, the definition of problems and solutions is a very complex matter. They are likely to be seen as related to the interaction between education and society, and as general matters that need to be addressed by schools as a whole rather than by administrative means. In this conceptualization, the institution as a social organization is likely to be regarded as a site of social, political and cultural interaction and negotiation. Management itself, therefore, becomes an area for investigation. It is just as likely to be part of the problem as part of the solution. The socially critical orientation is towards the implicit social, educational and political causes and effects of educational management, educational policy and educational practice. This means that management is never seen as neutral and educational participants are seen as social and political actors rather than as occupants of organizational roles.

Organizational cultures, in particular sites of struggle among social actors over the assertion of culture, reflect at least in part structural features of society at large, and also contribute to those structural features. Institutions are created within, and exist in relationship with, the social formation of society. This implies that society, despite its diversity, is characterized by micro and macro-cultures which are socially and historically constituted. Their ongoing constitution is always problematic and provisional, however, and occurs largely as a result of differential power relationships, cultural expectations and access to resources. Institutions such as schools contribute to macro-cultures in problematic ways because social relations in particular sites, as in society, cannot be simply assumed but must be continuously reconstituted as part of everyday life. Organizational culture is extraordinarily complex and dynamic – too much so to be rendered manipulable by organizational managers.

This chapter is intended to demonstrate that ongoing critique of conventional notions of organizational culture, administration and leadership in schools is needed. The focus of such critique could be upon the responsibility of schools, as social, cultural and political organizations, to enhance the interests of all their members. This would be perfectly consistent with current notions of 'sharing' in conventional perspectives on organizational culture. Instead of sharing coming about because of the imposition of uniform culture from above, however, the notion would refer to the importance of shared responsibility among participants for the production of organizational culture. It would not deny cultural contestation and negotiation in school sites, but would see all members as important participants in cultural politics. Indeed, administrators might recognize that participation is a cultural phenomenon, and that active participation is most likely to exist in a cultural milieu that accepts and encourages it – and sustains it in everyday practices – as an organizing principle of institutional life.

Such a perspective implies, as Benson (1977) pointed out some time ago, that we would understand an organization better if we did not regard it as a *thing* but as an ongoing *process of organizing*. This process, however, should not be seen as a regular, developmental, evolutionary pattern but as a somewhat messy and unpredictable process of micro and macro-politics. The emphasis would be on 'the ongoing interactions that continually reproduce the organization and/or alter it' (Benson 1977, p. 46), but the internal interactions would need to be seen and understood within the broader social and historical context. In this way organization patterns would be seen as being emergent. And if institutions, social structures, social relationships and organizations are seen as being in a continuous state of struggle, of 'becoming', we are then likely ask different questions about them than if we were trying to describe or explain what 'is'. Emphasis would be upon interactive processes by which institutional forms are produced, reproduced and transformed. Organizational analysis would therefore amount to the study of the ongoing process of organizing institutions, of the ongoing interactions and conflicts that produce, reproduce and transform organizations and their cultures, and of the historical and structural constraints on organizational dynamics and transformation.

If scholars in the field were to embrace such a perspective, there are several traditions of cultural work which might inform their analyses. I have already referred to the socially critical tradition in educational administration. The feminist tradition has also resulted in work which challenges hierarchical administration and advocates relational forms of school organization (Angus, 1993). A further tradition is that which has explored the nature of teachers' work in the context of school organization and investigated the emergence and assertion, and institutionalization in some cases, of democratic school practices (Apple, 1991). Emerging postmodernist approaches, although these are too complex for me to go into here, also raise interesting possibilities for the analysis of organization and culture (e.g. Parker, 1992). An organizing problematic of all of these approaches is that the relationship between school culture and power needs to be interrogated.

The implication is that the field of educational administration needs more studies of the dynamics of organizational life and micro-political activity. It would be especially important for such studies to investigate not only the ways in which administrators and other participants contribute to 'meaning-making' in schools, but also how administration and school culture mediate wider social influences. These multiple dynamics contribute to school cultures in complex ways. This means that a focus on internal micro-cultures of schools and organizations is important, but that such a focus should also examine the way in which schools, like other social organizations, contribute to broader cultures and society, and how inter-organizational dynamics influence wider power relations and widely shared social beliefs and practices. To do this, the analyst would need to regard power, like context, as a relational concept.

Power is embedded in power relationships and is everywhere. It is not something that operates simply between individuals, but through structures (such as bureaucracy, established organizational cultures, gender structures) that are characterized by formal and informal rules and expectations. We therefore need to recognize that power is not always exercised in order to bring about change. In fact, it is likely to act more often as a conserving force because it operates most subtly in ways that are taken for granted and which we do not recognize as the exercise of power. This means that power relationships, as part of the wide web of power, have the effect, without particular individuals nec-essarily deliberately trying to do so, of stabilizing and entrenching organizational and social arrangements and organizational meanings because, as Lukes (1974, p. 24) puts it so well, 'the most insidious exercise of power' is to 'prevent people, to whatever degree, from hav-ing grievances by shaping their perceptions, cognitions and preferences in such a way that they accept their role in the existing order of things, either because they can see or imagine no alternative to it, or because they see it as natural and unchangeable'. This is not to say, however, that everyone is hopelessly trapped in a web of power. As Angus and Rizvi (1989, p.2) put it, 'because we are participants in the network of power relationships we always retain the capacity to alter and influence those relationships. The problem is partly to overcome the insidious conservatism of established relationships with which we have become too comfortably familiar' (page 22). One way of trying to do this is by unpacking institutionalized meanings which have become taken for granted and which legitimate particular power relationships.

In a nutshell, within such a relational perspective, schools would be seen as sites in which the construction of culture is a social and politi-cal process. Rather than as a managerial device, then, organizational culture may be conceptualized as a social construct which both con-strains and enables organizational practice. In attempting to understand organizational culture in schools, therefore, we are attempting to understand how educational practice, including practices of adminis-tration, reflect organizational dynamics and the social and cultural location of schooling within a complex social formation. As Clegg (1988, p. 11) reminds us, we need to keep in mind that 'organizations are arenas of struggle and loci of calculations in which social relations of and in production are worked out with a degree of indeterminacy'. In other words, although organizations may appear at times as if they were solid, stable entities, this is often because a variety of meanings, rules and structures have become sedimented in such forms as 'organi-zational culture'. They become largely taken for granted, and they help to legitimate existing arrangements which then appear rather natural and systematic. But they are not *naturally* this way. Like all structures, organizational cultures have been *constructed* in particular ways and, in principle, could be reconstructed differently. This means that when it comes to investigating organizational culture, it is not enough to merely identify organizational culture – we must make organizational culture problematic and try to reveal what is taken for granted within it.

REFERENCES

Allen, R. F.: 1985, 'Four phases for bringing about cultural change', in R. H. Killman, M. J. Saxton and R. Serpa (eds.), *Gaining Control of the Corporate Culture*, San Francisco, Jossey – Bass, 332 – 350.

Anderson, G.: 1990, 'Towards a critical constructivist approach to school administration: Invisibility, legitimation and the study of non – events', *Educational Administration Quarterly*, 26(1), 38 – 59.

Angus, L.: 1992, "Quality' schooling, conservative educational policy and educational change in Australia', *Journal of Educational Policy*, 7(4), 379 – 397.

Angus, L.: 1993, 'Masculinity and women teachers at Christian Brothers' College', *Organization Studies*, 14(2), 235 – 261.

Angus, L. & Rizvi, F.: 1989, 'Power and the politics of participation', *Journal of Educational Administration and Foundations*, 4 (1), 6 – 23.

Apple, M. W.: 1991, 'The social context of democratic authority: A sympathetic response to Quantz, Cambron – mcCabe and Dartley', *The Urban Review*, 23(1), 21 – 29.

Apple, M. W.: 1992, 'Education, culture and class power: Basil Bernstein and the neo – marxist sociology of education', *Educational Theory*, 42(2), 127 – 145.

Bates, R.: 1980, 'Educational administration, the sociology of science, and the management of knowledge', *Educational Administration Quarterly*, 16(2), 1 – 20.

Bates, R.: 1987, 'Corporate culture, schooling, and educational administration', *Educational Administration Quarterly*, 23(4), 79 – 115.

Beare, H.: 1982, 'Education's corporate image', *Unicorn*, 8(1), 12 – 28.

Beare, H., Caldwell, B. and Millikan, R.: 1989, *Creating an Excellent School: Some New Management Techniques*, London, Routledge.

Bennis, W. & Nanus, B.: 1985, *Leaders: The Strategies for Taking Charge*, New York, Harper and Row.

Benson, J.: 1977, 'Organizations: A dialectical view', *Administrative Science Quarterly*, 22, 1 – 21.

Bernstein, B.: 1977, *Class, Codes and Control, Volume III*, London, Routledge.

Bottery, M.: 1988, 'Educational management: An ethical critique', *Oxford Review of Education*, 14(3), 341 – 351.

Bowles, S.: 1991, 'What markets can – and cannot – do', *Challenge*, July/August, 11 – 16.

Brizman, D.: 1986, 'Cultural myths in the making of a teacher: Biography and social structure in teacher education', *Harvard Educational Review*, 56(4), 442 – 456.

Burns, J.: 1978, *Leadership*, New York, Harper and Row.

Caldwell, B. & Spinks, J.: 1988, *The Self – managing School*, Lewes, Falmer Press.

Callahan, R.: 1968, *Education and the cult of efficiency*, New York, Sage.

Clegg, S.: 1981, 'Organization and control', *Administrative Science Quarterly*, 26, 545 – 562.

Clegg, S.: 1988, 'The good, the bad and the ugly', *Organization Studies*, 9(1), 7 – 13.

Coombs, R., Knights, D. & Willmot, H. C.: 1992, 'Culture, control and competition; towards a conceptual framework for the study of information technology in organizations', *Organization Studies*, 13(1), 51 – 72.

Deal, T. & Kennedy, A.: 1982, *Corporate cultures: The rites and rituals of corporate life*, 'Reading', MA, Addison – Wesley.

Erickson, F.: 1987, 'Conceptions of school culture: An overview', *Educational Administration Quarterly*, 23(4), 11 – 24.

Giddens, A.: 1976, *New rules for sociological method*, London, Hutchinson.

Giddens, A.: 1984, *The constitution of society: Outline of the theory of structuration*,. Berkeley, University of California Press.

Giroux, H.: 1981, *Ideology, Culture and the Process of Schooling*, London, Falmer Press.

Giroux, H.: 1984, 'Rethinking the language of schooling', *Language Arts,* 61(3), 33 – 40.

Golden, K.: 1992, 'The individual and organizational culture: Strategies for action in highly ordered contexts', *Journal of Management Studies*, 29(1), 1 – 21.

Goll, I. & Zeitz, G.: 1991, 'Conceptualizing and measuring corporate ideology', *Organization Studies*, 12(2), 191 – 207.

Greenfield, T.: 1973, 'Organizations as social inventions: Rethinking assumptions about change', *Journal of Applied Behavioural Science*, 9(5), 551 – 574.

Greenfield, T.: 1983, 'Environment as subjective reality'. Paper presented at the Annual Meeting of the American Educational Research Association, Montreal.

Gregory, K. L.: 1983, 'Native view paradigms; multiple cultures and culture conflicts in organizations', *Administrative Science Quarterly*, 28, 359 – 377.

Jackson, P.: 1968, *Life in Classrooms*, New York, Holt, Rinehart and Winston.

Johnston, Bill J.: 1991, 'Institutional and interorganizational contexts of educational administrator preparation', *The Urban Review*, 23(1), 31 – 38.

Kempner, K.: 1992, 'Getting into the castle of educational administration', *Peabody Journal of Education*, 66(3), 104 – 122.

Killman, R. H., Saxton, M. J., & Serpa, R. (eds.): 1985, *Gaining control of the corporate culture*, San Francisco, Jossey – Bass.

Kirby, P. C., Paradise, L. V. & King, M. I.: 1992, 'Extraordinary leaders in education: Understanding transformational leadership', *Journal of Education Research*, 85(5), 303 – 31.

Lorsch, J. W.: 1985, 'Strategic myopia: Culture as an invisible barrier to change', in R. H. Killman, M. J. Saxton and R. Serpa (eds.), *Gaining control of the corporate culture*, San Francisco, Jossey – Bass,. 84 – 102.

Martin, H. J.: 1985, 'Managing specialized corporate cultures', in R. H. Killman, M. J. Saxton and R. Serpa (eds.), *Gaining Control of the Corporate Culture*, San Francisco, Jossey – Bass, 148 – 162.

Meek, V. L.: 1988, 'Organizational culture: Origins and weaknesses', *Organization Studies,* 9(4), 453 – 473.

Meyer, M. and Rowan: 1977, 'Institutionalized organizations: Formal structure as myth and ceremony', *American Journal of Sociology*, 83(2), 340 – 363.

Millikan: 1984, 'School culture and imagery: What does it mean and what can it do for my school?', *The Secondary Administrator*, 2(1), 3 – 11.

Mills, A.: 1988, 'Organization, gender and culture', *Organization Studies,* 9(3), 352 – 369.

Mitchell, J. T. & Willower, D. J.: 1992, 'Organizational culture in a good high school', *Journal of Educational Administration*, 30(6), 6 – 16.

Parker, M.: 1992, 'Post – modern organization or postmodern organization theory?', *Organization Studies*, 13(1), 1 – 17.

Perrow, C.: 1979, *Complex Organizations: A Critical Essay (2nd edn.)*, Glenview, Ill., Scott – Forseman.

Peters, T. & Waterman, R.: 1982, *In Search of Excellence: Lessons From America's Best – run Companies,* New York, Harper and Row.

Purkey, S. & Smith, M.: 1982, 'Effective schools: A review', *The Elementary School Journal,* December, 64 – 69.

Purkey, S. & Smith, M.: 1985, 'School reform: The district policy implications of the effective schools literature', *The Elementary School Journal,* 85, 353 – 89.

Sachs, J. & Smith, R.: 1988, 'Constructing teacher culture', *British Journal of Sociology of Education,* 9(4), 423 – 436.

Schein, E. H.: 1985, 'How culture forms, develops and changes', in R. H. Killman, M. J. Saxton and R. Serpa (eds.), *Gaining Control of the Corporate Culture,* San Francisco, Jossey – Bass, 17 – 43.

Schein, E. H.: 1986, *Organizational Culture and Leadership,* San Francisco, Jossey – Bass.

Schultz, M.: 1991, 'Transitions between symbolic domains in organizations', *Organization Studies,* 12(4), 489 – 506.

Sergiovanni, T.: 1984, 'Leadership and excellence in schooling', *Educational Leadership,* 41(5), 4 – 13.

Sergiovanni, T.: 1991, 'Constructing and changing theories of practice: The key to preparing school administrators', *The Urban Review,* 23(1), 39 – 49.

Sergiovanni, T. & Corbally, J.: 1984, *Leadership and organizational culture: New perspectives on administrative theory and practice,* Urbana, University of Illinois Press.

Shaw, J.: 1992, 'School cultures: Organizational value orientation and commitment', *Journal of Educational Research,* 85(5), 295 – 302.

Sleezer, C. M. & Swanson, R. A.: 1992, 'Culture surveys', *Management Decision,* 30(2), 22 – 29.

Smircich, L.: 1983, 'Studying organizations as cultures', in G. Morgan (ed.), *Beyond Method,* London, Sage, 160 – 172.

Smith, P. B. & Peterson, M. F.: 1988, *Leadership, Organizations and Culture,* Newbury Park, CA, Sage.

Smyth, J.: 1993, *A Socially Critical View of the Self – managing School,* London, Falmer.

Starratt, R.: 1986, 'Excellence in education and quality of leadership', *Occasional Paper, No. 11,* Institute of Educational Administration, Geelong.

Vaill, P.: 1984, 'The purposing of high performing systems', in T. Sergiovanni and J. Corbally (eds.), *Leadership and Organizational Culture,* Urbana, Ill., University of Illinois Press.

Weick, K.: 1976, 'Educational organizations as loosely coupled systems', *Administrative Science Quarterly,* 21(1), 1 – 19.

Werlin, H. H.: 1988, 'The theory of political elasticity: Clarifying concepts in micro/macro administration', *Administration and Society,* 20(1), 46 – 70.

Willis, P.: 1977, *Learning to labour: How working class kids get working class jobs,* Westmead, Saxon House.

Wood, S.: 1985, 'Work organization', in R. Deem and G. Salaman (eds.), *Work, Culture and Society,* Milton Keynes, Open University Press.

Chapter 28: 'Breaking the Silence': Feminist Contributions to Educational Administration and Policy

JILL BLACKMORE

Deakin University

This chapter reviews how feminism has contributed to particular ways of theorising and practising educational administration and leadership, and reflects upon which feminisms have been more readily appropriated, which feminisms are ignored, and what different feminisms see as future issues in the field. It is also considers why 'other' bodies of literature in educational research on teachers' work and unions, curriculum and pedagogy have tended to be ignored by educational administrators and policymakers. A focus throughout will be upon equity and social justice. Feminism, in focusing upon women's inequality, could no longer ignore other forms of oppression based on class, race and ethnicity, sexuality and disability. By contrast, there is a significant silence in all aspects of educational administration with respect to social justice or equity in the theory and practice of educational administration and the training of administrators (Foster, 1986; Capper, 1993; Gosetti & Rusch, 1994). This chapter explores why administration in education, as a potential site of, and for, social justice, fails to address such issues.

THE READING AND THE TEXT

I pursued my focus on feminism and educational administration by first re-visiting and re-viewing my understanding of mainstream/malestream meta-narratives. Surprisingly little emerged from library searches cross referencing in multiple combinations educational administration and leadership to teacher unions, social justice and equity, restructuring and reform, gender and feminism, race and class, curriculum and pedagogy/instruction. Much of the 'women in leadership' literature was located in management. I resorted to substantive reviews, conference papers and monographs in the field as well as international colleagues to inform me of significant work. The result is

K. Leithwood et al. (eds.), International Handbook of Educational Leadership and Administration, 997-1042.
© *1996 Kluwer Academic Publishers, Printed in the Netherlands.*

a substantial, though still partial, mapping of trends, foci, interruptions, and silences. It is evident from the literature that while the under-representation of women has come to be seen to be 'a problem' in educational administration, as indicated in the increasing amount of research on and by women, much of it does not draw on *feminist* theory. A significant body of research on women in educational administration tends to treat gender as a variable and not an organising category (Jones, 1990).

I have focused on Canadian, New Zealand, English and Australian research, given the Amero-centric nature of the field of educational administration. Historically, educational administrators and policy-makers have readily crossed cultural/national boundaries and appropriated administrative models and solutions unproblematically. In particular, post-war Australia, New Zealand and Canada were fertile grounds for the importation of administrative theory from the USA, despite its ethnocentricity, given the assumption that administration was a value free science. The need for a post colonial perspective in the 1990s is even more urgent with the 'colonising tendencies' of global 'megatrends', encouraged by the World Bank and OECD, in educational restructuring and devolution (Sander, 1993).

The chapter is also critically self-reflective in that it considers where feminist educators focusing upon administration and leadership have come from, where we are now, and where we may possibly head. Feminism in the 1990s is not a monolithic movement. Tong (1989) broadly categorises the feminisms as liberal, marxist, radical/cultural, psychoanalytic, socialist, existentialist, cultural difference (i.e. black, Asian, ethnic specific), and the postmodern. These feminisms, as well as the disciplinary feminisms such as ecofeminism, overlap, contradict and build upon each other. Each has particular assumptions and perspectives about the nature, the causes and solutions for women's oppression. Each is partial in its explanation, has its own epistemological strengths and weaknesses, methodological and political implications (Alcoff and Potter, 1993). Each perspective has, in turn, a different way of conceptualising inequality and disadvantage.

In turn, definitions of disadvantage, inequality and social justice have also altered. Michelle Barrett and Ann Phillips (1992) view the western univeralising consensus seeking feminism of the 1970s as being framed by the modernist impulse which focused upon an agreed cause of women's oppression, the unproblematic nature of this oppression, and the emphasis on structural explanations (whether it be patriarchy, capitalism, the home/work divide) largely in response to the emphasis of conservatives on biological difference as played out in the sex/gender distinction. They see the destabilising postmodernist feminism of the 1990s arising from a fracturing of woman as a universal class with concerns about the 'politics of difference' as black and 'third world' feminists challenged the dominant voice of white middle class feminists as 'othering' black working class women, or women in Asian countries because of the Western, Anglo, classist and heterosexual nature of feminism itself (Collins, 1991; Hooks, 1984; Harasym, 1990).

This shift is now evident in studies focusing upon gender and educational administration in first, the recognition of how race, gender and class work in often contradictory ways in particular contexts. Second, there is a more positive view of the intransigence of sex differences which emphasises morality and care as positive form of gender identity, away from the quasi-androgynous view of 'I just want be a person'. Third, the postmodern turn of the late 1980s now links feminism into non-feminist strands of contemporary social, political and cultural theory. Central to this shift is the post modern critique of Enlightenment thought and 'its notion of the powerful unitary self conscious political subject, its belief in rationality and progress, in the possibility of grand schemes for reform' (Barrett & Phillips, 1992, p. 5).

The chapter is organised into three sections around the textual metaphors of 'silence', 'voice' and 'representation'. Silence represents the positioning of women in educational administration during the period well into the 1970s, a period characterised by the dominance of science then liberal humanism. Feminism then became one of the cacophony of voices of the paradigm wars of the 1980s, increasingly less marginal. Feminist thought in educational administration in the 1990s, I suggest, will struggle with the 'representations' of gender around notions of difference and community. In effect, the chapter considers specific feminist contributions to educational administration, and the relationship of these to other critical theories and mainstream theory.

SILENCE

In the search for a knowledge base, educational administration has drawn eclectically and selectively from outside education from the more 'foundational' disciplines of psychology, science, economics, politics. Histories of thought in educational administration clearly indicate how the metaphors of science, industry and philosophy, and sometimes the arts, have framed administrative practice (Campbell et al.,

1987; Beck & Murphy, 1994; Tyack & Hansot, 1983). In so doing, educational administration has, in ignoring educational research on curriculum, pedagogy, and teachers' work, been distanced from students and teachers, who have become the disembodied objects of research and reform (Blount, 1994). Patricia Yeakey and others (1986) attribute the failure of the theory movement in educational administration to its derivative origins not being rooted in school experience; its assumption of particular social science methods and concepts which were unaffected by the debates within social science; and its uncritical borrowing of Parsonian structural functionalism. Indeed, women, as students, were rendered invisible and silent by the totalising narratives of both science and humanism which universalised the experience of some men to all others and ignored women's contributions. Embedded in these metanarratives is the binary logic of the Enlightenment upon which women's exclusion was justified and naturalised, the dualisms between the public and the private, the mind and the body, reason and emotion, the universal and the particular, concrete and abstract (Lloyd, 1984). These dualisms were entrenched in administrative theory early in the twentieth century and naturalised by the later assertion that administration was a science, a position rectified by positivism's epistemological claims regarding objectivity and generalisability.

Fundamental to feminist critiques has been the recognition of this power/knowledge connection; of how power resides in the capacity to define what constitutes legitimate knowledge in educational administration. Feminism has contributed to the fierce epistemological debates and the proliferation of research methods which has meant 'the loss of positivisms' theoretic hegemony in the face of sustained and trenchant criticism of its basic assumptions (Lather 1991, pp 6-7). Early feminist critiques in administration during the 1970s can be located within the first of three strands of the feminist critique of science. Sandra Harding (1991) depicts these as the feminist empiricists reworking 'bad' science into 'good' science on its own terms of data collection and methodology; radical feminists rejecting all science as 'masculine' and constructing an alternative feminist science; and those working with feminist standpoint epistemology which begins with and works through women's experiences.

Within the first strand, feminists were quick to point out the androcentric bias in the theories, methodologies and policies of a social science and educational administration which arise from the exclusion of a large proportion of the population by theorising human behaviour in ways which either universalised the experiences of elite white middle class males or reproduced the binary oppositions upon which gender inequality was justified and naturalised (Shakeshaft & Nowell, 1984; Shakeshaft & Hanson, 1986). For example, Joan Acker (1992) illustrates how the Hawthorne studies, by ignoring gender, produced 'bad science' which in turn informed human relations theory. Systems theory in particular, rooted in biological metaphors of organisms, emphasised balance, consensus and integration and, by pathologising conflict and difference, defined women's difference to the male norm as deviance. Radical feminist philosophers challenged the epistemological assumptions of administrative theory, and the political and social implications of logical positivism's distinction between the 'is' and the 'ought', between 'fact' and 'value' (Lloyd, 1984). Yeakey et al. (1986) show how the universalising claims of value neutrality, of one 'truth' about what constituted normal science, and about administration's concern with power and control rather than educational issues, pseudo-included women's experiences. Functionalist models of organisational life naturalised hierarchies and the unequal distribution of goods, decontextualised organisations from social concerns and maintained the public/private divide. Such approaches ultimately divorced school organisational research from practical educational concerns and issues of equity and disadvantage arising from the civil rights, women's and post-colonial movements.

It is not surprising, perhaps, that the first significant pre-feminist challenges to mainstream educational administration during the 1980s originated amongst the 'colonised' on cultural, ethical and epistemological grounds (Young, 1993). Both the liberal humanism of Canadians Thom Greenfield and Chris Hodgkinson and the critical theory influenced by Habermas and Weber of Australian and ex-New Zealander Richard Bates were either 'ignored or treated with great hostility' by the orthodoxy centred in the USA. They had a disproportionate influence on both Canadian and Australian educational administration as a consequence (e.g. Evers and Lakomski, 1991; Duignan and McPherson, 1991). The liberal humanistic tradition has been particularly appealing to feminism since Hodgkinson, as Greenfield, places values and power as central to administration and argues that administration was about making choices and organisations were about shaping people and being shaped by people. Administration was redefined as a 'moral task' and leadership as appealing to a 'hierarchy of the good', clearly philosophical not scientific questions (Greenfield & Ribbins, 1993, p. 164-7; Hodgkinson, 1991).

More recent critical (Bates, 1994) and feminist (Young, 1993; Blackmore, 1990) analyses of Greenfield's work argue that, despite his humanist emphasis on values, culture and difference, it is flawed. In concurring with Hodgkinson in the view that administration 'is a matter of will and power; of bending others to one's will and of being bent in turn by others' position' (Greenfield & Ribbins, 1993, p. 166-7), Greenfield, as Hodgkinson, is hierarchical and antidemocratic. The assertion of individual will and authority over the collective is vindicated (Bates, 1994; Evers and Lakomski, 1991). The individualism of both, as of liberal social contract theory more generally, assumes that community is merely an aggregate of individuals who seek community merely to improve their self gain and for no other more altruistic or social purpose (Pateman, 1989). Certainly feminists would agree with Greenfield's damning of the exclusion of emotion, passion and morality from administrative theory, and humanist feminists with his appeal to interpretivism, yet most would still argue that women's realities differ from those of men.

While Greenfield marginalises issues of social justice, particularly with respect to gender, Hodgkinson's anti-feminism surfaces in his non-inclusive language and view that affirmative action programs are a 'pathology' (Young 1993, p.3). In part this is explained by his transcendental humanism which can be traced to Rawls's theory of justice, Kohlberg's theory of moral development and Plato's political theory (Benhabib, 1986). Feminist critiques have queried the gendered nature of the humanist claims embedded in such theories, in particular the capacity of the few to achieve a 'higher order' morality and of abstract, decontextualised rules to resolve concrete and particular issues of social justice (Blackmore, 1990) have proposed more relational and contextualised notions of morality and justice (Gilligan, 1982).

But as yet in educational administration the tension between feminism and liberal humanist perspectives is not resolved because of the latter's appeal to an ethics of justice and transformational leadership (e.g.Sergiovanni, 1987; Starrart, 1991). This is largely because the liberal feminism which has provided the underlying framework for the ways in which equity for women and girls in education has been conceptualised (Yates, 1993; Kenway, 1990) is itself a product of the Enlightenment (Harding, 1991). Rosemary Tong (1989) sees liberal feminism's main assumption being that it sees customary, structural and legal constraints blocking women's successful entrance into the public world. It tends to treat organisations and structures as neutral, and explains women's under-representation in leadership as being a consequence of the sex role socialisation of women and gender stereo-types about leadership. It emphasises discrimination and prejudice as forms of irrationality, and due process as the avenue of remediation. In so doing liberal feminism confirms male definitions of rationality, rights, interests and the common good, accepts the notion of the auton-omous rational individual and appeals to some gender neutral human-ism 'out there' (Tong, 1989, p. 31). Indeed, liberal feminism tends to focus upon changing women to become more like men rather than changing men or changing organisations and cultures. Other contem-porary feminisms have emerged both as derivatives of, and in reaction to, liberal feminism.

For example, feminists in educational administration have recently been attracted (e.g. Gosetti & Rusch, 1994) to feminist standpoint epis-temology (e.g. Smith, 1990), the third strand of the feminist critique of science, because it is both a product of, and reaction to, Enlightenment science. This is exemplified in concern about 'strong objectivity' (Harding, 1991), and, according to Gaby Lakomski, inherently inco-herent because of it (Lakomski,1989). Feminist standpoint epistemol-ogy begins with women's experiences and works outwards along the 'fault lines', seeking out the interruptions and contradictions, asking different questions, raising different issues and testing theories. The desire is not to substitute another 'master theory', nor to position men as lesser by privileging the 'feminine' over the 'masculine', but to maintain the instability of analytical categories such as gender, argua-bly a postmodernist position.

Ultimately, the silences, pseudo inclusions or distortions of women's experience through the meta-narratives of humanism and sci-ence have been made possible because administrative theory has worked through what Edith Rusch (1992) describes as a 'privileged lens' which refracts issues in particularly reductionist and gendered ways: power issues have been reduced to issues of legitimate authority or formal role; difference has been equated to deviance and the inca-pacity of individuals to become fully integrated into the organisation; values and beliefs become individual preferences outside organisa-tional life. It was this privilege which was significantly challenged dur-ing the 1980s.

VOICE

The 1980s has been characterised as a period of intellectual turmoil in educational administration with a cacophony of voices, amongst them feminism, rising out of the 'paradigm wars' of post-Kuhnian times. At one level these debates have focused upon whether paradigms are a valid conceptualisation (Evers and Lakomski, 1991) or about the incommensurability of paradigms (Foster, 1986). At another level, many feminists share with critical theorists anxiety about their positioning in the debate as one of many voices as they see the issue is not merely about the different epistemologies and methodologies underlying particular paradigms, but about the different political projects, often in direct antithesis, which give rise to new paradigms (Hennessey, 1993). Maria Calas and Linda Smirich (1992) see paradigm pluralism as two dimensional, recreating discrete models of binary logic, whereas feminism focuses upon the depoliticisation and neutralisation that pluralism produces. Feminism requires understanding, enunciating and working from gendered principles and political engagement with 'knowledge making' and is not just another paradigm.

This section, therefore, focuses upon how particular feminist theories have been working through, with and against other critical perspectives with regard to key concepts shaping women's marginality and issues of social justice in educational administration. It considers feminism's specific contributions to educational administration in critically analysing the gendered division of labour in education, in destabilising and redefining key administrative concepts such as career, leadership, ethics, care, inclusivity, difference, emancipatory practice, and in providing analyses of the contradictory and complex role of the state with regard to gender reform. In turn, there will be a self critical analysis of how different feminist voices have understood women's inequality in educational administration.

REDEFINING LEADERSHIP

Understandably, in seeking to give women a voice in educational administration, feminist researchers focused upon the few women in formal leadership. Various mythologies have portrayed women as incapable of leadership - their biology in the nineteenth century, their psychological deficiencies through the early twentieth century, their lack of career ambition and low self esteem during the 1970s. By then, empirical evidence suggested that the issue was more about structural and organisational discrimination, not lack of merit or aspiration. Early research on the behaviour of women administrators not only showed women to be highly competent, if not better, school administrators, but that they had a strong emphasis on the instructional process and teacher pupil dynamics, tended to be more democratic and seek community involvement, leading to higher teacher moral and parent approval and did not lack ambition (Adkinson, 1981). These early findings are still consistent with recent cross national research about women and educational administration (Adler, 1993; Ozga, 1993; Shakeshaft, 1987; Nixon 1987; Neville, 1988; Rees, 1990; Sampson, 1986; Court, 1992; Blackmore, 1995).

Significantly, the range of factors impeding women in the 1970s as in 1990s is similar: women's under-representation in leadership, biases in recruitment techniques, composition of selection committees, job progressions, different job titles and status for equivalent work, unequal sex-segmented distribution of extra curricular work, separate recreational activities, age and isolation on the job. What is different two decades later are the explanations of these phenomenon and the suggested strategies to remedy it. Now informed by radical feminism particularly, sex role socialisation theory and psychological factors have been displaced by more agential theories of action and a sense of context with a shift away from blaming the victim and individualising the problem of 'under-representation' to consider contextual organisational factors. Women's 'choices' in not applying for leadership, previously described as disguising their ability and abdicating from competition, have been reread as rejection of, and resistance, to male values (Adler, 1993). Fear of success is now seen to be as much avoidance of visibility under the male gaze and discrimination. Lack of career planning or 'intrinsic' work motivation is equally well explained by women's dual familial/work responsibilities (Biklen & Pollard, 1993; Acker, 1989).

These shifts also signify feminist challenges to the conceptual models of research which both justified and built upon androcentric concepts and epistemologies (Shakeshaft & Newell,1984). Shakeshaft (1986, 1987) illustrates the androcentric bias in central concepts in educational administration such as Getzels and Guba's model of social behaviour, Kohlberg's theory of moral development, Halpin's Leader Behaviour Description Questionnaire, Fiedler's theories of leadership effectiveness and Maslows concept of self-actualisation. Blackmore (1989) deconstructs the dominant masculinism embedded in leadership models, theories and epistemologies, with particular emphasis on how the notions of rationality, abstract morality and competitive individualism so central to liberal political theory excluded women. Both offer alternative feminist reconstructions of leadership which focus upon relationality, power through rather than over others, care and democratic process.

Much of the feminist work has sought to redefine notions of leadership, career and success, to make them more 'gender inclusive' (Middleton, 1992a; Evatts, 1989; Strachan, 1993; Acker,1989; Young, 1992). Often informed by labour process theory and interactionist approaches, but also life history, life narrative and cultural studies approaches, this research challenges the public/private divide, linear views of career and narrow definitions of success which construct women's choices as wrong or deficient (Marshall & Anderson, 1995). Instead, they query why men are not seen to be deficient because of their singular career outlook, narrow masculinist models of leadership and lack of interpersonal skills and student centredness (Sampson, 1986).

Yet liberal feminism has framed the 'woman question' in administration as being women's under-representation in leadership, and that a value change will occur as this is redressed. In so doing, liberal feminists have claimed equal political and ethical rights for women but left intact highly elitist and individualistic notions of leadership, administrative structures and cultures. A critical mass of women does not necessarily lead to greater equity in the distribution of jobs and power. Indeed, Christine Williams (1992) argues men are *advantaged* in female dominated professions, and rapidly rise into management positions on 'a glass escalator'. Furthermore, the paradox of focusing upon individual merit is that merit is itself a culturally constructed concept which historically has served some men's interests and not others (Burton, 1991; Young, 1990, pp.201-2). There is no reason why merit will not serve the same purpose for some women and not others.

In the leadership literature, cultural feminists, rather than focusing upon what was the same between men and women, focus upon gender difference: upon women's preferences for democratic leadership, their interpersonal skills and student/curriculum foci. This perspective is often read conservatively as women's 'special contribution' to leadership (Grant, 1988). But 'equal but different' and complementarity arguments do not challenge the binary logic of 'othering' and domination. It suggests women are not leaders because they have not engaged with dominant values or forms of rationality, but will bring a view from the periphery which may improve (but not fundamentally change) management. Certainly, cultural feminism has foregrounded the multi-faceted and multidimensional nature of leadership (Blount, 1994). But in its appropriation, this has been reduced to a debate over differences in male/female leadership 'styles', where style is equated to skill, which is a conceptually different position than the issues raised by the feminist ethics of care which arises out of substantively different moral positions.

Ultimately, the feminist critique has been framed by the malestream agenda which centres upon leadership, rather than power. Leadership is still treated as an institutional issue, and not an educational and political issue. Why, for example, are 'women's ways of leading' now being appropriated as 'good' leadership practice by mainstream theory in a period of economic constraint, the marketisation of education, a perceived leadership crisis in education and demographic change? (Blackmore, 1995; Ozga, 1993; Weiner, 1993;). The decontextualisation of leadership from issues of power and politics obstructs full understanding as to why so many eligible women do not seek formal leadership and why so many 'successful' women exit from the 'chilly climates' of executive administration. Strategies have focused upon individual rather than group equity, in part because of the failure to adequately theorise power as relational and thereby to connect leadership to broader social, political and economic arrangements.

Feminists have largely seen power in negative terms, as a possession, and often typify women as powerless. Critical theory and cultural studies have produced for feminists ways of considering how power works in organisations through cultural exclusion (Marshall & Mitchell,1989; Blackmore 1993); institutional ethos (Byrne, 1989); language and discourse (Luke & Gore 1992); capillary networks (Ferguson, 1984) and sexual politics (Bryson & Castells,1991). Feminist redefinitions of power range from a communitarian, radical perspective arguing that women view and practice power differently (power sharing not power over) through to a Foucaultian perspective which see no central unitary source or type of power, but in which power is dispersed arbitrarily and unevenly across multiple sites, working differently across different cultural contexts (McNay, 1992; Diamond & Quinby,1988). A communitarian perspective tends to assume equal power relationships between women in organisations. It denies the unequal power relationships between women in formal authority and their subordinates, and how women in leadership are often seen to be complicit in, and to have an investment in, maintaining current institutional arrangements which are patterned by race, class, ethnicity as well as gender. Post structuralist theories of power suggests the struggle against male dominance is often fundamentally different for different women. Equal opportunity legislation provides individual white women access to male dominated organisations only to face discrimination further up the organisation, whereas black or coloured women are less likely to get even initial access (Williams, 1987; due Billing & Alvesson, 1989). A feminist theory of power, Billing and Alvesson (1989) and Davies (1992) suggest, is central to producing greater distributional effects for all women by changing the nature of organisations and by playing down leadership as the core issue. The focus upon leadership and not on leader/subordinate relationships has been a major impediment to effective educational change with regard to gender equity.

THE GENDERING OF ADMINISTRATION AND TEACHING

Whereas liberal feminism has framed the feminist critique in educational administration, socialist feminism has sought to analysis the gendered division of labour in education in which men manage and women teach. Judith Glazer (1991) suggests that 'feminist theory building and testing are more pervasive in the literature on teaching than administration, which continues to adhere to theories of leadership and organisation that discourage collaborative models of leadership and reinforce patterns of male dominance-female subordination' (p. 337). Socialist feminism has informed much feminist theorising about the nature of teachers' work and unionism, for this is where women have been located and where feminist educational work itself, often as a subversive or oppositional activity, has been positioned (Weiler, 1988). Through research on women's life histories, unions and teachers' work, feminists are breaking down the public/private, administration/teaching and professionalism/unionism dichotomies which frame and sustain dominant versions of administration (Acker,1989; Middleton, 1986; Ozga 1988).

Historians have also challenged the linear progressivist view of change embedded in the modernist project by highlighting the often contradictory historical relationships between the wider social movements of educational progressivism, reform and feminism as well as between the bureaucratisation, feminisation and de-professionalisation of educational work (Tyack & Hansot, 1982; Ferguson, 1984). In the USA, for example, Kathleen Weiler, situates the acceptance of the 'gender-neutral ideology of professionalism' during the 1920s which effectively masculinised administration in teacher unions and universities, in the context of scientific management, the Red scare, pro-business and anti-union feeling, the decline of teachers' organisations and unions and the modernist new woman's emphasis on *human* equality (Weiler, 1994, p.11, Blount, 1994). In the UK, Australia, and New Zealand, socialist feminists have drawn from labour process and cultural theory, to illustrate how ideologies of both professionalism and unionism have sometimes advanced, sometimes undermined, women teachers' demands for equality (Ozga 1988; Middleton, 1986). Blackmore (1993) argues that historically it has been in particular male administrators' interests to construct and maintain the notion that unionism was anti-professional, and that administration was different from teaching.

Certainly the administrative literature does not reflect the pattern that in most Western societies, over 80% of teachers belong to teacher unions and unionism is an almost 'universal aspect of teachers' occupational identities' (Bascia,1994; Ozga, 1988). Unionism is relegated in the administrative literature to being an industrial issue, and not about the nature of teacher's work, professionalism and educational practice. Yet teacher unions in the UK, Australia, Canada and New Zealand have long been a source of educational ideas and individual and collective empowerment, active in educational restructuring and school based decision making, curriculum reform and policy development (Lingard et al. 1993; Ball et al., 1992). In the USA, teacher unions have been legally constrained from such involvement and recent 'Proposals by administrators, policymakers and scholars to 'professionalise teaching' have often drawn teachers' criticism for having failed to consider the realities of teachers' work or teachers' occupational values' (Bascia, 1994, p. 2). At the same time, while many women teachers find unions sites of empowerment through equal opportunity activities and professional development (Kenway 1990; Ozga, 1988); they have also been sites of male resistance to equal pay and female leadership claims (Cockburn, 1991; Arnot & Weiner, 1987). Administrative theory's neglect of the extensive studies of teachers' work which highlights the social complexity of teaching and learning, the role of teachers as change agents and the significance of professional collaborative cultures, have, as change theorists now recognise, resulted in inadequate theories of educational change (Lieberman et al. 1991; Little and McLaughlin, 1993;).

Furthermore, the administration/teaching dichotomy does not reflect the practice of female administrators who maintain student centred priorities (Shakeshaft, 1987; Weiler,1988; Ozga 1993; Adler et al., 1993; Blackmore 1995; Court, 1992). Helen Regan speaks of how 'much of feminist administering was really feminist pedagogy in another arena' which 'emphasises teacher empowerment and shared decision making' (Regan, 1990, p. 565). The feminist focus upon knowledge/power relationships in education positions the issue of curriculum at the 'very heart of the feminist critique of education' (Gaskell & McLaren, 1991, p. 222). Gender reform research clearly indicates for those seeking gender justice and social justice more generally, that the power relationships in schools amongst teachers cannot be separated from pedagogical issues, as they have particular political and material consequences in terms of who gets what jobs, and students' readings of gender power relations (Shakeshaft, 1993; Kenway et al., 1994; Arnot & Weiner, 1987). Despite these links, the feminist debates with regard to critical pedagogy, particularly in the USA, have remained within and around the women's studies programs in the academy and radical feminism (Ellsworth, 1989,1990; Culley & Portuges, 1985; Bryson & de Castells, 1991). In so doing they have failed to address teachers' practical concerns and to recognise the critical pedagogical work done earlier by radical educators in schools (Luke & Gore, 1992).

At the same time, the notion of administration as pedagogic practice is being asserted in a liberal humanist, though not necessarily feminist sense, by those advocating more reflective practices in administration. Lyn Beck (1994) argues that administrator preparation programs should focus upon pedagogy and professional development to produce caring administrators. But Judith Glazer (1991) suggests that while the restructuring of administrator training programs may introduce feminist pedagogies and new methods of research, 'the experience of women's studies indicates, they can only have a marginal impact unless those who control the profession - practitioners, policymakers and the professoriate- are willing to engage in a collaborative process through which both the professions and the institutions that support them are restructured to eliminate stratification based on gender' (p. 338) Indeed, as Elisabeth Al -Khalifa (1989) points out, one of the anomalies of the management literature is that performance in staff and pupil management or knowledge in gender linked issues is not a priority in selection criteria for principalships. Instead, when curriculum became the focus of reform during the 1980s, the aloofness of the critical pedagogy debates to school administrative practice provided space for more mechanistic, prescriptive and managerialist approaches to curriculum and pedagogy, as exemplified in much of the instructional leadership literature.

EMANCIPATORY POLITICS

At the same time, feminism(s) shares with the critical pedagogy, teacher-as -researcher and action research movements, as well as critical theory, a view that education is a form of emancipatory politics. Beyond that, and the shared dissatisfaction with technicist models of administration, each critical tradition has remained relatively distinct. Given its origins in Marxism and phenomenology, critical theory centred on issues of power, culture, equity, control, conflict, and rationality. Coming from an anthropological/cultural studies tradition, critical theorists rejected positivism's notions of value free facts and objective language and recognised that 'social research, no less than any other domain of human practice, is itself a form of cultural action containing both the potential for emancipation and oppression' (Codd, 1988, p. 23). It revealed social conditions through the analysis of opposing interests, and asked: whose interests are being served? (Bates, 1986; Foster, 1986)

Critical theory, therefore, shared many concerns with the feminism(s): ethics, culture, social justice, praxis and how power is exercised in 'unobtrusive ways' through knowledge and communication. Yeakey et al(1986) claim that it was the emergence of critical theory which refocused organisational research on larger equity concerns by analysing organisations structural, ideological and cultural features in ways which consider why certain individuals and groups were favoured in the distribution of goods, services and power (p. 119). A critical social science also proposed other than hypothetico-deductive research methods.

Two relatively distinct strands emerged within critical social science: one located in curriculum, evaluation and action research (Carr and Kemmis, 1986; Elliott, 1991) and another in educational administration (Bates, 1986; 1993; Foster, 1986; Codd, 1988). But as Weiner (1989) points out with regard to the action research movement, but also applicable to critical theory in educational administration, while absorbed into the largely feminised practices of teaching, nursing and welfare as well as educational administration, these continued to be male dominated, even ignoring other traditions of teacher-as-researcher which have arisen through gender equity work in schools amongst feminist teachers. Indeed, critical theorists have been criticised for their failure to work through how the 'transformative potential' of schooling in how they did not understand counter-hegemonic possibilities or practices or 'transformative' practice in critical pedagogy. Lather sees the early moves of gender 'into the margins' of critical theories analyses as more a tactical than theoretical one which did not dislodge the central Marxist orthodoxies (Lather, 1984). Giroux and McLaren's later attempts to reconcile feminism, critical theory and postmodernism under the rubric of critical pedagogy became the focus of harsh feminist criticism for their implicit resort to male authority and meta-narratives despite their emancipatory claims (Luke & Gore, 1992; Yates,1992;).

Feminist critiques of critical theory, Habermas in particular, have focused largely upon how the generalised concept of oppression fails to address the specificity of how different oppressions work in particular contexts and in relation to each other and how the analysis continues to prioritise class. More specifically, feminists such as Nancy Fraser (1989) consider Habermasian notions of communicative competence and action as idealised states, while recognising power inequities of age and cultural difference through the expression of interests in an 'ideal speech' situation, are still premised upon a desire for consensus which emphasises procedural logic not equitable outcomes. Certainly, Habermas' view of situated morality and communicative ethics go beyond other malestream philosophers in addressing feminist concerns about context and plurality, but he still vacillates between privileging the neutral standpoint of the 'generalised other' and the 'concrete other' (Benhabib, 1986, 327-51) and assumes a 'homogenous public' (Young, 1990, p. 7). His key concepts of dialogue, voice and consensus still tend to assume, as Rawls, that complex problems could be resolved by 'pure reason' (Capper, 1993) and maintain the public/private, universal/particular dichotomies which disenfranchise women.

Finally, there is the implicit notion of false consciousness embedded in a view of empowering 'others' (Ellsworth, 1989). Patti Lather and Lyn Yates argue that critical social theory is 'short on both explanatory and practical levels' (Lather, 1991 p. 37). While sharing with feminism the view of an emancipatory politics centred around the notion of a praxis which unites reflection and action in a dialectic manner, critical theory's view of praxis originated from the theory, whereas feminism originated in women's experience and its suspicions of malestream theory (Lather, 1986). Critical theory has 'largely focused upon critiquing and better understanding what is, rather than on action, change and possibility' (Yates 1986 p. 124; Kenway et al., 1994). While the critical pedagogy debates have tended to be American based, with little impact in mainstream educational administration, Australasian critical theorists, well aware of the disempowering aspects of critique alone, were also unwilling to fall into the trap of conventional educational administration by offering prescriptive and recipe book solutions. Strategies, it was argued, should arise out of ongoing context-situated ideology critiques.

More recently, feminists/critical theorists have brought together post-structuralism and Gramscian theories of culture with critical theory based upon the common identification with and interest in oppositional social movements (Lather, 1991 p. 3). Colleen Capper (1993), for example, seeks to incorporate feminist, critical, structuralist and liberal theory into her 'multi-paradigmatic' approach to educational administration. Largely drawing upon Bill Foster's work, she sees critical theory as not questioning the assumption that 'a leader' or position of authority is necessary and not criticising hierarchy. These specific criticisms hold less for the Australian critical tradition, which, while until recently gender blind, in drawing from Giddens, labour process and cultural studies theories, encourages the democratisation of educational administration and the equalisation of power relations (Rizvi, 1986); seeks to redefine administration and teaching as educational work by emphasising power/knowledge relations (Watkins, 1986); develops a notion of educational administration which sees curriculum and pedagogy as central (Smyth, 1989, 1993) and which redefines educational resources as culture and knowledge (Bates, 1986).

At the same time, feminists are understandably suspicious about the rationality/emotionality, objectivity/subjectivity divides embedded in Enlightenment theory as 'othering' women. And, as Nancy Fraser(1989) points out, Habermas' notions of life world and life systems are flawed because they are premised upon the public/private dichotomy embedded in Enlightenment thought in seeing child-bearing as symbolic reproduction and paid work as material production. At the same time, while feminists have pointed out to critical theorists the need for a better understanding of the specificity and historicity of acts of oppression, and the need for strategies of change and to reject the dualisms of Enlightenment thought, these debates have not been central to feminist work in administrative theory.

AN ETHICS OF CARE AND ADMINISTRATION

More significant has been feminism's struggle with its Enlightenment origins while seeking to deconstruct masculinist thinking and practice in educational administration. One response to both liberal feminism and universal models of man has been radical feminisms desire to revalue women's experience. In education, radical(cultural) feminism's influence is evident in strategies such as girl centred curriculum and pedagogies, single sex schools, self esteem and assertiveness training for girls and women (Kenway, 1990). In teaching it emerges in discussions about women's 'subcultures' as subversive and counter hegemonic (Lather 1984) and as 'subjugated knowledges' in bureaucracies (Ferguson, 1984). Cultural feminist accounts of education are derived from a view of patriarchy as a social power structure actively constructed by men and of consistent benefit to men and therefore an essential source of women's oppression. As liberal feminism, cultural feminism focuses upon what is the same amongst women, but considers women's oppression is actively constituted by men.

Whereas liberal feminism is premised upon a politics of access and success largely from a gender stratification perspective, cultural or radical feminists see educational institutions, values and the process of knowledge formation itself as being male biased and are therefore suspicious of all institutions and processes such as schooling (Tong, 1989). Lather sees cultural feminists as 'developing counter institutions, ideologies and culture that provide an ethical alternative to the dominant hegemony, a lived experience of how the world can be different' (Lather, 1984, pp. 55-6). They position the hegemonic values of males as being personified in competitive individualism, in socially constructed views of merit and skill, hierarchical and authoritarian structures, aggressive and rights oriented behaviours. This perspective therefore focuses upon power, language and knowledge and makes masculinity problematic. While a controversial one, cultural feminism is valuable in distinguishing between behaviours prescribed *for* women and activities arising *out* of women's lives

In seeking to 'humanise' educational administration, feminists have been informed in varying degrees by cultural feminism and feminist psychoanalytic theory, particularly that of Carol Gilligan (1982) and Nel Noddings (1988, 1992) and the emerging 'ethics of care' (Brabeck, 1989). Nel Noddings (1992) and Jane Roland Martin (1994) have elaborated on a form of moral education which revalues women's experiences; which emphasises the moral aspect of education in terms of personal relationships and civic responsibility and not just the public needs of men; which fosters caring attitudes in children (and administrators) by prizing kindness, compassion, and commitment; and which seeks to organise schooling around long term social relationships not differentiating disciplinary boundaries which serve the economy or an elite.

Despite its seeming convergence with the liberal humanist tradition in educational administration, particularly in its opposition to the dominant economistic and managerialist approach of the 1980s, the feminist tradition of an ethics of care derives from object relations theory, a strand of psychoanalytic theory developed from Nancy Chodorow's *Reproduction of Mothering* (1978); from Jean Ruddick's philosophical work on maternal thinking (1980); and from long term philosophical concerns about care and all its underlying 'male fear of effeminacy' (Noddings, 1992, p. 19). Object relations theory considers gender identity formation is not premised upon the presence or absence of the phallis, but upon parental relationships. The notion of an ethics of care as it is being incorporated into mainstream educational administration is not explicitly feminist. For example, Lyn Beck (1992, 1994) advocates an ethic of care in educational administration because emotions and interpersonal relationships are a significant aspect of educational work. Her analysis is unselfconsciously eclectic, although more within the liberal humanist tradition than the feminists tradition of an ethics of care or the cultural studies/critical theory tradition from which she draws her arguments. Likewise Beth Young et al. (1993) see the ethics of justice, ethics of critique, and ethics of care as complementary. In order to produce more inclusive communities they call upon Hodgkinson's notion of a moral art to develop a more humanly informed educational practice in administration which appeals to principles of affiliation, inclusiveness and justness. This desire to reconcile the ethics of care and justice is in part, I would suggest, arising out of feminism's difficulty in addressing its liberal origins. It is also, as David Corson points out, due to the lack of adequate theories of social justice which permits particular theories e.g. Rawlsian theories of justice, to remain unproblematic (Corson, 1994). Social justice has been the uncritical objective of feminist activity in education, but we have not asked *whose* moral order is embedded in this ethics of justice or *how* it is determined.

Also within the radical feminist tradition is the literature on 'women's ways of knowing' (Belenky et al., 1986) and organising out of which the notion of connected teaching and learning has emerged; in which teachers are 'genuine, flawed beings' and practice is a form of 'disciplined subjectivity'. The emphasis is on 'womancentred' analyses or 'womancultures'. The former demands a revaluing of women's experience as the prime object of study whilst 'womanculture' seeks to shift theory away from focus upon masculine systems and values. Whereas earlier versions of radical feminism saw all institutions as ultimately male-biased, the influence of cultural studies and critical theory, including hegemony theory, have provided new insights for feminists into the micro-politics of organisational life with the view that social negotiation and meaning are occurring within unequal and often hidden power relations' (Marshall & Anderson, 1995). Seeing organisations as cultural constructions has led to a focus upon how meanings frame decisions and actions as articulated through particular power relations, thus explicating the more subtle nuances of 'exclusionary cultures', and facilitating the shift in feminist analysis away from individuals and structures to context and values (e.g. Marshall & Mitchell, 1989; Blackmore, 1993; Ferguson, 1984). This perspective has greater explanatory power with regard to how particular hegemonic cultures of masculinity negotiate and work to maintain their hegemonic position, the seeming complicitness of subjugated groups in their own oppression, the integration between 'theorising and acting', and a strong sense of counterhegemonic cultures and agency.

But again much feminist work reflects the more general conceptual confusion with regard to how 'culture' is commonly understood in mainstream educational administration. 'Culture', most particularly in management theory, is used indiscriminately as a 'catch all' phrase to incorporate anything in organisational life which is amorphous, about shared values, views and experiences but which rests neither in the cultural/literary theory or anthropological traditions. Many feminists in educational administration have uncritically drawn from the consensual and homogenised view of culture articulated by management theorists which sees it to be a concrete and manipulable source, a tool for improving productivity. This version suggests leaders become 'culture builders' and use cultural artifacts, symbols, metaphors and language to motivate, incorporate and channel individual energies towards organisational ends (Deal & Peterson, 1990; Duignan & McPherson, 1991). It treats workers as the passive recipients of cultural values of leaders. This view is particularly evident in the literature on visionary leadership and many administrative texts (e.g. Beare, Caldwell & Millikan, 1989). Woman centred analyses, while speaking of suppressed rather than dominant cultures, often make similar assumptions about the unitary, consensual and cohesive nature of culture.

Consequently, socialist and poststructuralist feminists have expressed concern that the ethics of care and 'women' centred cultural analyses are prone to biological reductionism and essentialism, deny difference amongst women and indeed, many post-structural feminists would argue, produce totalising meta- narratives which are ahistorical (Fraser, 1989; Blount, 1994). Cultural feminists are also criticised for 'reverse' sexism by privileging 'feminine' values of nurturance and care over 'masculine' values and behaviours i.e. a form of 'new biologism' by idealising women's preferences for democratic organisation and care (Eisenstein, 1991). Indeed, cultural feminists' arguments about women's culture are readily co-optable to support the 'new conservative feminism' which rectifies traditional feminine and familial roles and mainstream management which portrays feminine values and skills as complementary, but not central, to dominant administrative practices (Burton, 1993; Blackmore, 1993; Kerfoot & Knights, 1993).

Feminisms' need to develop an ethics of care and women's ways of working have arisen out of a concern for community, a failure of top down 'patriarchal' reform to deal with social justice, an awareness of the limitations of liberal competitive individualism, and a recognition and celebration of gender difference. The question is whether an ethics of care or women's ways of working together can avoid women's self sacrifice, given that such views are prone to idealise women's oppression and implicitly lead to an 'equal but different' position. 'When people face oppressive conditions, they often develop strengths and attributes that may in our culture admire. Women may have developed qualities like caring and compassion as survival responses to society wide sexual oppression (Ferguson 1984, p. 92-9; Blount 1994; Brabeck, 1989). The issue is whether the world is seen to fall into the careers and the care for, those who 'prefer' democratic practice and those who see no need for such practices. The challenge feminism raises here, therefore, is for educational administration to develop a form of relational ethics or concrete morality inclusive of difference and not premised upon binary logic.

DIFFERENCE

Indeed, black feminist critiques arose to confront the totalising and universalising narratives of womanhood of liberal and cultural/radical feminism. Bell Hooks (1984) sees feminism as a movement largely of college educated, middle and upper class, married white women, who sought equal access to positions of power and careers, but who displayed little consciousness of the 'otherness' by race and class which create differences which the shared experiences of women cannot transcend. In educational administration, the differences which significantly divide women are magnified. For most women, liberal feminism's individualising discourse of social mobility has had little relevance. For the few who gain access, this discourse has not provided them with a sophisticated understanding of their political relationship to other women as a collective group. Black women, hooks argues, do not lack a sense of community, but do need to work through collective issues of domination. Linda Tuhiwai Smith (1993) points out how Maori women treat Pakeha (white) feminism with some scepticism, seeing that white women have been complicit beneficiaries of white colonialism in New Zealand.

Pre-1980, minority women administrators were seen to experience a 'double disadvantage' due to their colour and gender. Minority women administrators were not only isolated from other women, but also their minority constituencies (Adkinson, 1981). Flora Ortiz (1982) shows how race interfaced with schools differently for black and white administrators - minority administrators were positioned on special projects; they were socialised by minority groups to interact more with race/ethnic communities as their representative rather than with the organisation; they were confined by organisational definition to specific specialist tasks; they were generally appointed in lower status schools and therefore had lower status with colleagues; they were seen largely to be 'ethnic experts', often appointed to solve a particular problem in a minority school but not in a non-minority schools, and therefore expendable 'troubleshooters' rather than permanent administrators. Desegregation led to rapid reduction of black principals and the relegation of blacks to lesser 'race specific' administrative positions.

Whereas previously race was ignored or treated as 'other' (and thereby deviant or deficient) in this 'commotisation of difference', the multiple voices of cultural pluralism during the 1980s viewed all as 'equally ethnic'. Deborah Britzman (1993) sees multiculturalism as the liberal solution to conflict over race and ethnicity. By being positive about difference, it is assumed improved self concept will lead to improved performance. The emphasis is on sex role socialisation and works on the presumption that sufficient role models will encourage other individuals to follow. Helen Mirza, (1993) agrees with Britzman

(1993) 'idealised identities do not lend insight into the mobile and shifting conditions that make identity such a contradictory place to live' (p. 25-6). Role modelling arguments (Byrne, 1989), so common in educational administration, push normative concepts and ignore historical and generational issues which may mean one generation's role model may mean the nexts genderations deviant. The focus of this literature is upon culture and identity, on discrete and fixed categories, and on individualising difference, rather than considerations of how power and politics work in organisations. Consequently, Mirza (1993) argues, research idealises conceptions such as 'the strong black mother' which is translated into 'the black superwoman' in the leadership literature, a model which is paralysing for both women who do not 'fit' the image or highly stressful for those who appear to 'cope' (p. 33). It also assumes such women have the individual and cultural resources to 'cope' arising from their life histories, and thereby portrays their oppression as being a *beneficial* experience in producing 'strong' women.

Indeed, in culturally pluralist societies, minority women are increasingly being positioned as change agents in particularly difficult contexts, expected to bring 'something different' as both insider/outsider and also sharing commonality with particular communities. Studies of minority women in educational leadership in the USA and New Zealand indicate the double bind involved with their appointment-- that it is often symbolic as representing community views but also challenges existing school structures (Ortiz and Ortiz, 1994; Court, 1992). This contradictory positioning of minority women often means the 'potential benefits of diversity and alternative modes of leadership are lost' (Marshall, 1994, p. 173). It overly politicises the role and constructs levels of individual stress which token women feel obligated to suppress in what Marshall calls a 'politics of denial' (Marshall, 1994). Yet even exceptional educational or administrative performance does not mean success, as women and minority groups find; it merely makes them expendable. Such ameliorative multicultural approaches still assume a type of gender neutrality is possible through non-racist or non-sexist (i.e. gender neutral) administrative procedures or concepts such as merit, whereas indeed such notions have historically advantaged those in power, and can actively work against minority women.

Embedded in multiculturalist and pluralist approaches dominating administrative literature is the parallelist thesis which sees multiplicities of difference 'compounded' into double or triple oppression by gender, class and race. But merely 'adding on' oppressions' does not provide a full understanding of the 'qualitative' difference of life for a black female principal or teacher. Such an approach ignores the conflicts, tensions, contradictions and discontinuities which arise for a black female principal. The sexual and racial politics of organisations work differently, with, for example, black women being less 'threatening' than black men but more so than white women for white male managers (Ortiz and Ortiz, 1994). Elisabeth Al-Khalifa cites the current harassment facing black women administrators with the racist stereotypes about their sexuality, about being 'licentious and sexually active, very emotional and passionate, in the worst sense' or the Sikh teacher who felt she was seen as 'a lower creature... a 'bit of black'' (Al Khalifa, 1989, p. 91). Racial inequality has been treated theoretically in a reductionist and essentialist manner, which tends to see difference in a single cause or source and provide linear monocausal explanations of inequality. Both mainstream and radical writing tend to treat social groups as stable or homogenous entities by defining differences as 'transcendental essences' e.g. Asians, Latinos, Blacks, Chicana (de Lauretis, 1990). It also assumes that the white 'race' is culturally unified and homogenous with a cohesive culture, different not only from more recent arrivals but also aboriginal populations.

Educational policy and management, in drawing from such reductionist and essentialist mainstream theorising of issues of race, tends to reduce the issue of racial inequality to one overriding concern... the educatability of minorities and increasing the numbers of minority administrators. Jenny Williams (1987) sees race and gender policies as still defining gender as a female problem, race a black problem, and sexuality a gay and lesbian problem. The policy language leads us to forget the cultural origins of the terminology which associates race 'with some notion of cultural unity, captured in the term ethnic group' (p. 334). Administrative texts and educational policies refer to the categories of women and minorities as mutually exclusive 'special cases' (as deviant from the male norm). Christine Sleeter(1992) sees categorical definitions of difference and inequality in policies setting up women as competing with racial minority and low income groups, forgetting that many are women. This results in 'buttressing the relatively privileged positions of the white middle- and upper class- women, whilst removing from scrutiny the very privileged position of white professional men' (p. 221). Connell (1987) suggests categorical theory (race, gender and class) stresses conflict of interest, but fails to consider how such interests are constituted. For example, trying to raise the number of women in educational administration in a form of politics of access doesn't question the social arrangements that create such positions While categoricalism recognises power it deletes elements of practical politics: choice, doubt, strategy, planning, error, transformation.

Yet in the dominant administrative discourse, women and minorities, who together would constitute the majority, continue to be regarded as 'special interest' groups and the small elite of largely white middle class professional males are depicted as representing universal interests. Given that these hold leadership in most schools, it is not surprising. The grouping of women and minorities together in policies, argues Sleeter(1992), particularly under the new policy rubric of 'diversity', means that the appointment of another white woman is seen to be progressive and encouraging diversity in an already white milieu. Chantal Mohanty (1990) regards policies informed by feminist liberal cultural pluralism, such as the behaviour modification of individuals through 'prejudice reduction sessions' or 'managing 'diversity' policies, as reducing conflict to 'poor interpersonal relations' and not an issue of unequal power relations and the ways wider cultural, institutional factors legitimate harassment and discrimination. So while the feminist identity politics makes notions of cultural difference important in educational administration, it is, as post-colonial feminists point out, also problematic (Mohanty, 1990; Young, 1990). The lack of more sophisticated analyses is, according to Deborah Gewirtz (1993), impeded by the lack of specific theories of racism similar to those that exist in feminism, and, I would suggest failure of more recent theoretical debates to inform policy. Given that both race and gender politics is about change, the role of policy and the state, and about which voices are heard in policy texts, is central.

FEMINISTS THEORISING THE STATE AND POLICY

Feminists have relied not only upon their power as a movement, political lobbying through organisations and collective action in local communities to reduce sex discrimination against women, but they have also relied upon the state. In turn, the 'state' has played contradictory roles with respect to gender equity. On the one hand, the state is a major employer of women and enforces anti-discrimination and affirmative action laws (e.g. Title IX in the USA, Affirmative Action Act and Equal Opportunity legislation in Australia, Sex Discrimination Act in the UK); on the other hand, the state fails to provide adequate child care provisions which makes 'full' participation possible or leaves the implementation of gender equity laws up to male bureaucrats with an investment in existing arrangements. The relationship between 'the state' and gender equity reform is therefore an ambiguous one, and has become a point of contention amongst feminist theorists (Franzway, Court and Connell, 1989; Connell, 1990; Kenway, 1990).

There is range of views amongst feminists from one which sees the state as a monolothic entity captured by males to the view, as a site of/ for feminist change or that feminists no longer need a theory of the state (Watson,1990). From a Foucaultian perspective, Kathy Ferguson (1984) sees bureaucracies as sources of masculinist power positioning women's experiences as a form of 'subjugated knowledge' and feminism as a subversive activity. Anna Yeatman (1990; 1994) and Hester Eisenstein (1993) see the changing relationships between the state and its bureaucracies and the women's movement as providing a politics of new possibility for feminism in working in, with and through the state. Australian feminists particularly have sought to critically theorise the role of the state and bureaucracy largely because of the relatively unique relationship of the state to feminism exemplified by the role of feminist bureaucrats (femocrats) during the1980s initiating and institutionalising strong national gender equity policies (Burton, 1991).

Prior to 1975, most Western educational policy focused upon class rather than gender inequality. Even after 1975, strong state policy on gender equity was largely restricted to Australia and Sweden (Kenway, 1990; Yates, 1993), not the USA, England, Canada or New Zealand (Stromquist, 1993; Arnot 1987; Gaskell & McLaren, 1991; Middleton, 1986). In England, as the USA, race discrimination legislation provided precedents for later claims by women but with no central enforcement agency. English legislation relied upon local 'partnerships' between LEA's, Department of Education and Science and teachers to embrace race and sex discrimination legislation. The assumption was that 'sex discrimination would dissolve with increased knowledge of the issues, rational discussion and limited coercion i.e. proscription not prescription. It was reactive not proactive, and defined equality of opportunity as equal treatment' (Arnot, 1987, p. 316). Although by the mid 1980s it was accepted that it was indifference, hostility and lack of political will and not lack of information that led to non-action, there was no explicit policy statement on equal opportunities of either girls or women and no comparable committees of enquiry into gender as there were into race. In the USA, gender equity reform has largely been through coercive legislation seeking to remove sex discriminatory practices and targeting the presence of women in educational leadership under threat of withdrawal of federal funds. Nelly Stromquist (1993) argues that implementation has been limited because the legislation was minimalist, narrowly interpreted by the judiciary, had insufficient enforcement mechanisms, limited and reduced funding over time for related legislation, and low levels of research funding. In Canada, national debates on education are rare because of highly provincial orientation of education, and there is little funding of research on gender or critical scholarship (Gaskell & McLaren, 1991). As elsewhere, gender reform legislation has lacked coercive force and monitoring mechanisms and relied upon voluntary action by the states, organisations and individuals.

Equal opportunity policies have revealed the difficulty of 'resolving the tensions between demands for local autonomy and centralisation, between laissez faire and interventionist policies, between grassroots and top-down initiatives' (Arnot, 1987, p. 326). Feminist teachers and teacher unions, particularly in Australia, New Zealand and England, have been a powerful force for gender reform as activists in combination with 'top down' liberal initiatives arising from the lobbying of political parties and trade unions giving the move towards sex equality, rather than just EO, greater power (Kenway, 1990 Weiler, 1988; Arnot 1987). Change more often resulted from feminist teachers individually and collectively, often without formal power, using multiple strategies such as developing school based policy and publications, gaining funding for research, demanding non-sexist processes of promotion and selection and networking (Weiner, 1989; Gaskell and McLaren,1991; Middleton, 1990; Watson, 1988). Socialist feminists still tended to work more with the unions in developing local policies on industrial democracy and employment conditions, whilst black feminist and lesbian pressure for issues of racism and sexuality to be put onto the agenda (Middleton, 1992a).

Top down policy, on the other hand, has been largely been framed by both reactive and critical theories, but not theories of action (Yates, 1993; Arnot, 1991; Ozga, 1993; Bell and Chase, 1993). The eclectism of gender reform policy is evident. Although framed by liberal feminism, it is increasingly informed by cultural and socialist feminism with recognition of women's ways of leading, the significance of cultural contexts for women, and the centrality of childcare and flexible work arrangements. Mary Bryson and Suzanne de Castells (1993) fear that the discursive formation of action around notions of gender equity theory, policy and practice will inscribe 'women's ways' and other similarly preservationist liberal pluralisms as new 'regimes of truth' in educational policy' (p. 341-2). Furthermore, while the gender reform policies, premised upon social justice, provided disadvantaged groups with a voice, this voice has been increasingly overpowered by stronger and conflicting managerialist discourses of standards and efficiency promoted by the liberal right and market economics during the 1980s such that even the liberal feminist appeal to women's rights is subjugated to human capital economic theory and national economic needs (Henry & Taylor, 1991).

Gender equity policy thus highlights the inherent contradictions in liberalism between individualism and the government imperatives for planning and monitoring. The failure of equality of opportunity policies and professional development programs to achieve their promise by the late 1980s indicates that changing *individual* women to be more like men did not make a substantial difference (Burton, 1991). Most countries, even more so now, are reluctant to legislate in the same way for equity for women (e.g quotas) as for girls or on race (e.g.desegregation) (Marshall, 1994). Even where there has been widespread acceptance of the discourse of EO, feminist agendas do not permeate the mainstream policy process. The pattern of gender reform in the 1980s was largely symbolic policy statements, voluntary implementation, and delegation of responsibility to marginalised women's units with few resources or monitoring powers (Dickens, 1989; Watson, 1988). Now, in newly devolved educational systems, equity is being 'mainstreamed' and 'downstreamed', becoming everyone's and no-one's responsibility.

The failure of gender reform policy to attain its promise has led feminists to focus upon the nature of policy itself. Functionalist views of policy not only allow policymakers to instrumentally link the social functions of education to the economy in inequitable ways, but also inadequately theorise both the policy process and educational change. Catherine Marshall and Gary Anderson (1994) offer the notion of a feminist critical policy analysis which begins with assumptions that gender inequity results from purposeful choices to serve an in-group's interests. It asks how males benefit from current school practices and cultures and how each policy impacts on females. Kenway et al. (1994) offer a feminist poststructuralist view of policy as text, which considers how policy is read and acted upon by those it targets in ways which can often subvert, but also radicalise its intentions. How then will policy work for feminism and social justice in a period of uncertainty, change and self governance?

So while the 1980s was a period of unprecendented legislative and school based activity in equal opportunity, in which feminist voices on leadership, care, pedagogy and democratic practice have been heard and even incorporated, into mainstream administrative discourses, the effect has been limited. First, because strategies for change, largely framed by liberal feminism, sought to do what men did, but better. Emphasis was on leadership, mentorship, role models, assertiveness training, career planning, networking and building self esteem. While these strategies have been coupled with organisational strategies to make environments more amenable to women, feminist research has been rewritten in the process of its appropriation, for, as Gramsci suggests that hegemonic power relies upon its capacity to transform itself through the co-option of oppositional discourses. I would suggest that in part it is due to the lack of a feminist critical theory of social justice. In part, it is also in part due to the shifting context and the re-formation of educational administration. Increasingly the state relies upon self regulatory mechanisms of accountability: outcomes based management of schools, performance appraisal of teachers and standardised assessment of students. As we shift into an era of self governance with devolved school management operating in the context of deregulated educational markets, the relationship between the individual and the state, as mediated through education, is transformed. How does feminism address issues of representation and social justice in this context?

REPRESENTATION

In suggesting that the feminisms have shifted debate, I raised critical issues about future issues for the feminisms in educational administration with regard to conceptualising change, social justice and democracy- all key aspects to an emancipatory politics in education. Anna Yeatman argues that 'multiple interests in emancipation have tabled difference as a central axiom in the contemporary politics of justice. Not only do the various emancipatory movements have to accept each other's presence, but they have to work with this presence as part of their *internal* politics' (Yeatman, 1993, p. 228. Author's emphasis). Women in administration, as 'token' women, are caught, as Rita Felski (1989) argues, between needing to claim that they represent all women, and their awareness that their voice cannot adequately or morally represent 'other' women. Yeatman (1993, p.229) points out that white middle class women are positioned as the 'custodians of the established order *within* an emancipatory politics' (feminism). Representation also has cultural and textual significance for the positioning of women in various educational discourses with the shift from the politics of identity of the 1980s to a politics of difference.

FEMINISM /POST-STRUCTURALISM AND A POLITICS OF DIFFERENCE

Whereas the feminist politics of identity of the 1980s assumed the emancipatory universal subject, it has been postmodernism[1] which has rejected outright the Enlightenment dualisms between rationality/emotionality; rights/responsibilities; mind/body; public/private; universal/ particular. Some feminists see post-structuralism destabilising the shared feminist political project because of its potentiality for individualising difference (Bordo,1990). Others are more ambivalent. Hawkesworth (1989) sees post-structuralism providing a more sophisticated understanding of power/knowledge constellations, but argues that issues of poverty, rape, domestic violence and sexual harassment are not 'fictions' (p. 55). Calas and Smirich (1993) warn of the 'consequences of completely abandoning the modern principles when the powerful may still be performing and oppressing under these principles' (p. 244). And others see post-structuralism's emancipatory potential since postmodernism/post-structuralism shares a self conscious critical and historical relationship with feminism to dismantle the transcendental discourses of objectivity and reason which have separated mind and body, to undermine the claimed neutrality and objectivity of the academy; to celebrate fluidity of difference and negate categories; to view political engagement as temporary alliances (Flax, 1990).

Post-structuralism has much to offer to feminist analyses in educational administration by providing a capacity to become more openly self-reflective and self-critical and new ways of deconstructing masculinist discourses ((Blount, 1994), re-conceptualising subjectivity (Davies 1989; 1992) and revising organisational theory (Calas & Smirich, 1992). Feminists find post-structuralism seductive because of its emphasis on language and subjectivity, the notion of multiple subject positions of women, lived contradictions and discourse, of seeing power as having the potential for both oppression and emancipation (Ferguson, 1984; Davies, 1992). Colleen Capper (1993) values post-structuralism because 'power relations are viewed through language and its authority, history and availability; subjectivity in terms of identity, experience, process, access and selection; and power itself in terms of conflict and dissensus, covert modes of domination and resistance to power' (Capper, 1993, p. 103). This is not necessarily to neglect social justice. Feminist post-structural analysis is no new meta-narrative, but it considers how the stories contribute to or inhibit justice for traditionally oppressed groups' (Capper, 1993, p. 106).

There is evident in feminism's flirtation with post-structuralism a tension between the politics of difference and social justice (Young, 1990). 'Postmodernists offer theoretical tools for challenging essentialist feminist tendencies towards limited grand narratives; but on the other hand, feminists offer strong theories for social critique and political action geared towards dismantling an oppressive systems' (Blount, 1994, p. 49). Post-structuralism, in particular Foucault, has provided feminism with techniques to deconstruct the metanarratives of administration and articulate this with a politics of difference (Ferguson, 1984; Blount, 1994). But as yet the potential of post-structuralist theory to provide more sophisticated theories of subjectivity, in areas of leadership, for example, or to address strategic issues of change and social justice has not been fully explored in educational administration (Diamond & Quinby, 1988; McNay,1992; Sawicki, 1991). One exception is Capper (1994), who seeks to address both the politics of difference and social justice with her notion of 'otherist' post-structuralism which is founded on difference but no particular foundation e.g. gender/race/class. Utilising feminist critiques of critical pedagogy (Luke & Gore, 1992), she argues an Otherist post-structuralism would go beyond the interpretivist position of personal narrative and storytelling in educational administration so common to giving women voice to consider how localised contextualised knowledge and understanding would be cast against complex tapestries of historical structures of domination and exploitation. i.e. neither privileging the local or the global.

Feminist post-structuralism does ask different questions of educational administration arising out of its rejection of the male-female dualisms of Enlightenment thought, its focus upon the body and sexuality, its blurring of 'discrete categories' of difference, its view of power as process and relations not possession. One such question could be the possibilities of and for a post- masculinist politics in education?

A POST-MASCULINIST POLITICS?

Given that what is characterised as traditional 'patriarchal' models of organisations and leadership (hierarchy, specialisms, boundary maintaining) no longer constitutes 'best management practice' (Morgan & Knights, 1991; Hearn and Parkin,1992), there is surprisingly little theoretical or empirical research on masculinity in educational administration, with some exceptions. Feminist has traced the historical association between administration and particular hegemonic masculinities (Blount, 1994; Blackmore, 1993; Court 1994). Radical/cultural feminists and post-structural feminists have linked sexuality and the body to male dominance and resistance, thus highlighting the discursive formation of sexuality in institutions and through media and knowledge construction. Martin An Ghaill (1994) and Lyn Davies (1992) connect the re-gendering of teachers' and principals' work with the marketisation of schooling, the moral ascendancy of managerialism and entrepreneurship and hypercompetition between teachers, head teachers and schools. New associations are being made between a dominant 'masculine' authoritarianism legitimated by discourses of managerial efficiency and economic rationality and leadership - competitive, point-scoring, over-confident, sporting, career, and status conscious- which articulates with current shifts towards hierarchy, individuation and efficiency in the context of marketisation and globalisation of education.

Whilst it is evident that the presence of women in male dominated environments, particularly in upper levels of management, is a threat both to male peers and subordinates, research has concentrated upon the impact of this 'soft fear' upon women managers, not on male behaviour. Research has focused on how males seek to control the female presence and sexuality in management by reference to appearance, jokes and the male gaze, and how women in turn seek to make their 'stigmatization' invisible through conformity of language, dress and movement (Marshall, 1985; Adler, 1993; Ozga, 1993; Shakeshaft 1987; Weiler 1987; Blackmore, 1995). Black women in particular suffer stereotypic expectations about being 'exotic', in which traditional Asian or Caribbean or African hair styles and dress are treated as theatre or display rather than normal forms of dress (Ozga 1993). Exceptions are feminist work which show how masculinity is reworked and reconstituted in more subtle ways with shifts in modes of management and the subtle strategies of resistance against women which emerge (Cockburn, 1992). Feminism as a movement has been positioned defensively in continually justifying feminism's existence, relevance and intent rather than focusing upon how the 'politics of advantage' operates for men.

Likewise, sexuality have been explicitly addressed in curriculum and student relationships, but ignored in administration. Sexual preference amongst teachers has largely been addressed as a legal problem confronting administrators with respect to teacher-student relationships, and less an issue with respect to discrimination or the personal dilemmas confronting lesbian, gay or bisexual administrators or teachers, and how this impacts upon the quality of their work life (Sears, 1993). This is in part because overt displays of 'macho' masculinity and violence (whether against girls, lesbians or gays) are depicted as 'discipline' and 'authority' problems not issues of gender power relations in schools generally (Mac An Ghaill, 1994); in part because of the genderblindness of organisational theory (Acker, 1992); in part because, as Carrigan et al. (1987) suggests, the early development of the sociology of gender, was saturated with modernisation, the characteristic blindness to power and theoretical incoherence of sex role theory; and in part because 'one of the cultural supports of men's power is the failure to ask questions about masculinity' (Connell, 1993, p. 191). Many critical theorists and feminists have failed to recognise sexuality as a significant level of analysis in educational administration, sexuality being notable in its absence in the 'new leadership' paradigm which focuses upon reflective leadership (Sears, 1993).

It has been radical and then lesbian feminists who first focused in education upon masculinity. Initially this derived from concern about the impact of masculine biases in knowledge formation, representation and organisation on girls. Now the issue of violence has increasingly led schools to be seen as 'masculinizing agencies' in which the micro culture of management, teachers and students are key infrastructural mechanisms through which different masculinities and femininities are mediated and lived out, intersecting with beliefs about the relative sexism of other races, cultures and religions, but in which male heterosexuality is the dominant but unstable referent for all forms of sexuality (Mac An Ghaill, 1994). Increasingly, masculine heterosexuality is seen to be an important aspect of patriarchal culture in which a 'sexually passive gay' is as 'desirable' as a 'sexually submissive woman', in which hegemonic masculinity in particular contexts imposes its definitions of masculinity upon *other* masculinities and *all* femininities (Connell, 1987, 1990). Yet untapped is an emerging literature in organisational theory which sees organisations suffused with dominant forms of sexuality (or heterosexuality more accurately), which depicts how particular modes of administration desexualise and resexualise organisational work (Hearn et al., 1990). This is complemented by a developing sociology of masculinity by feminists (Segal, 1990) and pro-feminists (Hearn, 1991, 1992; Kimmel, 1987) and the new men's studies movement (Brod 1988, p. 62) which seeks not to see masculinity as a normative referent upon which all is judged but as a problematic concept. Homosexuality and lesbianism, even more than 'other' forms of difference, are particularly threatening to hegemonic masculinities and the homogenising tendencies of organisational elites (D'Augelli, 1991; Collinson & Hearn, 1992; Knights & Morgan, 1991). The sociology on masculinity has recognised the inadequacies of Parsonian functionalist sex role theory with its expressive/instrumental dichotomy. It is exemplified in the bureaucratically domesticated male of W. F White's *The Organisation Man* which typified males as either being too effeminate and lacking masculinity (homosexual) or hypermasculine as a defense against males 'unconscious feminine identification' and the negative effects of changing social and occupational roles of women. Recent empirically based work of Cynthia Cockburn (1992) for example, illustrates how hypermasculinity is sustained, of how hegemonic forms of masculinity drive women out, marginalised in the labour processes in which they remain, so as to sustain a strongly masculine 'work culture', and, in so doing subordinate other men (young men, unskilled workers).

The notion of a politics of difference, amongst men as well as women, therefore requires feminists in educational administration to think strategically, about how to work with those men who are 'othered' by such hegemonic masculinities so as to produce a post-masculinist organisational politics, about constructing new agendas which recognise that some men's interests are not aligned with dominant organisational cultures and there is a shared concern for social justice (Young, 1990; Yeatman, 1993).

RESTRUCTURING FOR THE 'POST MODERN'

The issue of a new form of feminist politics is also important in the context of changing relationships arising from educational restructuring. Gender has not been a focus in this global phenomenon of the 1980s (Sadker and Sadker 1988). The restructuring of nation-states and economies globally has led to changing relations between women, the state and education (OECD, 1993). Devolved education systems should be seen in the context of the dismantling of the welfare state in most Western capitalist societies. The trend has been to shift the cost of health, welfare and education from the state onto the individual, the family (usually women who care for the aged, young, sick and unemployed) and the community (voluntary) and remove these safety nets of national awards for less powerful workers with enterprise bargaining and individual contracts. This restructuring sets up the material and cultural conditions for new notions of citizenship and national identity. In particular, the marketisation of education equates citizenship to consumption of education as a private good, in a rights oriented framework, and does not address issues of community and social responsibility.

Feminism more generally sits uncomfortably with New Right politics of the market and the emphasis on traditional nuclear family, although liberal feminism is more comfortable with the emphasis on freedom of choice (Dickens p. 168-9, 1989). The state now mediates the market by guaranteeing individual choice and no longer directly intervenes to address group disadvantage and oppression (Kenway et al. 1993). Furthermore, the state, seeking to maintain its steering capacity, encourages an outcomes based rather than content and process orientation which exacerbates competitiveness between schools and individuals in anti-educative and anti-egalitarian ways. (Capper, 1993; Arnot, 1991)

Devolution to self managing/governing schools has been justified on the grounds, without empirical evidence, that it encourages flexibility and diversity in educational provision, imparts greater professional autonomy to teachers and administrators, increases parental choice, facilitates community involvement and ownership, and is therefore both efficient *and* equitable (e.g.Caldwell and Spinks 1992). Yet the effect of many 'reforms' has been to exacerbate teacher/administrator hierarchies through differential reward systems, poor motivating strategies for changing practice or producing equity (Shakeshaft, 1993). Devolution has been accompanied globally by reduced educational expenditure and countered by even stronger centralising tendencies resulting from increased surveillance of student, schools and teachers through outcome oriented accountability mechanisms of standardised testing, national curriculum, teacher appraisal and performance management. Cross-national research indicates that devolution, *in conjuncture with* the marketisation of education and reduced expenditure, more often undermines teacher collegiality and professionalism; increases inequality by class, race and locality between schools, teachers and students (Lingard, Knight & Porter, 1992; Bowe & Ball, 1992; Smyth, 1993; O'Shea, Kahane & Sola, 1990; Lieberman, Darling -Hammond and Zuckerman, 1991); produces school governing bodies largely composed of white middle class professional males; and results in equity disappearing from school-based charters and policies due to lack of strong top down policies (Deem, 1990, 1992; Middleton, 1992 a & b).

Early evidence suggests a new gendered division of labour is emerging in recently devolved education systems. In Israel (Goldring & Chen, 1994) and Australia (Blackmore, 1995) there is a feminisation of the principalship and teaching at the local level, yet the concentration of policy and financial power remains with the male dominated 'hard core' elite at the top. In this polarisation, women principals have been encouraged to become change agents as middle managers at the local level due to the shortage of range of skills required and not as a matter of fairness (Ozga, 1993, p. 3). They are then alienated and isolated from policy decisions and power as executive line management subverts their discretionary capacity and any preference for democratic practice. Women continue to do the 'emotional management' work for the system with little access to the power to change it fundamentally. At the same time, there is evidence in the USA and in New Zealand that devolution allows some minority groups (e.g. Maoris) to define and develop their own educational communities (Young, 1990; Yeatman, 1993).

I have sought in this chapter to raise what are some critical future issues for education's feminisms. In particular, I have suggested that in the context of the changing relationships between the state, education and the individual arising out of a post modern condition of heterogeneity, change and plurality, that a tension lies between a feminist politics of difference and social justice. A feminist politics of difference has already raised important questions about the relationship between liberty and equality, diversity/choice and social equality. The question, rarely asked in educational administration, is what type of citizen do we as educators wish to develop in post modern times? There are various feminist responses. Noddings (1992) and Beck(1992) suggest an ethics of care is a fundamental starting point to reframe and reorganize schools away from rationalist-economistic frameworks of school reform which counters emphasis on how ethics and pedagogical techniques which promote independence and achievement will produce more fully human beings. This is appeals to humanist/communitarian views of citizenship which highlights what is common and shared.

Anna Yeatman (1993) suggests a more heterogeneous and fractured view of the polity, due to the privatising aspects of market oriented forms of self governance. Feminists, she suggests, have been wrong-footed with neo-conservative attempts to selectively reduce the role of the state with devolution, user pays and consumer choice, for they have been left, on the one hand, to defend an outmoded masculinist, monocultural view of citizenship, organisation and leadership which assumes a homogeneous racial and ethnic (lingual) community, man the citizen and head of the patriarchal unity of the family and school. On the other hand, arguments about self governance have been seductive to feminists in that it would remove their dependence upon the state. Socialist feminists (Arnot, 1991) argue that foregrounding social justice in all educational decision making means first seeking a materialist base to their analysis of a feminist politics of change (e.g. Hennessey, 1993). Agreement lies amongst feminists about the need to reframe debates away from individual rights, but they dispute the process by which alternative forms of community may arise.

A view of social justice which addresses the issues raised in this chapter would perhaps begin with shifting the focus away from the traditional focus in social justice theory away from distribution to focus on domination and power. Young(1990) argues that feminists need to cultivate a form of political maturity which means recognising that we are all complicit in particular forms of domination and relationships which produce inequality. Only then can we build new bridges and multicultural alliances. This would require more sophisticated theories of power which would see power as relation and process, and interests as neither purely altruistic or selfish. A feminist politics of difference is also pushing for a view of difference which neither seeks to assimilate or separate, which names relations of similarity and dissimilarity, but which recognises difference as relational in contrast to the logic of 'pure' identity of Western thought which represses particularity and heterogeneity through rationalising and totalising dominant discourses such as that of management. A feminist politics of difference recognises the interdependence and interspersion of groups rather than essentialist notions of 'otherness'. But it is not just any difference, Mohanty (1990) argues, it is about the kinds of difference which is acknowledged and engaged. In terms of strategies for change, such a politics means feminists from diverse positions tend to agree that there are times to emphasise the multiplicity of female expression and preoccupations, and there are times when to emphasise the universal woman in what is called 'situated essentialism' where differences based on gender are sometimes foregrounded, and in other situations secondary (Tong, 1989, 237). It would also be a theory of justice which was premised upon a situated or concrete morality, rather than the abstract, transcendental view of Enlightenment thought (Benhabib, 1986); and upon reciprocity and responsibility, not just rights. While feminism has provided a critical edge to educational administration, it will be the conjuncture of feminism, post-colonialism and post-modernism which hopefully will require more fundamental rethinking of the field in strategic areas of citizenship, subjectivity, and of how the local/global relationships frame issues of rights *and* responsibility, of individuals and the state, with respect to educational administration.

FOOTNOTES

1. Patti Lather suggests postmodernism 'refers to the larger cultural shifts of a post-industrial, post-colonial era' which reject the tenets of the Enlightenment, and 'post-structural to mean the working out of cultural theory within the post modern context, particularly with respect to theories of representation' (Lather, 1991, pp. 4-5).

REFERENCES

Acker, J. (1992) Gendering Organisational Theory. In A. Mills & P. Tancred (eds) *Gendering Organisational Analysis*. New York: Sage.

Acker, S. (1989). *Teachers, Gender and Careers*. Lewes: Falmer Press,

Adkinson, J. (1981). Women in School Administration: a review of the research. *Review of Educational Research, 51*, 311-43.

Adler, S., Laney, J., & Packer, M. (1993). *Managing Women. Feminism and power in educational management*. Milton Keynes: Open University Press.

Al-Khalifa, E. (1989). Management by Halves: women teachers and school management. In H. De Lyons (Ed.), *Women Teachers* Milton Keynes: Open University Press.

Alcoff, L., & Potter, E. (1993). *Feminist Epistemologies*. London: Routledge.

Arnot, M. & Weiner, G. (1987) *Gender and the Politics of Schooling*. Lewes: Open University Press.

Arnot, M. (1991). Equality and democracy: a decade of struggle over education. *British Journal of Sociology of Education, 12*(4), 447-465

Arnot, M. (1993). A crisis in patriarchy? British feminist educational politics and state regulation of gender. In M. Arnot, & K. Weiler (Ed.), *Feminism and Social Justice* Lews, Sussex: Falmer Press.

Ball, S., Bowe, R., & Gold, A. (1992). *Reforming Education and Changing Schools*. London.: Routledge.

Barrett, M., & Phillips, A. (1992). *Destabilising Theory. Contemporary Feminist Debates*. Oxford: Polity Press,

Bascia, N. (1994) *What Unions Can Do For Teachers* New York: SUNY

Bates, R. (1986). *Management of Culture and Knowledge*. Geelong:, Deakin University Press.

Bates, R. (1994) The Bird that Sets itself Afire: Thom Greenfield and the Renewal of Educational Administration. 8th International Intervisitation Program, OISE, Toronto.

Beare, H., Caldwell, B and Millikan, R. (1989). *Creating an Excellent School. Some new management critiques*. London: Routledge,

Beck, L. (1994). *Reclaiming Educational Administration as a Caring Profession*. New York and London: Teachers College Press.

Beck, L., & Murphy, J. (1994). *Understanding the Principalship: a metaphorical analysis*. New York: Teachers College Press.

Belenky, M., Clinchy, B., Goldberger, N. R., & Tarule, J. M. (1986). *Women's Ways of Knowing. The Development of Self, Voice and Mind*. New York: Basic Books,

Bell, C. & Chase, S. (1993) The under-representation of women in leadership. In C. Marshall (ed.) *The New Politics of Race and Gender*. London: Falmer Press.

Benhabib, S. (1986) *Critique, Norm and Utopia*. New York: Columbia University.

Biklen, S. & Pollard, D. (1993). *Gender and Education. 92 Yearbook of the NSSE* Chicago: University of Chicago Press

du Billing, Y., & Alvesson, M. (1989). Four Ways of looking at Women and Leadership. *Scandinavian Journal of Management, 5*(1), 63-80.

Blackmore, J. (1989). Educational Leadership: A feminist critique and reconstruction. In J. Smyth (Ed.), *Critical Perspectives on Educational Leadership*, Lewes: Falmer Press.

Blackmore, J. (1990). Philosopher King or Fantasy Figure: *Images of Educational Administrators*. In F. Rizvi (Ed.), Images of Administration Geelong: Deakin University Press.

Blackmore, J. (1991). Changing from Within: Feminist Educators and Administrative Leadership. *Peabody Journal of Education, 61*(1), 19-37

Blackmore, J. (1993). 'In the Shadow of Men': Exclusionary theory and discriminatory practice in the historical construction of 'masculinist' administrative cultures. In J. Blackmore, & J. Kenway (Eds.), *Gender Matters in the Theory and Practice of Educational Administration and Policy: a feminist introduction* Sussex: Falmer Press.

Blackmore, J.(1995) 'Postmodern' leadership in self managing schools: a feminist analysis in B. Limerick & B. Lingard (Eds.) *Gender and Changing Educational Management*, ACEA Yearbook, Edward Arnold.

Blount, J. (1994) One postmodernist perspective on educational leadership. Ain't I a leader? In. S. Maxcy (ed). *Postmodern School Leadership: Meeting the crisis in educational administration*. London: Praegar.

Bordo, S. (1990). Feminism, Postmodernism and gender scepticism. In L. Nicholson (Ed.), *Feminism/Postmodernism* London: Routledge.

Brabeck, M. (1989). *Who Cares? Theory, research and educational implications of the ethic of care* New York: Praegar.

Britzman, D. (1993) Beyond Rolling Models: gender and multicultural education. In S. Biklen, & D. Pollard (Eds) *Gender and Education. 92 Yearbook of the NSSE* Chicago: University of Chicago Press

Brod, H. (1987). *The Making of Masculinities. The new men's studies*. London: Allen and Unwin,

Bryson, M & De Castells, S. (1991) En/gendering equity: on some paradoxical consequences of institutionalised programs of emancipation. *Educational Theory 43* (3) 341-355

Burton, C. (1991) *The Promise and the Price: The struggle for Equal Opportunity in Women's Employment*. Sydney: Allen and Unwin

Burton, C. (1993) Equal Employment Opportunity and Corporate Planning. In J. Blackmore, & J. Kenway (Ed.), *Gender Matters in the Theory and Practice of Educational Administration and Policy: a feminist introduction* Sussex: Falmer Press.

Byrne, E. (1989). Role modelling and mentorship as policy mechanisms: the need for new directions. In E. Byrne (Ed.), *Women and Science and technology in Australia. Policy Review Project* Brisbane: University of Queensland.

Calas, M., & Smircich, L. (1992). Rewriting gender into organisational theorising: directions form feminist perspectives. In M. Reed, & M. Hughes (Ed.), *Rethinking Organisation. New directions in organisation theory and analysis*. London: Sage.

Caldwell, B. & Spinks, J.(1992). *The Self Managing School* London, Falmer Press.

Campbell, R., Fleming, T., Newell, L., & Bennion, J. (1987). *A History of Thought and Practice in Educational Administration*. New York: Teachers College Press.

Capper, C. (1992). A feminist post-structuralist analysis of nontraditional approaches in educational administration. *Educational Administration Quarterly, 28*(1), 103-24.

Capper, C. (1993) Educational Administration in a Pluralistic Society: a multi-paradigm approach. In C. Capper (ed) *Educational Administration in a Pluralistic Society*. New York: SUNY.

Capper, C. (1994).'...and justice for all': Critical perspectives on outcomes - based education in the context of secondary school restructuring. *Journal of School Leadership, 4*(March), 132-55.

Carr, W. & Kemmis, S. (1986) *Becoming Critical: Knowing through action research*. Geelong: Deakin University Press.

Carrigan, T., Connell, R.W., & Lee, J. (1987). The sex role framework and the sociology of masculinity. In G. Weiner, & M. Arnot (Ed.), *Gender under Scrutiny. New inquiries in education*. London: Hutchinson.

Chodorow, N. (1978). *The Reproduction of Mothering: psychoanalysis and the sociology of gender*. Berkeley: University of California.

Cockburn, C. (1991). *In the Way of Women: Men's resistance to sex equality in organisations*. London: Macmillan.

Codd, J. (1988). *Knowledge and Control in the Evaluation of Educational Organisations* Geelong: Deakin University Press.

Collins, P. H. (1991). *Black Feminist Thought*. New York: Routledge.

Collinson, D., & Hearn, J. (1992). Men, masculinities and managements: unities, differences and their interrelationships. *Academy of Management Review, 17*,

Connell, B. (1987). *Gender and Power*. Sydney: Allen and Unwin.

Connell, R. W. (1990). Gender, state and politics: theory and appraisal. *Theory and society, 19*, 507-44.

Court, M. (1992). 'Leading from Behind': Women in educational administration. In S. Middleton, & A. Jones (Ed.), *Women and Education in Aotearoa 2* Wellington: Bridget William Books.

Court, M (1993) 'Macho masculinity' *Gender, Work and Organisation 1* (1)

Corson, D. (1993) Language, Minority Education and Gender: linking social justice and power. Toronto: Multilingual Matters/OISE

Culley, M., & Portuges, C. (1985). *Gendered Subjects. The Dynamics of Feminist Teaching*. New York: Routledge.

D'Augelli, A. (1989 (pub 1991)). Lesbians and Gay men on Campus: visibility, empowerment and educational leadership. *Peabody Journal of Education, 66*(3), 124-142.

Davies, B. (1992). The Concept of Agency: a feminist post-structuralist analysis. *Social Analysis, 30*, 42-53.

Davies, L. (1990). *Equity and Efficiency? School management in an international context*. London: Falmer Press.

Deal, T., & Peterson, K. (1990). *The Principals Role in Shaping School Culture*. Washington,: United States Department of Education.

Deem, R. (1990). Governing by Gender-the new school governing bodies. In P. Abbott, & C. Wallace (Ed.), *Gender, Sexuality and Power* London: Macmillan.

Deem, R., Brehony, K., & Hemmings, S. (1992). Social justice, social divisions and the governing of schools. In D. Gill, B. Mayor, & M. Blair (Ed.), *Racism and Education. Structures and Strategies* London: Sage and Open University.

Diamond, I., & Quinby, L. (19888). *Feminism and Foucault: reflections on resistance*. Boston, Mass.: Northeastern Press,

Dickens, L. (1989). Women- a rediscovered resource? *Industrial Relations Journal*, 167-173.

Duignan, P., & Macpherson, M. (1991). *Educative Leadership for the Corporate Managerialist World of Educational Administration*. ACEA.

Eisenstein, H. (1991). *Gender Shock: Practising feminism in two continents*. Sydney: Allen and Unwin.

Elliott, J. (1991). *Action research for Educational Change*. Milton Keynes: Open University Press.

Ellsworth, E. (1989) Why doesn't this feel empowering? Working through the repressive myths of critical pedagogy. *Harvard Educational Review. 59* (3). 297-324.

Evers, C. & Lakomski, G. (1991) *Knowing Educational Administration: contemporary methodological controversies in educational administration research*. New York: Pergamon Press

Felski, R. (1989). Feminist theory and social change. *Theory, Culture and Society, 6*, 219-40.

Ferguson, K. (1984). *The Feminist Case Against Bureaucracy*. Phil: Temple University Press

Ferguson, K. (1987). Work, Text and Act in Discourses of Organisation. *Women and Politics, 7*(2), 1-21.

Flax, J. (1990). Postmodernism and gender relations in feminist theory. In L. Nicholson (Ed.), *Feminism/Postmodernism* London: Routledge.

Foster, W. (1986). *Paradigms and Promises: new approaches to educational administration*. Buffalo: Prometheus.

Franzway, S., Court, D., & Connell, R. (1989). *Staking a Claim. Feminism, bureaucracy and the state*. Sydney: Allen and Unwin.

Fraser, N. (1989). *Unruly Practices. Power, discourse and gender in contemporary social theory*. Oxford: Polity Press.

Gaskell, J., & McLaren, A. (1991). *Women and Education: a Canadian perspective*. Calgary: Detselig

Gewirtz, D. (1991). Analyses of Racism and Sexism in Education and Strategies for change:. *British Journal of Sociology of Education, 12*(2), 183-201.

Gilligan, C. (1982) *In A Different Voice: Essays on psychological theory and women's development* Cambridge, Mass: Harvard University Press

Glazer, J. S. (1991). Feminism and Professionalism in Teaching and Educational Administration. *Educational Administration Quarterly, 27*(3), 321-42.

Goldring, E. & Chen, M. (1994) The feminisation of the principalship in Israel: the trade-off between political power and cooperative leadership. In C. Marshall (ed) *The New Politics of Race and Gender*. London: Falmer Press.

Gosetti, P., & Rusch, E. (1994). *Diversity and equity in educational administration: missing in theory and action*. New Orleans: Paper presented to the AERA.

Grant, J. (1988). Women as managers: what they can offer organisations. *Organisational Dynamics, Winter*, 56-63.

Grant, R. (1989). Heading for the Top: Career experiences of Women. *Gender and Education, 1*(2), 113-25.

Greenfield, T., & Ribbins, P. (1993). *Greenfield on Educational Administration*. London and New York: Routledge.

Hammond, S., & Hardbridge, R. (1993). The impact of the Employment Contracts Act on women at work. *New Zealand Journal of Industrial relations, 18*(1), 15-30

Harasym, S. (1990) *The Post-colonial Critics Interviews, Strategies, Dialogues*. New York: Routledge.

Harding, S. (1991). *Whose science? Whose Knowledge? Thinking from women's lives*. New York: Cornell University Press.

Hawkesworth, M. (1990). *Beyond Oppression: feminist theory and political strategy*. New York: Continuum.

Hearn, J., & Morgan, D. (1991). *Men, Masculinities and Social Theory*. London: Unwin Hyman,

Hearn, J., & Parkin, W. (1992). Women, men, and leadership: a critical review of assumptions, practices and change in industrialised nations. In N. Adler, & D. Izraeli (Ed.), *Women in Management World Wide* New York: M. Saharpe

Hearn, J., Sheppard, D., Tancred-Smith, P., & Burrell, G. (1990). *The Sexuality of Organisation*. London: Sage,

Hennessey, R. (1993). *Materialist Feminism and the Politics of Discourse*. New York/London: Routledge

Henry, M., & Taylor, S. (1993). Gender equity and economic rationalism: an uneasy alliance. In Lingard, B., Knight, J. & Porter, P. *Schooling Reform in Hard Times*. Lewes: Falmer Press.

Hodgkinson, C. (1991). *Educational Leadership: the moral art*. New York: SUNY.

hooks, b. (1984). *Feminist Theory: from margin to centre*. Boston: South End Press

Jones, B. K. (1990). The gender difference hypothesis: a synthesis of research findings. *Educational Administration Quarterly, 26*, 5-37.

Kenway, J. (1990a). *Gender and Education Policy: a call for a new direction*. Geelong: Deakin University Press.

Kenway, J., Bigum, C., & Fitzclarence, L. (1993). Marketing Education in the postmodern age. *Journal of Education Policy*.

Kenway, J., Willis, S., Blackmore, J., & Rennie, L. (1994). Making hope practical rather than despair convincing: feminist post-structuralism and change. *British Journal of Sociology, 15* 2, 187-210

Kerfoot, D., & Knights, D. (1993). Management, masculinity and manipulation: from paternalism to corporate strategy in financial services in Britain. *Journal of Management Studies, 30*(4), 659-77.

Kimmel, M. (1987). *Changing Men. New Directions in research on men and masculinity.* California: Sage,

Lakomski, G (1989) Against feminist science: Harding and the science question in feminism. *Educational Philosophy and Theory* 2 (1) pp. 1-11.

Lather, P. (1984). Critical theory, curriculum transformation and feminist mainstreaming. *Journal of Education, 166*(1), 49-62.

Lather, P. (1991). *Feminist Research in Education: Within/Against.* Geelong: Deakin University Press.

Lauretis, T. de (1990). Eccentric subjects: feminist theory and historical consciousness. *Feminist Studies, 16*(1),

Lieberman, A., Darling-Hammond, L., & Zuckerman, D. (1991). *Early Lessons in Restructuring Schools.* New York: Teachers College Press.

Lingard, B., Knight, J., & Porter, P. (eds) (1993) *Schooling Reform in Hard Times.* Deakin Series, 9. London: Falmer Press.

Little, J., & McLaughlin, M. (1993). *Teachers' Work: Individuals, colleagues and contexts.* New York: Teachers College Press

Lloyd, G. (1984). *The Man of Reason; 'Male' and 'Female' in Western philosophy.* London: Methuen.

Luke, C., & Gore, J. (1992). *Feminisms and Critical Pedagogy.* New York: Routledge,

Marshall, C. &. Ortiz., F. (1988). Women in educational administration. In N. Boyan (Ed.), *Handbook of Research in Educational Administration* New York: Longman.

Marshall, C., & Mitchell. D. (1989). Women's Careers as a Critique of the Administrative Culture., Paper presented to the AERA.

Marshall, C. (1994) Politics of denial: gender and race issues in administration. In C. Marshall (ed) *The New Politics of Race and Gender.* London: Falmer Press.

Marshall, C., & Anderson, G. (1995). Rethinking the Public and Private spheres: feminist and cultural studies perspectives on the politics of education. In J. Scribner & D. Layton (Ed.), *The Study of Educational Politics* London: Falmer Press.

Martin, J. R. (1994). Methodological essentialism: false difference and other dangerous traps. *Signs, 19*(3), 630-657.

McCarthy, C., & Apple, M. (1989). Race, class and gender in American Educational research: towards a nonsynchronous parallelist position. In L. Weis (Ed.), *Class, Race and Gender in American Education* New York: SUNY Press.

McNay, L. (1992). *Foucault and Feminism; power, gender and self.* Cambridge: Polity Press.

Middleton, S. (1986). Feminism and education in post-war New Zealand: an oral history perspective. In T. Openshaw (Ed.), *Reinterpreting the Educational Past* Wellington: NZ Council of Educational Research.

Middleton, S. (1992). Equity, Equality and Biculturalism in the Restructuring of New Zealand Schools: a life history approach. *Harvard Educational Review, 62*(3), 310-22.

Middleton, S (1992) Gender equity and school charters: theoretical and political questions for the 1990s in S. Middleton and A. Jones (eds) *Women and Education in Aotearoa 2.* Wellington, Bridget Williams Books.

Mirza, H. (1993) The social construction of Black Womanhood in British Educational Research: towards a new understanding. In M. Arnot & K. Weiler (eds) *Feminism and Social Justice*. London: Falmer Press.

Mohanty, C. T. (1990). On Race and Voice: challenges for liberal education in the 1990s. *Cultural Critique, 14*(Winter), 179-208.

Morgan, G. & Knights, D. (1991). Gendering Jobs: corporate strategy, managerial control and the dynamics of job segregation. *Work, Employment and Society, 5*(2), 181-200.

Neville, M. (1988). *Promoting Women: successful women in educational administration in New Zealand*. London: Longman Paul.

Nixon, M (1987) Few women in school administration: some explanations *The Journal of Educational Thought 21*(2), 63-70

Noddings, N. (1988). An ethic of caring and its implications for instructional arrangement. *American Journal of Education, Feb*, 215-230.

Noddings, N. (1992). *The Challenge to Care in Schools: an alternative approach to education*. New York: Teachers College Press.

O'Shea, C., Kahane, E., & Sola, P. (1990). *The New Servants of Power. A critique of the 1980s school reform movement*. New York: Praeger,

OECD. (1993). *Shaping Structural Change. The Role of Women*. Paris: OECD.

Ortiz, F. (1982). *Career patterns in education: women, men and minorities in public school administration*. New York: Praeger.

Ortiz, F. & Ortiz, D. (1994) Politicising executive action: the case of Hispanic female superintendents. In C. Marshall (ed) *The New Politics of Race and Gender*. London: Falmer Press.

Ozga, J. (1988). *Schoolwork. Approaches to the Labour Process of Teaching*. Milton Keyenes: Open University Press,

Ozga, J. (1993). *Women in Educational Management*. Milton Keynes: Open University Press.

Pateman, C. (1989). The 'fraternal social contract': some observation on patriarchal civil society. In C. Pateman (Ed.), *The Disorder of Women* Cambridge: Polity Press.

Prentice, A., & Theobald, M. (1991). *Women who taught: perspectives on the history of women and teaching*. Toronto: OISE

Ramsey, E., (1993). Linguistic omissions marginalising women managers. In D. Baker & M. Fogarty (eds) *A Gendered Culture. Educational management in the 1990s*. St. Albans: Victoria University of Technology,

Rees, R. (1990) *Women and men in education*. Toronto, Canadian Education Association.

Regan, H. (1990). Not for women only: school administration as a feminist activity. *Teachers College Record, 91*, 565-78.

Rizvi, F. (1986). *Administrative leadership and the Democratic Community as a Social Ideal*. Geelong: Deakin University Press.

Rusch, E. (1992). *Strategic Planning: looking through the lens of Foucault*. San Francisco: AARE

Sadker, M., & Sadker, M. (1988). *Equity and excellence in educational reform: an unfinished agenda*. Washington DC: American University,

Sampson, S. (1986). Equal opportunity, alone, is not enough or why there are more male principals in schools these days. *Australian Journal of Education, 31*(1), 27-42.

Sampson, S. (1987). But women don't apply: a discussion of teacher promotion in Australia. *Unicorn, 13*(3), 139-143.

Sander, B. (1993) Educational Administration and Developing Countries. In C. Capper (ed) *Educational Administration in a Pluralistic Society*. New York: SUNY.

Sawicki, J. (1991). *Disciplining Foucault: feminism, power and the body*. New York: Routledge.

Scheurich, J. & Imber, M. (1991) Educational reforms can reproduce social inequities: a case study *Educational Administration Quarterly 27*(3) 297-320.

Segal, L. (1990). *Slow Motion: Changing masculinities, changing men*. London: Virago Press.

Sergiovanni, T. (1987). *The principalship,. A reflective practice perspective*. San Antonia, Texas: Trinity University.

Shakeshaft, C. & Nowell, I. (1984) Research on theories, concepts and models of organisational behaviour: the influence of gender. *Issues in Education. 2*(3),186-203.

Shakeshaft, C. & Hanson, M. (1986) Androcentric Bias in the Educational Administration Quarterly *Educational Administration Quarterly 22*(1), 68-92.

Shakeshaft, C. (1987). *Women in Educational Administration*. Newbury Park, CA: Sage.

Shakeshaft, C (1993) Gender Equity in Schools. In C. Capper (ed) *Educational Administration in a Pluralistic Society*. New York: SUNY.

Sleeter, C. (1992). Power and privilege in white middle class feminist discussions of gender and education. In S. Biklen, & D. Pollard (Ed.), *Gender and Education* Chicago: University of Chicago Press.

Smith, D. (1988). *The Everyday World as Problematic.: a feminist sociology*. Milton Keynes: Open University Press.

Smyth, J. (ed) (1993). *A Socially Critical View of the Self Managing School*. Sussex: Falmer Press,

Smyth, J. (ed) (1989) *Critical Perspectives on Educational Leadership*. Sussex: Falmer Press.

Starrart, R. (1991). Building an ethical school: a theory of practice in educational leadership. *Education Administration Quarterly, 27*, 185-202

Strachan, J. (1993). Including the Personal and the Professional: researching women in educational leadership. *Gender and Education, 5*(1), 71.

Stromquist, N. (1992). Sex Equity Legislation in Education: the state as the promoter of women's rights. *Review of Educational Research 63*(4).379-408.

Tong, R. (1989). *Feminist thought: a comprehensive introduction*. Boulder Co: Westview.

Tyack, D., & Hansot, E. (1982). *Managers of Virtue: public school leadership in America 1820-1980*. New York: Basic Boo

Watson, H. (1988). The impact of the second wave of the women's movement on policies and practices in schools. In S. Middleton (Ed.), *Women and Education in Aotearoa* Wellington: Allen and Unwin.

Watson, S. (1990). *Playing the State Australian Feminist Interventions*. Sydney: Allen and Unwin,

Weiler, K. (1988). *Women Teaching for Change. Gender, class and power*. Massachusetts: Bergin and Garvey.

Weiler, K. (1993). Feminism and the struggle for democratic education. In M. Arnot, & K. Weiler (Ed.), *Feminism and Social Justice* London: Falmer Press.

1042

Weiler, K. (1994) Compulsory heterosexuality and the married teachers bar. Paper presented to AERA, New Orleans, April.

Weiner, G. (1989). Professional Self-knowledge versus social justice: a critical analysis of the teacher-researcher movement. *British Educational Research Journal, 15*(1), 41-51.

Weiner, G. (1993). A question of style of value? contrasting perceptions of women as educational leaders. Women and Leadership Conference, Perth: Edith Cowan University

Williams, C. (1992) The glass escalator: Hidden advantages for men in the 'female' professions. *Social Problems. 39* (3) pp. 253-65

Williams, J. (1987) The construction of women and black students as educational problems in M. Arnot & G. Weiner, (eds) *Gender and the Politics of Schooling.* London, Hutchinson.

Yates, L. (1992). Postmodernism, Feminism and Cultural Politics: or, if master narratives have been discredited what has Giroux think he has been doing? *Discourse, 13*(1), 124-33.

Yates, L. (1993). Feminism and Australian State Policy. Some questions for the 1990s. In M. Arnot, & K. Weiler (Ed.), *Feminism and Social Justice* London: Falmer Press.

Yeakey, C., Johnston, G., & Adkinson, J. (1986). In pursuit of equity: a review of research on minorities and women in educational administration. *Educational Administration Quarterly, 22*(3), 110-49.

Yeatman, A. (1990). *Bureaucrats, Technocrats, Femocrats.* Sydney: Allen and Unwin

Yeatman, A. (1993) Voice and representation in the politics of difference in S. Gunew & A. Yeatman (Eds.) *The Politics of Difference* Sydney: Allen and Unwin

Young, B. (1992) On Careers: themes from the lives of Four Western Canadian Women Educators, *Canadian Journal of Education 17* (2),148-61

Young, B. (1993) Not 'There' Yet: An Other Perspective on Canadian Educational Administration, Edmonton, University of Alberta

Young, B., Staszenski, D., McIntyre, S., & Joly, L. (1993). Care and Justice in Educational Leadership. *The Canadian Administrator, 33*(2),

Young, I. M. (1990). *Justice and the Politics of Difference.* Princeton: Princeton University Press

Chapter 29: Emancipatory Discursive Practices

DAVID CORSON

Ontario Institute for Studies in Education

INTRODUCTION

This chapter begins by introducing the 'discursive turn' now occurring
in the human sciences. It discusses the deep-level discursive reasons
that seem to lie behind the readiness of human beings to perceive the
world in hierarchical ways. It then reviews the international literature
in this developing area of research, treating the following topics: studies of informal administrative discourse in school settings, such as
supervisory conferences and staff meetings; studies of formal discourse in the official meetings of schools and educational systems;
oppressive and emancipatory policy discourse; the discursive practices
of teachers and students in classrooms; and theoretical matters relevant
to study in this area. Special attention is given to the ways in which
administrators exercise leadership through their discourse, the misuses
of power and authority that are possible in administrative discourse, the
forms of resistance that the 'administered' and the 'supervised' adopt,
and the uses of ideology and other distorting forms of dominance that
occur in situations of unequal power. The chapter focuses on ways of
resisting and escaping oppressive hierarchies and unwanted leaderships.

THE 'DISCURSIVE TURN' IN THE SOCIAL SCIENCES

Linguists, sociologists, historians, and anthropologists have long discovered major differences in the discursive practices of culturally,
socially, and historically remote peoples, differences that no doubt
have deep implications for differences in social cognition and human
interests. For many people from these disciplinary backgrounds, the
'discursive turn' now occurring across the social sciences could not
come soon enough. It has been delayed mainly by institutional forces
to do with the boundaries between academic disciplines and to do with
the vested interests of those tied to earlier ways of perceiving the

K. Leithwood et al. (eds.), International Handbook of Educational Leadership and Administration, 1043-1067.
© *1996 Kluwer Academic Publishers, Printed in the Netherlands.*

world. Now its arrival is having an impact even on the least dynamic and most conservative of disciplines.

In their important book, *The Discursive Mind*, Rom Harré and Grant Gillett (1994) signal the appearance and the rapid rise of a genuinely new psychology: 'discursive psychology'. Their book tries to make the main tenets and the initial research efforts of discursive psychology available to undergraduate and other interested non-expert readers. While the focus seems to be on psychology, this new field extends to all branches of the human sciences, involving anthropology, sociology and linguistics in a synthesis of trends that are already appearing or established. "It is both remarkable and interesting that the old psychologies continue to exist alongside the new" say the authors, and they begin their description with a critical look at "the traditional experimentalist psychology that still exists, particularly in the United States" (2).

The source of discursive psychology is in the idea of the social world as a discursive construction. The work of Jerome Bruner (1973; 1990) in cognitive psychology opened the way for thinking about human cognition in other than the methods and the metaphysics of the experimentalist tradition. Discursive psychology has already gone beyond Bruner's path-breaking work by discarding the twin dogmas of cognitive science: that inner mental states and processes exist; and that they are much the same for all human beings. As a result, discursive psychology acknowledges the reality and importance of those differences that linguists, sociologists, historians, and anthropologists have long discovered in the cognitive performances and practices of people.

Wittgenstein's idea of following a rule is at the root of the new cognitive revolution: Mental activity is not tied to some internal set of processes; it is a range of moves set against a background of human activity governed by informal conventions or rules, especially rules to do with the ways in which words and other symbols are used within the structures of a language (Corson 1995b). For Harré & Gillett, whatever existence the psychological world might have, it is not reducible or replaceable by explanations based on physiology, or any materialist discipline that does not get to grips with the structure of meanings in the lives of the cultural group to which a subject belongs. Getting inside those structures means getting inside the forms of life, norms, conventions, and rules, and seeing them as the subject does.

These ideas complement developments in a critical realist philosophy of the social sciences (Bhaskar 1986; Corson 1991a; 1991b) where the task in understanding human behaviour is one of interpretation and empathy, not prediction and control. Notably the self-reports of the people under study provide the real data for investigation, but these are not falsifiable reports of mind states; they are statements of how things really are to the 'subject'. They are ontologically real, and must be treated as true indicators of the social structures and cultural values that are important in the lives of subjects. Even the terms 'observer' and 'subject' become redundant in this account, to be replaced by the idea of co-participants who are making sense of the world and their experience of it.

As in discursive psychology, the subject matter of the social sciences in general is changing radically to include discourses, significations, subjectivities, and positionings, since this is where mental events are really located. As Harré & Gillett conclude: "the study of the mind is a way of understanding the phenomena that arise when different sociocultural discourses are integrated within an identifiable human individual situated in relation to those discourses" (22). This shift in direction alters the theoretical base of psychology. It threatens to destroy its subject matter entirely, since the mind of an individual becomes a nexus or meeting point of social relations, integrating the multifaceted subjectivity that arises from this intersection of influences. The mind or personality is embedded in contexts that have unique historical, political, cultural, social and interpersonal determinants: a unique intersection of discourses and relationships, or a 'position' which largely determines mind.

If the influences that shape individual cognition are social and interpersonal, then discourse has a formative influence on the development of individual psychology: social influences shape brain function, as Harré & Gillett argue. But it is a corollary of their argument that seems central to a critical realist account of the world: If social influences shape brain function, which shapes social influences, this provisionally explains the workings of ideology, propaganda, stereotypes, religious and political indoctrination, the insular practices of many bureaucrats, and other forms of groupthink. Doubtless it increases the prospects of emancipation from some of these influences.

Discursive psychology is arriving on the scene rather late. For some time, discourse analysts, ethnomethodologists, conversation analysts, and sociologists of language have been setting this new course for the social sciences, which promises to lower even further the rapidly disappearing social science disciplinary boundaries. Consistent with this rising interdisciplinarity, the 'discursive turn' is now beginning to have a wider impact on educational studies, where the study of educational problems and issues is becoming one of working across disciplinary boundaries, rather than within and from their narrow subject matters. This chapter tries to show some of the relevance of the 'discursive turn' to one area of educational studies: educational administration and leadership.

RESEARCH ON POWER RELATIONSHIPS IN EDUCATIONAL ORGANIZATIONS

A central interest in educational studies is the relationship between discursive power and the administration of educational organizations. Although this is among the important applied topics in the social sciences, it remains relatively unexplored in the annals of critical and emancipatory research on power. Three structural factors combine to insulate educational administrative research from wider critical examination. Their influence is easy to discern.

Firstly, in many countries educational studies itself is a relatively new field of study in universities, having only recently escaped from the hold that teacher training institutions and educational bureaucracies had over its subject matter. Its reputation within universities is still developing and it is certainly regarded almost everywhere as among the 'softer' of academic fields. Since educational administration itself, as a sub-field of educational studies, has been little examined until recently by mainstream sociologists of education and critical educational theorists (with the notable exception of the works cited in the section in which this chapter appears), it is clear why the critical study of educational organizations, as agencies of great overt and latent power, remains underdeveloped.

Secondly, since its inception in the 1950s, educational administration research has been largely dominated by scholars following a logical empiricist approach to their work. As a result, a diluted form of positivism has ruled the field of inquiry almost everywhere. Since the search for answers in educational administration research has been channelled in this way by a single, highly distorting ideology, the organs of power in the field, including scholarly journals, research networks, and professional organizations, are still much influenced by that ideology. Although its influence is waning, the effects of positivism block progress towards emancipatory and critical research. This dominance is reinforced by educational policymakers who continue to insist on 'hard' data as a basis for their activities. Thirdly, cultural and gender factors still directly influence the selection of scholars into university faculties of educational administration. Often a criterion for appointment has been that the candidate has had experience in educational administration. This has all but excluded minorities and women from the professoriate until recent years. It has also meant that relatively few empathetic mentors are available to guide minorities and women in their academic progress, and to point them towards positions in the field (Shakeshaft, 1989). Because of all this, few members of these outgroups have been able to break into the professoriate. At the same time, their work has suffered all the problems of marginalization that arise when a single Zeitgeist is dominant in an area of inquiry.

Clearly the field of 'discourse and power in educational organizations' (Corson 1995a) offers a challenge to the rather monadic account of power that emerges from the structuralist/functionalist and logical empiricist traditions that continue to inform much of the work in educational administration. Quite simply, in those traditions, power in organizations is said to depend either on formal authority or on prestige, and it is demonstrated through dominance over others. The alternative to this monadic view is a much more provocative, optimistic, and emancipatory one. It bypasses many earlier approaches to studying educational administration: approaches that accept contemporary forms of education uncritically; approaches that often seem divorced from a concern for the quality and relevance of curriculum, for the humanity of pedagogy, for the moral consequences of policies, and for the wishes and interests of the diverse sociocultural communities now reaching into schools from every side.

Although this alternative view is an unsettling one, it cannot be ignored for much longer since it is largely consistent with contemporary and emerging positions in the philosophy and practice of the social sciences. Educational administration theorists may risk obsolescence by failing to grapple with these contemporary positions. In general, the alternative view grows from critical, poststructuralist, and postpositivist conceptions of the relationship between discourse and social reality. It sees social reality, including relations of dominance, as constituted subjectively: social realities cannot be identified in abstraction from the language in which they are embedded. Language, as always, is the prime data in social research. In fact, it is the *only* truly emergent data to understand the social world, since everything, including information and reports about values, attitudes, ideologies, and preferences, has to be put into a language before it can be shared and used.

PRIMITIVE SEMANTIC NOTIONS ABOUT HIERARCHY

In spite of the remarkable emancipatory potential that language has always had, it also possesses an insidious and oppressive quality: It can snare people into beliefs, perceptions, and practices that are not of their own making or choice. Some of these things are of the most basic kind imaginable, and they link directly into the way that people conceive of human organizations and of the potential for reforming them.

Wherever human groups take up permanent residence, a culture is established; where a culture forms, human organizations are created to manage, protect, and transmit that culture; and when organizations are planned, hierarchies are devised to provide the ubiquitous tiered arrangements of organizational structures. Critical theorists advance the following views: that hierarchical arrangements in education and elsewhere, are a direct reflection of macro social arrangements and historical forces; that wider social structures are reproduced in institutional power hierarchies; and that ruling groups in societies maintain their hegemonic influence by imposing hierarchical structures on key organizations that reflect wider social formations. Plainly powerful groups in societies and cultures do seek to protect their hegemony by controlling key organizations and shaping them to suit their vested interests. That they do all this is not in doubt. But in non-totalitarian societies, what structured aspects of social cognition and perception, on the part of the controlled, actually allow the controllers to do all this, often to their own surprise?

Social theorists seem to agree that Antonio Gramsci (1948) was on the right track. He highlights the non-coercive aspect of domination, comparing it with the more obvious coercive forms of power more typical of totalitarian systems. His concept of 'hegemony' describes the organization of consent through invisible cultural dominance, rather than through visible political power. In developed modern societies, control is exercised in a modern way which gives stability by basing power on wide-ranging consent and agreement. This non-coercive 'force' is said to penetrate consciousness itself, so that the dominated become accomplices in their own domination. So it is argued that hierarchies and unwanted leaderships are reinforced from both sides of the power relationship: The non-dominant adhere to the norms created by dominant groups, while not recognizing that they are being 'voluntarily coerced'. How does this happen?

It is the case that human beings cannot easily conceive of organizations except in hierarchical terms. Our propensity to view and treat the

world in a hierarchically structured way, seems to owe much to our linguistic socialisation (our earliest sociocultural positioning, as Harré &
Gillett would put it) and also to the inescapable fact that complex
world entities are hierarchically structured. It is certain that we receive
broad primitive notions about hierarchy from our earliest linguistic
experiences. In fact humans may experience little that is not hierarchically structured (Corson 1986a) and, as a result, we come to have difficulty in thinking non-hierarchically. There are two likely 'causes' of
this common human mind-block.

Firstly, our views as a species may be largely shaped by *universal
semantic primitives*. These are structures in the brain that we inherited
from our hominid ancestors that help impose meaning on the world,
but only in the most basic of ways. These universal primitives provide
given 'items of knowledge' that all humans bring to bear, both as a perspective on concrete reality and as a heuristic template that we use to
'overlay' metaphysical space. These *a priori* items are thought to be
innate basic elements of semantic structure, biologically given to us
through the structure of the human organism. They facilitate and relate
in other important ways to the perceptual structuring patterns that
humans apply in segmenting the perceived universe along hierarchical
lines.

I am not saying that we are controlled in a determined fashion by
these primitives, only that we have strong innate inclinations to perceive and often to think in hierarchical patterns. This is because we
have inherited the categorization scheme evolved by our ancestors, a
scheme that served them well during the more than 99% of human history in which humans were hunters and gatherers. During all this time
they were without the daily intellectual need to step outside that
scheme. Today these structural invariants that evolved as a response to
a world that most humans no longer inhabit, equip us with *innate prejudices* about the world. But these are distortions that we can still accept
or reject, on the basis of higher level reasoning processes.

Secondly, our views as individuals are no doubt largely shaped by
acquired semantic primitives which we begin developing no later than
our first contacts with language. The environment gives us primitives
when we first come to talk about it and to hear talk in reply. We learn
very early from trial-and-error encounters with the world, to divide
things into hierarchical patterns, whether or not the impetus for that
learning is an innate disposition to do so, or the result of discursive
positioning and socialisation. These acquired primitives are hierarchically structured in an habitual way, since we meet nothing complex in

the world in our early lives that is not structured hierarchically (although this is not apparent to us in our early encounters). As a result of these early experiences, people go on to impose similar hierarchical structures on things and situations as a fairly habitual part of their linguistic and cognitive interaction with the environment. Almost always, the environment reinforces this habit.

These predispositions towards a hierarchically structured world view are causally related as well to our fondness, as a species, for imposing 'order' and control upon the world. They are also related to our general reluctance to tolerate anarchy as a widespread variable in human affairs. These predispositions affect the way we view and create complex formal organizations. Since they are human creations, framed in line with human dispositions, then the uncritical perceptions that all individuals have of them are more alike than we realise, since they are created in line with those predispositions and perceived in line with them as well. Even our perceptions of abstract things, like school knowledge categories, are influenced by our strong, shared inclinations to rank and order even the most abstract of entities, adding, as further criteria for that ranking and ordering, whatever rationale is to hand.

A critical realist account tries to identify the actual structures that constrain human action, structures whose identification and modification can prove emancipatory for human beings in general. I am using the word 'structure' to refer to the intractability of the social world. Structures set limits to freedom, often in hidden ways, through a complex interplay of powers within diverse social institutions. I have argued above that among the most basic of these structures are the inherited or the acquired semantic primitives that constrain human beings into thinking hierarchically, for much of the time. But like all structures of power, these primitive dispositions have no existence separate from the activities that they govern and from agents' discursive reports of those activities.

While it is true that the discourse of individuals is heavily influenced by institutional practices and the effects of these constraints often show up in stereotyped and unjust oppositions that severely disadvantage females, sociocultural minorities, or those of little power more generally (Corson 1993), it is also true that structures, in their turn, are reconstructed, reinforced, or reformed by acts of critical discourse in micro settings. I have argued this point already, as a corollary of Harré & Gillett's work. Indeed the very possibility of emancipation from oppressive ideologies and structures, depends on this being so.

EMANCIPATORY DISCURSIVE PRACTICES: A REVIEW OF THE
LITERATURE

One problem for a critical realist and emancipatory account of the
world, is how to overcome these inherited and acquired dispositions
towards hierarchy, whenever the need, wish, or opportunity to do so
exists: how to avoid collaborating in one's own oppression by accepting unwanted hierarchies and leaderships. What kind of emancipatory
discursive practices in educational organizations help defeat these
inbuilt prejudices that often frustrate people's real interests as autonomous moral agents? The answers seem to lie in encouraging individuals and groups to create emancipatory discursive 'positions' for
themselves, which is the most universal form of communicative action.
Examples of what I mean are beginning to appear in the educational
studies literature.

Communicative Action and Teacher Resistance in School Administration

Charol Shakeshaft and Andy Perry (1995) address questions of power
relationships between speakers of different statuses, related especially
to gender differences in administrative discourse. Setting the 'language
of power' alongside the 'language of empowerment', they examine the
performance of women as school managers, and the gender differences
in communication, evaluation, and feedback that accompany that performance. Their study proposes that one explanation for the difference
in effectiveness and style of women administrators lies in the language
used by women themselves, which emphasizes power with, rather than
power over others. Ruth Wodak (1995) also uses a real world context
for her study of power, discourse, and styles of female leadership in
school committee meetings. After considering the relationship between
power, hierarchy, and interaction in public institutions, she reports
studies carried out in three schools where statutory committees were
established to conform with a school/community partnership law. In
these conventionally hierarchical institutions, female principals adopt
contrasting discursive strategies to justify, legitimize, and achieve their
administrative agenda.

Access to power is the great variable that often distinguishes men
and women, and in the analysis of discourse, power seems to be a more
powerful variable than gender in determining discursive forms (Corson, 1993). Supporting this claim, Cathryn Johnson (1994) systemati-

cally examines the language produced in simulated laboratory 'organizations' in which subjects are grouped in power contexts of unequal status. Some three-person-groups are all female or male, with a same-sex leader; others are all female or male, with a different-sex leader. Her analysis confirms that formal authority (power) is more influential than gender in predicting conversational patterns. At the same time, paralinguistic patterns (smiling and laughing) seem to be more gender related, with only slight links to the power variable.

Jo Roberts Blase and Joseph Blase (1995) capture some of the complexities involved in exercising discursive power as a school administrator, and in resisting that administrative power as a teacher. They examine the micropolitics of supervisor-teacher interaction in instructional conferences, noting the lack of systematic research in the literature that goes beyond the bureaucratic and technical character of the supervisory conference. Early research on actual conference texts (Blumberg & Amidon 1965; Blumbers & Cusick 1971) aimed only to extend hierarchical control and manipulative power; it asked administrators to work with teachers to replace defensiveness with supportiveness; and it found ways in which administrator influence could be enhanced. After reporting interactions of novice and experienced supervisors with teachers in instructional conferences, Roberts Blase & Blase suggest that hierarchical factors at work in the setting often put the key goals of supervisors out of reach. Their study contrasts control-oriented with empowering discursive strategies and their role in the development of successful conferencing.

Roberts Blase (1992) also examines the use of face-threatening acts by supervisors, and the interaction of these acts with politeness levels. These face-threatening acts by supervisors are imbued with elements of distance, power, and threat which intrude into areas of professional autonomy. The job experience of supervisors seems a key variable in the use of face-threatening acts. Roberts Blase (1994) also discusses the relevance of discourse analysis to administrative and leadership problems in education. She gives further attention to politeness phenomena in the supervisor-teacher exchange, but does not address the emancipatory dimension of her data very much. Similarly Zeichner & Liston (1985) examine the quality of discourse between university supervisors of teachers-in-training, and the trainees themselves. But they do this without addressing issues of power or any tensions that might be associated with the difference in status between the supervisors and the student teachers. While they get themselves ready to analyse 'critical discourse' (158-164), Zeichner & Liston do not take this framework very far in their actual analysis.

Perhaps much of the problem about power imbalances in supervision, lies in the use of the term 'supervision' itself to describe relationships between colleagues. 'Supervision' is not widely used outside North America. This lexicalization of the activity suggests to me that the power relationship is dysfunctionally formulated from the outset. I find the use of terms like 'instruction' or 'instructor' similarly dysfunctional, since they imply a form of teaching and a kind of relationship that many teachers would like to leave behind, if they could. These words 'supervision' and 'instruction' suggest that subjugation to the wishes of the supervisor or the instructor is the only way to self-improvement for the supervised or instructed. This seems a discursive practice of great distorting power, for teachers, and for pupils in classrooms.

Also writing in response to the growing use of instructional conferences as a device of administration, Duncan Waite (1992; 1995) examines administrator-teacher conferences. Although the teacher supervision literature presents supervision as 'growth-inducing' for teachers and as a way of improving instruction, Waite tries to deal more adequately with the balance of power in these conferences, especially the problem of facilitating teacher resistance. One finding of his 1992 study, is that genuine collegial relations between supervisor and teacher are highly problematical. By using conversational analysis in his 1995 study, he presents the tactics and resources available to teachers for asserting counter-control in conference settings and for making them more cooperative and empowering administrative activities.

More oblique to the theme of this review, since his data is all paralinguistic and has only impressionistic value, Barry Kanpol (1988) describes teachers' actions motivated by their resistance to 'informal routine realms'. These actions seem to be acts of perversity or ritualistic disobedience, in response to administrator demands, rather than challenges to dominant ideology. So Kanpol suggests that the teachers in his study were not really furthering their own emancipation or transforming their consciousness as teachers and citizens, although their actions may be a first step towards an emancipatory practice. Elsewhere, however, Kanpol (1991) uses classroom and interview discourse to argue a contrary position. He sees the collective willingness of teachers to bend rules and test the principal's authority as evidence of incipient political resistance: "probing hierarchical relationships and structural facets of school, such as petty rules" and strongly resisting "the institutional authority structures and official components of schooling" (p. 143). Although he is ambivalent about whether or not these actions constitute forms of resistance that improve the human condition in some way, he still sees the teachers as "transformative intellectuals" who have potential to "generate a counter hegemonic agenda" (p. 147).

The earlier literature on educational administration presents only a few analyses of actual discourse used in administrative contexts. This is not surprising given the recency of developments in discourse analysis and given the fact that educational administration as a field of study has been rather isolated from many developments in the parent disciplines of the social sciences. This includes those developments in the philosophy of the social sciences, mentioned above, that increasingly license researchers to recognize human reasons and accounts in language as the priority social scientific data. Here I mention two sets of school-based studies that appear in the early literature. These have their origins in the late 1970s and are linked no doubt to the quickening of interest in discourse analysis that began at that time. Peter Gronn (1983; 1984) and Andy Hargreaves (1981) both use transcribed analyses of administrator or teacher talk in schools as brute data for their theorizing.

Gronn's two case studies analyse extracts from transcripts of talk recorded by the researcher. The first study (1983) concentrates on informal talk by and with the principal of a school, recorded in corridor, office and staffroom. Gronn argues that this talk that takes up so much of the principal's day, is really 'the work' of educational administration; that through his use of discourse the principal relaxes and tightens his administrative control. The second study (1984) concentrates on semi-formal talk, recorded at a school council meeting where the principal and the councillors debate the allocation of money for teaching aids. In this case study, Gronn goes beyond the discourse itself by consulting the participants after the council meeting, and inviting their reflections on his data. He also argues that his study is useful for understanding the internal dynamics of the leader-follower relationship.

Hargreaves (1981) attends to teacher staffroom talk of two types. The first type he characterizes as 'contrastive rhetoric': 'the introduction into discussion of outrageous and stereotyped examples of alternative practice which, by implication, quickly serves to mark the boundaries of reasonable and acceptable decision-making' (p. 215). He compares this contrastive rhetoric with what he calls 'extremist talk':

'deployed by certain junior members of staff to push the boundaries of discussion outwards' (p. 215). The main point of the study is that both these forms of talk affect staff decision making processes and educational innovation, either by limiting or enlarging the range of educational practices considered 'acceptable'.

The Gronn and Hargreaves studies are of considerable value and relevance. But from this distance, they seem less than perfect in the range, precision, and depth of their analyses. For example, in the transcriptions that Gronn and Hargreaves provide for their readers there is very little prosodic information. By this I mean any transcribed detail related to intonation, speed of delivery, stress, timing, interruption patterns etc. The absence of this detail limits the quality of the message that readers can take from the transcripts and obviously makes them imperfect replicas of their originals. Now that formal linguistic studies have moved a little away from their former preoccupation with syntax and phonology, the semantic and pragmatic dimensions of human communication have assumed greater importance. In particular prosodic features are now regarded as much more important, both as signs with semantic significance and as instruments of domination and resistance. As a result, the information content of prosody, coupled where possible and necessary with the non-verbal language of gestures, laughter, and other body language, now figures much more prominently in the analysis of texts than was the case a decade ago. At the same time, it is still important to keep distracting symbols to a minimum in transcripts, depending on the sorts of research questions being asked.

Interviews with interactants after the analysis of their discourse, help confirm that their interpretations of what was said are consistent with the researcher's interpretations. This view is supported not just by discourse analysts themselves (Potter & Wetherell 1987) but also by the very course that the philosophy of the social sciences has been taking in the last decade. As mentioned already, researchers must make allowances in their methods and their theorizing for the distinctly human capacity for second-order monitoring. This capacity enables people to reflect on their discourse and render an interpretation of those practices in a new account which has priority as evidence over other accounts that may be offered by a researcher who is unable to perform that monitoring (Hughes 1990).

'Ideology' does not appear as an explicitly discussed concept in either of Gronn's studies. In Hargreaves' study there is a reference to those 'psychiatric ideologies' used by practitioners in medicine, which are protective of professional occupational identities in psychiatry, in much the same way as his teachers' 'contrastive rhetoric' consolidates their own views of themselves as professionals. Although Hargreaves gives only this limited attention to ideology, his study is much concerned with ideological practices: things like symbolization, distorted communication, the use of stereotypes, inexplicit messages etc.

Nicholas Burbules (1986) describes the characteristic features that ideologies bring together: "they are ambiguous and elliptical enough to allow a fairly wide range of interpretation and so are resistant to falsification; they combine descriptive and evaluative effects by using highly emotive and connotative terms; and they are attractive because they help persons make sense of the social world and their place in it. Ideologies explain, reassure and motivate" (p. 106). A key observation to make about ideologies, is that it is often wrong to believe that the best way to confront them is by simply opposing their falsehoods and distortions with facts. What ideology critique involves is a questioning of unspoken assumptions, vagueness, rhetoric, misrepresentation, and half-truths. It is also important to ask the question 'who benefits?'.

Combining prosody, ideology, and follow-up interviews, David Corson (1993b) examines discursive bias and ideology in the administration of minority group interests. Like Ruth Wodak (1995), he studies a formal school meeting and suggests how easily distorted communication can arise in formal administrative discourse when the interests of those with some stake are not represented among participants in the discourse. Using three episodes of discourse, the study generalizes, from the unjust use of discursive power in the treatment of one cultural out-group, to other culturally different minorities whose views and interests are not often represented among administrators and policy makers in education. He recommends how discursive power could be exercised more fairly and more generally, along lines recommended earlier in this chapter.

Very relevant to the interests of researchers in educational administration, Viviane Robinson (1995) considers the problems of identifying and evaluating power in discourse. She argues the need for a normatively neutral theory of power for use in studies on the exercise and evaluation of power in administrative discourse. She also critiques the practices of discourse analysts who make normative judgments about the negative or oppressive use of power in texts. Using an administrative case study, she examines the usefulness of her normative theory of power for evaluating actual staff interaction in a school meeting.

Communicative Action in School Policies, Communities, and Classrooms

Policies adopted across an educational system ideally begin with principles as norms for use at system level; they elaborate on the ways in which these principles can be related to one another; and they lay out what makes different principles appropriate to different situation types. Having done all this, good system-level policies devolve as much policy decision making and power as possible to schools themselves so that fair compromises can be reached appropriate to local contexts and consistent with the original normative principles.

There are clear reasons why the devolution of decision making down to local levels is important in specific areas of policy making: Firstly, devolution is needed to establish sub-norms for determining local compatibility between interest groups, whose views may not be well represented at whole system level because of the degree of pluralism that most political systems contain. Secondly devolution is needed to agree on any necessary compromises, should genuine incompatibility exist. For example, incompatibility will arise when the values of cultural or religious minorities support pluralist versions of 'the good life' that are very different from the norm. A just form of policy action does not need a conception of what *the* just society would be. Rather, it requires as many conceptions of justice as there are distinct possible conditions of society or subsets of society or culture.

Thirdly, devolution is often the only practical way to focus attention on the outcomes of any implemented process of change. Only rarely do the utopian intentions that lie behind complex centralised policies, marry up with the final outcomes of their implementation (Corson, 1986b). In recommending that more attention be given to the likely results of reforms, Cleo Cherryholmes (1995) links pragmatism with the limits of modernity and its impact on educational change. After critiquing a review by Michael Fullan of hundreds of studies of planned educational change, he finds that the methodology of many of the change efforts displays key weaknesses reflecting these limits of modernity. He advances pragmatism, in its classical form, as a remedy for the modernist assumptions and social practices of conventional reform processes in education. A pragmatic approach to change focuses attention wholistically on likely outcomes.

Local schools, collaboratively managed through critical policies that are continually revised using the best available discursive evidence about changing circumstances (Corson, 1990), are more likely to be places of staff and community commitment. This is because community and staff participation has to be deliberately sought in order to get at that evidence. But participation is an end in itself as well as a device for producing other ends. When people come together to plan something, there is obvious value to them in the feedback, skill development, social interaction, and knowledge growth that they receive. More than this, participation usually fosters a commitment in people to the results or product of their participation, as they position themselves in relation to new and creative discourses, provided those results seem reasonable to them. This form of critical policy making can have rewards for a school at several levels.

For example, using democratic and relational management practices, schools tend to escape the trap of having their procedures and styles of operation modelled only on dominant and often outdated points of view. By implementing genuine collaborative management, involving staff, parents, and community, schools limit the degree to which the wider system of education can constrain social action within them. In other words, collaborative management lessens the extent to which wider social formations, like the relationships that exist between schools, the economy, and the state, create the ideological framework that constrains discourses of reform and initiative within them. Those same external and constraining relationships can be challenged by school policy makers to advance the interests of the school and its community. When challenged in this way, unjust social formations themselves can often be transformed and their undesirable impact elsewhere may also be lessened. At the same time by lending approval and support, schools can reinforce worthwhile and desirable values in wider social formations.

There is evidence to support claims of this kind. For example, it has been found that active parent-involvement in decision making can bring children from minority culture or class groups closer to their teachers, who often come from the dominant class and culture. Also parents themselves grow in confidence and develop a sense of their own efficacy which impacts positively on student learning; and harmful teacher stereotypes about pupils fall away, as teachers begin to collaborate with parents (Comer, 1984; Cummins 1986; Garcia & Otheguy, 1987; Greenberg 1989; Haynes, Comer & Hamilton Lee, 1989; May, 1994; Rasinski & Fredericks, 1989). In the eyes of the public, autonomous schools run through parent participation are also more 'legitimate' places. Open parent participation prevents powerful participants from abusing their superior bargaining power, if everyone, as far as possible, is asked to propose and defend arrangements that they sincerely believe ought to be acceptable to everyone affected. For some purposes, parent participants think of themselves as representatives of groups in the wider society, although not if this means excluding the real representatives of minorities or other social groups. Very often these groups will have views and interests that are systematically different. Not only will they have interests that others do not understand, but often too interests that others cannot understand.

As an example of this point, Jan Branson and Don Miller (1995) discuss sign language and the discursive construction of power over the Deaf through education. They argue that the discourse on sign language in education is vital to the assertion of symbolic power by the hearing establishment over the Deaf community. Using case studies of policies for the Deaf from Western countries, they show the educational and political processes at work, as individual Deaf communities, with their own distinct native sign languages, confront the ideology that education can only proceed through the dominant language and the accredited modes of the hearing. Deaf communities are increasingly seizing the emancipatory opportunities of managing schools for themselves, making them more organic to the culture of local Deaf communities.

A look at the history of modern schooling helps explain some of the discursive limitations of conventional schools and classrooms. The concentration on control and passive student activities in classrooms, reflects the ethos of control that is still an outstanding feature of most school organizations. In this respect, modern schools have not changed very much in their general aim since their inception, in the middle of the nineteenth century. The political architects of modern universal schooling were contemporaries of the political architects of modern prisons, asylums for the insane, and hospitals for the diseased poor. It is no accident that all four types of institution use the word 'superintendent' to describe their executive officers, and operate through hierarchical and controlling structures. In education, beginning in English-speaking countries in the decades around the Taunton Report in Britain (1864-1868), these policy architects were acting in direct response to fears about what many children would otherwise become if attempts were not made to control their socialization through compulsory schooling.

These architects had before them recent memories of the democratic revolutions across Europe and North America in 1848 and earlier, and they were mindful of the bitter and costly contemporary uprisings of culturally and linguistically different subject peoples in defence of their cultural and language rights. They were anxious to avoid any extension of similar experiences. So they saw schooling for the masses as a way of initiating their own lower orders into the technologies, meaning systems, and values of the mainstream culture, and as a way of assimilating and taming the culturally and linguistically different. These architects saw schooling as a way of making children 'better': as a way of 'civilizing' them in line with the canons for civilized Man that the architects themselves, or people very like them, had established.

Structurally schools remain very much in this mould. Often in spite of teachers' best efforts, classrooms tend to reflect the controlling structures of the wider institution. These structures in their turn, often reflect wider discourses of repression that persevere in modern states, as many theorists contend. Jim Cummins (1995) discusses the role of wider social formations in shaping bilingual policies for minority language users. After reviewing the present policy norms for speakers of minority languages in English-speaking countries, he locates those norms within wider discourses of economic and political oppression in capitalist nation states, especially the "competing and conflicting discourses blown in by the winds of changing political fashion" in the United States. While suggesting how those policies work to constrain socially just reforms at national, regional, school, and classroom levels, he makes clear recommendations for reform. These range across matters of cultural/linguistic incorporation, community participation, critical pedagogy, and sensitive assessment policies.

Looking more directly at the impact of these policies on classrooms, Alan Luke, Joan Kale, and Michael Garbutcheon Singh (1995) show how these wider structures of power impact on culturally different children in classrooms, right from their earliest years of schooling. They use critical discourse analysis to examine a key element of early schooling for many culturally different children: how literacy instruction makes available particular discourses for talking and thinking about cultural identity. Their study describes an array of spoken and written texts generated by students, teachers, and textbooks that position and construct children and their culture in ways that mark out cultural difference at the same time as they silence it.

Many teacher interaction styles that are compatible with the values and discursive practices of culturally different children, are also relevant to interactions with girls and young women in general (Corson 1993). Female discursive norms are often different from male norms. Because females tend to place high value on strengthening affiliative links between people, their discursive norms seem to be different in broadly the same directions as are the discursive interests of many ancestral minority peoples. Indeed it would seem that dominant male norms of interaction are really the 'marked' variety in spite of their dominance: they constitute a norm which most people would not prefer if allowed the choice. Perhaps the real interests of boys and men would also be served by changes in teacher-pupil interaction practices to eliminate imbalances in the use of power, such as the following: the unrestrained use of the imperative; the use of the (absolute) right to speak last; the use of the (absolute) right to contradict; the use of the (absolute) right to define the world for others; the use of the (absolute) right to interrupt or to censure; the use of the (absolute) right to praise or blame in public. These negative discursive practices are deeply ingrained habits that many teachers consider to be part of the very stuff of teaching. I believe that this is a teacher ideology that would not withstand critical inspection and challenge.

Jill Blackmore and Jane Kenway (1995) offer a poststructuralist account of gender regimes and organizational culture in schools. They argue for the importance of considering gender dynamics as part of organizational culture, and examine elements of the gender regime of schools and the position of teachers and students in that regime, concluding with policy recommendations for reform that would impact on curriculum and pedagogy, challenging many harmful and taken-for-granted ideologies. There are many positive steps that can be taken. Michelle Stanworth (1983) recommends that teachers give higher priority to reshaping the sexual distribution of interaction in classrooms: by singling girls out for more recognition; by remembering their names, and using them; by creating a comfortable and non-threatening environment for interaction (by sitting down in a child's desk to address the class, for example; or relaxing the posture). Girls themselves, of course, are often adept at finding ways of resisting unjust discursive practices in classrooms and schools. Öhrn (1993) describes girls' patterns of resistance in Scandinavian schools, which vary by social class as well as by gender. Typically girls are more oriented towards personal relations, while boys fit more readily into activities and hierarchical structures that can make girls feels powerless and which girls have to counter by imposing a personal component on situations.

As part of a growing movement of critical linguists, Norman Fairclough (1995) sees the capacity for critique of language as a prerequisite for effective democratic citizenship. He describes two elements of an approach to the general societal problematic of language and power:

The first involves the overdue development of a critical tradition within language studies; the second is the application of this critical theory and method in developing critical language awareness work in schools and in other educational settings. He offers examples of critical language awareness at work in schools. But if critical language awareness is to find a place in classrooms, teachers will have to reduce their heavy reliance on several favoured approaches to teaching.

One major 'pedagogy of disempowerment' spans and affects the entire process of education. The conventional classroom questioning technique of the 'initiation – response – feedback' cycle (IRF) is the basis of most teaching acts. Robert Young (1995) begins with a critique of the relevance of poststructuralist/postmodernist theorizing to practice and reform. He examines the ideology-producing processes of classrooms, especially that universal cornerstone of traditional pedagogy: the IRF cycle. His study of the IRF cycle shows that the possibility of rational responses by students to the validity claims in teachers' questions, is actually excluded in principle. Typical patterns support a form of strategic action by teachers, appropriately labelled 'instructional action', rather than the 'educational action' necessary for learning aimed at the learner's eventual autonomy. Students are seduced or indoctrinated, not educated. Young offers some possibilities for reform.

Stanton Wortham (1995) discusses another widespread and taken-for-granted pedagogy: 'experience-near examples'. These objects or events from a student's own experience are introduced into lessons to illuminate curriculum content. From his data, Wortham argues that the superficiality of many experience-near examples reflects larger historical ways of thinking and speaking to do with the peculiar character of products and social relations in capitalist society. Rather than creating pedagogical moments that are productive, this commodification of classroom discourse may be leading schools to produce passive, not critically reflective students.

CONCLUSION

Several of the references, towards the end of this review of the literature, from Stanton Wortham, Bob Young, and Alan Luke and his colleagues, trace the impact of wider processes and structures operating through classroom discourses and onto the subjectivities of children. They focus discussion on the *function* of educational organizations, as distinct from their *purpose*. In other words, they address the way that modern schooling typically positions children so that they are prepared for uncritical admission into hierarchical sociocultural conditions discursively constructed well in advance of that admission. Rather than preparing children for 'initiation into a worthwhile form of life', schools offer them filtered immersion in the discursive practices in which schools themselves are positioned; they reflect onto children a sanitized version of the social formations that surround them; and by doing all this, they represent *sectional* sociocultural, political, and economic interests to children as though they were *universal*.

In the face of such a dire, disturbing, and uncomfortable description, this chapter is very short on solutions, since the real work has only just begun. The social sciences in general is only beginning to stumble onto this problem, helped now by the discursive turn, mentioned in the opening paragraphs of this chapter, and by the obsolescence of what this new initiative replaces. In this chapter, I have tried to raise and focus aspects of the problem in challenging and direct ways. Although the chapter presents a disconnected narrative, it does suggest strongly that wider discursive structures and processes filter into school organizations, and then into classrooms to recreate four things: ideology-producing classroom processes; instructional rather than educational action; a commodification of classroom discourse; and a reproduction of unjust sociocultural arrangements. In all this, there are obvious winners and losers, as my discussion illustrates. The fact that the losers are almost always the same people who start out from behind, is a startling indictment of the institution of education itself, and of its management in the broadest sense.

As part of its purpose, this chapter tries to show how links can be made between the researcher's interests and the interests of practitioners. The ideas found in many of the references suggest that we need a new research and policy agenda. It must be an agenda that involves practitioners and researchers as co-participants at every point. It must encourage students of education to reflect critically on the good practices of critical practitioners, and then use evidence of those good practices not as data to be copied, but as insights to be learned from. Above all, it must attempt to trace the seamless links between the discourses of wider social formations, the discourses of educational policy and administration, and the discourses of classrooms.

What we need are more wideranging critical ethnographies like Stephen May's study of Richmond Road School (1994). We also need more conventional ethnographies comparing community and school discursive practices, like Shirley Heath's *Ways With Words* (1983). But following the discursive turn, future ethnographies need to be broadened so as to connect political, economic, and organizational discourses with the discourses of home, community, and classroom since it is the former that often position the latter, creating 'mind' in the process. We also need critical discourse analyses that try to improve on those reviewed here. Mixed with the ever-present need for high quality studies, is the demand that research look outward in every direction, since discursive practices permeate every 'closed' context and every 'closed' system.

The postmodern condition that we now find ourselves in, is emancipatory in one respect above all others: It reveals a world where orthodoxies, ideologies, disciplinary boundaries, and closed contexts exist only in the minds of those positioned by them. Awareness of this fact allows us to begin to 'reclaim reality' at last. Freed by this knowledge, researchers can begin to enlarge their aims and scope considerably. Future emancipatory studies in educational administration will link the administration of schools with wider social processes and policies, but also with what really happens in classrooms and communities. There is much to be done, but the discursive turn in the social sciences is at last pointing us in genuinely emancipatory directions.

REFERENCES

Bhaskar, Roy (1986). *Scientific Realism and Human Emancipation*. Verso: London.

Bhaskar, Roy (1989). *Reclaiming Reality: A Critical Introduction to Contemporary Philosophy*. Verso: London.

Blackmore, Jill & Kenway, Jane (1995) Changing schools, teachers and curriculum: but what about the girls? Theorising change and feminist post- structuralism. In D. Corson (Ed.) *Discourse and Power in Educational Organizations*. Hampton Press, Cresskill, NJ/OISE Press, Toronto, 233-256.

Blumberg, Arthur & Amidon, Edmund (1965) Teacher perceptions of supervisor-teacher interaction. *Administrator's Notebook*. 14: 1-4.

Blumberg, Arthur & Cusick, Philip (1971) Supervisor-teacher interaction: an analysis of verbal behaviour. *Education*. 91: 126-134.

Branson, Jan & Miller, Don (1995) Sign language and the discursive construction of power over the deaf through education. In D. Corson (Ed.) *Discourse and Power in Educational Organizations*. Hampton Press, Cresskill, NJ/OISE Press, Toronto, 167-190.

Bruner, J.S. (1973) *Beyond the Information Given: Studies in the Psychology of Knowing*. New York: Norton.

Bruner, J.S. (1990) *Acts of Meaning*. Cambridge, Mass: Harvard University Press.

Burbules, Nicholas C. (1992) Forms of ideology critique: a pedagogical perspective. *International Journal of Qualitative Studies in Education*. 3: 7-17.

Cherryholmes, Cleo H. (1995) Pragmatism, modernity and educational change. In D. Corson (Ed.) *Discourse and Power in Educational Organizations*. Hampton Press, Cresskill, NJ/OISE Press, Toronto, 149-166.

Comer, J. P. (1984) Home/school relationships as they affect the academic success of children. *Education and Urban Society* 16: 323-337.

Corson, David (1986a). Primitive semantic notions about hierarchy: implications for educational organizations and educational knowledge. *Journal of Educational Administration*. 24: 173-186.

Corson, D. (1986b) Policy in social context: a collapse of holistic planning in education. *Journal of Education Policy* 1: 5-22.

Corson, D. (1990) *Language Policy Across the Curriculum*. Clevedon, Avon: Multilingual Matters

Corson, David (1991a) Bhaskar's critical realism and educational knowledge. *British Journal of Sociology of Education*. 12: 223-241.

Corson, David (1991b) Educational research and Bhaskar's conception of discovery. *Educational Theory*. 41: 189-198.

Corson, David (1993a). *Language, Minority Education and Gender: Linking Social Justice and Power*. Clevedon, Avon: Multilingual Matters/Toronto: OISE Press.

Corson, David (1993b) Discursive bias and ideology in the administration of minority group interests. *Language in Society* 22: 165-191.

Corson, David (Ed.) (1995a) *Discourse and Power in Educational Organizations*. Hampton Press, Cresskill, NJ/OISE Press, Toronto.

Corson, David (1995b) *Using English Words*. Kluwer: Boston.

Cummins, Jim (1986) Empowering minority students: a framework for intervention. *Harvard Educational Review*. 56: 18-36.

Cummins, Jim (1995) Discursive power in educational policy and practice for culturally diverse students. In D. Corson (Ed.) *Discourse and Power in Educational Organizations*. Hampton Press, Cresskill, NJ/OISE Press, Toronto, 191-210.

Fairclough, Norman (1995) Critical language awareness and self-identity in education. In D. Corson (Ed.) *Discourse and Power in Educational Organizations*. Hampton Press, Cresskill, NJ/OISE Press, Toronto, 257-272.

Garcia, O. and Otheguy, R. (1987) The bilingual education of Cuban-American children in Dade County's ethnic schools. *Language and Education* 1: 83-95.

Giddens, Anthony (1979). *Central Problems in Social Theory*. Berkeley: University of California Press.

Gramsci, Antonio. (1948) *Opere di Antonio Gramsci (Quaderni Del Carcere)* Turin: Einaudi.

Greenberg, P. (1989) Parents as partners in young children's development and education: a new American fad? why does it matter? *Young Children* 44: 61-75.

Gronn, P. C. (1983). Talk as the work: the accomplishment of school administration. *Administrative Science Quarterly* 28: 1-21.

Gronn, P. C. (1984). 'I have a solution...': administrative power in a school meeting. *Educational Administration Quarterly* 20: 65-92.

Hargreaves, A. (1981). Contrastive rhetoric and extremist talk. In A. Hargreaves & P. Woods (Eds) *Classrooms and Staffrooms: The Sociology of Teachers & Teaching*. London: Open University Press.

Harré, R. & Gillett, G. (1994) *The Discursive Mind*. Thousand Oaks, California: Sage.

Haynes, N. M., Comer, J. P. & Hamilton-Lee, M. (1989) School climate enhancement through parental involvement. *Journal of School Psychology* 27: 87-90.

Hughes, John (1990). *The Philosophy of Social Research*. London: Longmans.

Johnson, Cathryn (1994) Gender, legitimate authority, and leader-subordinate relations. *American Journal of Sociology*. 59: 122-135.

Kanpol, Barry (1988) Teacher work tasks as forms of resistance and accommodation to structural factors of schooling. *Urban Education*. 23: 173-187.

Kanpol, Barry (1991) Teacher group formation as emancipatory critique: necessary conditions for teacher resistance. *The Journal of Educational Thought*. 25: 134-149.

Luke, Alan, Kale, Joan & Garbutcheon Singh, Michael (1995) Talking difference: discourses on aboriginal identity in grade one classrooms. In D. Corson (Ed.) *Discourse and Power in Educational Organizations*. Hampton Press, Cresskill, NJ/ OISE Press, Toronto, 211-232.

May, Stephen (1994) *Making Multicultural Education Work*. Clevedon, Avon: Multilingual Matters/Toronto: OISE Press.

O'Barr, W. (1982) *Linguistic Evidence: Language, Power and Strategy in the Courtroom*. Academic Press: New York.

Öhrn, Elisabet (1993) Gender, influence and resistance in school. *British Journal of Sociology of Education*. 14: 147-158.

Potter, M. & Wetherell, M. (1987) *Discourse and Social Psychology*. London: Longman.

Rasinski, T. V. & Fredericks, A. D. (1989) Dimensions of parent involvement. *Reading Teacher* 43: 180-182.

Roberts Blase, Jo (1992) Face threatening acts and politeness theory: contrasting speeches from supervisory conferences. *Journal of Curriculum and Supervision*. 7: 287-301.

Roberts Blase, Jo (1994) Discourse analysis of supervisory conferences: an exploration. *Journal of Curriculum and Supervision*. 9: 136-154.

Roberts Blase, Jo & Blase, Joseph (1995) The micropolitics of successful supervisor-teacher interaction in instructional conferences. In D. Corson (Ed.) *Discourse and Power in Educational Organizations*. Hampton Press, Cresskill, NJ/OISE Press, Toronto, 55-70.

Robinson, Viviane (1995) The identification and evaluation of power in discourse. In D. Corson (Ed.) *Discourse and Power in Educational Organizations*. Hampton Press, Cresskill, NJ/OISE Press, Toronto, 111-132.

Shakeshaft, Charol. (1989) *Women in Educational Administration*. Newbury Park, Cal.: Corwin Press.

Shakeshaft, Charol & Perry, Andy (1995) The language of power vs the language of empowerment: gender differences in administrative communication. In D. Corson (Ed.) *Discourse and Power in Educational Organizations*. Hampton Press, Cresskill, NJ/OISE Press, Toronto, 17-30.

Stanworth, Michelle (1983) *Gender and Schooling: A Study of Sexual Divisions in the Classroom*. Hutchinson: London.

Thompson, John (1984). *Studies in the Theory of Ideology*. Cambridge: Polity Press.

Waite, Duncan (1992) Supervisor's talk: making sense of conferences from an anthropological linguistic perspective. *Journal of Curriculum and Supervision*. 7: 349-371.

Waite, Duncan (1995) Teacher resistance in a supervision conference. In D. Corson (Ed.) *Discourse and Power in Educational Organizations*. Hampton Press, Cresskill, NJ/OISE Press, Toronto, 71-86.

Wodak, Ruth (1995) Power, discourse, and styles of female leadership in school committee meetings. In D. Corson (Ed.) *Discourse and Power in Educational Organizations*. Hampton Press, Cresskill, NJ/OISE Press, Toronto, 31-54.

Wortham, Stanton (1995) Experience-near classroom examples as commodities. In D. Corson (Ed.) *Discourse and Power in Educational Organizations*. Hampton Press, Cresskill, NJ/OISE Press, Toronto, 283-300.

Young, Robert E. (1992) *Critical Theory and Classroom Talk*. Multilingual Matters: Clevedon, Avon.

Young, Robert E. (1995) Dancing, seducing or loving. In D. Corson (Ed.) *Discourse and Power in Educational Organizations*. Hampton Press, Cresskill, NJ/OISE Press, Toronto, 273-282.

Zeichner, Kenneth M. & Liston, Dan (1985) Varieties of discourse in supervisory conferences. Teaching and Teacher Education. 1: 155–174

Chapter 30: Critical Theory and the Social Psychology of Change

VIVIANE M.J. ROBINSON
University of Auckland

The purpose of this chapter is to evaluate the adequacy of the theory of change that is embedded within critical theory, by examining both the record of its practical achievements and the conceptual resources it provides. Both evaluative criteria are required, since there are reasons for practical failure which have no bearing on theoretical adequacy. For example, if the conditions specified by the theory as necessary for change are not present, the correct conclusion is that the theory has not been tested, not that it has failed. Some critical theorists make this point when they argue that schools are so constrained by economic and political forces that they are inappropriate sites for the type of transformative effort prescribed by critical theory (Burbules 1986). If, however, one can attribute practical failure to inadequacies in the conceptual resources provided by the theory, then the criticism is all the more telling, because it implies that change would not occur under the conditions specified by the theory, even if they were present.

The position taken in this chapter is that weaknesses in the theory of change embedded within critical theory have seriously limited its transformative achievements in education. Those weaknesses can be broadly described as a mismatch between critical theory and the social psychology of change. The mismatch includes both the way the target of change is formulated and the conceptualization of the change process itself. The methodology employed to defend this argument will not be that of the typical literature review, for despite their passionate espousal of change, few critical theorists in education, with the notable exception of Freire and his colleagues, (Freire, 1985; Shor & Freire, 1987; Torres, 1992), have conducted, or at least published, a change project. I develop the argument, firstly, by summarizing various critical theorists' expositions of change. Secondly, I construct an analysis of the target of change using the frequently criticized practice of streaming (known as 'tracking' in North America) as a practical example. The analysis employs Nickles's (1981; 1988) constraint inclusion account of problems to show their generic features and the implications of

K. Leithwood et al. (eds.), International Handbook of Educational Leadership and Administration, 1069-1096.
© *1996 Kluwer Academic Publishers, Printed in the Netherlands.*

those features for educational change. Thirdly, I embed this problem-solving process in a dialogical framework, having argued that that provided by such social psychologists as Chris Argyris is to be preferred to that of Habermas. Finally, I show how social psychological research on the impact of problem size and on the resolution of social dilemmas confirms the utility of incorporating a more problem-oriented approach to change within critical theory.

CRITICAL THEORY AS A THEORY OF CHANGE

Critical theory incorporates both a theory of change and an account of the purposes to which change should be directed, namely the promotion of social arrangements which enable actors to collectively determine what constitutes their enlightened self interest and how it may be attained (Fay 1987, ch. 4). Commitment to these purposes alerts educational leaders to the ways in which learning institutions may, through their governance, curriculum, assessment and disciplinary systems, serve the interests of some groups better than others, while at the same time denying those who are disadvantaged the opportunity to reshape those same systems. Critical theory requires that the reform of such institutional arrangements is not undertaken by leaders on behalf of their constituents, but rather that it be undertaken as a collaborative project with those who suffer under the existing arrangements. Critical theory, in other words, requires that the change process itself, as well as its eventual result, serve the emancipatory values of the theory.

Several major writers on critical theory agree on the broad parameters of the change process (Comstock 1982; Fay 1987, ch.2; Geuss 1981, ch.3; Young 1989, p. 41). Comstock summarizes what is involved as follows:

> Critical social research begins from the life problems of definite and particular social agents who may be individuals, groups, or classes that are oppressed by and alienated from social processes they maintain or create but do not control. Beginning from the practical problems of everyday existence it returns to that life with the aim of enlightening its subjects about unrecognized social constraints and possible courses of action by which they may liberate themselves. Its aim is enlightened self-knowledge and effective political action. Its method is dialogue, and its effect is to heighten its subjects'

      self-awareness of their collective potential as the active agents
      of history. (p. 382)

The starting point of a critical project is the frustration or unhappiness
of a group of people and an analysis of their suffering in terms of the
conditions, including their self understandings, which maintain their
unhappiness. This analysis phase is followed by a period of education
(ideology critique) in which false understandings are replaced by alternatives which better serve the real interests of those addressed by the
critical theory. Ideology is seen to be operating when minority students, for example, explain their own educational failure in terms of a
deficit theory which better serves the interests of official agencies than
their own. The role of ideology is exposed by demonstrating either how
insider understandings are incompatible with relevant evidence, or how
they lead actors to behave against their own interests, or how they were
adopted for reasons that, if known, would be unacceptable to the actors
themselves (Geuss 1981, p. 12-22).

    The educative phase of the change process continues with debate
about the accuracy of the critical theorist's analysis, and about the
desirability of alternative understandings and actions. In the process,
the audience may accept the analysis, alter their understandings, and
plan to act to change the conditions which are, at least in part, causally
involved in their unhappiness. According to Comstock (1982), the
model of education which is appropriate to this process:

      is not the familiar one of formal schooling but, rather, a model
      of dialogue in which the critical researcher attempts to either
      problematize certain meanings, motives or values accepted by
      his or her subjects or to respond to issues which are already
      perceived by them as problematic. (p. 385)

The educative phase of a critical project is followed by a social action
phase, in which participants collaborate to redress the problems that
were the subject of the analysis. Critical research is not idealist, for it
recognizes that changed understandings do not in themselves change
material circumstances; action and ideas are interdependent in the
process of understanding and changing the world (Fay 1987, pp. 24-
25).

    More needs to be said about the last phase of transformative action if
we are to correctly understand the contribution of critical research in
education. Although the basic structure of a critical theory incorporates

a distinction between the phases of education and social action, the process of critical analysis can itself be construed as a type of social action for it may shift taken for granted assumptions about the nature and desirability of the educational activities in which one is engaged. The tendency to interpret critical theory's call for social action as a call for new meanings and new language is seen in some recent writing on educational leaders as agents of transformation. Foster (1994), building on the account of Brian Fay (1987), interprets the change mandate of critical theory as requiring the creation of new 'narratives' which better embody the values of a critical theory.

> For the administrative leader this presents a challenge. It means not only the raising of consciousness, but the establishment of a new narrative order in a school... A narrative order means that one's experience in an institution forms a coherent whole rather than an interrupted series of largely disconnected events. There is, in other words, a narrative or story that expounds on the meaningfulness of the schooling experience. This living history puts the administrative act into context; administration can be shown to have a beginning and an end. When the experiences of successful teachers and administrators are captured in books or film, it is the narrative quality of their experiences that helps us to resonate with them and to understand their struggle.(p. 48)

How does the call for 'new narratives' fit critical theory's approach to change? Foster needs to specify at least in broad outline, the origins of the vision, the reasons why the community should find it attractive, and the steps needed to attain it. What are the limits that need to be overcome and the possibilities of success? Critical theorists who fail to address these questions are being idealist; that is acting as if shifts in meaning and language are all that is required to achieve change. This is not to say that, in some cases, such shifts are not profoundly important. It is unlikely, however, given the deep seated nature of change advocated by most critical researchers, that shifts in language and ideas will prove sufficient to transform educational institutions in the ways advocated.

CRITICAL THEORY AND THE ACHIEVEMENT OF CHANGE

Given the practical commitment of critical theory, it is appropriate to ask about its contribution to the resolution of the problems it addresses. A review of critical research projects reveals that many critical research projects in education stop short of the social action which is supposed to be one of the hallmarks of this approach. The critically informed empirical literature in education shows that with the exception of the work of Ira Shor and Paul Freire and his colleagues, most critical researchers do not carry their critique through to a stage of education and social action. Unless substantial numbers of intervention efforts are going unreported, few critical researchers in education are conducting their research as a change process.

This criticism is applicable across two types of critical research in education (Anderson 1989, p. 262; Young 1989). The first type of such research, according to Burbules (1986), involved the analysis of schooling as a process of social reproduction, in which schools were seen to reproduce a class based labour market and economy through differential provision for and treatment of children from different social classes (Bourdieu & Passeron, 1988; Bowles & Gintis, 1976).

The subsequent second type of critical research in education challenged the portrayal of teachers and students as passive victims of wider economic forces by attempting to show how these forces could be resisted, or even transformed, by the active participation of teachers and students in the creation of schools and their cultures (Anyon 1980, 1981; Willis 1977). By highlighting the relative autonomy of classroom cultures from economic forces, this type of research seemed to offer critical researchers and educators more hope of achieving some of their school-based reform agenda. Despite this theoretical difference, similar criticisms have been levelled at these less deterministic versions of critical research. Very little such research has been able to move beyond critique to the more difficult process of laying the theoretical basis for transformative modes of practice, let alone to initiating such practice (Anderson 1989, p. 262; Aronowitz & Giroux 1985, p. 154). Has the transformative as opposed to the critical potential of critical inquiry been overplayed?

There is a major difficulty with providing a definitive answer to the question, for until more critical researchers incorporate a change process into their projects we will have insufficient evidence from which to evaluate the change potential of the theory. In the meantime, I suggest it is worth exploring the possibility that the practical promise of critical theory is jeopardized by certain counterproductive features of the theory itself.

CRITICAL THEORY AND PROBLEM RESOLUTION

My argument, which will be illustrated with reference to research on streaming, (known in North America as 'tracking'), is that aspects of critical theory are mismatched to the generic features of practical problems and to the social psychology of change. Professor Jeannie Oakes, one of the leading North American researchers on tracking, defines it as a sorting process 'whereby students are divided into categories so that they can be assigned in groups to various kinds of classes' (Oakes 1985, p. 3). Critical researchers problematize the practice, as does Jeannie Oakes, because their normative theory alerts them to the way it violates values of equal opportunity and social justice. Students from the most disadvantaged groups are further handicapped by being located in tracks which typically receive the poorest curricular and pedagogical resources. Despite describing the research on tracking as mostly of good quality and remarkably consistent in its findings, Oakes (1992) suggests it has as yet little to offer the growing number of practitioners and policy-makers who are interested in alternatives to tracking. She writes:

> Reform-minded policy-makers and practitioners have responded to this work with hard, but reasonable, questions about what alternatives might ameliorate tracking-related problems, and at the same time be compatible with other efforts to increase the quality of schools. They want to know what good 'detracked' schools look like and what strategies might foster such schools.

> Researchers have few answers. We have learned much about the complex and problematic nature of tracking, but little about promising alternatives or how they might be implemented. We have not addressed the effects that altering this school structure has on students, school faculties or parents and communities. (p. 12).

Why is it that a body of research that is of clear relevance and high quality, and that has attracted the attention of decision-makers, has so little to offer? One way of answering the question involves examining the difference between the problems pursued by tracking researchers and the problems pursued by practitioners. Tracking researchers have asked four different types of question: 'What are the social correlates of membership in particular tracks?' 'What factors influence track placement?' 'What are the effects of various track assignments on students' school and classroom experience?' 'What are the consequences of being in a particular track, for academic achievement, attitudes, peer relations and life chances?' Practitioners, in contrast, focus on the quite different problem of how to organize students of varying interest and abilities in ways that they believe to be educationally efficient and effective. Their problem is a practical one about what to do (Gauthier 1963); the researchers' questions are about what is the case. Tracking is the practitioners' solution to their practical problem, and while they may acknowledge that that solution has some or all of the unintended consequences that researchers have identified, they will not abandon it until they have another which satisfies the practical, normative and political constraints which they perceive to be relevant.

In short, the limited contribution of tracking research is due, in part, to the fact that it studies the practice in isolation from the problem-solving processes that gave rise to it. Casual accounts which bypass those process will not capture the ways in which policy-makers and practitioners believe they are impelled to continue a practice they judge as less than ideal; critique that does not explicitly recognize all the conditions which practitioners believe to be relevant, will be judged as simplistic and unfair.

If research is to make an impact on practice, we need to understand and engage the beliefs, values and implicit theories that inform the way policy-makers and practitioners solve their practical problems. This requires a research methodology, as I argue in the subsequent section, that incorporates a theory of problems and of how they are solved.

THE NATURE OF PRACTICAL PROBLEMS

If we understand the generic features of practical problems like student allocation, we are in a better position to understand what is involved in solving them, and, therefore, in re-solving them when we reject the solutions that are already in place. The constraint inclusion account of problems developed by the philosopher of science Thomas Nickles (1981; 1988), provides a theory of problems and of how they are solved that helps one to understand the limits of critical theory as an approach to change. Thomas Nickles, defines a problem as 'all the conditions or constraints on the solution (variously weighted) plus the demand that the solution (an object satisfying the constraints be found' (1988, p. 54). Constraints are conditions which must be satisfied, or at least partially so, by solution candidates. They may comprise values, goals, or practical limits on resources such as time, money or skill. Constraints should not be construed simply as external barriers or obstacles to acting as one would otherwise wish. This common sense understanding of a 'constraint', differs from Nickles's approach in two significant ways. First, constraints in Nickles's sense, are simply solution requirements, whether those requirements are set by problem solvers themselves, or are, in some sense, externally imposed. Second, constraints, as solution requirements, both rule in and rule out solution candidates. The requirement that any solution to the problem of student allocation satisfy the constraint of pedagogical effectiveness, for example, might rule in streaming for math and rule it out for English teaching.

A problem is solved by finding strategies that satisfy the whole constraint set. Dewey (1992, p. 194) calls the process one of imaginative deliberation, in which the problem solver tests informal hypotheses about how the constraint set can be integrated. Such integration will involve tradeoffs between the various constraints, and there will, of course, be debate about the adequacy of both the specification of the constraint set, and of its integration.

Nickles makes clear that constraints are not external factors operating upon the problem, but the very constituents of the problem. Without constraint specification problems are unsolvable. For example, an educational leader can not resolve the problem of writing a curriculum plan until constraints are set which specify what counts as an adequate plan. Adequacy could be defined by a set level of expenditure, compatibility with the school's philosophy, and acceptability to the community. The goal is to produce the plan; the problem is how to do so in a way that meets the constraints which define it as such.

METHODOLOGICAL IMPLICATIONS OF A PROBLEM FOCUS

Nickles's constraint inclusion account shows why critical researchers who want to have an impact on tracking, or on any other problematic practice for that matter, should not isolate it from the constraint set that gave rise to it, for it is those constraints that define it as a solution, and that will, unless altered, provide the evaluative framework for judging alternative practices. One gains access to that constraint set via the reasoning of relevant practitioners, and that reasoning, in turn, will signal the institutional structures which sustain and are sustained by those reasoning processes. The implication of Nickles's account for the interpretive phase of critical inquiry is that its goal should be to reconstruct the reasoning processes that led to the employment of the problematic practice; in that way we discover the nature of the problem for which the practice is a purported solution.

The constraint inclusion account of problems also helps one to understand what would count as a convincing critique of a practice like tracking. Typically, critical theorists use the values selected by their theory to judge the desirability of the practice. Tracking is judged to be undesirable because it violates values of equal provision and social justice. Now, this is a perfectly reasonable evaluation, and no doubt one of the main contributions of critical research to education has been increased awareness of the way current provision violates such evaluative criteria. Such critique is not entirely convincing to practitioners, however, because while they may accept its validity, it proceeds from an incomplete evaluative framework. The constraint structure of the problem which practitioners face is far richer than that usually employed by critical researchers, who typically ignore such constraints as cost, skill level of teachers and the additional pedagogical challenges involved in teaching untracked classes. Critique of tracking would be more convincing if it was based on an argument about how alternative arrangements could better satisfy the set of *constraints* that critical theorist and practitioner deemed important, rather than those few constraints that are selected by critical theory. It is precisely such selectivity that leads to the charge that critical research is impractical and over simplified.

Finally, the constraint inclusion account of problems has important implications for processes of change. If change is to proceed non-coercively, as is required by the values of critical theory, then change must be motivated by an intellectual commitment to the process. If the reasoning that sustains the current practice is incompatible with the researcher's suggested alternative, that reasoning will be the source of objections and a block to the development of commitment. A process of change that directly targets the problematic practice without engaging with the reasoning processes that gave rise to it is unlikely to succeed. All parties to the change must agree, at least in broad outline, that an alternative solution is both more desirable than current practice, and able to be implemented.

One of the limitations of Nickles's constraint inclusion account of problems is that it is based on scientific problems about which there is generally far less uncertainty than is true for problems of practice. Having discovered the constraint set that provides practitioners with the justification for tracking, and evaluated it against a possible alternative set, one is left with the question of how to determine the adequacy of the competing solutions that they yield. Critical theory seems to provide ambiguous if not contradictory guidance about what is involved. On the one hand, it conceptualizes change as a non impositional educative process, that requires engagement with the understandings of those involved. On the other, it assumes the false consciousness and misunderstanding of its audience. One can not conduct an educative change process if it is only the theories of the audience that are subject to test, and only they that are in need of education. The result will be at best persuasion, and at worst authoritarianism. What is needed is a dialogical process in which differing constraint structures are treated as competing theories of the problem. The goal of such dialogue is warranted agreement among all relevant stakeholders about the appropriate constraint set and about the solution that best satisfies it. Critical researchers have typically turned to the work of Habermas for a model of such dialogical processes. In the following section I argue that his model is too sketchy and abstract to guide the conduct of a dialogue directed towards the development of a shared formulation of a practical problem.

HABERMAS AS A LIMITED DIALOGICAL RESOURCE

Critical researchers in education have turned to Habermas for his critique of instrumental reasoning, for his advocacy of an expanded concept of rationality, and for his defence of the latter in what he calls the formal presuppositions of speech. It is his analysis of speech which has laid the groundwork for the dialogical models so frequently employed by critical researchers in education (Burbules 1993; Corson 1993; Young 1992).

Instrumental reasoning, as Habermas defines it, is concerned with administrative procedures, efficiency and taken-for-granted ends rather than with the desirability of the ends and of the standards used to judge the means. While this form of reasoning has allowed humankind to successfully dominate nature, Habermas argues that it has been inappropriately applied to areas of human and social activity. Acceptance of instrumental reasoning as the only form of rationality, relegates the search for consensually defined forms of authority, standards, and shared meanings to the realm of arbitrary and relativist decision arenas. The result is an impoverished public domain, loss of community, and the alienation of citizens from the institutions which control their lives. Habermas's thirty year project has been to reveal the one-sided nature of this form of rationality, and to argue for a much broader concept, which can be the basis of emancipatory critique.

Habermas grounds his expanded notion of rationality in what he calls the formal presuppositions of speech. Any communicative action, that is action directed towards understanding, presupposes a concept of rationality that overcomes the limitations of the much narrower instrumental version. Every speech act undertaken in a context of communicative action, embodies three different types of validity claim, only one of which falls within the factual claims embraced by instrumental reasoning. Yet the very act of making such claims, Habermas argues, presupposes the ability, if required, to redeem them through the provision of reasons. It is our very status as competent speakers that commits us to the rational redemption of claims about the world, about ourselves, and about what is right (Habermas, 1984, pp. 306-307). Habermas (1990) summarizes these ideas in the following explanation of communicative action:

> I call interactions communicative when the participants coordinate their plans of action consensually, with the agreement reached at any point being evaluated in terms of the intersubjective recognition of validity claims. In cases where agreement is reached through explicit linguistic processes, the actors make three different claims to validity in their speech acts as they come to agreement with one another about something. Those claims are claims to truth, claims to rightness, and to truthfulness, according to whether the speaker refers to something in the objective world (as the totality of existing

states of affairs), to something in the shared social world (as the totality of the legitimately regulated interpersonal relationships of a social group), or to something in his own subjective world (as the totality of experiences to which one has privileged access). (p. 58)

In short, Habermas is arguing that the rationality of claims about the world, about ourselves, and about what is right are all redeemed through appeal to relevant argument and evidence.

A speaker's ability to demonstrate the rationality of these claims is usually taken for granted, because everyday communication takes place against a background consensus. For example, when someone states in a meeting that time is running short, we usually accept the claim because we know what the time is, when the meeting usually finishes, and what else is still to be discussed. If however, we want participants to reconsider the conventions that have developed about the use of time, we might challenge such a claim. If such challenges can not be met immediately by appeal to relevant evidence or norms, then the speakers have recourse to a meta-level discourse, in which the disputed claims, including the language in which they are expressed, can be critiqued. Disputes are adjudicated via discourse, when evidence is indeterminate and initial arguments fail to compel (Dews 1986, p. 162).

At the same time as defending his normative ideal, Habermas (1990) is clear that it is counterfactual, that is, that discourse is seldom conducted in the manner suggested by the ideal. In discussing practical discourse (the form of discourse in which disputes about normative claims are resolved), he writes:

> Like all argumentation, practical discourses resemble islands threatened with inundation in a sea of practice where the pattern of consensual conflict resolution is by no means the dominant one. The means of reaching agreement are repeatedly thrust aside by the instruments of force. Hence, action that is oriented towards ethical principles has to accommodate itself to imperatives that flow not from principles but from strategic necessities. (p. 106)

One of the forces that precludes discourse is that of strategic action. Habermas describes the difference between strategic and communicative action as follows:

> Whereas in strategic action one actor seeks to *influence* the behaviour of another by means of the threat of sanctions or the prospect of gratification in order to *cause* the interaction to continue as the first actor desires, in communicative action one actor seeks *rationally* to motivate another by relying on the illocutionary binding/bonding effect (*Bindungseffekt*) of the offer contained in his speech act. (p. 58)

Strategic action in other words involves the unilateral control of another, through inducement or sanction, in order to achieve the purposes of the controller.

How relevant is Habermas's work on dialogue to the educative and action phases of critical inquiry? In answering this question it is important to remember that Habermas's primary purpose is the normative justification of his expanded concept of rationality, not the empirical examination of its practice. His appeal to language provides, in his view, a universal grounding for the concept which protects it against the charge that it is the product of, or only applicable to, a particular reading of Western culture. In a similar vein, the purpose of his discussion of strategic action, is to show how, despite its frequency, its presence does not undermine the normative foundations of his theory of rationality. Even assuming the accuracy of Habermas's claim that all validity claims are redeemable through discursive practice, critical researchers must go well beyond this account to investigate why such practices are displaced by forms of strategic action, and how discursive practice can be restored in particular circumstances by particular actors.

Habermas (1990) explains his interest, or rather lack of it, in the 'choice' between strategic and communicative action as follows:

> The possibility of *choosing* between communicative and strategic action exists only abstractly; it exists only for someone who takes the contingent perspective of an individual actor. From the perspective of the lifeworld to which the actor belongs, these modes of action are not matters of free choice. The symbolic structures of every lifeworld are reproduced through... processes [which] operate only in the medium of action oriented toward reaching an understanding... That is why they, as individuals, have a choice between communicative and strategic action only in an abstract sense, i.e., in individual cases. They do not have the option of a long term

absence from contexts of action oriented toward reaching an understanding. That would mean regressing to the monadic isolation of strategic action or schizophrenia and suicide. In the long run, such absence is self destructive. (p. 102)

It is precisely what Habermas calls the 'individual cases' that concern change oriented critical researchers, for despite the long term self destruction that may come with sustained strategic action, appeal to that possibility has little motivational force in a situation where strategic action appears to serve immediate self-interests. What is needed instead is a challenge to this self-perception, and a demonstration of how discourse is both possible, and more satisfying, than strategic interaction. Habermas provides few resources for this task, since the ideal he is concerned to defend can not be directly applied to everyday situations. As Habermas himself says, formal pragmatics, which is concerned with the identification of the formal presuppositions of speech is 'hopelessly removed from actual language use' (Habermas 1984, p. 328). Robert Young (1989) summarizes the difference between formal pragmatics, and empirical pragmatics, which is concerned with the communicative practice of everyday life, as follows; '... the theory of universal pragmatics [...] is an abstract or general theory developed against the background of an undifferentiated and notional social context' (p. 105). Empirical pragmatics, by contrast, is the study of actual utterances in specific, differentiated social contexts (Young, p. 105). Young goes on to say that this would involve analysing sequences of naturally occurring dialogue, investigating how the background of speakers influences their interpretations and recognizing instances of distorted (strategic) communication.

In summary, Habermas's work on language provides a very limited resource for critical researchers who want to learn how to create the conditions under which all relevant parties can reach warranted agreement about how a particular educational problem is best understood and resolved. While pointing to the possibility that all validity claims, including normative claims, can be discursively redeemed, he has little to say about the institutional, interpersonal and intrapersonal conditions that work against this possibility in particular situations, and even less to say about how these barriers could be overcome (Benhabib 1990, p. 18; Forester 1993, p. 13). Given that these are not Habermas's purposes, these comments can not be construed critically. More pertinent is the question of why critical researchers in education have been so drawn to a model of dialogue which was never intended to serve their practical purposes.

IMPROVING THE CHANGE POTENTIAL OF CRITICAL THEORY

The earlier work on the nature of a practical problem and of what it is to solve it, enables one to identify the ways in which critical theory is mismatched to practice, and to evaluate how it may be strengthened by other theories of change. One obvious need is to find a way to embed Nickles's constraint inclusion account of a problem in an interpersonal and institutional context.

RESOURCES FOR PROBLEM-BASED DIALOGUE

If educational leaders are to foster the involvement of all stakeholders in the development of a constraint inclusion account of an educational problem, they need the interpersonal and cognitive skills and values to support the process. In the following, I begin with an account of the cognitive skills and then move to the interpersonal values and skills required when problem solving occurs in an interpersonal context.

Cognitive skills

The first skill involved is the interpretive one of understanding how the various stakeholders understand the problem. For a problem like tracking, these various understandings will probably reveal an extensive and apparently irreconcilable set of solution constraints. Those constraints need to be evaluated and the surviving ones integrated by a solution that best satisfies their various demands. Constraint evaluation is conducted in the way Habermas describes; that is by evaluating the empirical and normative claims that they represent. Is it the case that these teachers in this school will not accept multi-level teaching? If so, what is that claim based on? Is it reasonable that parents of high track children don't want them 'held back' by low track children in the same class? Alongside the evaluation of constraints runs a search for ways of integrating them. The process of integration is not accomplished by seeking to maximize one or two favoured constraints or by reaching a compromise between them all. How then is it accomplished when components of the constraint set might be in conflict? Compatibility can be improved by seeking to understand the underlying value that a constraint seeks to preserve. This strategy increases flexibility and opens up options which may allow other constraints, which initially appeared to be in conflict, to be at least partially satisfied. For example, reform of tracking may seem impossible while a group of teachers refuses to countenance mixed ability classes. If the leader discovers, however, that their reason for nominating this constraint is their past difficulty with such teaching, particularly in math classes, considerably more options become available about how this constraint may be satisfied without foreclosing on the satisfaction of others. If participants understand the underlying purpose of each nominated constraint, they are more likely to be able to see ways of integrating them. The problem solution constitutes the action that all agree best integrates the final constraint set.

In summary, the cognitive skills involved in the resolution of practical problems are the ability to specify and evaluate constraints, the ability to understand their point at a deep rather than surface level so that they can be transformed in ways that maintain their integrity, and the ability to generate and test hypotheses about how they may be integrated.

These cognitive processes are very similar to those described in Ury, Fisher and Patton's (1991) account of principled negotiation. Their emphasis on the need to understand the interests behind statements of position, is very similar to my emphasis on discovery of the point and purpose of a nominated constraint. In each case, the strategy is designed to understand the reasoning behind the position, in order to open up more possibilities about how it may be satisfied without sacrificing other legitimate constraints. The difference between the constraint inclusion account of problem solving and Habermas's account of discourse should now be clear. While Habermas describes how *individual* validity claims are evaluated in discourse, the process of problem solving involves, in addition, the transformation and integration of many such validity claims so that a particular problem may be solved. Habermas has little to say about these transformative and integrative processes.

Interpersonal values and skills

Given that the resolution of any educational problem requires co-ordinated action, and that critical theory demands that such co-ordination be achieved consensually, a complete model of dialogical problem-solving must show how the above cognitive skills can be embedded into a mutually educative interpersonal process. My account of the interpersonal values and skills required is based on the work of Chris Argyris, a Harvard based social and organizational psychologist who for the last thirty years has been concerned with describing and creating interpersonal and organizational environments conducive to learning and problem-solving (Argyris 1982; 1993). Other writers who are closer to the critical tradition, such as Burbules (1993) and Young (1992) have also offered dialogical models, but unlike Argyris they have not, as yet, provided the methodological and empirical detail required to forge the links between normative theory and actual practice.

I suggest that participants in a problem-solving discourse must be committed to three discourse values. The first, that of respect, ensures what Habermas calls the general symmetry requirement: fair opportunity to speak, to challenge or to continue any line of inquiry, to express one's feeling and to be in general unconstrained in one's dealings with the other parties in the discourse. Respect is important for the enhancement of cognitive and imaginative resources – if points of view are suppressed, the quality of information and hypotheses may be reduced. Respect also increases participants' commitment to the process and outcome of the problem-solving process. The value of respect alerts us to the way discourse may be thwarted both by institutional structures which prevent people from participating in discourse or by various inequalities which arise within discourse itself. While critical researchers in educational administration have documented the former in several recent case studies, (Corson 1993; Scheurich & Imber 1991), far less work has been done by them on the latter. Many of the inequalities that are attributable to ineffective interpersonal processes are traceable to an attitude, frequently unconsciously exercised, that privileges one's own goals and opinions over those of relevant others. Such an attitude can be seen in a leader who treats others as people to be won over, rather than as contributors to a debate about the adequacy of the views of all parties.

The second discourse value is that of commitment to valid information. It involves commitment to the conduct of discourse in ways that increase the chances of detection and correction of error in one's own and others' claims about the nature of a problem and how to solve it. When dialogue participants seek to enhance valid information, they welcome rather than discourage different perspectives, because only by pitting their views against alternatives and objections can they determine whether they are worthy of their commitment. This value is an essential addition to that of respect. To embrace respect without also being committed to valid information is to foster unexamined consensus; to embrace valid information without respect is to undermine the trust and openness needed for a free and full debate of differing points of view.

The third value, that of commitment to the process and outcomes of dialogue is a corollary of the first two values of the model rather than independently derived. It involves being motivated to expend the intellectual and emotional effort required until all parties can proclaim to each other and to third parties that they have a solution that is the best they can construct, given their mutually agreed constraints on the problem.

Despite the high level of espousal of these interpersonal values, there is considerable evidence that actors do not behave accordingly, particularly in situations where they have something at stake and disagreement is anticipated (Argyris 1982, p. 43; Bifano 1989). Progress requires, therefore, a careful specification of the practices that reflect these values, of the barriers to their employment and of the educative processes involved in learning them. The first skill is that of disclosure, that is the ability to say what one thinks in a way that enables others to do the same. Problem-solving is enhanced when all relevant information is put on the table, including that which is potentially threatening or embarrassing. Since all competent adults are capable of saying what they think and why, the significance of this skill lies in understanding why it may not be exercised. No amount of espousal of the desirability of disclosure will motivate a person who wants to protect his or her views from critical scrutiny, or who unilaterally decides to protect another from embarrassment.

The second set of interpersonal skills concerns the ability to publicly test the claims made during the process of problem resolution. The point of disclosure is not only to reveal one's perspective, but also to facilitate its testing by examining the reasoning and evidence on which it is based. While private examination of one's own views can result in detection and correction of error, it is no substitute for public testing, for the same reasoning processes that lead us to believe as we do, are likely to inform our examination of our beliefs.

The third set of skills involves facilitation of the participation of others in quality problem-solving. Such facilitation is required on the part of educational leaders to counteract imbalances of power which would otherwise militate against critique of the taken-for-granted, or prevent the inclusion in dialogue of those who experience the worst consequences of current practices. Against such a background, many actors will either not expect their views to be taken seriously, or lack confidence in their articulation and defence.

Combined with the cognitive skills outlined earlier, these interpersonal skills are designed to improve problem-solving effectiveness, through an increase in quality information and in the commitment of those involved in the process. While most of the work on the model has been done in non-educational settings (Argyris 1990; 1993), there is some evidence available that educational leaders both espouse its values and have difficulty putting them into practice (Bifano 1989; Robinson & Absolum 1990). Despite the difficulties involved, we also know that with specialist help, dialogical skills can be learned and successfully employed in the collaborative resolution of long-standing school-based problems (Robinson 1993).

The Scale of the Problem

The problem-based approach to change advocated in this chapter runs counter to much critical research in education in at least two respects. First, many researchers eschew problem solving approaches because they see them as narrowly instrumentalist, and thus as incompatible with the value commitments of a critical theory. Second, critical analyses in education are typically much grander in scale than can be accommodated within the constraint inclusion framework I am advocating. In this section, I argue that Nickles's theory of problem solving is not instrumental, and that there are considerable practical advantages in tackling problems of a modest rather than grand scale.

The idea of problem-solving has acquired a pejorative connotation among many critical theorists (Cox, 1981; Forester, 1993). The criticism stems from the view that problem-solving is a search for the most efficient and effective means to given ends, and thus an exclusively technical or instrumental activity which rules out critique of the assumptive framework within which the problem is understood. The limitations of this view are obvious. It may be impossible to find a solution to the problem of truancy, for example, while it is assumed that any such solution must be directed towards increasing student attendance at existing class programmes. These criticisms do not apply to the constraint inclusion account of problem-solving advocated in this chapter because that view treats the process of problem formulation and problem-solving as one and the same. Problem solving is not a process of finding a solution that meets a taken-for-granted set of constraints; it is a process of formulating a constraint set so that a solution is possible.

The problem-based approach to educational change requires intensive collaborative investigation of the factors that sustain particular problematic practices, and of the ways those practices may be rethought and reconstructed. This requirement can not be met by the grand scale theorizing, typical of critical theory, in which the causes of problematic practices are located in an ever widening circle of institutional, social and economic contexts. Cox (1981) contrasts the scope of critical and problem-solving approaches as follows:

> As a matter of practice, critical theory, like problem-solving theory, takes as its starting point some aspect or particular sphere of human activity. But whereas the problem-solving approach leads to further analytical sub-division and limitation of the issue to be dealt with, the critical approach leads towards the construction of a larger picture of the whole of which the initially contemplated part is just one component, and seeks to understand the processes of change in which both parts and whole are involved (p. 129).

The critical theorist's tendency to widen the scope of the analysis, with its accompanying increased abstraction, works against the integration of constraints that is central to the problem-solving process. An abstract formulation of a constraint structure robs it of the richness of empirical detail that makes it possible to both understand the principles at stake in this particular case, and to create options about how those principles can be met in the context of the whole constraint set. Put more generally, problems that are grandly rather than modestly formulated stretch the limits of our information processing capacities. Tighter analyses can be formulated when cause and effect linkages operate on a smaller scale, when critical evidence can be determined and detected, and when formal and informal experimentation can provide the feedback required for theory revision. When problems are formulated on a grand scale, it is very difficult to do the type of intensive analyses required to identify precisely how they arise and are sustained in the concrete practices of those involved in the situation (Weick 1984).

Moving from analysis to intervention, Weick (1984) also argues that many social reform efforts have failed because they were too massive in scale. He compares, for example, the success of feminist attempts to desex the language with the relative failure of their attempt to desex legislation through the Equal Rights Amendment to the U.S. Constitution (p. 42). The reasons for failure are both task-related and psychological. Large tasks require more careful coordination than small ones and are thus more sensitive to breakdowns in timing, to political defections, and to failure to achieve subordinate goals. Psychologically, the chances of success are increased when massive social problems are recast into smaller ones, because problem solvers are more likely to judge the challenge as within their capacities and as less risky. As Weick puts it, aiming for small wins produces a more functional level of arousal for those involved.

> A small win reduces the importance ('this is no big deal'), reduces demands ('that's all that needs to be done'), and raises perceived skill levels ('I can do at least that'). When reappraisals or problems take this form, arousal becomes less of a deterrent to solving them (p. 46).

A preference for tackling modest rather than grand-scale problems does not imply a preference for a technical rather than a more radical approach to their solution. Where one sets the boundaries of a problem is independent of the degree of change required to solve it. Indeed, more radical solutions may be more easily achieved with problems that are modestly rather than grandly formulated because such problems provide better conditions for learning precisely what is required to resolve them and for recruiting the required resources.

A related criticism of problem-solving approaches to change, even when not construed in a limited technical sense, is that such a piecemeal approach can not possibly address the social structures and wider formations that shape the administrative practices that we seek to change. Do such criticisms reflect a call for critical researchers to engage in large scale revolutionary social change? If not, then do they ask researchers to be alert to the way wider social processes may be reflected in more local, contextualized practices such as tracking? If so, such investigation of the causal links between social structure and the reasoning and action of agents in particular contexts, is precisely the type of analysis that is called for by a problem-based approach. Rather than start with the wider social context, and imply or assume the consequences for local problems, the constraint analysis approach requires the reverse, namely, the careful investigation and empirical demonstration of the way a problematic practice is sustained by the reasoning of relevant practitioners and how that reasoning may be sustained, in turn, by certain social structures. Such careful retroductive causal analyses provide convincing empirical demonstrations of the connections between agents and social structure, and of the possibilities for altering those linkages.

The call for critical theorists to turn to the analysis, let alone the resolution, of specifically located problems is not new. In 1987, Brian Fay concluded his trenchant critique of the ontology of critical theory with a call that it eschew its aspiration to capture the essence of liberation and offer instead 'an account of the ways in which it is inherently and essentially contextual, partial, local, and hypothetical' (p. 213). Six years later, from a more sympathetic vantage point, John Forester (1993) made a similar call. He wrote:

> The glass of critical theory is surely half-empty: we are still missing a good deal of guidance about the most fruitful ways to carry out empirical, historically situated, phenomenologically cogent, normatively insightful analyses. Here surely the balance must now shift from necessarily abstract methodological analyses toward the effort to assess specific cases, concrete attempts to work out the implications of a critical communications framework in particular cases...(p. 13).

CRITICAL THEORY AND THE CREATION OF COMMON INTERESTS

The dialogical problem-solving process outlined above, is intended to be inclusive; that is to involve either directly or indirectly, all relevant parties in the problem situation. Its goal is a problem solution which satisfies, better than the current practice, the critically examined interests of all. It challenges educational leaders, in the context of debate on school tracking, for example, to involve the parents and teachers of both low and high track children in a re-examination of current allocation practices. For many critical researchers, these goals will seem both naive and unrealistic, for they run counter to the theory of conflicting interests that is central to much critical theory. Burbules (1994) writes that despite the fact that many critical theorists have moved away from Marxist analyses of schooling, '– what remains is still an image of society bifurcated between oppressors and the oppressed, and of perpetual struggle against a 'ruling class' of disproportionate power and privilege' (p. 3620).

Critical theorists' assumption of conflicting interests translates into their paradoxical tendency to exclude from the problem-solving process the very groups they see as responsible for the situations they seek to redress. Comstock (1982, pp. 379 388), for example, who provides one of the most detailed and frequently quoted accounts of critical research in education, omits the powerful (in his terms the non-progressive group) from his educative processes. Paulo Freire (1970, pp. 28, 39), in similar fashion, sees the suffering of the oppressed as the result, at least in part, of social structures and processes which are controlled by the powerful, yet he excludes them from his emancipatory pedagogy. The dialogical model presented earlier requires that rather than prejudge the degree of conflict or compatibility between various groups, that educational leaders learn how to encourage such groups to publicly test the extent to which their interests are, or can become compatible. The constraint inclusion account of problem-solving provides one model for such public testing, through the search for a solution which integrates the constraints that all have accepted as appropriate for the problem.

Guidance about the conditions which foster resolution of apparently irreconcilable interests comes from recent research on social dilemmas, that is, those situations in which individual and common interests are believed to be in opposition (Liebrand, Messick & Wilke 1992). Many of the most serious social problems facing us today are of this type. The population crisis and problems of pollution and resource management take this form because their resolution requires individuals to make choices which are more costly than current self-interested choices, yet, if not taken by a critical mass of the population, will leave everyone worse off than they are at present. The concept of a social dilemma is also not irrelevant to many of the issues addressed by critical theorists in education. Take, for example, the issue of disproportionate representation of the children from poor and indigenous minority backgrounds in statistics of school disciplinary actions. Pressure from various community groups might lead educational administrators to consider how the curriculum and assessment practices of the district contribute to a cycle of failure, alienation and disciplinary problems, and how various new initiatives might alter the punitive and exclusionary practices currently employed. For any individual classroom teacher, however, whose use of the detention and suspension systems has been contributing to the statistics, the attempt to alter his or her classroom management and curricular practices is far more costly than the removal of students who are disruptive in class or in breach of rules. In addition, the success of the change requires the co-operation of others, so any one teacher's sacrifice will prove doubly costly if others choose not to co operate. In the long run, however, failure to change will leave everyone worse off as the cycle of student alienation and punitive reaction escalates to the point where teaching becomes impossible.

Recent research on naturally occurring dilemmas has revealed some of the conditions which lead people to make choices that are in the long term interest of all, rather than in the short term interest of a few (Klandermans 1992). Actors are more likely to make co-operative choices if they believe that their own choice can make a difference to the problem, that sufficient other people will choose co-operatively, and that such choices will solve the problem at hand. In the context of the earlier educational example, the relevant factors are whether the teachers believe that their own actions can make a difference to the problem of minority student alienation, whether they believe their colleagues will cooperate to learn the new disciplinary and curricular strategies, and whether such strategies, even if successfully implemented, are likely to be successful in solving the problem.

Expectations about one's own contribution in solving a problem are influenced by its size and the number of people involved. As each of these factors increases, personal efficacy reduces as responsibility is diffused among many actors or as dependency on others' co-operation increases. Once again, we see how the large scale problem formulation typical of critical theorists can be counterproductive to the achievement of change unless subgoals are formulated that lead people to believe that they can still make a difference (Klandermans, p. 314).

There is also a close connection between the expectation of others' co-operation and one's own social choices. Actors who attribute conflicting interests and nefarious motives to others are less likely to co-operate in the resolution of a social dilemma than those who make more charitable attributions. Attributions are likely to create self-fulfilling prophecies as their holders act in ways that create the reactions they have predicted. There are obvious lessons here for critical theorists, since they are more likely to attend to the politics, conflict and self-interest at work in a social problem than to the possibilities for common ground. In so doing, their theoretical framework may itself exacerbate any conflict of interest that is otherwise present. While a naive idealism can be as dysfunctional to transformative action as a cynical politics, the social psychology of self-fulfilling prophecies suggests that the presumption of goodwill is more functional than its opposite.

We know that individual choices in a social dilemma are influenced by the value placed on the problem as well as by expectations about whether it will be solved, because a few individuals contribute to its solution regardless of personal costs and benefits (Klandermans, p. 312). On the whole, however, emphasis on the importance of a social problem and its moral implications is an inadequate motivator for the great majority of individuals whose choices depend, in addition, on their expectations that the problem can be solved. While critical theorists have rendered problematic many educational practices, they have contributed far less towards increasing the expectations of relevant publics that such problems can be solved, and it is these expectations that are crucial to transformative action. As Jeannie Oakes has pointed out in the context of research on tracking, change requires the development of adequate alternatives as well as critical awareness of its necessity.

CONCLUSION

In one sense, the conclusion to be drawn from this chapter is very simple; critical research will continue to offer little to educational leaders who wish to go beyond critique of school practices to their reconstruction, until its exponents learn how to intervene in the systems that are the subject of their analyses. In another sense, this conclusion is oversimplified, for I have argued that even if more change projects were conducted, their success would be hampered by serious mismatches between critical theory itself, and the practices it seeks to transform. Indeed, some writers have expressed concern that these very features, for example, the grand sweep of its theorizing, its prejudged problem analyses, and its assumptions about implacable conflict, may produce a change process that violates critical theory's own educative and collaborative ideals (Ellsworth 1989; Fay 1987).

The limited reconstructive, as opposed to critical contribution of critical research in education, can be attributed to mismatches between the generic features of the practical problems it seeks to resolve, and to what we know about the social psychology of change. I have argued that those mismatches can be addressed by the inclusion of a dialogical model of problem-solving within critical theory. The inclusion of such a model would considerably reduce the mismatch, because it requires researchers to embed the practices that they select as problematic in the problem-solving processes that gave rise to them and that continue to sustain them. Those processes, along with the conditions that sustain them, need to be uncovered, debated and reconstructed, if change is to be achieved. This requires engagement with *all* the constraints deemed by key players to be relevant to the situation, rather than with only those constraints selected by critical theory. One of the central advantages of Nickles's constraint inclusion account of problems is that it encourages engagement with a total constraint set, and thus with the need to solve a problem, rather than to maximize preferred values.

Finally, it is puzzling that critical researchers have engaged so little with traditions that offer far more substantial empirical and conceptual resources on change than their own. While some of this literature may embrace values that are incompatible with critical theory, much of it may not, and in any case, I would argue that the compatibility of its technical insights with the values of critical theory needs to be debated in the context of specific problems rather than judged in the abstract. Critical theory has made a huge contribution to raising the consciousness of its audience, including educational leaders and administrators. However, since consciousness raising is an incomplete approach to changing most educational problems, it is time to engage seriously with traditions that have a more secure record on the achievement of change.

REFERENCES

Anderson, G.: 1989, 'Critical Ethnography in Education: Origins, Current Status and New Directions', *Review of Educational Research 59* (3), 249 – 270.

Anyon, J.: 1980, 'Social Class and the Hidden Curriculum of Work', *Journal of Education 62*, 67 – 92.

Anyon, J.: 1981, 'Social Class and School Knowledge'. *Curriculum Inquiry 2*, 3 – 41.

Argyris, C.: 1982, *Reasoning, Learning and Action*, Jossey Bass, San Francisco.

Argyris, C.: 1990, *Overcoming Organizational Defenses: Facilitating Organizational Learning*, Allyn and Bacon, Needham MA.

Argyris, C.: 1993, *Knowledge for Action: A Guide to Overcoming Barriers to Organizational Change*, Jossey Bass, San Francisco.

Aronowitz, S., & Giroux, H.: 1985, *Education under Siege*, Bergin and Harvey, South Hadley, MA.

Benhabib, S.: 1990, 'In the Shadow of Aristotle & Hegel: Communicative Ethics and Current Controversies in Practical Philosophy', in M. Kelly (ed.), *Hermeneutics and Critical Theory in Ethics and Politics*, MIT Press, Cambridge, 1 – 32.

Bifano, S.L.: 1989, 'Researching the Professional Practice of Elementary Principals: Combining Qualitative Methods and Case Study', *Journal of Educational Administration, 27* (1), 58 – 70.

Bourdieu, P. & Passeron, J.C.: 1977, *Reproduction in Education, Society and Culture*, Sage, Beverly Hills.

Bowles, S., & Gintis, H.: 1976, *Schooling in Capitalist America*, Basic Books, New York.

Burbules, N.: 1986, Review article – 'Education under Siege', *Educational Theory, 36* (3), 301 – 313.

Burbules, N.: 1993, *Dialogue in Teaching: Theory and Practice*, Teachers College Press, New York.

Burbules, N.C.: 1994, 'Marxism and Educational Thought', in T. Husen & N. Postlethwaite (eds.), *The International Encyclopedia of Education* (Vol. 6), Pergamon, Oxford, 3617 – 3622.

Comstock, D.: 1982, 'A method for critical research', in E. Bredo and W. Feinberg (eds.), *Knowledge and Values in Social and Educational Research*, Temple University Press, Philadelphia.

Corson, D.: 1993, 'Discursive bias and ideology in the administration of minority group interests', *Language in Society, 22*, 165 – 191.

Cox, R.W.: 1981, 'Social Forces, States and World Orders: Millenium. *Journal of International Studies, 10* (2), 126 155.

Dewey, J.: 1922, *Human Nature and Conduct*, Henry Holt, New York.

Dews, P. (ed.): 1986, *Habermas: Autonomy and Solidarity: Interviews*, Verso London.

Ellsworth, E.: 1988, 'Why doesn't this feel empowering?' Working through the repressive myths of critical pedagogy', *Harvard Educational Review, 59* (3), 297 – 324.

Fay, B.: 1987, *Critical Social Science: Liberation and its Limits*, Polity Press, Cambridge.

Fisher, R., Ury, W., & Patton, B.: 1991, *Getting to Yes: Negotiating Agreement Without Giving In.* (second edition), Houghton Mifflin, Boston.

Forester, J.: 1993, *Critical Theory, Public Policy and Planning Practice: Toward a Critical Pragmatism*, SUNY Press, New York.

Foster, W.: 1994, 'Administration of Education: Critical Approaches', in T. Husen & T.N. Postlethwaite (eds.), *The International Encyclopedia of Education (Vol. 6)* Pergamon, Oxford, 60 – 67.

Foster, W.: 1994, 'School Leaders as Transformative Intellectuals: Toward a Critical Pragmatism', in N.A. Prestine & P.W. Thurston (eds.), *Advances in Educational Administration (Vol. 3)*, 29 – 51.

Freire, P.: 1970, *Pedagogy of the Oppressed*, Herder and Herder, New York.

Freire, P.: 1985, *The Politics of Education: Culture, Power and Liberation*, Bergin and Harvey, South Hadley, Ma.

Gauthier, D.P.: 1963, *Practical Reasoning*, Oxford, London.

Geuss, R.: 1981, *The Idea of a Critical Theory. Habermas and the Frankfurt School.* Cambridge University Press, Cambridge.

Habermas, J.: 1984, *The Theory of Communicative Action (Vol. 1, Reason and the Rationalization of Society)*, Beacon Press, Boston.

Habermas, J.: 1990, *Moral consciousness and communicative action*, MIT Press, Cambridge.

Klandermans, B.: 1992, 'Persuasive Communication: Measures To Overcome Real – Life Social Dilemmas', in W. Liebrand, D. Messick & H. Wilke (eds.), *Social Dilemmas: Theoretical Issues and Research Findings*, Pergamon Press, Oxford, pp. 307 – 318.

Liebrand, W., Messick, D., & Wilke, H. (eds.): 1992, *Social Dilemmas: Theoretical Issues and Research Findings*, Pergamon Press, Oxford.

Nickles, T.: 1988, 'Questioning and Problems in Philosophy of Science: Problem – Solving Versus Directly Truth – Seeking Epistemologies', in M. Meyer (ed.), *Questions and Questioning*, Walter de Gruyter, Berlin, 43 – 67.

Nickles, T.: 1981, 'What is a Problem That We May Solve It?', *Synthese, 47* (1), 85 – 118.

Oakes, J.: 1985, *Keeping Track: How Schools Structure Inequality.* Yale University Press, New Haven.

Oakes, J.: 1992, 'Can Tracking Research Inform Practice? Technical Normative and Political Considerations. *Educational Researcher, 21* (4), 12 – 21.

Robinson, V.M.J., & Absolum, M.: 1990, 'Leadership Style and Organizational Problems: The Case of a Professional Development Programme', in N. Jones & N. Frederickson (eds.), *Refocusing Educational Psychology*,: Falmer Press, London, 31 – 54.

Robinson, V.M.J.: 1993, Problem – Based Methodology: *Research for the Improvement of Practice*, Pergamon, Oxford.

Scheurich, J.J., & Imber, M.: 1991, 'Educational Reforms Can Reproduce Societal Inequities: A Case Study'. *Educational Administration Quarterly, 27* (3), 297 – 320.

Shor, I. & Freire, P.: 1987, *A Pedagogy for Liberation: Dialogues on Transforming Education.* Macmillan, Basingstoke.

Torres, C.A.: 1992, 'Participatory Action Research and Popular Education in Latin America', *Qualitative Studies in Education, 5* (1), 51 – 62.

Weick, K.: 1984, 'Small Wins: Redefining the Scale of Social Issues', *American Psychologist, 39,* 40 – 50.

Willis, P.: 1977, *Learning to Labour*, Gower Publishing, New York.

Young, R.: 1989, *A Critical Theory of Education: Habermas and our Children's Future*, Harvester Wheatsheaf, New York.

Young, R.: 1992, *Critical Theory and Classroom Talk*, Multilingual Matters, Clevedon.

Chapter 31: The Socially Just Alternative to the 'Self-Managing School'

JOHN SMYTH

Flinders Institute for the Study of Teaching, Flinders University of South Australia

In this paper I want to, first, briefly sketch out what is happening with regard to the devolution as expressed in the concept of the 'self-managing school'. It is prevalent in almost all western democracies at the moment (USA, England and Wales, Canada, New Zealand, and Australia), and there are important commonalities not only in what is claimed to be in the best interests of public education, but also what is not being disclosed in respect of this worldwide phenomenon, or the alternatives to it. The basic argument is that moves towards devolution, in most cases, are not fundamentally about grassroots democratic reform of education aimed at giving schools and their communities more power – rather, they are about precisely the reverse, namely, the intensification of central control, while seeming to be otherwise.

Second, and ironically, I want to propose that if schools are to be saddled with what appear to be mandated forms of self-management, then this ought to occur on a very different theoretical and philosophical terrain than is happening at the moment – one that is less driven by economic agenda, and that is more informed by educational, social, and dare I say it, democratic, ideals.

THE PROBLEM WITH THE SELF-MANAGING SCHOOL

Around the world at the moment, we are being led to believe that as educational bureaucracies bite the dust, that schools and educational institutions stand to become more empowered. In other words, they will get more control over their work and their institutions – and in a sense, that's right. What we are not being told is that this is to occur in a context of sharply reduced central provision of resources for public education, as the bureaucratic structures that have traditionally supported the work of teaching are progressively dismantled, and schools are converted into stand-alone institutions in which there is only an illusion of a shift in power and control. As a teacher in New South

K. Leithwood et al. (eds.), International Handbook of Educational Leadership and Administration, 1097-**1131**.
© *1996 Kluwer Academic Publishers, Printed in the Netherlands.*

Wales so aptly put it in the opening statement in my book *A Socially Critical View of the Self-Managing School:*

> I feel like we have been taken to the cleaners. When you go to the dry cleaners you get a note that says: 'All care but no responsibility'. With this devolution and self-management stuff, 'it's all responsibility and no power (Smyth, 1993a, p. 1).

Ball (1993) characterised the move to school self-management as part of a discursive trick – one in which things are not so much done *to schools*, as done *by schools* to themselves, with the consequence that the state is left in the 'enviable position of having power without responsibility' (p. 77). Self-management, he says, really amounts to those being cut, doing the cutting to themselves, while believing that it is for the best, because that way, they control their own decline (p. 77). As Hartley (1994) put it succinctly:

> The surface impression given is that devolved school management is all about local control and the quest for quality. At root, however, is a new mode of regulation, a new discourse, whereby government retains strategic control of funding, curriculum and assessment, whilst it devolves to headteachers (*not* school boards, who will merely be consulted) the tactics for implementing that strategy (p. 139).

The strategy for doing this is that self management has a different Bill of Sale, depending upon who it has to be sold to:

To Teachers: it is put as a form of empowerment, made possible by the miracle of removing red tape and bureaucracy. Decisions about schools are supposedly able to be brought much closer to classrooms and children.

To Parents: it is portrayed as a way of giving them a greater say over what is happening to their children, and making schools more accountable.

To Administrators: it is presented as a way of re-claiming control over the day-to-day running of the school, uninhibited by intrusive and distant external control. Global budgeting has a certain degree of superficial appeal to administrators who have long suffered under what they regard as stifling central strictures.

To Business: it is held up as a shining example of the way schools are introducing competition and market forces into education, appearing to make schools more responsive to the needs of industry, and in the process more efficient and effective.

To Policy Makers: it is a way of evading impossible decisions, in a context of sharply declining tax bases. At the same time, they are able to convince the wider community that as politicians they are really in control, because they have leverage over outcomes through performance measures.

As educational reforms go, this is a pretty attractive package, and it has widespread appeal because it is:

- participatory – in that the rhetoric is that of giving individuals and schools autonomy over their own affairs;
- economical – in that it appears to be cost-neutral, and there is even the hint that it might be cost saving, because it makes schools more efficient through competition;
- compelling – in the sense that no rational person could possibly be against allowing the 'consumers' of education a greater say, by removing self-seeking 'producers' (educators); and is
- inclusive – in the way it incorporates all the major players, leading each to believe that self-management will advance their own particular individual positions.

The manner in which this notion is addressed in the research literature in various countries, is informative. Below are a few illustrative instances of what seems to be emerging.

Canada

It is the subtlety, the ambiguity, and the contradiction implicit in self-management that make it far from a straight-forward notion, as the Canadian experience shows. The idea does have some decided and potential pluses. For example, so-called 'operational decisions' can be made closer to the work of schools; red tape and other negative aspects of bureaucracy can be minimised; schools, when the have resource control, can make decisions about how best to deploy [resources] to fulfil their purposes (Somerville, 1981). But, as Somerville (1981) has noted from the Canadian experience in Edmonton:

> The extent to which any of these advantages do or do not materialise seems to depend in part on the nature of the staff in the school, and more particularly on the skill and the disposi-

tion of the principal. Much of the positive reaction generated within the pilot project [in Edmonton] seemed to depend on the careful selection of a few administrators who were prepared to put a great deal of time and effort into working with their staffs, involving teachers in budget development and ensuring that priorities were established that the school would accept. In such circumstances, most or all of the above advantages could be realised (p. 74).

There are also some disadvantages that weigh heavily against these. As Somerville (1981) points out, because of the heavy emphasis on budgeting and resource allocation, a great deal of time of teachers can be diverted away from the primary task of teaching and learning. The energies of the principal can also be diverted away from being the educational leader and 'convert him/her into a glorified business manager' (p. 75). The emphasis on the 'management' of schools brings with it a fanatical pre-occupation with 'management by objectives' and 'performance outcomes', a feature that highlights a concern with 'product', almost to the exclusion of 'process'. From an equity point of view, school-based management also inevitably leads to a reduction in the overall quality of educational provision, when there is no longer any provision for ensuring 'an equitable balance of services and facilities within the system' (p. 76). In other words, schools have to buy services from 'out-sources' and when confronted with severe financial constraints, specialist services disappear.

The most fundamental point in all of this is that resources will be allocated to schools *before* educational needs are assessed, no matter what formula is used. That is to say, funding allocations occur in a vacuum, or in the context of what is considered politically prudent at the time. The evidence accumulating from various sources is that there are winners and losers, and that cutting schools loose from equitable centrally provided resourcing may seem to serve certain rhetoric about competition and efficiency, but in the final analysis it will be deeply destructive of schools.

From the place that has reputedly had the most extensive experience of devolution, and which is held out as the most virtuous example of its implementation, the Edmonton Public School System, the story is less than positive:

... after 13 years, it has become quite institutionalised within our system. The whole business of setting District and School priorities, community meetings to review proposed budgets etc., has become the new bureaucratic modus operandi.

... the only difference [over time] is that so-called decentralization is harder to live with as economic conditions deteriorate. School-based budgeting protects the trustees and senior administration from having to make and face the consequences of funding cuts. They simply turn the tap down by changing the ratio between allocation and unit costs, and then leave the schools to contend with and be responsible for what results.

In many respects, the effect of school-based budgeting has been to consolidate centralised decision making rather than to promote decentralisation. The central authority is less encumbered and now has more time to devote to exercising control (Somerville, 1993).

Larry Booi (1992) in a paper entitled 'The emperor's new clothes and the myth of decentralisation', reports on what has really gone on inside the 'Edmonton Experience', or as it has been described by others, 'the quiet revolution' (McConaghy, 1989). The evidence is quite overwhelming:

While it is true (and laudable) that schools now can more easily purchase supplies and equipment with less 'red tape', to pretend that schools and teachers actually make significant budget decisions borders on delusion. After salaries, utilities, and a few other fundamentals are paid for (at rates determined by the central authority), how much is left? Those few decisions that can be made 'on-site' are generally made by the principal. The lack of structures to guarantee meaningful teacher involvement in these decisions is glaring testimony to the nature of the real decision making process...

But the myth involves much more than the budget process; it reaches into virtually every aspect of the school culture, as it is designed to do. We are told constantly that the schools have been 'freed' to make all of the big decisions. Of course, with this alleged freedom comes the responsibility for the 'outcomes' – particularly for the difficult ones. If staff are declared surplus, it is 'the school's decision'. If there is not enough money for professional development, that is 'the school's choice'. If school results on achievement tests are low, the culprits are near at hand. In reality, power, control and resources are kept at the centre; responsibility, blame and guilt are decentralised to the schools (p. 3).

The point to be taken from the Edmonton experience is that there is indeed a quite revolution going on in terms of schools having a greater sense of ownership – but it is ownership of the wrong things. Giving schools a capacity to control dwindling resources, making their own priorities, and winding back allocations when times get tough, amounts to forcing them to find funding from elsewhere, produce divisiveness within local communities, or even worse, close schools down. And finding funding from corporate sponsorship and partnerships has its own package of moral and ethical problems.

United Kingdom

John Murphy (1990) from the Department of Accounting, University of Hull, has undertaken research into the three alleged virtues of SBM (or LMS as they call it in the UK):
– that it enables schools to be more responsive to the needs of their clients and the community;
– that it promotes responsiveness in schools, giving schools more control over their resources; and
– that it reduces the administrative burden associated with central control.

As to the first of these, 'responsiveness to clients', Murphy (1990) found that: 'Whatever potential LMS might offer in this respect, it was insignificant in comparison to the limitations imposed by the delegated budget' (p. 4). In other words, the budget cutbacks that accompanied devolution frustrated schools – which was supposedly one of the major reasons for the devolution in the first place. As to the second, the capacity of schools to be more accountable by virtue of having control over their own resources, Murphy (1990) found 'some support for this, however this was qualified by the constraint of inadequate budget' (p. 4). It was also true that the 'extra freedom regarding staffing, was welcomed' (p. 4). On the third count of whether or not LMS reduced the administrative burdens associated with central bureaucracy, there was no equivocation at all. 'Every Head said that LMS had increased their administration. The only variation in the responses was in the size of the estimated increase, 100% and 200% being commonly reported' (Murphy, 1990, p. 5). There was unanimous agreement among principals 'that LMS had substantially increased administration'. This was brought about by the legal requirement that the centre had to check up on local expenditure, so that all administrative machinery was effectively duplicated. A great deal of work was required to complete the management plan (or charter) with exactly the same demands being made on all schools, a process that was particularly burdensome for small primary schools. On the matter of 'formula funding', Murphy (1990) says, in England 'there were very distinct winners and losers' (p. 6). What Murphy found was that there was no indication as to how the 'unspecified attribute (of quality) was to be detected or evaluated' (p. 7). There was certainly a lot of testing, measurement, and reporting, but it resembled more of a smokescreen, than any genuine attempt to reflect changes in the quality of teaching or learning.

Real questions exist, then, in the UK research, about the extent to which delegation of responsibility to schools had actually occurred. Murphy's (1990) respondents questioned whether 'the arrangements constitute[d] delegation in any real sense, or whether it was 'a paper tiger?'. Statistics indicated that around 80% of the cost of running a school are labour costs, and that the size of the budget is mainly determined by the number of pupils and their ages. Therefore, the degree of influence schools can exert on staffing is marginal. As Murphy (1990) says:

> The degree of controllability is small... [The] major portion of school costs is committed. The existence of a school, necessarily implies the employment of teaching and non-teaching staff. They are the essence of the organisation, and cannot be wished away by the most cost-conscious of Governors without compromising the objectives of the school (p. 13).

In this kind of context it seemed that there was little potential for schools to 'manage' costs, because detailed parameters were laid down centrally, and schools were unable to challenge the basis of apportionments. The whole process resembled more a form of 'stewardship', rather than control by schools. Overall, what Murphy (1990) found in respect of England was that while devolution was supposed to diminish the extent of central control, the detailed responsibilities given to schools resulted in the role of central authorities 'being strengthened'; principals had become managers not educationists; and [school council members] had their jobs considerably increased, making it difficult to recruit such people in the future.

Evetts' (1993) study of the headship also found that in respect of Locally Managed Schools (LMS) in England, there had been an 'expansion of managerial and executive tasks and [a] reduction in educational leadership aspects' (p. 53). She summarised it in these terms:

> Heads, their senior management teams and governing bodies are having to think in commercial terms. They are increasingly engaging in negotiations with industrial and commercial organizations in order to expand their resources. They are renting their buildings and charging for services. They are seeking sponsorship from industry and local business for both capital expenditure and to meet running costs... All recognised the necessity for such activities but in general they were reluctant to welcome such schemes (p. 61).

Evidence from another study in the UK by Marren & Levacic (1994) provides remarkably similar findings – from interviews in 11 schools with senior managers, teachers and governors. While senior management responded positively, there were perplexing but as yet unanswered questions:

> The evidence gathered in this study confirms the findings of other research on the impact of LMS on school decision-making and staff roles... that LMS is leading to a concentration of financial tasks within a small elite group of senior managers and governors, with governors playing a subservient role' (p. 52).

> [There was a view that] financial management is a task for senior management and that it should only impinge on teachers to the extent that it affects their immediate job' (p. 52).

The crucial questions to emerge were:

1. To what extent is class teacher involvement in financial decision making required in order for local management to result in the improvement to teaching and learning expected of it by its proponents?
2. How best can such involvement be achieved? (p. 52).

Finally...

> Our case study evidence suggests that teachers need to be involved in resource management decisions and to have a degree of empowerment through controlling their own budgets if they are to respond favourably to local management' (p. 52).

Operating from within a declared 'economic' perspective of explicitly dealing with issues of 'efficiency' and 'effectiveness' within self-management, Simkins (1994) examined the empirical literature on the self-managing school and concluded that while such moves might be 'efficiency enhancing' in that they made schools more economical:

> there is little evidence concerning the impact... on school effectiveness, beyond the examples of schools responding to parental choice through 'image enhancing' and 'substantive' changes in curriculum and organization (p. 30).

In other words, it is the effectiveness of schooling that is crucial, and to date moves towards the self-managing school have failed to come to grips with the 'dynamic and contested' (Simkins, 1994, p. 31) nature of schools and their goals, and how moves towards self-management adequately addresses the widening equity chasm between 'winners' and 'losers'.

One of the consistent features emerging across the research cited so far, is that because devolution is essentially a cost-cutting exercise, schools are forced to supplement their funding from private sources – and herein lies the equity issue. Schools, because of their socio-economic make-up, have vastly different capacities to do this – some take to the freedom and flexibility given them (usually the better off schools), and flourish as a consequence. Working class schools, on the other hand, do not have the financial and cultural capital to do this and end up as 'sink', 'residue' or 'ghetto' schools. What we are dealing with here in cutting schools loose from being part of an 'education system', is something very much less than a level playing field.

The comments of headteacher Mike Davies (1992), in England, summed it up nicely:

> I cannot believe that hundreds of headteachers, whose professional and job satisfaction has come through working with teachers and children so they can walk along the road towards empowerment and liberty, can so quickly swap all of this for the keyboard, spreadsheet and bank balance... [W]e seem to have entered a new era of managerialism without ever being clear what it is that we are managing (p. 4).

> ... [M]uch of our orientation since the end of the last decade has led us to serve the mythical customer, who is thought to have an insatiable appetite for statistics and league tables, and providing information to boards of governors (p. 4).

> What this move to 'delegation' and 'autonomy' means in reality is that schools have become relatively autonomous cost centres, but forfeit the right to be in control of their heart, i.e. the curriculum. They can determine the number and regularity of the heartbeats but not the quality of the blood pouring through the system (p. 4).

> We need urgently to readdress the question of what we are managing and to what end (p. 5).

> ... [I]t is hardly surprising that staffroom conversation is about management, systems and procedures, rather than about the excitement of the last lesson and looking forward to the next. The ubiquitous way in which money and financial considerations can dominate management is a real coup for a government determined to stratify the system and deny that schools are for social change. Such change could only come through a more challenging, flexible and active pedagogy – the anthesis being the definition of knowledge-bound subjects which are crudely tested through pencil and paper... I fear that headteachers and their colleagues [are being directed] away from their core activity and that they have been seduced by short-term illusions of power, and freedom...

This obsession with pseudo-power, control over spending and the fine tuning of administrative systems has been a wonderful diversion, ensuring that discussion and debate is never curriculum-centred (p. 6).

It is utterly fickle for a school to accept 'devolution' when all that accrues is the freedom to veer between the various buttons on the calculator (p. 8).

United States of America

In the USA, Lindquist & Mauriel (1989) similarly report that:

... despite the overwhelming demand by outsiders to establish such a management system and the espoused acceptance of it on the part of many educational administrators, School Based Management (SBM) does not seem to have been widely adopted... (p. 403).

The empirical evidence from the American sites (e.g. Dade County, Florida; Rochester, New York; Hammond, Indiana; Salt Lake City, Utah) indicates that the process of SBM is only beginning. As of yet, there has not been a specific delegation of full and meaningful authority to make key decisions in all three areas of curriculum, budget and personnel (p. 413).

These commentators conclude:

... there is a disparity between the theory and clearly articulated intentions of SBM and the practice of SBM as conducted... (p. 403).

What is intriguing about these local outbreaks of 'devolutionism' is that they are always accompanied by a claim that this is the route to follow because it is 'international best practice' – yet this is not borne out at all by the evidence. For example, Judy Codding (1993), Deputy Director of the U.S. National Alliance for Restructuring Education, in her paper entitled 'The need to build a new infrastructure for American education', said in Australia recently:

Some people [in the USA] want to go as far as you have in
Australia and do away with local school districts and put the
authority and accountability in the hands of schools. In the
United States, (however), we are far from this becoming a
reality... A different state-federal structure and a strong history
of local school boards work against full devolution along Australian lines. Unfortunately today in the United States site-
based management ideas are found everywhere, yet in a real
sense nowhere. Site-based management has rarely been implemented in United States public schools... (p. 12).

Where there is support for it in the U.S.A, it tends to come from school
administrators, not from teachers and the wider school communities,
but even that seem to be wavering in places, too. Some see it as a process that could well be 'doomed to failure' (Lindquist & Mauriel, 1989).

Australia

One of the most ardent supporters of devolution in Australia has had
second thoughts, if not actually recanted. Fenton Sharpe (1993), the
major architect of devolution in New South Wales (the second largest
school system in the world to California) in his period as Director General of Education, said recently:

[The movement to devolution is] characterised by a paucity of
formal evaluation and a lack of objective data on its effects...
Devolution remains largely an act of faith... No longer should
such a major structural and social change be promulgated as
an axiom of faith without substantial supporting evidence (p.
20).

According to Australian zealots like Caldwell and Spinks (1988;
1992), such moves amount to a logical and desirable separation of
administrative means from the social ends of education, with consensus about educational policy being presumed, and the whole business
merely being a matter of getting the administrative strategies, tactics
and budgetary mechanisms right. But, according to Hartley (1994):

Because Caldwell and Spinks's self-managing school is based
on economic, not educational principles, it is the *financial*

audit which will matter in the new spreadsheet society of the school; the *educational* audit will be a mere by-product (p. 131).

New Zealand

In New Zealand, where the ideas of devolution have been trialed most extensively in recent times, the research is far from conclusive. As Alcorn (1991) notes in her introduction to a publication that reports on the extensive changes to educational management in that country, there is no doubt that the changes have significantly increased the workload of principals, but none of them 'wished to return to the old system' (p. 62). Mitchell, Jefferies, Keown and McConnell (1991) analysed the issues surrounding devolution in New Zealand eighteen months into the experiment and found that the 'score card' was very mixed:

> For some, the reforms offered new possibilities and undoubt-edly heightened expectations... Many Maori would fall into this group who felt the reforms would have allowed them to have a greater effect on their children's education... [but] for some of those who held out high expectations the reforms have been disappointing, and we are detecting a note of cyni-cism among such people.

> For others, the reforms represented a natural extension of what they had been doing for some years... [most notably] schools which already had considerable parent input onto their activi-ties... [and] secondary schools, which had always enjoyed fairly high levels of administrative autonomy in the previous system (p. 60).

While there was a feeling emerging from this research that schools were 'coming to grips' with the reforms in New Zealand, there was also widespread agreement that the reforms 'have been more complex to implement than most people originally envisaged' (p. 60). Reflect-ing the mixed outcomes, Mitchell and associates (1991) concluded that 'the jury is still out on whether the administrative reforms are condu-cive or antagonistic' to the educational experiences of New Zealand's children (p. 60).

Overall, it seems that we have reached the point worldwide with many countries well into devolved school systems, that doubts are beginning to surface, and that the time is indeed ripe for a thorough review of what is happening in respect of devolution. Put quite simply, 'there is little evidence that school-based management improves student achievement' (Malen et al., 1990, p. 323 – Hartley, 1994, p. 135).

The notion of 'choice' as expressed in the self-management of education is by no means new. As Hartley (1994) has noted, in the 1960s, we saw this take expression through 'educational theory' in the form of 'pupils managing their own learning' (p. 130). The difference between *then* and *now*, is that it is parents as 'consumers' who are allegedly doing the choosing, through the mechanism of the market – the 'choice is being driven by economic theory in order to prevent the fiscal overload of the state' (p. 130). This is not a frenzy driven by the quest for a more democratic structure for schooling, but a 'free-market economy based on parental choice' (p. 130) aimed at releasing schooling from the so-called dead hand and redtape of centralised bureaucratic control.

SELF-MANAGING SCHOOLS THAT ARE MORE *JUST, DEMOCRATIC* AND *EQUITABLE*

If it is the case as Hartley (1994) argues, that the 'self-managing school is an idea whose time has come' (p. 129), then the underlying agenda of what this might mean needs to be re-construed according to a broader and different set of principles than those espoused by proponents like Caldwell and Spinks (1988; 1992). Rather than self-management being a device by which the state attempts:

> ... to curb without coercion the level of public expenditure on education at a time of fiscal overload... [and in the process] minimise its invisibility in order to maximise it control over education (Hartley, 1994, p. 129)

then we need a qualitatively different approach, one that is informed by ideas like the following:
   (i)   Schools should be driven much less by a quest for possessive and competitive individualism within and between themselves, and instead be characterised by a concern for community and collective action.

(ii) Decisions about schooling need to be informed much more by educational considerations, rather than those of economics, entrepreneurialism, marketing, image, impression management, and the like.

(iii) Schools need to be engaged in questioning what it is they are doing, not from an accountant's point of view, but from the perspective of how their agenda fits with a broader view of what constitutes a just society. If there is any auditing of schools deemed necessary, then it needs to be *educational, moral,* and *democratic* forms of auditing.

A way of describing this is in terms of a 'socially critical orientation' to the self-managing school. This is a perspective characterised by a genuinely democratic agenda in which decision making and control extends to parents, teachers and students collectively. It is an approach that moves on a 'whole school change' front, rather than being limited to the opportunistic few who see it in their individual interests to make a running. Kemmis, Cole and Suggett (1983) claim that this involves a preparedness to take on 'big issues' like: regarding 'society as problematic' in how it operates, and schools as having a social and 'moral philosophy' with which to understand the wider picture (p. 15). What this means, in effect, is that there is a commitment to helping students and communities 'understand the structures and values of our society, and to evaluate them' with a view to making improvements in society (p. 15). This is done though 'critical self-reflection' on what schools are for, and how they do it (p. 15).

Schools as Discursive Communities

The one indispensable element to the socially just self-managing school is what Strike (1993) describes as 'local deliberative or discursive communities' (p. 226). His argument is that we need to understand schools as democratic institutions based on the nature of collective deliberations that ensue within them, rather than according to the way they represent the interests of citizens. He sees the notion of teacher professionalism which celebrates teachers as a self-regulating 'guild of practitioners', with an 'esoteric' knowledge base, as working against democratic control over the work of teachers' because gains in efficiency are at the expense of 'diminishment of democratic authority' (p. 258). The basis of Strike's (1993) claims is a Habermasian view of the ideal speech community 'in which practical arguments are made and in which all relevant considerations can be aired, and all competent speakers are heard' (p. 263). The consequence is a process of discursive redemption of social norms through consensus and open 'undominated discourses' in an 'ideal speech community' (p. 263). As far as schools are concerned, Strike (1993) claims that:

> These aspirations might be pursued in schools by transforming them into local deliberative communities [where] the social relations between members of the community will have to be characterised by equality, autonomy, reciprocity, and a high level of respect for the construction of rational consensus. Discursive communities require a supportive culture (p. 266).

Corson (1993) carries this notion of 'communicative action' in 'discursive communities' considerably further, particularly as it relates to issues of how power is exercised dialogically in sociocultural settings. Drawing upon Habermas' insights, Corson (1993) argues that institutions tend to have a certain in-built pathological, distorted, even dysfunctional quality about them when it comes to the norms of most communicative situations, and it is this which makes them inherently unjust. It is when people within institutions, schools included, strive towards the ideal of 'sort[ing] out their real interests from their illusory ones' (Corson, 1993, p. 36), that the possibility of pursuing discursive communities begins to become a reality – especially in the ways incompatible interests 'are resolved through compromise' (p. 39). Without pursuing this in excessive detail, Corson (1993) argues that the 'ideal speech situation' is central to discussion, from which can emerge 'the true interests of the participants' (p. 156) and hence a 'critical measure' of the quality and extent of interaction that informs democratic public discussion (p. 157). Having as a starting point a well-rounded understanding and appreciation of the nature of society, its character and materiality, is regarded by Young (1981) as a crucial knowledge pre-requisite for any such discursive community.

The features of such discursive communities, are that:
- the work of teachers and administrators is characterised by team work;
- scale requirements are such that they allow for formations that permit the kind of face-to-face discourse that characterises and permits intense dialogue;

- parents are included as members of the community, and are not conceptualised as clients;
- no relevant argument in such decision-making communities is barred, and no competent and interested speaker is excluded;
- everyone acknowledges that decisions are the property of the community as a whole, and that proposals for change are publicly discussed;
- the burden of justification is not met until a reasoned consensus has been achieved (adapted from Strike, 1993, 206 – 7);
- the question of 'who (or what) is the community?' is still open to debate because 'school communities have vague boundaries' (p. 276);
- the role of teachers is characterised as 'first among equals' (p. 267) and;
- 'educational authorities' enact a role of 'sovereign of last resort' in a context where the 'primary deliberative forum' is the school as a whole.

In sum, what Strike is saying is that schools need to be restructured along lines that decentralise and debureaucratise decision making.

Curriculum is a particular illustration of what local deliberation and discursive community might mean in terms of the management of knowledge and culture. Ashenden, Blackburn, Hannan & White (1984) express this as a 'Manifesto for a Democratic Curriculum' where the touchstones are principles of equality, commonality, and making the curriculum public. They propose the following hallmarks of the curriculum as being consistent with the nature of knowledge and learning in a socially just self-managing school:

- It should be common, in that all students are able to progress consistently through all areas of the course. Choices or groupings within major areas should not impede this progress or close off other options irrevocably.
- It should be premised on co-operation rather than competition, and on success rather than failure.
- It should be worthwhile, in that it offers something of enduring relevance to the learners.
- It should be coherent in that its structure shows how human knowledge grows and builds on itself.
- It should be systematic in the way that student growth and autonomy is steady and widespread, rather than haphazard and limited to the few.

- It should be reflective in that knowledge is open to question, and its application to one's framework of meaning is actively explored.
- It should be moral rather then neutral, and is critical in the way it addresses conceptions of right and wrong, truth, compassion and justice.
- It should be inclusive in its coverage of the everyday experience of all of its students, and reflects the diverse character of its community.
- It should be practical in the way it combines doing and reflecting, so as to make learning accessible to the largest possible range of students.
- It should be doable and structured in a way that is not a mechanism for selecting or spotting students (p. 16).

Whole School Change

Self-managing schools that are committed to taking on curriculum change of this type have a strong sense of the importance of 'whole school change'. As Connell, White and Johnston (1990) put it, '[This] implies participation of the whole staff and parent groups in planning, which challenges the conventional authority relations in schools and has significant costs of time and effort' (p. 10). Hattam (1994) argues that whole school change is inextricably connected to conceiving of what it means to work in socially just ways:

> Whole school change in response to educational disadvantage has been an attempt to generate more democratic structures and processes in schools. It is difficult to imagine how a school can improve the lack of power of certain groups in society without implementing measures to 'empower'. The term whole school change implies that the whole school community is involved in the process of deciding what is an appropriate curriculum. More than that, whole school change is about ensuring the curriculum reflects the concerns, life experience and aspirations of the whole school community. In essence whole school change is a process or a struggle to actively involve the whole school community in the curriculum process, to ensure all students are actively engaged and being successful, that the school actively works to include

groups that have been traditionally marginalised or silenced (p. 4).

Kretovics et. al., (1991) provide further practical detail on what such communities might look like. Described as 'reform from the bottom up that aims to empower teachers to transform schools', they identify three key features, in a high school they worked in Toledo, Ohio:

(i) creating a sense of family – which amounted to structuring 'the school day to keep students and teachers in the program for a continuous block of time' (p. 296);

(ii) facilitating collaboration between teachers – through providing them with a 'common work period each day' (p. 296);

(iii) establishing an extensive program of professional development – this was an opportunity for teachers 'to examine research in a collegial atmosphere and to develop strategies appropriate to the students with whom they would be working' (p. 296).

Developing a community in which students felt they had a close bond, was a crucial first step. The project by Kretovics assigned each student 'to a pod of no more than 100 students. Within this pod, the students were divided into sections of no more than 25 members' (p. 296). Each section had a 'group mentor' to assist with student problems and to maintain contact with the students' families:

> Teachers, parents, and students have proved by their actions that the sense of family and commitment to the group are taking hold... The key to academic success... is students, parents, administrators, and the community working together as a family to improve academic achievement (p. 296).

Strategies included 'co-operative learning', 'group work', and 'peer tutoring', and students were encouraged to work together such that when they had finished their work, they offered assistance to other students.

Working together so as to learn from each other was crucial, and Kretovics et. al., (1991) found teachers who, when provided with a common work period, were able to collaborate to 'solve problems and make decisions concerning the programs... [and] discuss student progress and problems' (p. 297):

> Teachers... examine[d] themselves and their students in an attempt to find a philosophical foundation for teaching. They raise[d] questions about expectations, biases, differing cultures, tracking, achievement, teaching strategies, learning styles, and assessment. Using these questions as starting points, they then examine[d] relevant research in an attempt to reach consensus concerning the development of the program, its potential problems, and some possible solutions (p. 297).

Matters dealt with included approaches to discipline, linking concepts and content of learning to student experiences, reading and writing across the curriculum, co-operative learning, and problem posing:

> Teachers were not only able to discuss the strengths and weaknesses they found in these approaches, but they were able to use their individual planning periods to observe their peers in practice (p. 297).

They also arrived at explanations for the barriers to student learning, the theory and research related to these problems, devising research-based solutions, trialing them to see what happened, and re-focusing and modifying as required.

Neither the creation of a sense of family, nor collaboration between teachers were sufficient, without professional development aimed at reversing the stultifying effects of teacher training programs, teacher-proof curriculum, and standardised testing. Professional development was engaged in by teachers so as 'to reclaim the intellectual heritage of teaching' (p. 298) with two ends in mind:

> First, [that] the nature and function of the professional teacher needs to be reconceptualised around the idea of the teacher as intellectual... [involving] assist[ing] teachers in studying experiences to instil in students the confidence, academic skills, cultural tools, knowledge, and vision necessary to face today's challenge...

> Second,... teachers must be given the time and resources to work together to restructure classroom practice... [in this case] through the professional development program... and the common work period (Kretovics, et. al., 1991, p. 298).

The idea that what is being managed in this kind of self-managing school is knowledge, culture and discourse, is not a new notion in organizations that have a commitment to being 'learning communities' (Senge, 1992; Lieberman, 1988). What is different, however, is that such schools also have a well developed commitment to asking poignant questions about the broader context within which such learning and schooling is occurring, and the nature of the society to which schools are contributing. Questions include:

- what's happening here?
- what do we know about this?
- who says this is the way things should be?
- what overall purposes are being served?
- whose vision is it anyway?
- whose interests are being served?
- whose needs are being met?
- whose voices are being excluded, silenced, denied?
- how come some viewpoints always get heard?
- why is this particular initiative occurring now?
- what alternatives have or should have been considered?
- what kind of feasible and prudent action can we adopt?
- who can we enlist to support us?
- how can we start now?
- how are we going to know when we make a difference? (Smyth, 1994a)

Schools committed to the kind of core values represented in questions of this type depart markedly from the traditional view of how teaching occurs, by 'teaching against the grain' (Cochran – Smith, 1991; Simon, 1992). In other words, teachers engage with the social. intellectual, ethical and political aspects of what it means to teach. Cochran – Smith (1991) claims that what distinguishes these schools is that they have a strong commitment to developing the kind of structures that produce 'critical dissonance' and 'collaborative resonance' (p. 304). That is to say, they generate 'intensification of opportunities to learn from teaching through the co-labour of communities' (p. 304) that focus on how school participants themselves might begin to 'bear upon the institutional and instructional arrangements of schooling' (p. 282). The process of collaborative resonance involves, she says, participants in 'critiqu[ing] the cultures of teaching and schooling, research[ing] their own practices, articulat[ing] their own expertise, and call[ing] into question the policies and language of schooling that are taken for granted' (p. 283).

Drawing from Clifford and Friesen (1993) I recently made an attempt at trying to summarise what whole school change committed to a wider social agenda might look like, if we resisted the 'return to traditional images and practices' (p. 341) and used instead a different set of principles or touchstones (Smyth, 1993 b). This is what I came up with:

- We need to resist the conversion of fundamental moral and political questions, into technical and administrative problems to be solved (Ghaill, 1991, p. 310)
- We need to listen to one another's' voices as teachers' more and publicly defend, them against the cries to unthinkingly follow the model of industry;
- We need to work in ways that not only acknowledge but loudly celebrate our theories of what works, and why;
- We need to actively pursue the notion that teaching is a form of 'intellectual struggle' (Reece, 1991) – and put to rest the notion that teaching is mere technical work;
- We need to ensure that teachers as an occupational group are treated in more trusting ways, and that means acknowledging that teachers are in control of what they do, and that they have workable ways of being accountable to one another;
- We need to be more vociferous at proclaiming the complex nature of the work we do as teachers – in a context where segments of the community and the media believe that teaching is something any fool can do;
- We need to convince a sceptical public and a hostile media that when students don't learn as well as might be expected, we should be less hasty in pointing the finger at teachers, and at look more closely at the context within which teachers work, and ask if they are being properly supported;
- Through whatever means at our disposal, we need to make the point that curriculum should be constructed around the 'lived experiences' of children and teachers, rather than crafted around national profiles that are allegedly aimed at making us more internationally competitive, or that aim to reduce the balance of payments.
- We need to encourage 'deliberate improvisation' in teaching, so that we can move beyond mindless processes that produce 'compliant' and 'defiant' kids (Clifford & Friesen, 1993, p. 345);

- We need to promote the kind of circumstances in our schools in which we feel comfortable with and compelled to call into question the basic assumptions about teaching and learning – and to radically change those if experience tells us otherwise Clifford & Friesen, 1993, p. 341);
- We need to make the point resoundingly, that teaching and schooling ought to be about engaging with the 'big questions' that fire the 'imagination', the 'spirit', the 'feelings', and the 'intellect' (Clifford & Friesen, 1993, p. 346).

Consistent with this view of seeking to locate teaching, learning and what schools do in a broader arena, Haberman (1991) describes what I argue we should be moving away from, as a 'pedagogy of poverty' – the view that teaching constitutes a series of basic traditional core functions, such as 'giving information, asking questions, giving directions, monitoring seat work, assigning homework, settling disputes, punishing non-compliance, giving grades' (p. 291).

Haberman argues that pedagogy of poverty does not work because:

> The classroom atmosphere created by constant teacher direction and student compliance seethes with passive resentment that sometimes bubbles up into overt resistance. Teachers burn out because of the emotional and physical energy that they must expend to maintain their authority every hour of the day (p. 291).

Good teaching, on the other hand, says Haberman (1991), has quite a different genre that is much clearer about what it is that is being managed – namely, learning, life chances, and the opportunity to challenge entrenched and oppressive views. In Haberman's (1991) terms:

- Whenever students are involved with issues they regard as vital concerns, good teaching is going on;
- Whenever students are involved with explanations of human difference, good teaching is going on;
- Whenever students are being helped to see major concepts, big ideas, and general principles and are not merely engaged in the pursuit of isolated facts, good teaching is going on;
- Whenever students are involved in planning what they will be doing, it is likely that good teaching is going on;

- Whenever students are involved with applying ideals such as fairness, equity, or justice to their world, it is likely that good teaching is occurring;
- Whenever students are actively involved, it is likely good teaching is going on;
- Whenever students are directly involved in real-life experience, it is likely that good teaching is going on;
- Whenever students are actively involved in heterogeneous groups, it is likely that good teaching is going on;
- Whenever students are asked to think about an idea in a way that questions common sense or a widely accepted assumption, that relates new ideas to ones learned previously, or that applies an idea to the problems of living, then there is a chance that good teaching is going on;
- Whenever students are involved in redoing, polishing, or perfecting their work, it is likely that good teaching is going on;
- Whenever teachers involve students with the technology of information access, good teaching is going on;
- Whenever students re involved in reflecting on their own lives and how they have come to believe and feel as they do, good teaching is going on (pp. 293 – 4).

Leadership: In Search of a Different Metaphor

Both Corson (1993 a; 1993b) and Cazden (1989) have described Richmond Road School, a multi-ethnic school in New Zealand, as an example of a school that appears to have a history of having worked towards the kind of socially just self-managing alternative which is based on communicative action. It was a school that had a strong image of itself, was able to convey that to others, and use it as a way of stemming the intrusion of mindless non-educational nonsense. It was a learning organization in which people were able to take risks and make mistakes without fear of loss of face, or retribution, that was inclusive in the ways it operated, and that worked in a self-reflexive ways that involved asking itself questions like:

- why do we do what we do here?
- are we doing what we think we are doing?
- are we incorporating a range of viewpoints?
- how might we do things differently? (Smyth, 1994 b)

In part, Richmond Road's success was due to a long history of people in the school community having deeply-rooted ideas about what kind of school they were (see May, 1994 for a full account of this), and a clear conception of what kind of practices were therefore appropriate. For example, they no longer worked on the notion of the single cellular way of organising the school. Rather, the school had developed a process of 'critical policy making' (Corson, 1993a), that involved a concerted and extended process of dialogue and debate about educational ideas. There was also extensive use of paired teaching, immersion classes, dispensing with ascribed statuses, and the view that expertise could come from anywhere in the school including students, parents and even the janitors. The teaching staff placed a great deal of stress on staying up to date with the latest theoretical developments, and people operated in ways in which they shared what they learned with one another. The idea that individuals could develop individual private granaries of knowledge in the school, was unheard of; what one person knew, was available to all.

Change was slow and carefully considered at Richmond Road School, and even then, occurred only after extensive debate, a piloting of new ideas, and then a formulating policy in a way in which everyone had a stake it. The mode of operation was to 'problematise' what was occurring so that dominant ways of doing things were continually challenged, and new possibilities forged that everyone felt comfortable with. Conflict, when it occurred, was seen as having a positive dimension to it as people tested out ideas, and explored why they were doing what they did. Above all, this was a school that was continually in the process of communicating to its constituent parts (most of all its parent community), and people were given time to think and work things through together.

The lessons from this one school are clear enough!!

There needed to be ways of creating collaborative ways of analysing and sharing what it is that is going on in classrooms and schools, questioning how this intersects with the broader structures within which the work of schooling proceeds. Successful cases of opposition and resistance, as in the Richmond Road example, occur where people see their work as being inextricably connected to wider social and institutional structures, and are able to successfully convince colleagues that this ought to be central to what the school exists for.

A large part of what is required here is the restoration of the notion of community – amongst ourselves as teachers, and within the extended networks within which we work. Sergiovanni (1994) has made a significant advance on this front recently by arguing that leadership in schools needs a metaphor that is more indigenous to schools, rather than being derivative of formal organization theory, as at the moment. He argues that the notion of the family, community, or the neighbourhood would be more appropriate. The metaphor that comes from the prevailing view of leadership and administration as applied unquestioningly to schools, is highly derivative of a largely abandoned and outmoded Newtonian view of mechanics, the military, and business. It is about missioning, controlling, commanding, operational and strategic planning, and surveillance. If we were to depart from this militaristic metaphor, there is a distinct chance several things might happen, according to Sergiovanni (1994):

- – there would be much less pre-occupation with who is in control;
- – there would be less emphasis on contractual relationships;
- – there would be much less equating of hierarchy with expertise.

Sergiovanni (1994) says:

> In communities... the connection of people to purpose and the connections among people are not based on contracts but on commitments. Communities are socially organised around relationships and the felt interdependencies that nurture them. Instead of being tied together and tied to purposes by bartering arrangements, this social structure bonds people together in special ways and binds them to concepts, images, and values that comprise a shared idea structure. This bonding and binding are the defining characteristics of schools as communities. Communities are defined by their centres of values, sentiments, and beliefs that provide the needed conditions for creating a sense of *we* from a collection of *Is* (p. 217).

If we were to follow Sergiovanni's suggestion, and see schools as being more like families than military platoons, then we might finish up in quite a different place. We would, for example, rely less on 'external control, [and] more on norms, purposes, values, professional socialisation, collegiality, and natural interdependence'... 'more on the commitments, obligations and duties that people feel towards each other and the school' (p. 217). We might also see the members of our schools as community members, 'connected to each other because of felt interdependencies, mutual obligations, and other emotional and normative ties' (p. 218). From this kind of vantage point, we come to a theory and practice of leadership which Sergiovanni (1994) says would be:

> ... more in tune with children and young adults; sandboxes and crayons; storybooks and interest centres; logarithms and computer programs; believing and caring; professional norms and practices; values and commitments; and other artefacts of teaching and learning (p. 218).

We would have invented a new source 'of authority for what we do, a new basis for leadership' (p. 218).

Questions likely to emerge, according to Sergiovanni (1994), would include:

- What can be done to increase the sense of kinship, neighbourliness and collegiality among the faculty of a school?
- How can the faculty become more of a professional community where everyone cares about each other and helps each other to learn together and to lead together?
- What kinds of relationships need to be cultivated with parents that will enable them to be included in this emerging community?
- How can this web of relationships exist among teachers and between teachers and students so that they embody community?
- How can teaching and learning settings be arranged so that they are more family-like?
- How can the school itself, as a collection of families, be more like a neighbourhood?
- What are the shared values and commitments that enable the school to become a community of mind?
- How will these values and commitments become practical standards that can guide the lives of community members who want to lead, what community members learn and how, and how community members treat each other?
- What are the patterns of mutual obligations and duties that emerge in the school as community is achieved? '(pp. 220–21).

In changing the metaphor we live by in schools, and therefore, the discourse of schooling in this way, we would be working actively to put the educative in all its facets back to central place so that the managerial takes its rightful secondary place. We would also be working to consistently, in and through the ways we work, re-assert the prominence of the participative – something that is rapidly being evacuated in this new era of self-management driven by competitive and possessive individualism.

The socially just self-managing school being described here, is not concerned either *only* with aspects of functional literacy of students, but it takes on big issues as Kemmis, Cole and Suggett (1983) point out, like:

- regarding society as problematic in how it operates, and schools needing to have a social and moral philosophy with which to understand the wider picture (p. 15);
- helping students and communities understand the structures and values of our society, and to evaluate them with a view to making improvements in society (p. 15);
- doing this is though critical self-reflection on what schools are for, and how they do it (p. 15)

Schools like these are places in which parents too, feel comfortable that their experiences and what they have to offer, are valued and valuable. They are not treated in ways that make them feel as if their contributions are less important than those of teachers or the administration. Parents have an equal opportunity to express a viewpoint, to question, and to give reasons for what they think is best for their children and the society of which they are a part. Furthermore, the quality of what passes as public discussion between teachers, administrators, parents and students is regarded as being crucial, and is judged against criteria like:

- who is allowed to speak – only those in positions of power and status;
- whether decisions are arrived at on the basis of genuine consensus;
- whether some viewpoints are privileged, while others are denied, ignored, or silenced?
- whether participation and collaboration genuine, or is it forced and contrived?
- whether or not deliberate moves are adopted to search out the views of minority groups, and whether their voices are being heard? and
- whether all participants are respectful of the language, customs, culture and histories of others.

In such schools the motto is 'the kids come first' (Cazden, 1989). Things come unstuck rapidly when schools place other things first. For example: when schools exist for teachers; when schools are regarded as being for national economic reconstruction or for the restoration of international competitiveness; when schools exist for the convenience of the educational system or bureaucracy; or when schools exist to satisfy the needs of the business community.

Schools characterised in these ways are places that are continually experimental in the widest and best sense of that term. They are sufficiently confident of themselves, of one another, and of the society of which they are a part, to be able to try out new approaches, and to learn from the experience without feeling excessively threatened. Above all, schools committed to being socially just places, understand that improvement is not possible through individual action – 'collective action capable of confronting unjust and irrational social structures' (Kemmis, Cole & Suggett, 1983, p. 9) is needed. '[T]he socially critical school seeks to locate and interpret culture within an historical context as well as through the immediate process of action and reflection' (p. 9).

The question as to 'who is a teacher?', is not a settled question in such schools. It may be that for much of the time, teachers are people who have formal status and authority – but this is always open to the possibility that 'whoever has knowledge teaches' (Corson, 1993 a, p. 162). For example, there may be occasions in which parents and members of the community, because of experience, background, special knowledge, or whatever, are the people best qualified to teach students. At Richmond Road, the school's caretaker (janitor) was involved in the educational work and was a valued colleague!

A school that is socially just as well as self-managing is open to the possibilities that teachers need to work with one another in innovative and open ways. This means: paired teaching; joint preparation of teaching materials; sharing materials and ideas across the entire school; and, continuous discussion about teaching and learning among all teachers. When teachers work together in these ways, it sends powerful messages to students and parents about what is considered important in the school. As a teacher at Richmond Road School, put it: 'I think that's why the children work together here, because they can see us working together' (Cazden, 1989, p. 150).

It is worth noting that some of these are ideas that are decidedly out of fashion at the moment, as students are urged to compete against one another. The claim is that if we make students compete against each other, then we will have competitive and more efficient schools (the ones that aren't will disappear), and that this will make us internationally able to out-compete other nations.

One of the most compelling features that characterises socially just self-managing schools, is that they have a strong sense of 'caring' – it permeates relationships at all levels – between teachers, students, parents and administration. To put it another way, they are 'relational schools' (Skilbeck, 1984) characterised by 'pedagogical caring' (Hult, 1979). That is to say, not only do they show a 'concern and appreciation for the special uniqueness and circumstances of the person' that involves 'overcoming obstacles and difficulties' (p. 239), but they are also about caring for ideas as well:

> Pedagogical caring refers to the careful... manner or style by which a teacher operates. In doing his [her] professional job with due care, the teacher demonstrates serious attention, concern, and regard for all his [her] duties. And what is especially ingredient to pedagogical caring is the teacher's commitment to develop and maintain his [her] style throughout his or her professional career, even under conditions of adversity (p. 169).

Restoring 'Educative Leadership' to the Self-Managing School

Leadership is, therefore, not simply about charisma, or acting decisively, in the way the educational literature talks of these matters. The style or image of leadership being spoken about here, is first and foremost educative (Smyth, 1989). There is a clear sense of what it is that school communities regard as being valuable and worthwhile, and the mode of operating reflects and project those understandings. Leadership in these schools is about assisting teachers and parents to search out alternatives which the wider community is prepared to own;

Leaders of socially just self-managing schools are able to enthusiastically carry people along with them, and they do this primarily by assisting the school and its community 'to uncover meaning in what they do, while investing in them the capacity to change, improve and transform what they do' (Smyth, 1989, p. 179). The Richmond Road School makes this point well. Leadership consisted of: developing tentative plans, trialing what happened, and adopting or discarding them; involving teachers and the community in initial decision making; moving very slowly, with small changes, and then only with consultation; making it clear, that there are no simple answers to complex policy questions; demonstrating success at each stage, and making modifications based on consultation, before moving on; and being able to convince the community that what is underway is genuine reform (Corson, 1993 a, p. 167).

Leaders of socially just schools are 'intellectuals' in the sense that Herbert Kohl (1983) uses that term. They know their field and have a wide breadth of knowledge about other aspects of the world. They use experience to develop theory, and question theory on the basis of further experience and they have the courage to question authority and refuse to act counter to their own experience (p. 30). In this they are prepared to take a strong stance against external agencies who hold impositional views, and they are vigorous advocates for what they believe works best for their schools. They have a well developed sense of what is socially just and how to work with a school community to develop policies that reflect this.

There is an acute understanding of change in such institutions, what is feasible, what is manageable, and of the need to fully explore issues from multiple directions before acting. Teachers, parents and students are viewed as being capable of working towards theorised accounts of what they do.　School participants are regarded as being active constructors of their own realities, rather than passive recipients of other people's realities. For leaders in these school events in the wider community are considered important – so important in fact that they actually initiate community activity rather than letting such events happen. Part of this involvement is also the process of assisting people to see that conflict and criticism are inevitable and productive (Corson, 1993 b). Difference and diversity is something that has to be embraced through 'commitment building' and dialogue, within a context of clear agreement and understanding of whose interests are being served.

At a practical level this means providing the time whereby teachers can be released from teaching to engage in the policy making process, identifying, and testing possible solutions against what is prudent, based on knowledge and the experience of the participants. The views, wishes, aspirations, and lived experiences of the people in the school are the most important – not what the education system believes to be important.

For parents, the consequence of operating in these ways is that they 'feel drawn to contribute to policy making, to teaching, and to other activities... 'They feel free to observe or participate in class activities any time'. Another way of saying this, is that parents are given a real measure of power, not the illusion of power.

CONCLUSION

Overall, the model of a socially just self-managing schooling is one that is fundamentally and qualitatively at variance with what is rapidly becoming the mainstream econometric notion of self-management. The alternative I have sketched out here:

(i) has a democratic decision making framework among teachers and parents;
(ii) has an established consultation process with the local community; and
(iii) that does all of this in an environment that builds on and strengthens students' own contact with their own cultures (Corson, 1993 a, pp. 167 – 8).

Such schools are organised in ways that are open – to parents, as well as open to themselves as critical, reflective, analytical communities. As Cazden (1989) put it, in such schools the 'kids always come first' and there is 'an agenda for children; but actually it is an agenda for everyone'. 'Whoever has knowledge teaches' – authority is non-hierarchical and provisional. There is learning about teaching, learning about other people and other cultures, and above all, learning about what it means to be part of a learning community.

Kemmis, Cole and Suggett (1983) describe such a school in not dissimilar terms when they portray it as a community which learns individually socially and collectively through collaborative intervention that focuses on common work, common language, and joint participation in decision making. There is a concern for negotiation of curriculum between teachers, students, and parents as to what is considered to be educationally worthwhile. There is a form of institutional self-reflection on actions and processes, on habits and customs, and on what the school believes places limits and constraints on what it can do. But, above all, there are the kind of self-understandings at multiple levels – of: individual practice classroom practice whole school activity school – community relations social and political organization of society (Kemmis, Cole & Suggett, 1983)

Such schools, as distinct from their mainstream self-managing look-alikes, are small research communities, collaboratively researching their own practices, understandings and situations; providing students with learning experiences that allow them to question and learn about society; avoiding competitive academic curriculum, and pursuing instead democratic emancipatory tasks; regarding learning as a co-operative task; structuring time for teachers to negotiate and reflect; developing in teachers a pervading commitment to extending their own and their students' skills; regarding knowledge as being constituted through interaction; taking the problems of society as a starting point for discussion – not as a given; and working so that social justice becomes something that happens in *all* schools, not something learned about in isolation in *some* of them (see Kemmis, Cole & Suggett, 1983).

REFERENCES

Alcorn, N.: 1991, 'Introduction to the First New Zealand conference on Research in Educational Administration', *New Zealand Journal of Educational Administration* 6, 62 – 63.

Ashenden, D. Blackburn, J. Hannan, B. & White, D.: 1984, 'A Manifesto for a Democratic Curriculum *Australian Teacher* 65 (4), 13 – 20.

Ball, S.: 1993, 'Culture, Cost and Control: Self – Management and Entrepreneurial Schooling in England and Wales', in J. Smyth (ed.), *A Socially Critical View of the Self – Managing School*, Falmer Press, London, 63 – 82.

Booi, L.: 1992, 'The Emperor's New Clothes and the Myth of Decentralization', *The Bell, Book and Candor* 12 (2),1 – 4.

Caldwell, B. & Spinks, J.: 1988, *The Self – Managing School*, Falmer Press, London.

Caldwell, B. & Spinks, J.: 1992, *Leading the Self – Managing School*, Falmer Press, London.

Cazden, C.: 1989, 'Richmond Road; A Multi – lingual/Multi – cultural Primary School in Auckland', *Language and Education: An International Journal* 3, (3), 143 – 66.

Clifford, P. & Friesen, S.: 1993, 'A Curious Plan: Managing on the Twelfth', *Harvard Educational Review* 63 (3), 339 – 54.

Cochran – Smith, M.: 1993, 'Learning to Teach Against the Grain', *Harvard Educational Review* 61 (3), 279 – 310.

Codding, J.: 1993, 'The Need to Build a New Infrastructure for American Public Education', paper to the annual conference of the Australian Council for Educational Administration, Adelaide, September.

Connell, R. White, V. & Johnston, K.: 1990, *Poverty, Education and the Disadvantaged Schools Program (DSP)*, Macquarie University, Sydney.

Corson, D.: 1993 a, *Language, Minority Education and Gender: Linking Social Justice and Power*, Multilingual Matters, Clevedon.

Corson, D.: 1993 b, 'Critical Policy Making: Emancipatory School – site Governance in Multi – ethnic Schools, unpublished manuscript.

Davies, M.: 1992, 'The Little Boy said... the Emperor still isn't Wearing any Clothes *Curriculum Journal* 3 (1), 3 – 9.

Evetts, J.: 1993, 'LMS and Headship: Changing the Contexts for Micro – politics *Educational Review* 45 (1), 53 – 65.

Ghaill, M.: 1991, 'State – school Policy: Contradictions, Confusions and Contestation', *Journal of Education Policy* 6 (3), 299 – 313.

Haberman, M.: 1991, 'The Pedagogy of Poverty versus Good Teaching', *Phi Delta Kappan* 73 (4), 290 – 94.

Hartley, D.: 1994, 'Devolved School Management: the 'New Deal' in Scottish Education', *Journal of Education Policy* 9 (2),129 – 40.

Hattam, R.: 1994, 'The Socially Just School in the 90s: Where is it? and What Does it Look Like?' Discussion Paper, Flinders Institute for the Study of Teaching, Adelaide, August.

Hult, R.: 1979, 'On Pedagogical Caring', *Educational Theory* 29 (3), 237 – 43.

Kemmis, S. Cole, P. & Suggett, D.: 1983, *Orientations to Curriculum and Transition: Towards the Socially – Critical School*, Victorian Institute of Secondary Education, Melbourne.

Kohl, H.: 1983, 'Examining Closely What We Do', *Learning* 12 (1), 28 – 30.

Kretovics, J. Farber, K. & Armaline, W.: 1991, 'Reform from the Bottom up: Empowering Teachers to Transform Schools', *Phi Delta Kappan* 73 (4), 295 – 99.

Lieberman, A.: 1988, *Building a Professional Culture in Schools*, Teachers College Press, New York.

Lindquist, K. & Mauriel, J.: 1989, 'School – based Management: Doomed to Failure?', *Education and Urban Society* 21 (4), 403 – 16.

Malen, B. Ogawa, R. & Krantz, J.: 1990, 'What Do We Know About School – based Management?' in W. Clune and J. White (eds), *Choice and Control in American Education* Volume 2, Falmer Press, London.

Marren, E., & Levacic, R.: 1994, 'Senior Management, Classroom Teacher and Governor Responses to Local Management of Schools', *Educational Management and Administration* 22 (1), 39 – 53.

May, S.: 1994, *Making Multicultural Education Work*, Multilingual Matters, Clevedon.

McConaghy, T.: 1989, 'The Quiet Revolution: School – based Budgeting', *Phi Delta Kappan* 70 (6), 486 – 7.

Mitchell, D. Jefferies, R. Keown, P., & McConnell, R.: 1991 'Monitoring 'Today's School': a score card after 18 months' *New Zealand Journal of Educational Administration* 6, 48 – 60.

Murphy, J.: 1990, 'Delegation, Quality and the Local Management of Schools', Unpublished manuscript, Department of Commerce, University of Adelaide,.

Reece, P.: 1991, 'Teachers' Work as Intellectual Struggle', *Critical Pedagogy Networker* 4 (1), 1 – 5.

Senge, P.: 1990, *The Fifth Discipline: the Art and Practice of the Learning Organization*, Doubleday, New York.

Sergiovanni, T.: 1994, 'Organizations or Communities? Changing the Metaphor Changes the Theory', *Educational Administration Quarterly* 30 (2).

Sharpe, F.: 1993, 'Devolution – Where Are We Now)?, paper to the annual conference of the Australian Council for Educational Administration, Adelaide, September.

Skilbeck, M.: 1984, *School – Based Curriculum Development*, Harper and Row, London.

Simkins, T.: 1994, 'Efficiency, Effectiveness and the Local Management of Schools', *Journal of Education Policy* 9 (1),15 – 33.

Simon, R.: 1992, *Teaching Against the Grain: Texts for a Pedagogy of Possibility.* Bergin & Garvey, Amherst.

Smyth, J.: 1989, 'A 'Pedagogical' and 'Educative' View of Leadership', in J. Smyth (ed), *Critical Perspectives on Educational Leadership*, Falmer Press, London,179 – 204.

Smyth, J. (ed): 1993 a, *A Socially Critical View of the Self – Managing School*, Falmer Press, London.

Smyth, J.: 1993 b, 'What is Happening to Teachers' Work?', keynote address to the 'Teachers Reclaiming Teaching', Third International Teacher Development Conference, Adelaide, November.

Smyth, J.: 1994 a, 'Thinking Critically, Acting Politically', paper to the National Australian Primary Principals Association Conference, Adelaide, October.

Smyth, J.: 1994 b, 'Administering Schooling that is Open to Parents: Schooling for Democracy', keynote address to the 'Parents and Teachers for a Better Education' conference, Malta, 11 – 13 April.

Strike, K.: 1993, 'Professionalism, democracy, and discursive communities: normative reflections on re – structuring', *American Educational Research Journal* 30 (2), 255 – 75.

Young, I.: 1981, 'Towards a Critical Theory of Justice', *Social Theory and Practice* 7, 279 – 302.

M

W

NAME INDEX